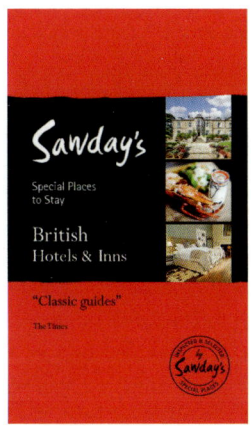
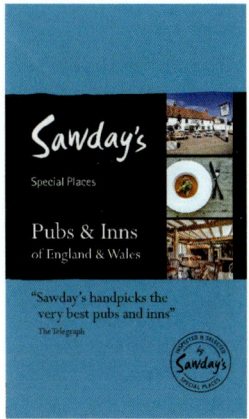
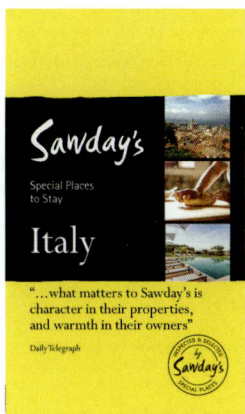
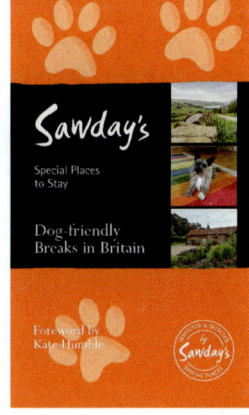

Twenty-third edition
Copyright © 2018
Alastair Sawday Publishing Co. Ltd
Published in September 2018
ISBN-13: 978-1-906136-89-5

Alastair Sawday Publishing Co. Ltd,
Merchants House, Wapping Road,
Bristol BS1 4RW, UK
Tel: +44 (0)117 204 7810
Email: info@sawdays.co.uk
Web: www.sawdays.co.uk

All rights reserved. No part of this publication may be used other than for the purpose for which it is intended nor may any part be reproduced, or transmitted, in any form or by any means, electronically or mechanically, including photocopying, recording or any information storage or retrieval system, without prior written permission from the publisher. Requests for permission should be addressed to: Alastair Sawday Publishing in the UK.

A catalogue record for this book is available from the British Library. This publication is not included under licences issued by the Copyright Agency. No part of this publication may be used in any form of advertising, sales promotion or publicity.

Alastair Sawday has asserted his right to be identified as the author of this work.

Series Editor Alastair Sawday
Editor Wendy Ogden
Production Coordinators Sarah Barratt, Antonica Jones, Melissa Wiseman
Writing Claire Baranowski, Becca Bill, Jo Boissevain, Chris Elmes, Nicola Crosse, Carmen McCormack, Sue Nottingham, Wendy Ogden, Honor Peters, Annie Shillito
Inspections Jan Adam, Edna Allbrooke, Mandy Barnes, Sue Birtwistle, Neil Brown, Becky Brunning, Angie Collings, Anne Cousin, Carmen McCormack, Nicola Crosse, Mary Dixon, Fiona Duby, Trish Dugmore, Beverley Edge, Peter Evans, Julie Franklin, Catherine Gledhill, Naomi Gorvin, Becca Harris, Auriol Marson, Veronique Nelson, Wendy Ogden, Valerie Penny, Margot Rawson, Aideen Reid, Scott Reeve, Pamela Romano, Annie Shillito, Heather Stephenson, Kate Soar, Nicky Tennent, Gilly Unwin, Gwen Vonthron
Marketing & PR
0117 204 7801
marketing@sawdays.co.uk

We have made every effort to ensure the accuracy of the information in this book at the time of going to press. However, we cannot accept any responsibility for any loss, injury or inconvenience resulting from the use of information contained therein.

Production: Pagebypage Co Ltd
Maps: Maidenhead Cartographic Services
Printing: Pureprint, Uckfield
UK distribution: The Travel Alliance, Bath
kholmes@pelotongrey.com

Cover photo credits.
Front 1. Hooppells Torr, entry 85 2. Low Mill, entry 390 3. The Summerhouse, entry 258

Back: 1. Greenwood Barn, entry 422 2. Fauhope House, entry 431 3. Bilton Barns, entry 242

Spine: Davenport House, entry 272

Sawday's

Special Places
to Stay

British
Bed & Breakfast

Contents

Front	Page
A word from Alastair Sawday	6
How we choose our Special Places	7
Inspections	7
Feedback	7
Subscriptions	8
Disclaimer	8
Using this book	10
Finding the right place for you	10
Maps	10
Symbols	10
Quick reference indices	11
Practical matters	12
Types of places	12
Rooms	12
Meals	12
Prices and minimum stays	14
Booking and cancellation	14
Payment	15
Tipping	15
Arrivals and departures	15
Closed	15
Maps	17–39

Guide entries	Entry	Map
England		
Bath & N.E. Somerset	1-5	3
Bedfordshire	6-7	9
Berkshire	8-9	4
Birmingham	10	8
Bristol	11-14	3
Buckinghamshire	15	8
Cambridgeshire	16-21	9
Cheshire	22-24	7
Cornwall	25-46	1
Cumbria	47-64	11, 12
Derbyshire	65-71	8, 12
Devon	72-104	2
Dorset	105-126	2, 3
Durham	127	12
Essex	128-130	10
Gloucestershire	131-151	3, 8
Hampshire	152-159	3, 4
Herefordshire	160-166	7
Hertfordshire	167	9
Isle of Wight	168-170	4
Kent	171-189	5
Lancashire	190-191	11, 12
Leicestershire	192-193	8, 9
Lincolnshire	194-200	9, 13
London	201-219	4, 22
Norfolk	220-236	9, 10
Northamptonshire	237-240	8, 9
Northumberland	241-249	12, 16
Nottinghamshire	250-251	9
Oxfordshire	252-263	4, 8
Rutland	264-265	9
Shropshire	266-278	7
Somerset	279-313	2, 3
Staffordshire	314-315	8
Suffolk	316-325	9, 10
Surrey	326-331	4

Guide entries	Entry	Map
England contd.		
Sussex	332-347	4, 5
Warwickshire	348-358	8
Wiltshire	359-370	3
Worcestershire	371-373	8
Yorkshire	374-401	12, 13
Channel Islands		
Guernsey	402	4
Scotland		
Aberdeenshire	403	19
Angus	404	19
Argyll & Bute	405-408	14, 17
Ayrshire	409	14
Dumfries & Galloway	410	11
Edinburgh	411-416	15
Glasgow	417	15
Highland	418-420	17, 18
Isle of Skye	421-422	17, 20
Lanarkshire	423-424	15
Midlothian	425	15
Moray	426	18
Perth & Kinross	427-429	15, 18
Scottish Borders	430-432	15, 16
Stirling	433-434	15
Western Isles	435	20
Wales		
Carmarthenshire	436-437	7
Conwy	438	7
Flintshire	439-440	7
Gwynedd	441-443	6, 7
Monmouthshire	444-446	7
Pembrokeshire	447-453	6
Powys	454-459	7
Wrexham	460	7

Back	Page
Quick reference indices	279
Wheelchair-accessible	279
Children of all ages welcome	279
Pets welcome	280
Credit cards accepted	281
Special Places to Stay series	283
Index by property name	284
Index by town	296
What's in each entry?	304

A word from Alastair Sawday

Photo: Tom Germain

Claire Cohen questioned in the Telegraph recently whether Britain has lost the art of B&Bing. Expectations of pillow menus, Hungarian goose down and roll top tubs have driven out, she affirms, those B&B owners who simply throw open the doors of their homes and hope that guests will like what they find. She has a point – but that's exactly what we're looking for here at Sawday's.

We're now hovering on a rejection rate of 40% of the places who apply to us – the highest it has ever been and I blame it on lack of confidence. We're inundated with applications from B&Bs which all look exactly the same because they have been 'created' rather than been allowed to stay as somebody's home. Anything personal, everything that reflects the owners' characters has been whisked out of sight in favour of a bland, incredibly dull landscape lifted straight from a magazine. And that's not what we're looking for.

You'll find much diversity in this book – from grand to humble and lots in between. And while you will come across some that are more in the boutique style, we're proud to say you'll still find the odd candlewick bedspread, places with cobwebs, houses which are not beautifully photographed, some which haven't got a website yet so you have to take pot luck and some others where family life bumps along in its boisterous way almost unaware of the 'rules' between guest and host. Those will always be our favourites.

Because it's not just about what you get – it's about who you are with and how you feel. Some of our owners have been with us for over twenty years, others are young and just starting out. But at every single Sawday's B&B you'll be looked after beautifully. You'll experience real generosity of spirit and meet some truly interesting people – some even a tad eccentric – all of whom have the confidence to keep their home a proper home and love to share it with other people. Happy B&Bing.

Alastair Sawday

How we choose our Special Places

It's simple. There are no rules, no boxes to tick. We choose places that we like and are fiercely subjective in our choices. We also recognise that one person's idea of special is not necessarily someone else's so there is a huge variety of places, and prices, in the book. Those who are familiar with our *Special Places* series know that we look for comfort, originality, authenticity, and reject the insincere, the anonymous and the banal. The way guests are treated comes as high on our list as the setting, the architecture, the atmosphere and the food.

Inspections

We visit every place in the guide to get a feel for how both house and owner tick. We don't take a clipboard and we don't have a list of what is acceptable and what is not. Instead, we chat for an hour or so with the owner and look round. It's all very informal, but it gives us an excellent idea of who would enjoy staying there. If the visit happens to be the last of the day, we may stay the night. Once in the book properties are sometimes re-inspected, to keep things fresh and accurate.

Feedback

In between inspections we rely on feedback from our army of readers, as well as from staff members who are encouraged to visit properties across the series. This feedback is invaluable to us and we always follow up on comments. So do tell us whether your stay has been a joy or not, if the atmosphere was great or stuffy, the owners cheery or bored. The accuracy of the book depends on what you, and our inspectors, tell us. A lot of the new entries in each edition are recommended by our readers, so keep telling us about new places you've discovered too. Please email us at info@sawdays.co.uk to tell us about your discoveries.

However, please do not tell us if the bedside light was broken, or the shower head was scummy. Tell the owner, immediately, and get them to do something about it. Most owners are more than happy to correct

Photo: Upper Red House, entry 444

problems and will bend over backwards to help. Far better than bottling it up and then writing to us a week later!

Subscriptions

Owners pay to be part of Sawdays, but we only include places we find special so it is not possible for anyone to buy their way onto these pages. Nor is it possible for the owner to write their own description. We will say if the bedrooms are small, or if a main road is near. We do our best to avoid misleading people.

Disclaimer

We make no claims to pure objectivity in choosing these places. They are here simply because we like them. Our opinions and tastes are ours alone and this book is a statement of them; we hope you will share them. We have done our utmost to get our facts right but apologise unreservedly for any mistakes that may have crept in. The latest information we have about each place can be found on our website, www.sawdays.co.uk.

You should know that we don't check such things as fire regulations, swimming pool security or any other laws with which owners of properties receiving paying guests should comply. This is the responsibility of the owners.

Photo above: The Old Parsonage, entry 26
Photo right: Wellies, entry 308

10 Using this book

Finding the right place for you
All these places are special in one way or another. All have been visited and then written about honestly so that you can take what you like and leave the rest. Those of you who swear by Sawday's books trust our write-ups precisely because we don't have a blanket standard; we include places simply because we like them. But we all have different priorities, so do read the descriptions carefully and pick out the places where you will be comfortable. If something is particularly important to you then do check when you book: a simple question or two can avoid misunderstandings.

Photo above: Hartland Mill, entry 78
Photo right: Bay House, entry 38

Maps
Each property is flagged with its entry number on the maps at the front. These maps are a great starting point for planning your trip, but please don't use them as anything other than a general guide – use a decent road map for real navigation. Most places will send you detailed instructions once you have booked your stay.

Symbols
Below each entry you will see some symbols, which are explained at the very back of the book. They are based on the information given to us by the owners. However, things do change: bikes may be under repair or a new pool may have been put in. Please use the symbols as a guide rather than an absolute statement of fact and double-check anything that is important to you – owners occasionally bend their own rules, so it's worth asking if you may take your child or dog even if they don't have the symbol.

Children – The 👶 symbol shows places which are happy to accept children of all ages. This does not mean that they will necessarily have cots, high chairs, etc. If an owner welcomes children but only those above a certain age, we have put these details at the end of their write-up. These houses do not have the child symbol, but even these folk may accept your younger child if you are the only guests. Many who say no to children do so not because they don't like them but because they may have a steep stair, an unfenced pond or they find balancing the needs of mixed age groups too challenging.

Pets – Our symbol shows places which are happy to accept pets. Do let the owners know when booking that you'd like to bring your pet – particularly if it is not the usual dog! Be realistic about your pet – if it is nervous or excitable or doesn't like the company of other dogs, people, chickens, children, then say so.

Owners' pets – The symbol is given when the owners have their own pet on the premises. It may not be a cat! But it is there to warn you that you may be greeted by a dog, serenaded by a parrot, or indeed sat upon by a cat.

Quick reference indices
At the back of the book you'll find a number of quick reference indices that will help you choose the place that is just right for you.

In this edition you'll find listings of properties where:
- at least one bedroom or bathroom is accessible for wheelchair users
- children of all ages are welcome. Cots, highchairs etc are not necessarily available
- guests' pets are welcome
- credit cards are accepted

Practical matters

Types of places
Some houses have rooms in annexes or stables, barns or garden 'wings', some of which feel part of the house, some of which don't. If you have a strong preference for being in the throng or for being apart, check those details. Consider your surroundings when you are packing: large, ancient country houses may be cooler than you are used to; city places and working farms may be noisy at times; and that peacock or cockerel we mention may disturb you. Light sleepers should pack ear plugs, and take a dressing gown if there's a separate bathroom (though these are sometimes provided).

Some owners give you a front door key so you may come and go as you please; others like to have the house empty between, say, 10am and 4pm.

Rooms
Bedrooms – We tell you if a room is a double, twin/double (i.e. with zip and link beds), suite (with a sitting area), family or single. Most owners are flexible and can juggle beds or bedrooms; talk to them about what you need before you book. Staying in a B&B will not be like staying in a hotel; it is rare to be given your own room key and your bed will not necessarily be made during your stay, or your room cleaned. Make sure you are clear about the room that you have booked, its views, bathroom and beds, etc.

Bathrooms – Most bedrooms in this book have an en suite bath or shower room; we only mention bathroom details when they do not. So, you may get a 'separate' bathroom (yours alone but not en suite) or a shared bathroom. Under certain entries we mention that two rooms share a bathroom and are 'let to same party only'. Please do not assume this means you must be a group of friends to apply; it simply means that if you book one of these rooms you will not be sharing a bathroom with strangers. If these things are important to you, please check when booking. Bath/shower means a bath with shower over; bath and shower means there is a separate shower unit.

Sitting rooms – Most B&B owners offer guests the family sitting room to share, or they provide a sitting room specially for guests, but do not assume that every bedroom or sitting room has a TV.

Meals
Unless we say otherwise, a full cooked breakfast is included. Some owners – particularly in London – will give you a good continental breakfast instead. Often you will feast on local sausage and bacon, eggs from resident hens, homemade breads and jams. In some you may have organic yogurts and beautifully presented fruit compotes. Some owners are fairly unbending about breakfast times, others are happy to just wait until you want it, or even bring it to you in bed.

Apart from breakfast, no meals should be expected unless you have arranged them in advance. Although we don't say so

Photo right: Davenport House, entry 272

on each entry — the repetition a few hundred times would be tedious — all owners who provide packed lunch, lunch or dinner need advance notice. And they want to get things right for you so, when booking, please discuss your diet and meal times. Meal prices are quoted per person, and dinner is often a social occasion shared with your hosts and other guests.

Do eat in if you can — this book is teeming with good cooks. And how much more relaxing after a day out to have to move no further than the dining room for an excellent dinner, and to eat and drink knowing there's only a flight of stairs between you and your bed. Very few of our houses are licensed, but most are happy for you to bring your own drink.

Photo above: The Old Manor House, entry 357

If you do decide to head out for supper, you can find recommendations of our favourite pubs on our *Special Places to Eat and Drink* website: www.sawdays.co.uk/pubs. If a B&B has a pub nearby, you can see this on their page on our website, too.

Prices and minimum stays

Each entry gives a price PER ROOM for two people. We also include prices for single rooms, and let you know if there will be any extra to pay, should you choose to loll in a double bed on your own.

The price range for each B&B covers a one-night stay in the cheapest room in low season to the most expensive in high season. Some owners charge more at certain times (during regattas or festivals, for example) and some charge less for stays of more than one night. Some owners ask for a two-night minimum stay and we mention this where possible. Most of our houses could fill many times over on peak weekends and during the summer; book early, especially if you have specific needs.

Booking and cancellation

You may not receive a reply to your booking enquiry immediately; B&Bs are not hotels and the owners may be away. When you speak to the owner double-check the price you will pay for B&B and for any meals.

Requests for deposits vary; some are non-refundable, especially in our London homes, and some owners may charge you for the whole of the booked stay in advance. Some cancellation policies are more stringent than others. It is also worth noting that some owners will take the money directly from your credit/debit card without contacting you to discuss it. Ask them to explain their cancellation policy clearly before booking to avoid a nasty surprise.

Payment

Most of our owners take cash and UK cheques with a cheque card. Some take credit cards; if they do we have given them the appropriate symbol. Please check that your particular credit card is acceptable.

Tipping

Owners do not expect tips. If you have been treated with extraordinary kindness, write to them, or leave a small gift. Please tell us, too – we love to hear, and we do note all feedback.

Arrivals and departures

Say roughly what time you will arrive (normally after 4pm), as most hosts like to welcome you personally. Be on time if you have booked dinner; if, despite best efforts, you are delayed, phone to give warning.

Closed

When given in months this means the whole of the month stated.

Photo bottom: Two Hillside Crescent, entry 414
Photo overleaf: Northcourt, entry 169

General map   17

© Maidenhead Cartographic, 2018

18   Map 1

Map 2

Map 3

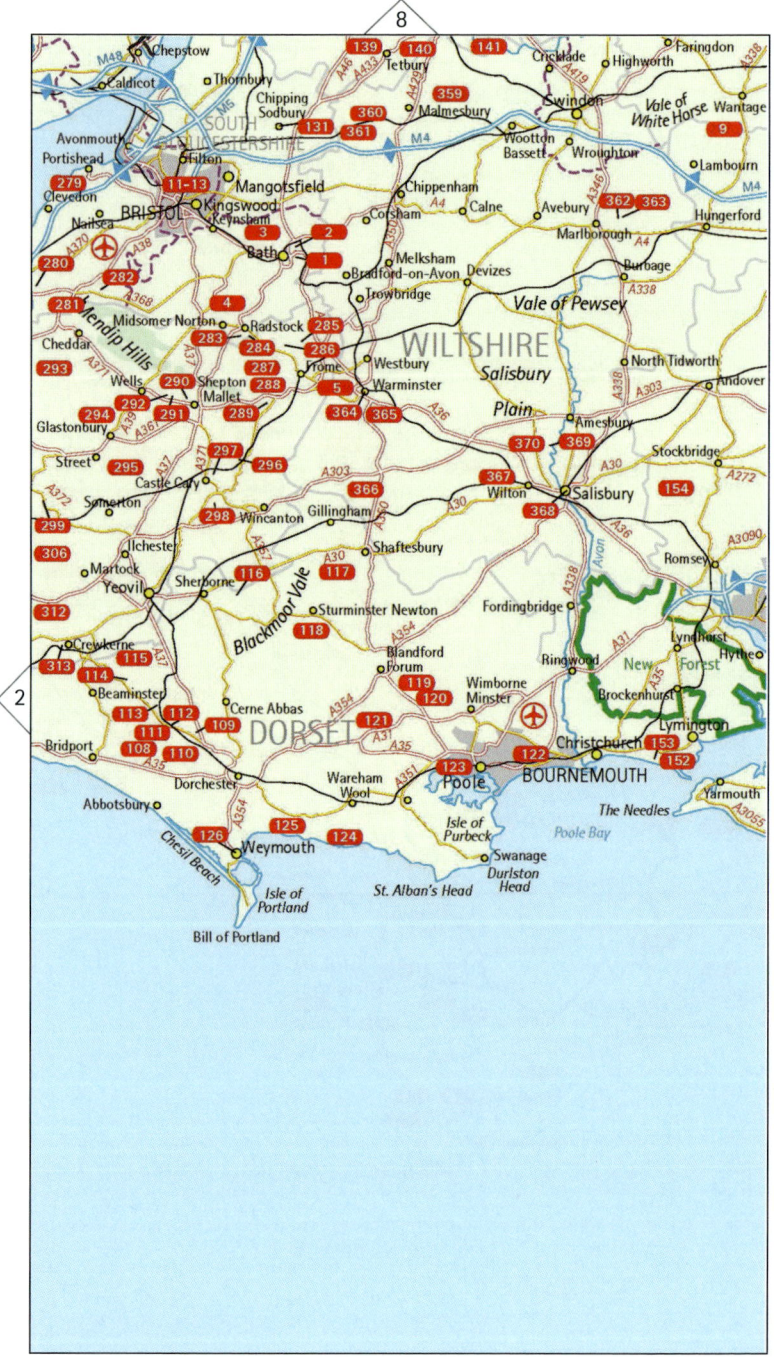

Map 4   21

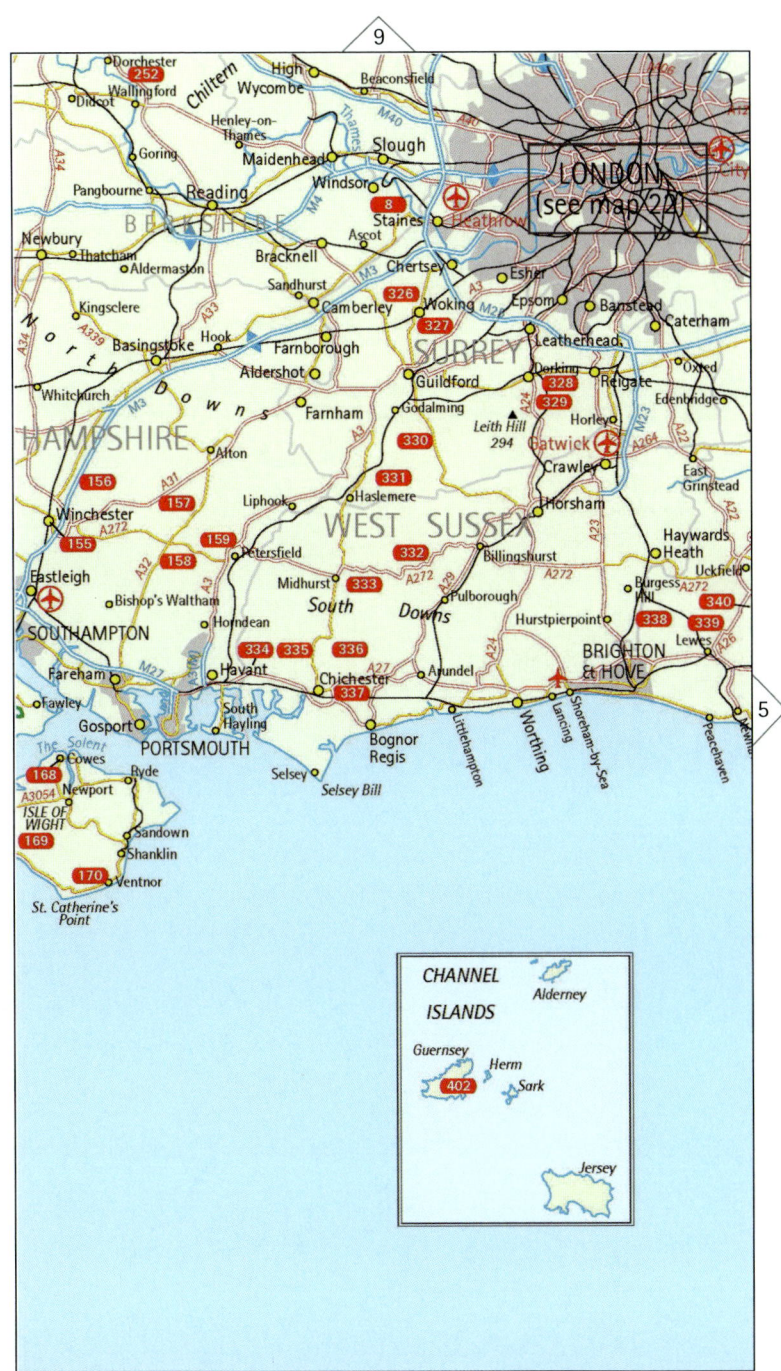

Map 5

Map 6

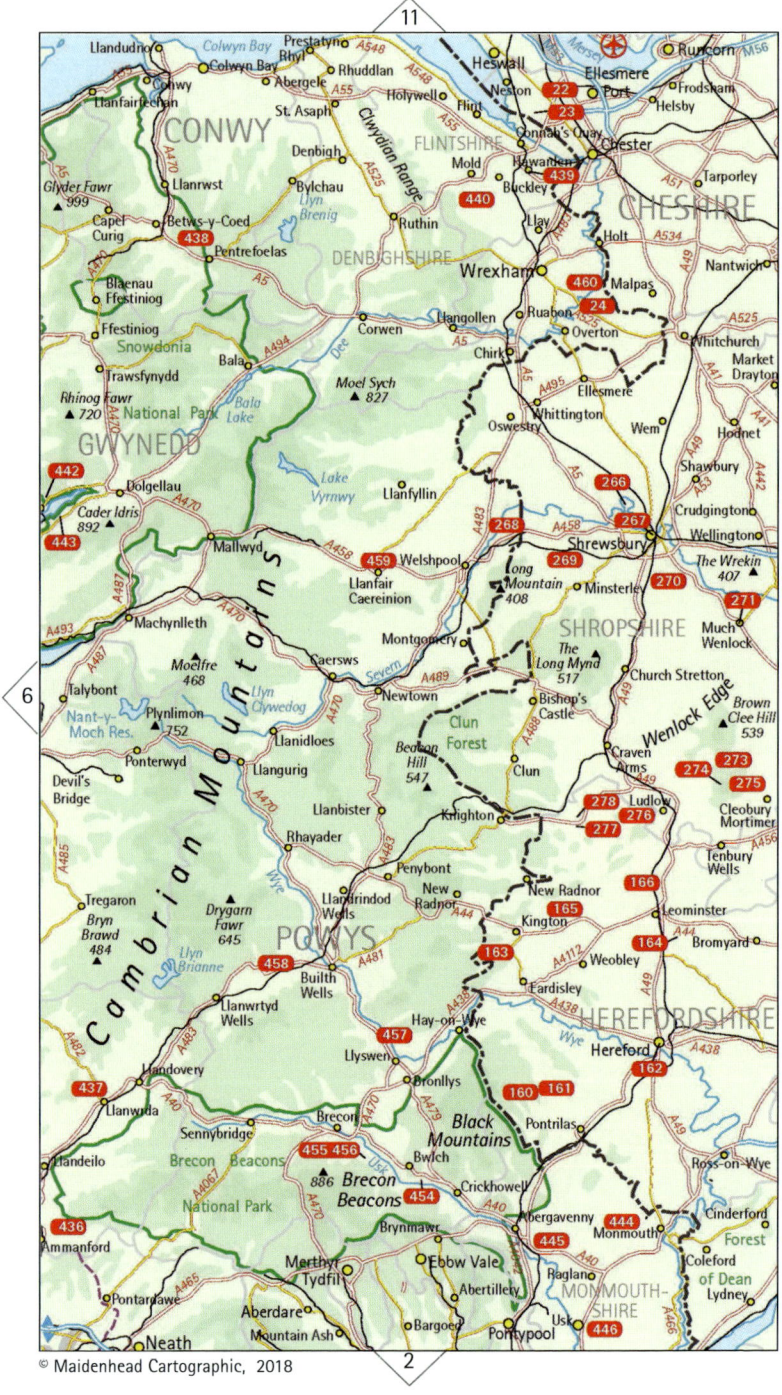

Map 8

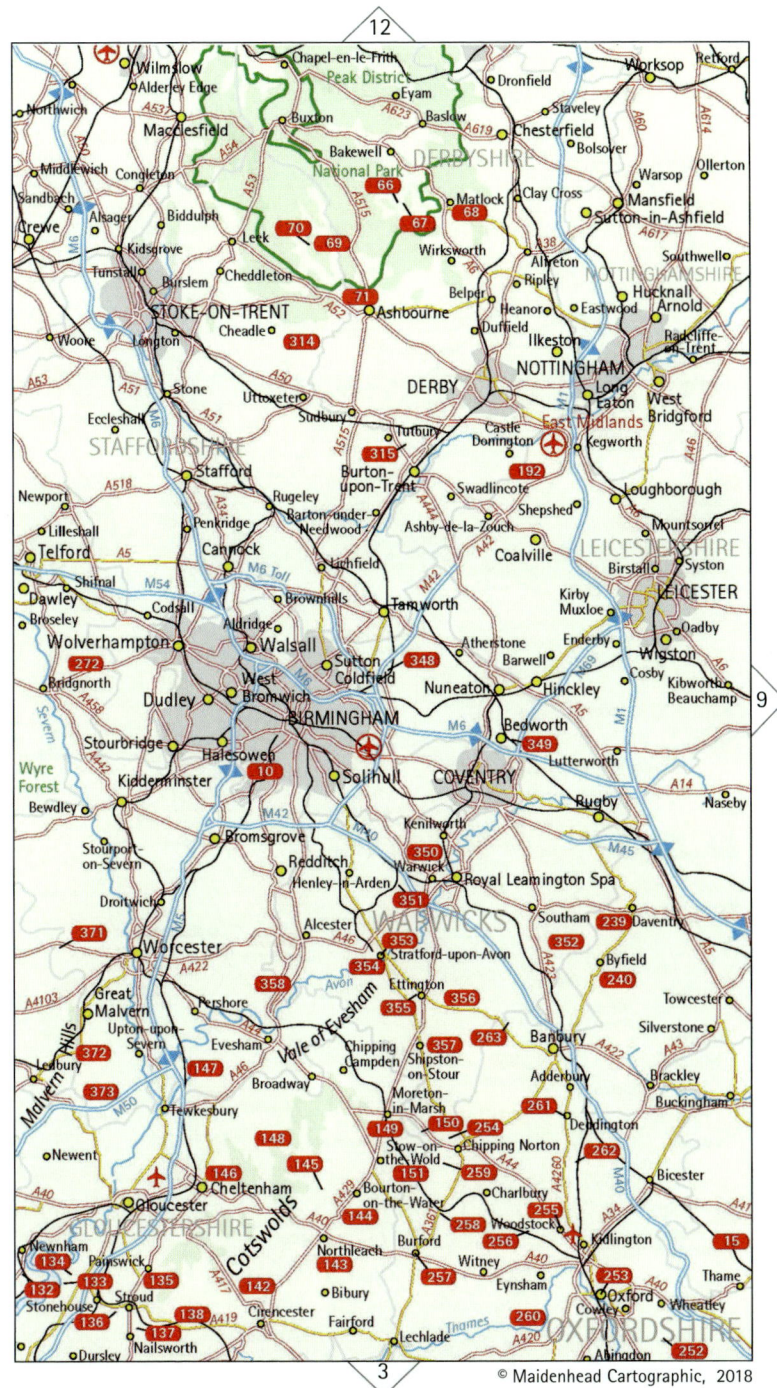

Map 9

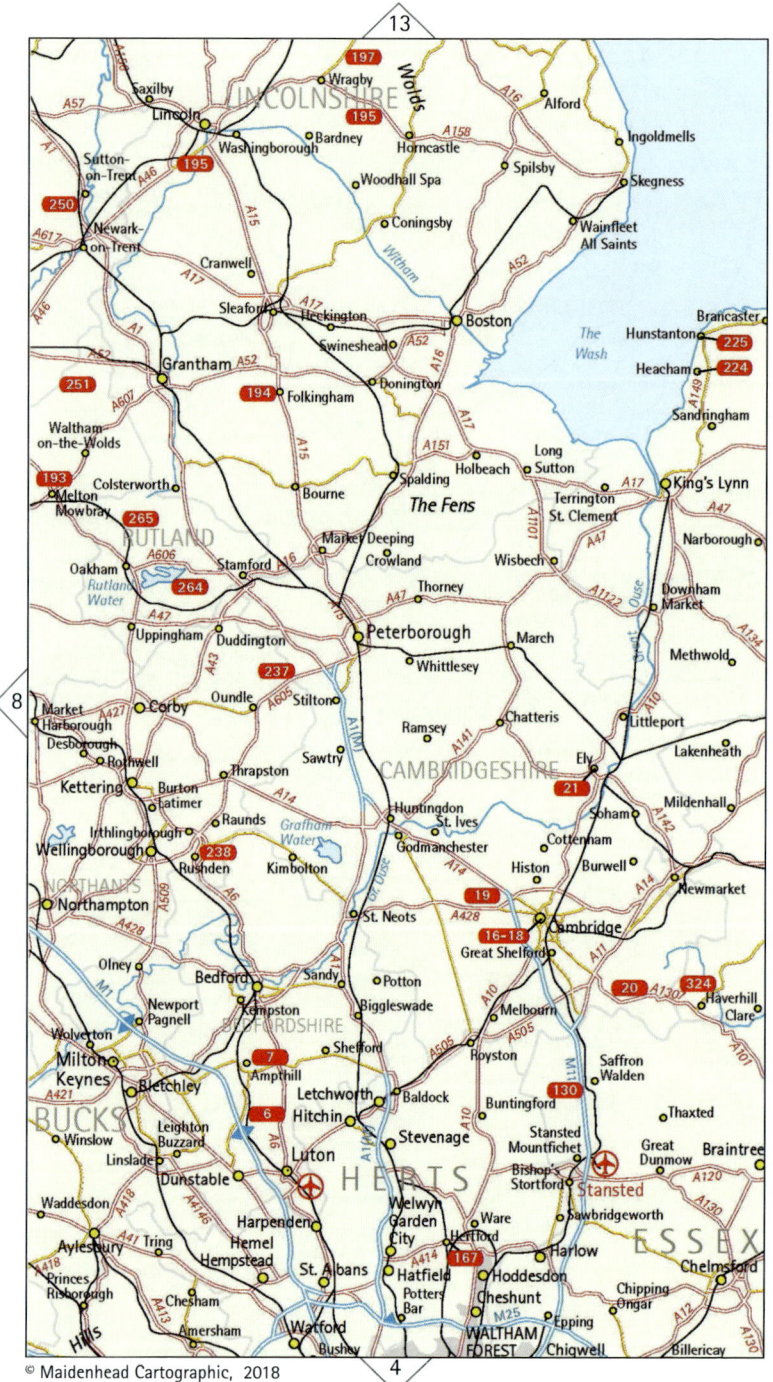

Map 10

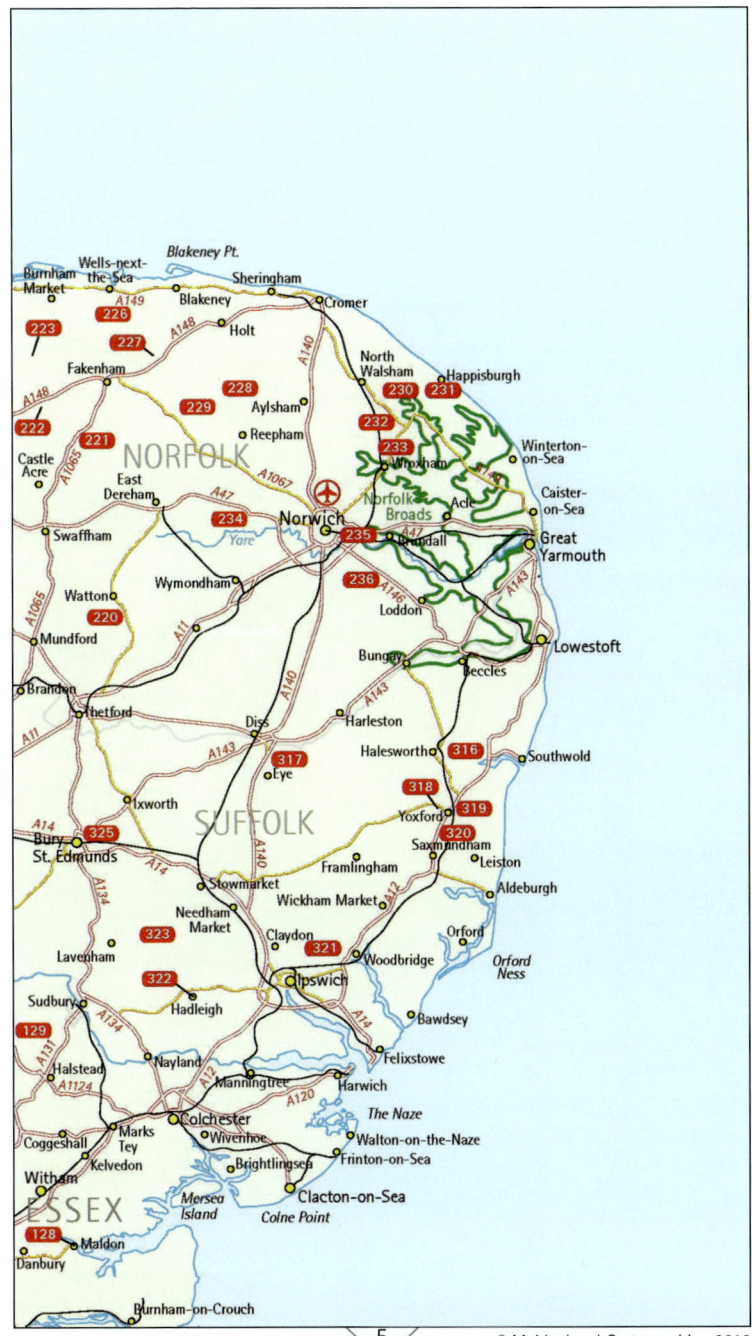

Map 11

Map 12

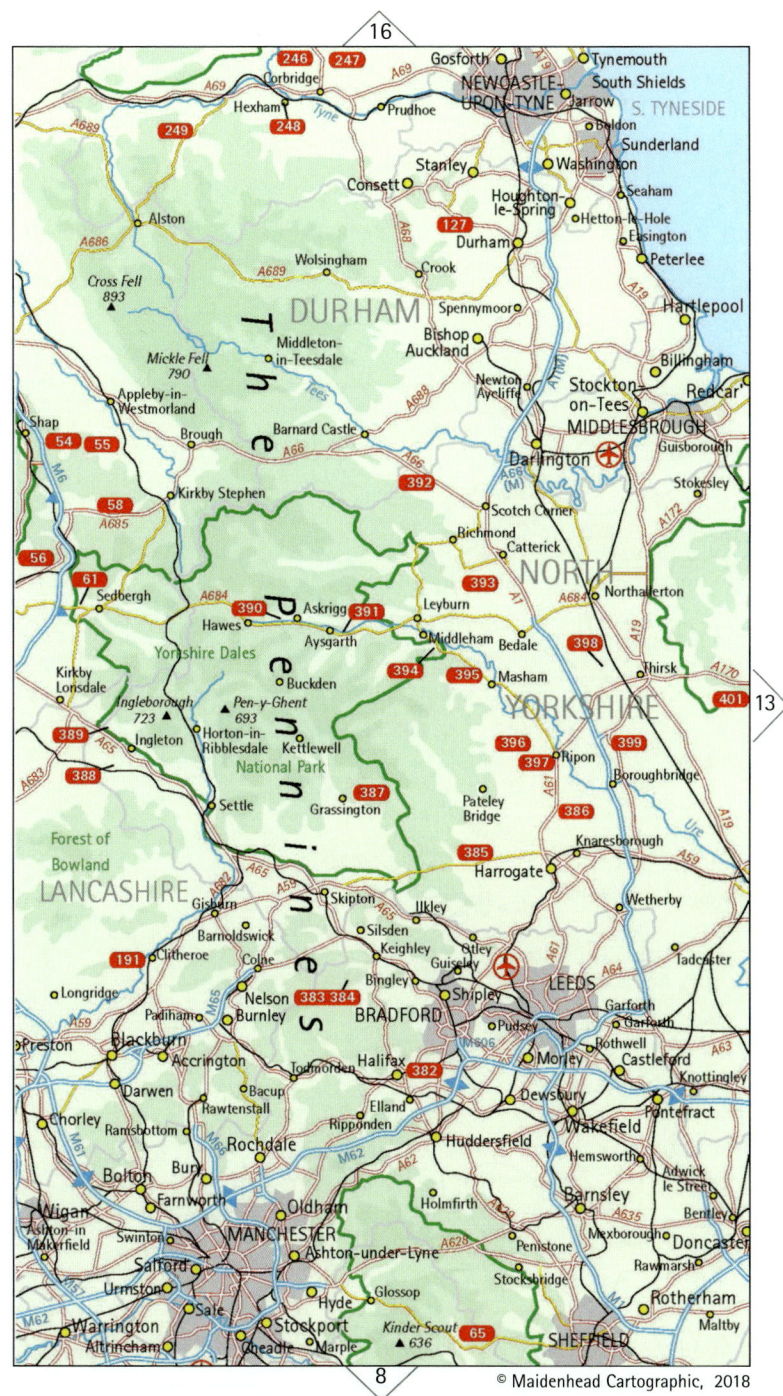

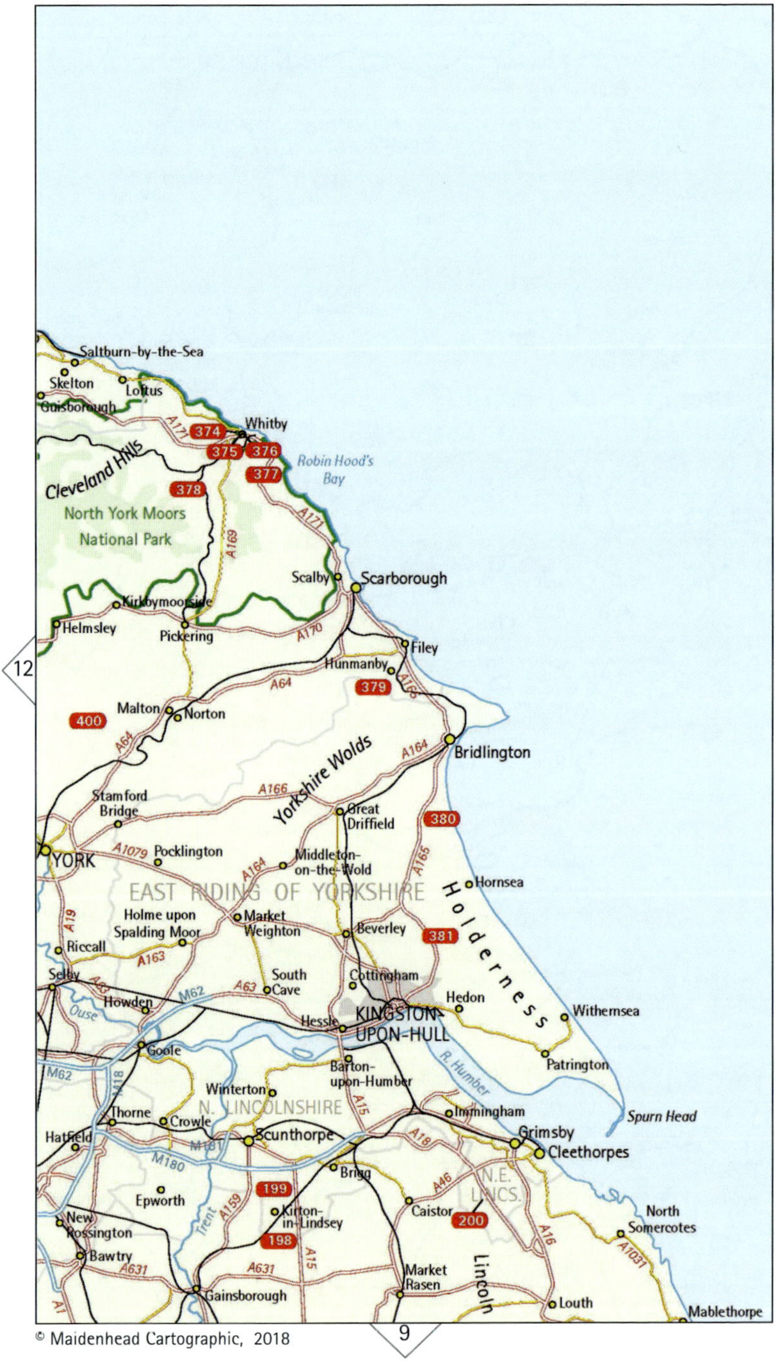

Saltburn-by-the-Sea
Skelton
Loftus
Guisborough
Whitby
374
375
376
377
378
A171
Robin Hood's Bay
Cleveland Hills
North York Moors
National Park
A169
Scalby
Scarborough
Kirkbymoorside
Helmsley
Pickering
A170
Filey
Hunmanby
379
A64
12
Malton
Norton
400
Bridlington
A164
Yorkshire Wolds
Stamford Bridge
A166
Great Driffield
380
YORK
A1079
Pocklington
Middleton-on-the-Wold
A165
Hornsea
EAST RIDING OF YORKSHIRE
Holderness
Holme upon Spalding Moor
Market Weighton
Beverley
381
A19
Riccall
A163
Selby
South Cave
Cottingham
A63
Howden
M62
Ouse
Hedon
KINGSTON-UPON-HULL
Hessle
Withernsea
Goole
Barton-upon-Humber
R. Humber
Patrington
A18
Winterton
N. LINCOLNSHIRE
A15
Thorne
Crowle
Immingham
Spurn Head
Hatfield
M181
Scunthorpe
Grimsby
Cleethorpes
M180
Brigg
Epworth
199
A159
Trent
A46
N.E. LINCS.
Caistor
200
Kirton-in-Lindsey
New Rossington
198
North Somercotes
Bawtry
A631
A16
A1031
Market Rasen
Lincoln
Gainsborough
Louth
A1
Mablethorpe
9

Map 14

32 Map 15

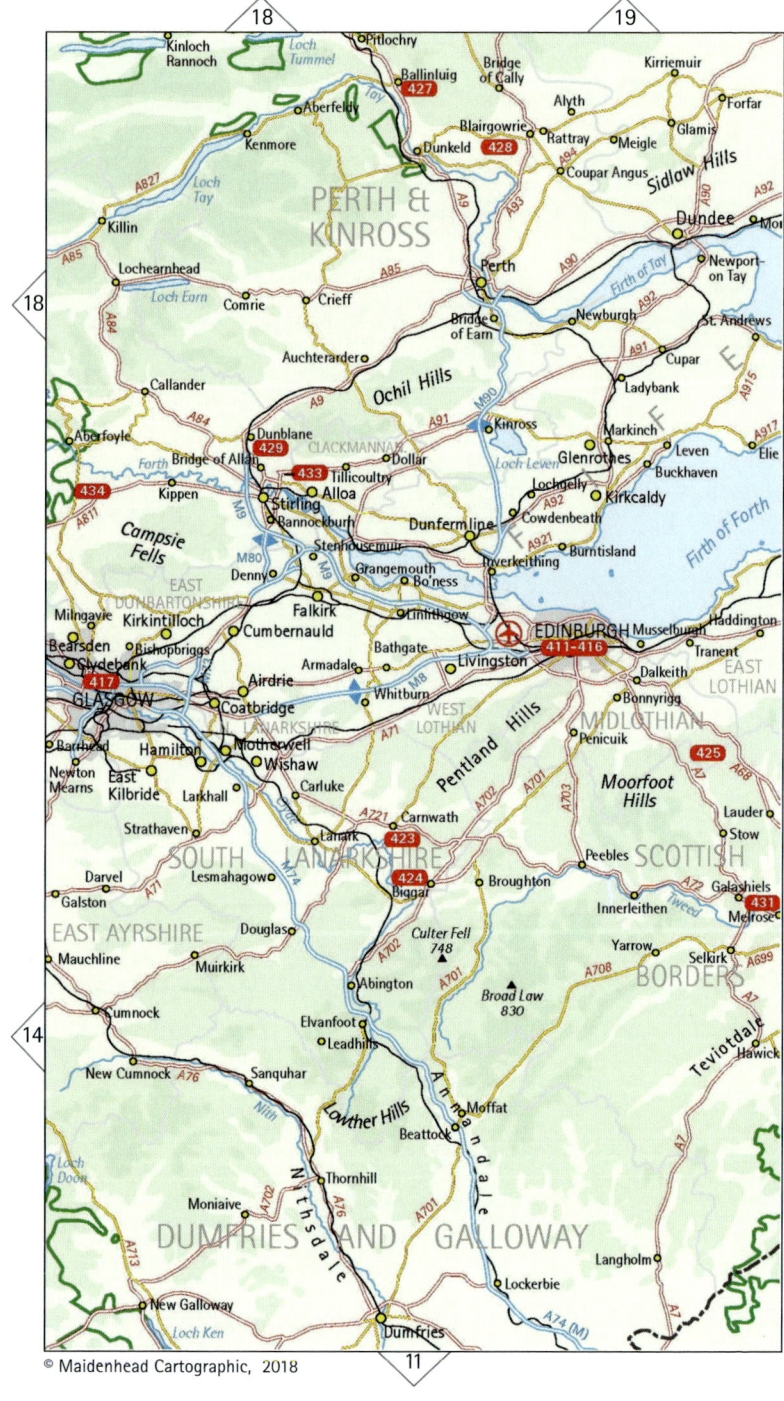

Map 16

34 Map 17

Map 18

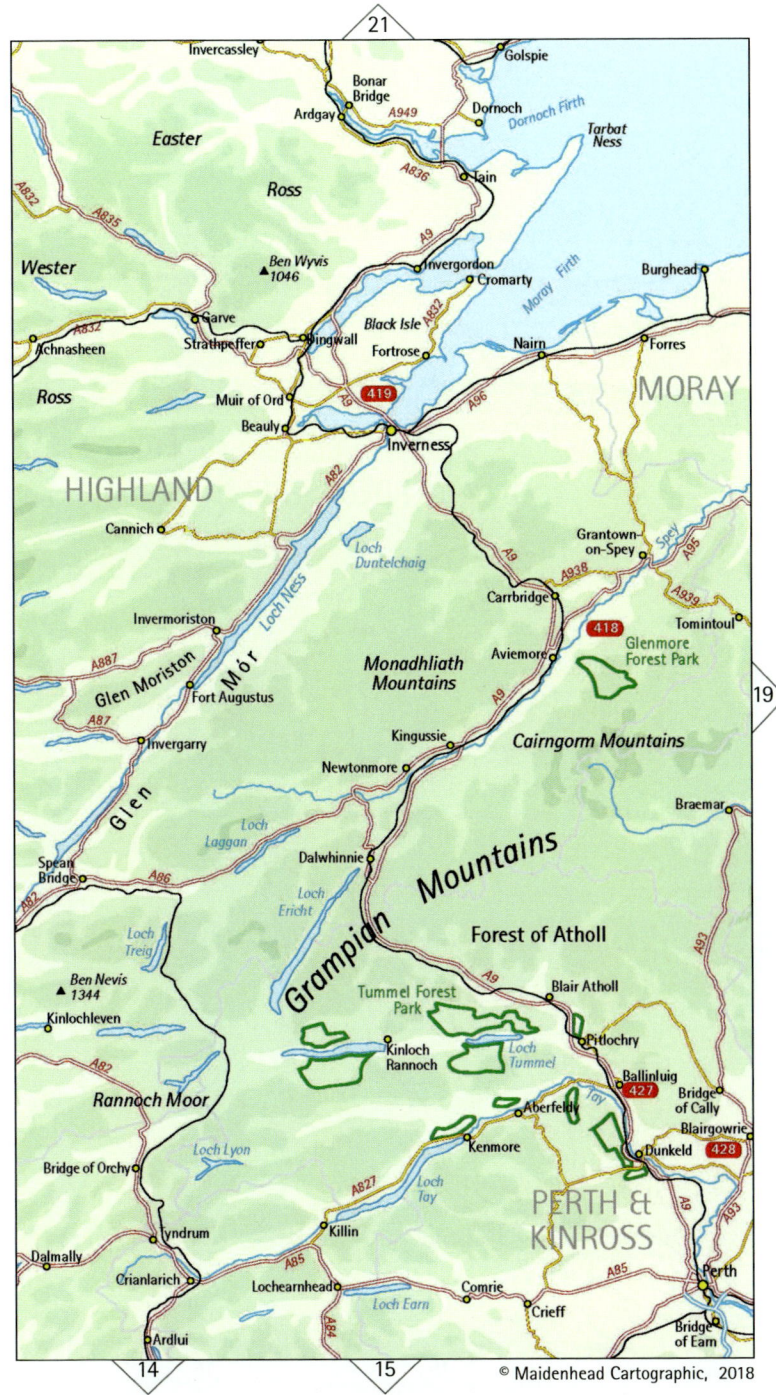

36　Map 19

Map 20

Map 21

Map 22

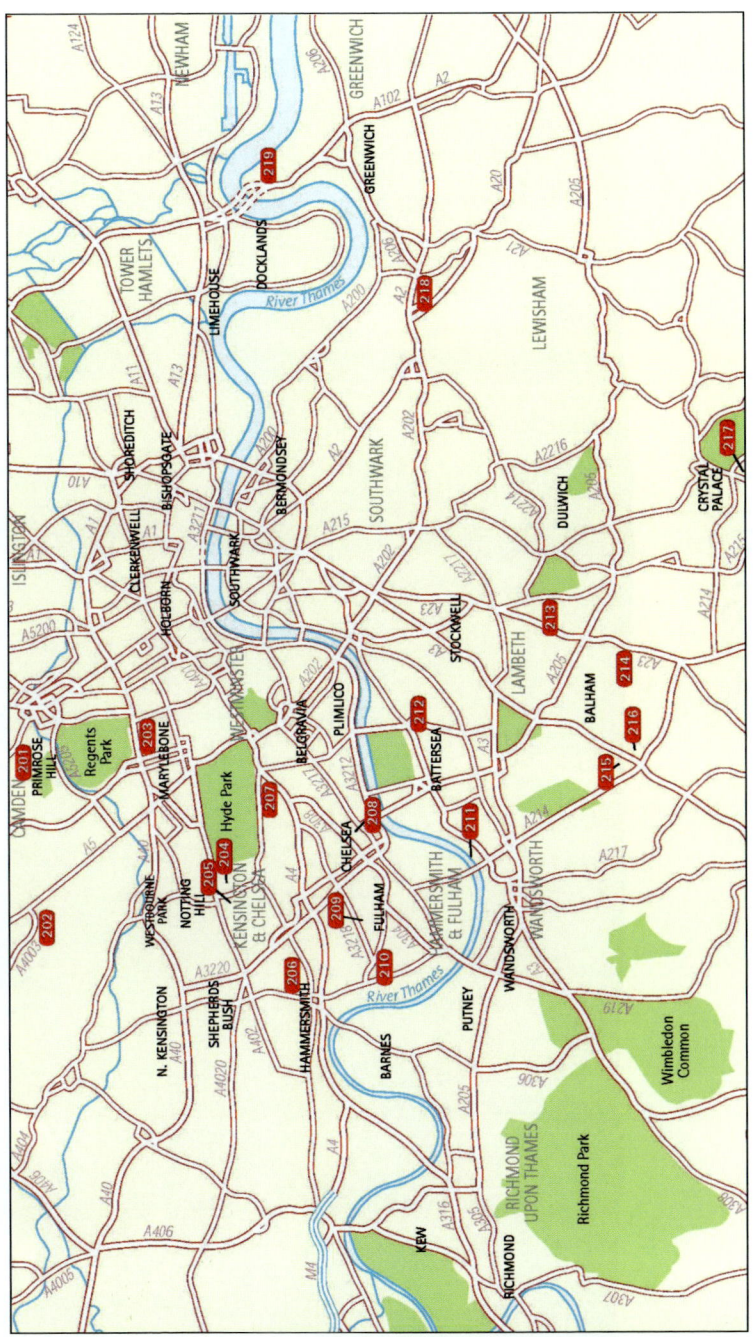

39

England

Photo: Ansford Farm Cottage, entry 297

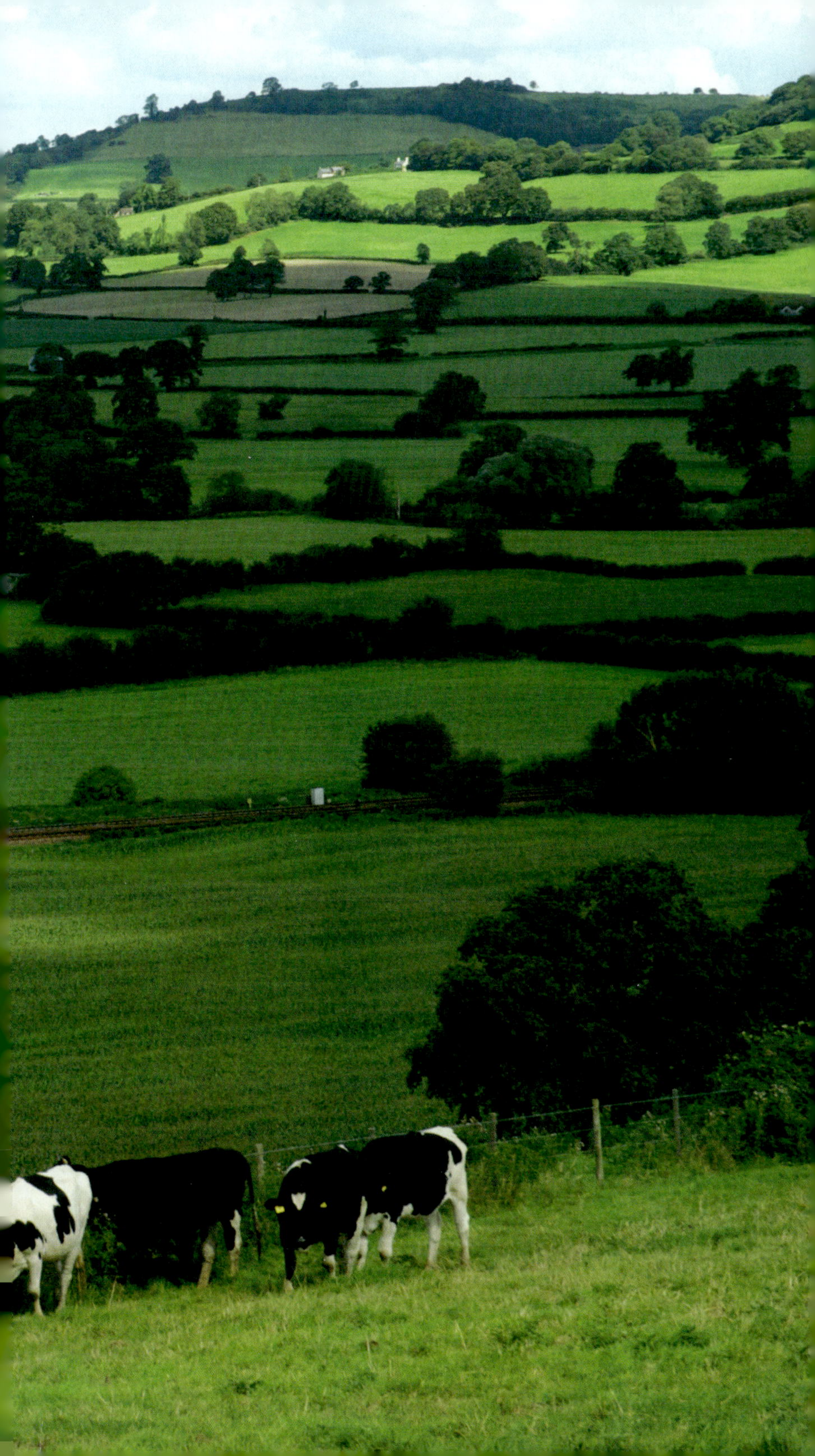

Bath & N.E. Somerset

Grosvenor Villa

This listed Georgian villa was built to house the former high altar of Bath Abbey, which now forms part of the impressive entrance hall. Quiet bedrooms (up quite steep stairs) have super king-size beds with fine linen, robes, TVs and WiFi. Breakfast is continental with fruit salad, pain au chocolat, cheeses, boiled eggs; a convivial affair in the Georgian dining room. Your hosts are generous and you're welcome to relax in the garden or by the wood-burner in the upstairs sitting room. It's a short taxi ride or 20-minute stroll along the canal tow path to the centre for all the bustle of shops, restaurants and theatre.

Rooms	1 double; 2 doubles with separate bathrooms: £109-£179.
Meals	Pubs/restaurants 5-minute walk.
Closed	Christmas & New Year.

Minimum stay: 2 nights at weekends & in high season. One parking space; additional in nearby roads (no charge).

Richard Sweet
Grosvenor Villa,
Grosvenor Bridge Road,
Bath, BA1 6BB
Tel   +44 (0)1225 330092
Email   info@grosvenorvillabath.co.uk
Web   www.grosvenorvillabath.co.uk

Entry 1   Map 3

Bath & N.E. Somerset

Sir Walter Elliot's House

Utterly wonderful hosts at this Grade I-listed house. On one of Bath's finest Regency terraces, it has been so beautifully restored that the BBC filmed it for *Persuasion*; Jane Austen Society members often stay. Up several stairs are bedrooms flooded with light, two with views over Sydney Gardens, one with a bathroom in marquina marble, cherrywood and ebony. Have breakfast in the convivial family kitchen, or in the plant-filled conservatory. For the adventurous, Mechthild will serve an Austrian alternative – cold meats and cheeses, fresh rye breads and homemade cakes. Herrlich!

Rooms	3 twin/doubles: £135-£200.
Meals	Pub/restaurant 300 yds.
Closed	Rarely.

Minimum stay: 2 nights at weekends.

Julian Self
Sir Walter Elliot's House,
95 Sydney Place, Bath, BA2 6NE
Tel   +44 (0)1225 469435
Mobile   +44 (0)7967 471085
Email   visitus@sirwalterelliotshouse.co.uk
Web   www.sirwalterelliotshouse.co.uk

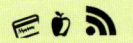

Entry 2   Map 3

Bath & N.E. Somerset

The Power House

On top of Bath's highest hill lies Rikki's Bauhaus-inspired home, its glass walls making the most of a magical spot and a sensational view; on a clear day you can see the Welsh hills. In the vast open-plan living space – homely, inviting, inspiring – are treasures from a lifetime of travels: ancient Tuareg camel sacks, kitsch Art Deco pots, gorgeous Persian chests. Bedrooms in the house are airy, with doors onto a huge balcony; the snug, colourful studio room has a wood-burner and little kitchen. Rikki is an incredible chef and uses the finest ingredients from Bath's farmers' market, ten minutes away. Breakfasts are superb – good coffee too.

Bath & N.E. Somerset

Pitfour House

Georgian gentility in a village near Bath. This is where the rector would live in an Austen novel: it's handsome, respectable, and the feel extends inside, where convivial hosts Frances (a keen cook) and Martin (a keen gardener) put you at ease in their elegant home. The creamy guest sitting room gleams with period furniture, the dining room is panelled and parqueted, fresh flowers abound. The two bedrooms – one with en suite shower, one with a private bath – are compact but detailed with antiques. Take tea in the neat walled garden, admire the vegetable patch, then taste the spoils in one of Frances's fine suppers.

Rooms	1 double: £100–£120. 1 studio for 2 with kitchen: £100–£120. 1 single: £70. 2 further small doubles available, sharing bathrooms.	Rooms	1 twin/double; 1 twin/double with separate bath: £98–£100. Singles £78–£80.
Meals	Dinner £25. Pubs/restaurants 3-minute drive.	Meals	Dinner, 2-3 courses, £30–£38. Supper £25. Restaurant 1.5 miles.
Closed	Rarely.	Closed	Rarely.

Self-catering available in studio.

Minimum stay: 2 nights.

	Tiana Jacout The Power House, Brockham End, Lansdown, Bath, BA1 9BY		Frances Hardman Pitfour House, High Street, Timsbury, Bath, BA2 0HT
Tel	+44 (0)7974 222666	Tel	+44 (0)1761 479554
Mobile	+44 (0)7974 222666	Email	pitfourhouse@btinternet.com
Email	rjacout@gmail.com	Web	www.pitfourhouse.co.uk

Entry 3   Map 3

Entry 4   Map 3

Somerset

Reeves Barn

Drive under the willow to find a prettily converted studio barn, a gorgeous shepherd's hut and an away-from-it-all feel. The studio comes with limed beams, a romantic bedroom, a simple wet room with scented oils, and a mini kitchen cleverly tucked into a cupboard. Or choose to sleep under the stars in the snug and woody shepherd's hut. You can order dinner for your arrival, and artist Barbette leaves a breakfast hamper for you – wake and eat when you want! Sit in the sun by pots of flowers, curl up by a wood-burner, enjoy the rustic vibe in the hut. Bath, Wells, Frome and Bruton's Hauser & Wirth are nearby.

Rooms	1 double with sitting room & kitchenette: £100–£115. 1 shepherd's hut for 2: £85. Extra bed/sofabed/cot £15 per person per night.
Meals	Dinner, 3 courses for studio guests, £35. Dinner, 2 courses & bottle of prosecco for shepherd's hut guests, £65 for 2.
Closed	Rarely.

Barbette Saunders
Reeves Barn,
17 Whitbourne Springs, Corsley,
Warminster, BA12 7RF

Tel	+44 (0)1373 832106
Mobile	+44 (0)7796 687806
Email	barbettesaunders@gmail.com
Web	reevesbarn.com

Entry 5   Map 3

Bedfordshire

Harlington Manor

Charles II may have stayed, and his bedroom has changed little... Off a busy street yet an ancient dream of a manor house, David's home is a dramatic trove of antiques, art, rich colour, grand piano, rose carvings, gorgeous bedrooms – be swept along by his enthusiasm and generosity, marvel at the attention to detail. Breakfast is served in the magnificent Tudor dining room at one long table: continental with compotes and yogurt, home-baking, tea in heirloom china. David's a good cook, and dinner with the family might include a harpsichord recital. A pretty garden, guided local tours... hop on a train from St Pancras and arrive in time for drinks.

Rooms	2 doubles; 1 double with separate bathroom: £88–£120.
Meals	Continental breakfast on weekdays, cooked breakfast at weekends. Dinner, 4 courses with glass of champagne & port, £40. Restaurants 2-minute walk.
Closed	Rarely.

Public transport 2-minute walk.

David Blakeman
Harlington Manor,
Westoning Road,
Harlington, LU5 6PB

Mobile	+44 (0)7788 742209
Email	blakeman.david1@gmail.com
Web	www.harlingtonmanor.com

Entry 6   Map 9

Bedfordshire

Forge Cottage Barn

A sweet pea and lavender-clad pergola leads to your own barn... Carmel and David give you a fresh bedroom with tip-top linen and cheerful bedspread on a seriously comfy bed; they have an interesting library that you're welcome to browse too. Breakfast is a moveable feast – have it outside the barn in the sun, over in the main house or on the deck by a stream; tuck into locally sourced everything with homemade marmalade and jams. Masses to do nearby – gardens, cycling, rowing on the river Ouse, walks on the Greensand Ridge. Return to explore the pretty cottage garden, and then curl up with a book on the sofa in your room.

Rooms	1 double: £85. Friday & Saturday: £90. Extra child's bed and travel cot available.
Meals	Pub 3-minute walk.
Closed	Christmas.

Carmel Golding
Forge Cottage Barn,
Forge Cottage, The Knoll, Maulden,
Bedford, MK45 2DB

Tel +44 (0)1525 840485
Email carmel@dandcgolding.com
Web www.forgecottagebarn.com

Entry 7   Map 9

Berkshire

Monks Walk

On a quiet, genteel cul de sac tucked away in Old Windsor, Marion has created a cosy, self-contained bolthole for guests. Your annexe is just 200 yards from the Thames and overlooks a pretty garden; the elegant bedroom has down pillows and white linen, fine china tea set and an old treadle sewing machine serving as a dressing table. The shower room sparkles and is replete with handmade smellies. You get sole use of an unashamedly traditional sitting room with open fire in the main house, near the dining room where Marion serves impressive full Irish breakfasts, along with an unending supply of her delicious baking.

Rooms	1 double with separate shower room: £100.
Meals	Pubs/restaurants 15-minute walk.
Closed	Rarely.

Parking on-site.

Marion Clark
Monks Walk,
The Friary,
Old Windsor, SL4 2NR

Tel +44 (0)1753 841202
Mobile +44 (0)7931 500645
Email marion.clark@hotmail.com

Entry 8   Map 4

Berkshire

Long Acre Farm

You have your own entrance to a converted pigsty and your hosts are charming, so join in as much, or as little, as you want. Joanna is a great cook and organic breakfasts include homemade granola and apple juice, often home-baked bread, a full English if you want it – eat at the family dining table or in the private kitchen. She'll happily rustle up a packed lunch, so hikers can walk up to White Horse Hill or join the Ridgeway for miles of glorious downland. Bedrooms have underfloor heating, books and speedy broadband; relax and watch a DVD by the wood-burner in the Stable barn. Sit in the walled garden on balmy days, visit nearby Buscot Park with its Faringdon Collection or walk up to the gallops on the edge of the farm to watch the horses train; return for an organic dinner.

Rooms	2 doubles; 1 twin with separate bathroom: £95. Cot available.
Meals	Lunch on request, £5-£20. Dinner, 2-3 courses, £35-£30. Pubs/restaurants 5 miles.
Closed	Christmas & New Year.

Joanna Preston
Long Acre Farm,
Seven Barrows,
Lambourn, RG17 8UH
Mobile +44 (0)7815 782518
Email joannapreston@cheynehouse.com

Entry 9   Map 3

Birmingham

Woodbrooke

A pleasure to find ten tranquil acres (woodlands, lawns, lake and walled garden) so close to the centre of Birmingham – run by such special people. This impressive Georgian mansion was donated by George Cadbury to the Quakers in 1903, as a place for study and contemplation. And so it remains. There are corridors aplenty and public rooms big and small: a library, a silent room, a lovely new garden lounge, and a dining hall where organic buffet meals feature fruit and veg from the grounds. Bedrooms, spread over several buildings, are carpeted, comfortable, light and airy, and most have en suite showers. Welcoming, nurturing, historic.

Rooms	5 doubles, 7 twins, mostly en suite: £69-£99. 1 family room for 5, 1 family room for 6: £135-£179. 53 singles, mostly en suite: £49-£79. 2 triples: £95-£119.
Meals	Breakfast included. Lunch & dinner £11. Pubs/restaurants 15-min walk.
Closed	Christmas & Boxing Day.

Please note the reception is not open 24hrs.

Marc Harbourne-Bessant
Woodbrooke,
1046 Bristol Road, Selly Oak,
Birmingham, B29 6LJ
Tel +44 (0)121 472 5171
Email enquiries@woodbrooke.org.uk
Web www.woodbrooke.org.uk

Entry 10   Map 8

Bristol

The Bristol Wing

It's a hostel, but not as you know it, and it couldn't have a friendlier vibe. You've a choice of places to sit and work or chat; reception has a busier buzz with folk wandering in and out, music, help-yourself coffee and tea; the downstairs sitting room has interesting books. Upstairs find eclectic art on the walls, fresh white doubles, family rooms and shared dorms, some en suite, some with shared bathrooms. Ethical credentials here are impressive: this is the second brilliant social enterprise scheme initiated by Ben Silvey. The first is The Kitchen, an award-winning café just over the courtyard, where you have breakfast. Both are owned and managed by YMCA Bristol, and any profits made are re-invested in supporting homeless young people. Excellent value, and will equally suit single travellers, couples or families.

Rooms	1 family room for 3: £54. 2 family rooms for 4: £80. 2 family rooms for 4, sharing bathroom: £70. 2 family rooms for 5: £90. 1 family room for 6: £102. 1 6-bed mixed bunk room, 1 6-bed female bunk room, 1 9-bed mixed bunk room, 1 9-bed female bunk room, 1 12-bed male bunk room: £18 p.p.p.n.
Meals	Pubs/restaurants 2-minute walk.
Closed	Never.

Ben Silvey
The Bristol Wing,
9 Bridewell Street, Bristol, BS1 2QD
Tel: +44 (0)117 428 6199
Email: enquiries@thebristolwing.co.uk
Web: thebristolwing.co.uk

Entry 11   Map 3

Bristol

9 Princes Buildings

A super city base with comfortable beds, charming owners and, without a doubt, the best views in Clifton. You're a hop from the elegant Suspension Bridge, restaurants, shops and pubs of the village and a ferry to whisk you to town or the station; yet all is quiet and the garden is large and leafy. You walk in to a big square hall; the drawing room has a peaceful feel and a veranda for the views. Bedrooms are sunny and traditional: one downstairs overlooks the garden, the top floor double is furnished more simply. Simon and Joanna give you a good, leisurely breakfast too: local sausages and bacon, homemade jams and marmalade.

Rooms	2 doubles, 1 twin/double; 1 twin/double with separate bath: £105-£125. Singles £75-£79.
Meals	Pub/restaurant 100 yds.
Closed	Rarely.

Simon & Joanna Fuller
9 Princes Buildings,
Clifton,
Bristol, BS8 4LB
Tel: +44 (0)117 973 4615
Email: info@9pb.co.uk
Web: www.9princesbuildings.co.uk

Entry 12   Map 3

Bristol

Victoria Park Rooms

Light streams into every room of this end of terrace Edwardian townhouse – and it overlooks big, leafy Victoria Park. It's a young, interesting household and you'll feel very much part of the family. There's a choice of two rooms – escape to the top floor if you want a bit more privacy. Both rooms are large, bright and homely and have books, tea, coffee and a drawer of snacks. You can hop down to the wood-burner warmed sitting room for breakfast, or stay put and have it in your room; the continental spread includes homemade granola, pastries and good bread. Sit outside in the front garden with your coffee on sunny mornings. An easy place to stay if you want to be in Bristol without the bother of the town centre. In the summer there's a café in the park so if you fancy a bacon butty you can stroll over there.

Rooms	1 double; 1 double with separate shower room: £70–£110.
Meals	Pub 100 yards.
Closed	Rarely.

	Stewart & Celia Wright
	Victoria Park Rooms,
	36 Nutgrove Avenue,
	Bristol, BS3 4QF
Email	celiaowright@gmail.com

Entry 13   Map 3

Cluckinghamshire

Roost

Here's a new one for Sawday's – a B&B where hen parties are positively welcome! Inside, there's a cosy, artisan feel – almost as if the whole place had been knocked together from a couple of old doors – with rickety ladders leading to rows of wooden beds complete with straw mattresses and a communal sitting area where guests perch for a wattle wag. Owner, Roger, is proud of his reputation as a ladies' man. "I know it's not pc these days but I just LOVE the chicks," he crows as he struts about his yard. He's been known to ruffle a few feathers locally with his early morning wake up calls but hey, he couldn't give a cluck.

Rooms	One shared between 20.
Meals	Thrown in.
Closed	Night times only; make sure you're in by dusk.

Minimum stay: 2 nights

	Roger Peckham
	Roost
	Cornworthy
	Cluckinghamshire, PO1 TRY
Tel	Please do – anytime, anywhere ;-)
Email	rise@dawnandmakesomenoise.co.uk
Web	www.cockadoodle.co.ck

Entry 14   Map

Buckinghamshire

Long Crendon Manor

Masses of history and oodles of character at this timbered listed house with high chimneys, dating from 1187... no wonder film companies are keen to get through the arched entrance and into the courtyard! The vast dining room is a dramatic setting for breakfast: sausages from Sue's pigs, home-baked bread, plum and mulberry jam from the gardens. Windows on both sides bring light into the fire-warmed drawing room with leather sofas, gleaming furniture, family bits and bobs, pictures galore. Sleep soundly in comfortable, country-house style bedrooms (one with gorgeous yellow panelling). Peaceful.

Rooms	1 double, 1 double with extra twin in dressing room, 1 four-poster: £100-£200. Singles £80-£100.
Meals	Supper £30. Pubs/restaurants 3-minute walk.
Closed	Occasionally.

	Sue Soar Long Crendon Manor, Frogmore Lane, Long Crendon, Aylesbury, HP18 9DZ
Tel	+44 (0)1844 201647
Email	sue.soar@longcrendonmanor.co.uk
Web	www.longcrendonmanor.co.uk

Entry 15   Map 8

Cambridgeshire

Cambridge University

Buses, bicycles and punting on the Cam: huge fun when you're in the heart of it all. Enter the Great Gate Tower of Christ's College to be wooed by tranquil, beautiful quadrangle gardens, breakfasts beneath portraits of hallowed masters, and a serene chapel. At smaller Sidney Sussex – 1598-old with additions – you can play tennis in gorgeous gardens, picnic on perfect lawns and start the day with rare-breed sausages. Churchill has a great gym, Downing has Quentin Blake paintings on the walls, St Catharine's has a candlelit chapel. Bedrooms (some shared showers) and lounges are functional; well-informed porters are your first port of call.

Rooms	60 doubles, 206 twins: £75-£128. 804 singles: £49-£79. 3 apartments for 2: £85-£150.
Meals	Breakfast included. Some colleges offer dinner from £7 (details on website).
Closed	Mid-January to mid-March, May/June, October/November; Christmas. A few rooms available throughout year.

Rooms spread across 23 colleges.

	University Rooms Cambridge University, Cambridge
Web	www.universityrooms.com/en-GB/city/cambridge/home

Entry 16   Map 9

Cambridgeshire

Duke House

Opposite Christ's Pieces, one of the city's oldest green spaces, and right in the centre: perfect! This house has been refurbished from top to toe and all is gleaming and generous. Settle into the guest sitting room (chandelier, Regency style furniture, calm colours) and sleep soundly under Irish goose down in beautiful bedrooms all named after dukes; top-floor's Cambridge suite has a romantic balcony. The lovely breakfast room has separate tables with fabric-backed chairs overlooking a little plant-filled courtyard; Liz serves an excellent organic and homemade spread. Shops, botanical garden, restaurants… a happy stroll.

Rooms	4 doubles: £140-£170. 1 suite for 2 (extra sofabed available): £160-£250. Singles £125-£160.
Meals	Pubs/restaurants 5-minute walk.
Closed	Rarely.

Minimum stay: 2 nights at weekends. Children over 10 welcome.

Liz Cameron
Duke House,
1 Victoria Street,
Cambridge, CB1 1JP
Tel +44 (0)1223 314773
Email info@dukehousecambridge.co.uk
Web www.dukehousecambridge.co.uk

Entry 17   Map 9

Cambridgeshire

5 Chapel Street

Exemplary! Where: in a lovely, comfortable, refurbed Georgian house 20 minutes' walk from Cambridge centre. How: with warmth, pleasure, intelligence and local knowledge. Bedrooms have good quality mattresses, bedding and towels. Characterful pieces too – antique brass bed, freestanding bath, oriental rugs on polished floors – with flowers and garden views. The breakfasts are delicious, largely organic and local: fresh fruit salad, kedgeree with smoked Norfolk haddock, home baking (three types of bread; gluten free, no problem). If you'd like to swing a cat book the biggest room; borrow vintage bikes and thoroughly enjoy your break.

Rooms	2 doubles, 1 twin: £100-£130. Singles £90-£120.
Meals	Pubs/restaurants 5-minute walk.
Closed	Rarely.

Minimum stay: 2 nights. Children over 11 welcome.

Christine Ulyyan
5 Chapel Street,
Cambridge, CB4 1DY
Tel +44 (0)1223 514856
Email christine.ulyyan@gmail.com
Web www.5chapelstreet.com

Entry 18   Map 9

Cambridgeshire

Crafts Hill Barn

Two inviting bolt holes in the grounds of a Victorian granary. Each has a sitting/dining space, airy with soaring beams, restful colours and a fresh contemporary feel. There's a sofa, TV and nifty kitchenette and, through white curtains, a cow hide underfoot in The Cowshed and a king size bed topped with luxurious linen. Jo brings over breakfast: homemade granola, muffins and bread; at the weekends you can order a delicious Aga-cooked spread – lots of choice. Cambridge is an easy drive, and your escape a treat to come back to: sit on the pond's jetty and watch the moorhens while sipping a glass or two.

Rooms	The Cowshed & The Pigsty: £90-£100.
Meals	Pub/restaurant 1 mile. Continental breakfast included; cooked breakfast £5-£8 (weekends only).
Closed	Christmas & occasionally.

Minimum stay: 2 nights.

Jo Ward
Crafts Hill Barn,
31 Oakington Road, Dry Drayton,
Cambridge, CB23 8DD
Tel   +44 (0)1954 488534
Mobile +44 (0)7977 275501
Email joclareward@gmail.com
Web   www.craftshillbarn.co.uk

Entry 19   Map 9

Cambridgeshire

Springfield House

The former school house hugs the bend of a river, its French windows opening to delightful rambling gardens with scented roses... and a yew garden, and a mulberry tree that provides fruit for breakfast. It's an elegant home reminiscent of another age, with fascinating history on the walls and big comfortable bedrooms for guests; one is reached by narrow stairs and has steps out to the garden. The conservatory, draped with a huge mimosa, is an exceptional spot for summer breakfasts, and the breakfasts are rather delicious. Good value and peaceful, yet close to Cambridge, of which Judith is a fund of knowledge.

Rooms	2 doubles; 1 twin/double with separate bath: £70-£90. Extra bed/sofabed £15-£30 per person per night.
Meals	Pubs 150 yds.
Closed	Rarely.

Judith Rossiter
Springfield House,
14-16 Horn Lane,
Linton, CB21 4HT
Tel   +44 (0)1223 891383
Email springfieldhouselinton@gmail.com
Web   www.springfieldhouselinton.com

Entry 20   Map 9

Cambridgeshire

Peacocks Fine B&B

Above their delightful riverside tearoom in the heart of Ely, George and Rachel have created two suites. Each has its own sitting room stocked with books and squashy sofas. Brewery House has a fireplace and river views; Cottage is cosy and pretty with flowery wallpaper. Both have goose down duvets and tea trays. Enjoy breakfast by the Aga: perhaps savoury crumpets, omelette or delicious Croque Madame. Browse the nearby antique centre, visit the cathedral, stroll out for dinner or explore Cambridge and the Fens; but make sure to leave time for tea – there are 70 kinds! The Peacocks are friendly and funny – lovely hosts.

Rooms	1 suite for 2; 1 suite for 2 with separate bathroom & wc: £135-£160. Singles £110-£135. Extra bed/sofabed £50-£70 per person per night.
Meals	Pubs/restaurants 3-minute walk. Tearoom closed Monday & Tuesday.
Closed	Rarely.

Rachel Peacock
Peacocks Fine B&B,
65 Waterside,
Ely, CB7 4AU

Mobile +44 (0)7900 666161
Email peacockbookings65@gmail.com
Web www.peacockstearoom.co.uk

Entry 21   Map 9

Cheshire

Goss Moor

Crunch up the gravelled drive to the big white house, a beautifully run family home. Bedrooms are light, bright and decorated in creams and blues; bathrooms are spotless and warm. Be cosseted by fluffy bathrobes, biscuits or flapjack, decanters of sherry – all is comfortable and inviting. After a day's exploring the Wirral and Liverpool, historic Chester and the wilds of north Wales – a short drive all – return to a kind welcome from Sarah. Expect a generous and delicious breakfast by the sunny bay window; in the summer, you are free to enjoy the garden and pool (not always heated!).

Rooms	1 twin/double; 1 double with separate bath: £90-£95. Singles £55-£60.
Meals	Pub/restaurant 2 miles.
Closed	Never.

Chris & Sarah White
Goss Moor,
Mill Lane, Willaston,
Neston, CH64 1RG

Tel +44 (0)151 327 4000
Mobile +44 (0)7771 510068
Email sarahcmwhite@aol.com
Web www.gossmoor.co.uk

Entry 22   Map 7

Cheshire

Trustwood

Small and pretty and wrapped in beautiful country, Trustwood stands in peaceful gardens with National Trust woods at the end of the lane. Outside, sweetpeas flourish to the front in the summer, while lawns run down behind to a copse where bluebells thrive in spring. Inside, warm, fresh, contemporary interiors are just the ticket: super bedrooms, fabulous bathrooms, and a wood-burner and sofas in the sitting room. Free-range hens provide eggs for delicious breakfasts, Lin accounts for the lovely scones. As for the Wirral, much more beautiful than you probably imagine; coastal walks, botanic gardens and the spectacular Dee estuary all wait.

Rooms	2 doubles: £80. Singles £55.
Meals	Restaurants 2 miles.
Closed	Occasionally.

Lin & Peter Friend
Trustwood,
Vicarage Lane, Burton,
Neston, CH64 5TJ

Tel +44 (0)151 336 7118
Mobile +44 (0)7550 012462
Email lin@trustwoodbnb.uk
Web www.trustwoodbnb.uk

Entry 23   Map 7

Cheshire

Mulsford Cottage

Delicious! Not just the food (Kate's a pro chef) but the sweet whitewashed cottage with its sunny conservatory and vintage interiors, and the green Cheshire countryside that bubble-wraps the place in rural peace. Chat – and laugh – the evening away over Kate's superb dinners, lounge by the fire, then sleep deeply in comfy bedrooms: cane beds, a bright red chair, a vintage desk. The double has a roll top bath, the twin a tiny shower-with-a-view. Wake for local bacon, sausages and honey and just-laid bantam eggs. Walk the 34-mile Sandstone Trail to Shropshire; Wales starts just past the hammock, at the bottom of the bird-filled garden.

Rooms	1 double; 1 twin with separate bath/shower: £90. Singles £65. Dinner, B&B £18–£25 per person.
Meals	Dinner from £18. Pub 1.5 miles.
Closed	Rarely.

Kate Dewhurst
Mulsford Cottage,
Mulsford,
Sarn,
Malpas, SY14 7LP

Tel +44 (0)1948 770414
Email katedewhurst4@gmail.com
Web www.mulsfordcottage.co.uk

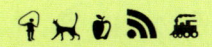

Entry 24   Map 7

Cornwall

Trevigue

Not far up the single track road from Crackington Haven and close to wildly beautiful Strangles Bay you'll find Trevigue hunkering down, as it has for 700-ish years. There's history in the stone floors, oak beamed ceilings and crackling open fires, but it's the Crockers' love for the place that shines most brightly. Their passion for sustainable living is infectious. All furnishings are locally sourced and some of the cushion covers are made from recycled water bottles. Much of the food served is home-grown – Gayle's dad's sausages and bacon for breakfast and hearty dishes, with a Mediterranean twist for dinner (on request). Pack up your swimmers and take the path that snakes down the cliff to a very nearly private beach for swimming or sunbathing. Say hello to the farm animals on your way back.

Rooms	1 double, 3 twin/doubles: £80–£99. Singles £70–£86. Extra bed/sofabed £35–£45 per person per night.
Meals	Dinner, 2 courses, £24.95. Wine £16. Pubs/restaurants 1.5 miles.
Closed	Christmas.

Children over 7 welcome.

	Gayle Crocker
	Trevigue, Crackington Haven, Bude, EX23 0LQ
Tel	+44 (0)1840 230492
Mobile	+44 (0)7903 110037
Email	trevigue@talk21.com
Web	www.trevigue.com

Cornwall

The Old Parsonage

On the southern fringe of Boscastle lies this handsome Georgian parsonage, a grand base for exploring the Cornish coast. Behind the picture-perfect exterior find elegant, light-filled spaces and four big, bright, modern bedrooms. After a restful sleep take a seat at the convivial table in the pine-floored dining room for a breakfast well worth waking up for. Jon and Delyth are big foodies and like to show off local produce, so along with their homemade bread it's the perfect fuel for your seaside adventures. Hikers can stride out onto a spectacular stretch of the South West Coast path, boat spotters can wander down to Boscastle harbour, and the more laid back may relax with an afternoon tea watching the Cornish world go by.

Rooms	4 twin/doubles: £108–£135.
Meals	Packed lunch £6.95. Pub/restaurant 600 yds.
Closed	November – January.

Over 12s welcome.

	Jon & Delyth Ward
	The Old Parsonage, Forrabury, Boscastle, PL35 0DJ
Tel	+44 (0)1840 250339
Mobile	+44 (0)7377 063722
Email	enquiries@old-parsonage.com
Web	www.old-parsonage.com

Cornwall

The Corn Mill

This restored mill in a quiet Cornish valley is a relaxed and friendly home. Step inside and find a country cottage medley of flowers and family furniture, antique rugs and interesting market finds. Artist Suzie has her studio in a folly in the pretty garden; ducks and geese wander in the orchard. Cosy bedrooms have flowery fabrics, warm blankets and good cotton; bathrooms are simple and fresh with fluffy towels. Breakfast well in the farmhouse kitchen on a locally sourced spread and bread fresh from the Rayburn. Exceptional coastal walking, music festivals, great beaches and Port Isaac are all nearby.

Rooms	1 double: £90–£120.
	1 family room for 2-4: £90–£120.
Meals	Pub/restaurant 2 miles.
Closed	Christmas & New Year.

Susan Bishop
The Corn Mill,
Port Isaac Road,
Trelill,
Bodmin, PL30 3HZ
Tel   +44 (0)1208 851079
Email jemandsuzie@icloud.com

Entry 27   Map 1

Cornwall

Higher Lank Farm

Families rejoice: this 500-year old, eco-run farmhouse is as child friendly as they come and has all the kit you need. Bring the whole gang (must include an under seven) for an action-packed stay. Nursery teas begin at 5pm, grown-up suppers later and Lucy will cheerfully babysit while you slink off to the pub in between. Bedrooms have toys and large TVs, farm-themed playgrounds are safe and fun: baby animals to play with, eggs to collect, pony and trap rides, tractors, a sand barn, a police house and cream teas in the garden. Wander down to the private woods to spot wildlife, or try fishing on the river Camel. Daily children's swim sessions leave you to relax by the biomass-heated endless pool or take a dip in the jacuzzi.

Rooms	3 family rooms for 4: £125–£170.
	Singles by arrangement.
Meals	Supper £23. Nursery tea £7.
	Pub 1.5 miles.
Closed	November-Easter.

Minimum stay: 3 nights, 5 in high season.

Lucy Finnemore
Higher Lank Farm,
St Breward,
Bodmin, PL30 4NB
Tel   +44 (0)1208 850716
Email lucyfin@higherlankfarm.co.uk
Web   www.higherlankfarm.co.uk

Entry 28   Map 1

Cornwall

Trewornan Manor

Drive through the white gate and listed pillars to a house that began in 1211. You'll fall in love the moment you arrive, and your hosts' enthusiasm is infectious. Guests are spoiled in off-beat boutique style in one beautiful, sprawling wing: dining and lounging downstairs, and bedrooms up. It is sumptuous and gorgeous but definitely not swanky and the attention to detail is delightful: hot water bottles, sweets, biscuits, natural toiletries, bikes and breakfast that tastes as good as it looks. Lose yourself in 25 acres of woods, water meadows and historic gardens – or sally forth, to Padstow and Rock.

Rooms	5 twin/doubles: £120-£210. Singles £100-£170.
Meals	Pubs/restaurants 1 mile.
Closed	Rarely.

Paul & Lesley Stapleton
Trewornan Manor,
St Minver,
Wadebridge, PL27 6EX
Tel   +44 (0)1208 812359
Email   enquiries@trewornanmanor.co.uk
Web   www.trewornanmanor.co.uk

Entry 29   Map 1

Cornwall

Myrtle Cottage

Sue's warm welcome and cream teas set the tone – you'll feel relaxed and happy, even if you've been stuck behind a tractor on the way. This is a chocolate box cottage in a proper Cornish village. The house is cosy too. Bedrooms have uneven white walls, quilts on beds, fresh flowers from the garden and distant sea views. After a peaceful night Sue lays on a great breakfast: tuck into homemade bread, muffins and preserves, local eggs and bacon, in the dining room, the conservatory, or out on the sunny patio. You can stroll to join the coastal path in either direction, pick up a map to find the best secret coves. Walk half a mile to the foodie pub in the village for dinner.

Rooms	1 double, 1 twin: £80-£90. Singles from £60.
Meals	Pub/restaurants 0.5 miles.
Closed	Rarely.

Minimum stay: 2 nights weekends & in high season.

Sue Stevens
Myrtle Cottage,
Trevail, Cubert, Newquay, TR8 5HP
Tel   +44 (0)1637 830460
Mobile   +44 (0)7763 101076
Email   enquiries@myrtletrevail.co.uk
Web   www.myrtletrevail.co.uk

Entry 30   Map 1

Cornwall

House at Gwinear

An island of calm, this grand old rambling vicarage sits in rare bird-filled acres, just a short drive from St Ives. Come for peace and quiet and a classic Cornish welcome from owners Charles and Diana who are devoted to encouraging the arts and crafts. Find English shabby chic with loads of character and no stuffiness – fresh flowers on the breakfast table, a piano in the corner, rugs on polished floors, masses of books. Your bedroom is in a separate wing with its own sitting room and a fine view of the church from the bath. In summer you can eat breakfast in the Italianate courtyard, play a game of tennis on the ancient courts and wander the large, lawned gardens. Ask for supper or walk half an hour to the pub.

Rooms	1 twin/double with separate bath & sitting room: £85-£95.
Meals	Supper, 2 courses with wine, £25. Pub 1.5 miles.
Closed	Rarely.

French and Italian spoken.

Charles & Diana Hall
House at Gwinear,
Gwinear,
St Ives, TR27 5JZ
Tel +44 (0)1736 850444
Email charleshall@btinternet.com

Cornwall

The Firs

This attractive Edwardian villa was author Rosamunde Pilcher's childhood home. There are dreamy views of the garden from airy bedrooms, and Marie greets you with tea and cake. Breakfast is served at a sunny table overlooking the garden: a generous continental spread including fruit, yogurt, cheese and meats – or you can order a daily cooked special if you fancy more. Walk to the flawless sands of Porthkidney, spot the many birds on the estuary, play golf at the local course. At the end of the terraced lawns you'll find a tiny station – hop on a clifftop train and enjoy one of the most scenic routes in the country. Eight minutes of spectacular coastal views later and you can be exploring the galleries and beaches of St Ives. Stay for dinner or head back to one of Lelant's cosy village pubs.

Rooms	2 doubles: £125.
Meals	Continental breakfast. Restaurants 5-minute walk.
Closed	Occasionally.

Parking on-site.

Marie Britten
The Firs,
Riverside, Lelant, TR26 3DW
Tel +44 (0)1736 757830
Email stay@thefirslelant.com
Web www.thefirslelant.com

Cornwall

Cove Cottage

Down a long lane to a rose-clad cottage in the most balmy part of Cornwall... peace in a private cove. Your own door leads up steps to a gorgeous suite with luxurious linen on an antique four-poster, art, sofas... and a flowery balcony with spectacular views of the sea and subtropical gardens. Settle in happily to the sound of the waves. Sue is friendly and serves a great breakfast in the garden room: home-laid eggs, homemade jams and their own honey. The Penwith peninsula hums with gardens, galleries and stunning sandy beaches; Minack Theatre and Lamorna are close. Arrive to a salad supper chosen from a small but special menu. Paradise!

Rooms	1 suite for 2: £145.
Meals	Salad suppers from £12.50 available on the night of arrival. Pub/restaurant 3 miles.
Closed	November – February.

Minimum stay: 3 nights in high season

Sue White
Cove Cottage,
St Loy, St Buryan,
Penzance, TR19 6DH

Tel	+44 (0)1736 810010
Email	thewhites@covecottagestloy.co.uk
Web	www.covecottagestloy.co.uk

Entry 33   Map 1

Cornwall

The Old Pilchard Works

Hidden down the side of Tracey's house are two little flats each with their own door. One has stairs to an airy bedroom and a glimpse of the sea. Find a calm, sleek feel with modern white furniture, cool linen, snug wool blankets; zinc coat hooks, bright cushions, clever lighting add interest. Tracey leaves you a niftily upcycled 7UP box stuffed with homemade granola, croissants, pain au chocolat, homemade compote and yogurt, fruit, organic oatmeal porridge, agave syrup... Eat outside on the shared suntrap terrace – or in bed if you fancy. Stroll along the harbour, book a boat trip; St Ives and atmospheric Minack Theatre are nearby.

Rooms	1 twin/double; 1 double with separate shower room: £80–£105.
Meals	Pubs/restaurants 2-minute walk.
Closed	Rarely.

Minimum stay: 2 nights. Nearby car park £3 for 24 hours

Tracey Wearne
The Old Pilchard Works,
6 Chapel Street,
Mousehole,
Penzance, TR19 6SB

Tel	+44 (0)1736 732699
Email	tracey.wearnes@gmail.com

Entry 34   Map 1

Cornwall

Venton Vean

Everything at Venton Vean is tip-top. Immensely helpful owners Philippa and David moved from London with their family and have transformed a dilapidated Victorian house into a supremely cool and elegant B&B. Moody colours, mid-century design classics and interesting reclamation finds make for a stunning and eclectic interior. Food is a passion – expect freshly ground coffee in your room and some of the most tantalising breakfasts around: Mexican, Spanish, even a good old full English will have you dashing down in the morning. Arty Penzance is a joy as is the craggy-coved beauty all around.

Rooms	4 doubles: £72–£100.
	1 family room for 4: £110–£140.
	Singles £71–£87.
Meals	Packed lunch from £5.
	Cream tea £4.
Closed	Christmas.

Minimum stay: 2 nights.

	Philippa McKnight
	Venton Vean,
	Trewithen Road,
	Penzance, TR18 4LS
Tel	+44 (0)1736 351294
Email	info@ventonvean.co.uk
Web	www.ventonvean.co.uk

Entry 35   Map 1

Cornwall

Ednovean Farm

There's a terrace for each fabulous bedroom (one truly private) with views to the wild blue yonder and St Michael's Mount Bay, an enchanting outlook that changes with the passage of the day. Come for peace, space and the best of eclectic fabrics and colours, pretty lamps, Christine's sculptures, fluffy bathrobes and handmade soaps. The beamed open-plan sitting/dining area is an absorbing mix of exotic, rustic and elegant; have full breakfast here (last orders nine o'clock) or continental in your room. A footpath through the field leads to the village; walk to glorious Prussia Cove and Cudden Point, or head west to Marazion.

Rooms	2 doubles, 1 four-poster: £100–£145.
Meals	Pub 5-minute walk.
Closed	Rarely.

Over 16s welcome.

	Christine & Charles Taylor
	Ednovean Farm,
	Perranuthnoe,
	Penzance, TR20 9LZ
Tel	+44 (0)1736 711883
Email	info@ednoveanfarm.co.uk
Web	www.ednoveanfarm.co.uk

Entry 36   Map 1

Cornwall

Halzephron House

The coastal path runs through the grounds of this former smugglers' house and the view is to die for – you can see St Michael's Mount on a clear day. Be greeted by homemade treats and coffee roasted in Cornwall: lovely Lucy and Roger are foodies as well as designers. A contemporary and quirky suite awaits you, throw open the drawing room door and there's a big private deck overlooking the garden where you can soak up the stunning sunsets. Drift off in a big antique French bed to the sound of the waves. The handsome house sits in four acres of lawns and wildflower meadow and has a 'secret' cliff top garden and amphitheatre. You can walk to three amazing beaches, a 13th-century church, a golf course and a gastropub. Your hosts will happily chat about the house and area over breakfast at the sunny communal table.

Rooms	1 suite for 2 with sitting room: £130-£150. Extra bed/sofabed £30-£45 p.p.p.n. Self-catering cottage available + 2 cabins on Canopy & Stars.
Meals	Pub 0.25 miles. Continental/Cornish breakfast in the drawing room: enquire with owner.
Closed	Rarely.

Minimum stay: 2 nights; 7 nights in high season.

Lucy Thorp
Halzephron House,
Gunwalloe,
Helston, TR12 7QD
Mobile +44 (0)7899 925816
Email   info@halzephronhouse.co.uk
Web   www.halzephronhouse.co.uk

Entry 37   Map 1

Cornwall

Bay House

This is almost as close to the sea as you can get and there are Atlantic views at every turn. Watch the sunset from the west-facing terrace that juts out over the very edge of Cornwall. Inside, the attention to detail is immaculate. You'll feel smart wearing a Ralph Lauren dressing gown in your antique and art-filled bedroom. Space too for lounging with DVDs and an iPod dock. Scramble down to secluded beaches; play golf nearby; stroll to the famous Lizard Lighthouse just yards away and join the coastal path that leads you in both directions. You can hear the waves breaking from the garden, so rest here under rustling palms and hovering kestrels. Breakfast is outstanding – choose almost anything, all sourced locally and served with John's homemade bread and jams.

Rooms	2 twin/doubles: £125-£195.
Meals	Pubs/restaurants 5-minute walk.
Closed	Christmas.

Carla Caslin
Bay House,
Housel Bay, The Lizard, TR12 7PG
Tel   +44 (0)1326 290235
Mobile +44 (0)7740 168505
Email   carla.caslin@btinternet.com
Web   www.mostsoutherlypoint.co.uk

Entry 38   Map 1

Cornwall

The Hen House

A generous, peaceful oasis. Sandy and Gary have oodles of local information on places to visit, eat and walk – with OS maps on loan. Your big ground floor room, in its own barn, has bright fabrics, a king-size bed and stable doors to the courtyard; there are self-catering guests on-site too. Relax in the hot tub in the wildflower meadow, bask on sun loungers, wander by the ponds and watch the ducks' antics; the central courtyard is fairy-lit at night. Scrumptious locally sourced breakfasts are served in the dining chalet surrounded by birdsong. Tai-chi in the meadow, reiki and reflexology in the Serpentine Sanctuary... bliss.

Rooms	1 double: £85-£95.
Meals	Pub/restaurant 1 mile.
Closed	Rarely.

Minimum stay: 2 nights. Over 12s welcome.

| | Sandy & Gary Pulfrey
The Hen House,
Tregarne, Manaccan, Helston, TR12 6EW |
|---|---|
| Tel | +44 (0)1326 280236 |
| Mobile | +44 (0)7809 229958 |
| Email | henhouseuk@btinternet.com |
| Web | www.thehenhouse-cornwall.co.uk |

Entry 39   Map 1

Cornwall

Trerose Manor

Follow winding lanes through glorious countryside to find the prettiest, listed manor house, a warm family atmosphere and welcoming tea in the beamed kitchen. Large, light bedrooms, one with floor-to-ceiling windows, sit peacefully in your own wing and have views over the stunning garden. All are dressed in pretty colours, have comfy seats for garden gazing and smartly tiled bathrooms. A sumptuous breakfast can be taken outside in summer, there are wonderful walks over fields to river or beach and stacks of interesting places to visit. Tessa is an engaging host, and you're looked after very well – guests love it here.

| Rooms | 2 doubles, 1 twin/double: £135-£145.
Singles from £80. |
|---|---|
| Meals | Pubs/restaurants within walking distance. |
| Closed | Occasionally. |

Pets by arrangement.

| | Tessa Phipps
Trerose Manor,
Mawnan Smith,
Falmouth, TR11 5HX |
|---|---|
| Tel | +44 (0)1326 250784 |
| Email | info@trerosemanor.co.uk |
| Web | www.trerosemanor.co.uk |

Entry 40   Map 1

Cornwall

Bosvathick

A huge old Cornish house that's been in Kate's family since 1760 – along with Indian rugs, heavy furniture, ornate plasterwork, portraits and a piano... even a harp. Historians will be in their element: pass three Celtic crosses dating from the 8th century before the long drive finds the imposing house (all granite gate posts and lions) and a rambling garden with grotto, lake, pasture and woodland. Bedrooms are traditional, full of books, antiques and pots of flowers; bathrooms are spic and span, one small and functional, two large. Come to experience a 'time warp' and charming Kate's good breakfasts. Close to Falmouth University, too.

Rooms	2 twin/doubles: £110.
	2 singles: £70. Extra bed/sofabed £25-£35 per person per night.
	1-night stays: £10 surcharge per person.
Meals	Supper, from £25.
	Packed lunch £5-£10. Pubs 2 miles.
Closed	Rarely.

French spoken.

Kate & Stephen Tyrrell
Bosvathick,
Constantine,
Falmouth, TR11 5RZ
Tel   +44 (0)1326 340103
Email   kate@bosvathickhouse.co.uk
Web   www.bosvathickhouse.co.uk

Entry 41   Map 1

Cornwall

Trevilla House

Come for the position: the sea and Fal estuary wrap around you, and the King Harry ferry gives you an easy reach into the glorious Roseland peninsula. Inside find comfy bedrooms with homemade quilts on the beds – the twin with a sofa and old-fashioned charm, the double with stunning sea views. Jinty rustles up delicious locally sourced breakfasts with homemade jams, and you eat in the conservatory that looks south over the sea. Trelissick Gardens, with its intriguing newly opened house, is a 20-minute walk – worth visiting for the view down the Fal alone. From there you can catch the ferry to Truro, St Mawes or Falmouth.

Rooms	1 double, 1 twin: £85-£95.
	1 single, sharing bath with double (let to same party only): £50-£55.
Meals	Pubs/restaurants 1-2 miles.
Closed	Christmas & New Year.

Jinty & Peter Copeland
Trevilla House,
Feock, Truro, TR3 6QG
Tel   +44 (0)1872 862369
Mobile +44 (0)7791 977621
Email   jinty.copeland@gmail.com
Web   www.trevilla.clara.net/accom.html

Entry 42   Map 1

Cornwall

Hay Barton

Giant windows overlook many acres of farmland, and Jill and Blair look after you so well! Breakfasts are special with the best local produce, homemade granola, yogurt and more. Arrive for tea and lovely home-baked cake, laid out in a comfortable guest sitting room with a log fire and plenty of books and maps. Bedrooms are fresh and pretty with garden flowers, soft white linen on big beds and floral green walls. Gloriously large panelled bathrooms have long roll top baths and are painted in earthy colours. You can knock a few balls around the tennis court, and you're near to good gardens and heaps of places to eat.

Rooms	3 twin/doubles: £90-£100. Singles £70-£75.
Meals	Pubs 1-2 miles.
Closed	Rarely.

Minimum stay: 2 nights in summer.

	Jill & Blair Jobson
	Hay Barton,
	Tregony, Truro, TR2 5TF
Tel	+44 (0)1872 530288
Mobile	+44 (0)7813 643028
Email	jill.jobson@btinternet.com
Web	www.haybarton.com

Entry 43   Map 1

Cornwall

Antonia's Pearls, The Studio

Tucked behind a handsome listed Georgian villa is a small yet stylish bolthole for two with a private, sunny garden. Artistic owners have created a contemporary, fun space: white walls and rafters, painted floorboards, quirky touches here and there, a charcoal sofa in a corner and a lovely big bed. A nifty galley kitchen has all you need to rustle up meals – Antonia can bring you a breakfast hamper including croissants, homemade granola and Cornish smoked salmon; supper too if you fancy – or there are heaps of great cafés nearby. Smell the salt on the air, wander down to Charlestown's bustling quay…

Rooms	1 studio for 2: £145-£185
Meals	Breakfast on request, £15. Dinner on request, 2 courses, £20. Pubs/restaurants 2-minute walk.
Closed	Never.

	Antonia Shields
	Antonia's Pearls, The Studio,
	Charlestown Harbour,
	Charlestown, PL25 3NX
Tel	+44 (0)1726 68966
Email	antonia@antoniaspearls.co.uk
Web	www.antoniaspearls.co.uk

Entry 44   Map 1

Cornwall

Tredudwell Manor

Winding lanes lead to this handsomely refurbished Queen Anne style house. Surrounded by lawns and mature trees the views are south to the sea and the total peace is just the tonic. Inside is a marble bar for more reviving and the mix of sofas, mini-ottomans, parquet floors with Persian rugs and family portraits make for a genteel atmosphere. First floor bedrooms are large enough to waltz in with toile de Jouy wallpaper, antiques and views. In the roof space are more compact but delightful rooms – uncluttered and calm with low beams, shuttered windows and modern bathrooms. Breakfast is a treat with the best produce from nearby Fowey.

Rooms	6 doubles: £70-£130.
	1 family room for 4: £125-£165.
	Singles £75-£100.
	Extra bed/sofabed £10-£20 per person per night.
Meals	Pubs/restaurants 2 miles.
Closed	Rarely.

Pets by arrangement.

Justin & Valérie Shakerley
Tredudwell Manor,
Lanteglos,
Fowey, PL23 1NJ
Tel   +44 (0)1726 870226
Email justin@tredudwell.co.uk
Web   www.tredudwell.co.uk

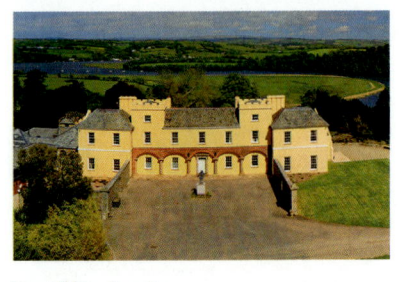

Entry 45   Map 1

Cornwall

Pentillie Castle

The approach is gorgeous with Dartmoor National Park in the distance, a long flower-lined drive, then the river Tamar comes into view and lastly the romantic castle. It's as well run as any hotel (with a chef and smiley staff) but it's got an informal family feel with 'help yourself' suppers in an Aga-warmed kitchen along with a note saying, 'don't wash up!'. Bedrooms are a dream; wake to fill up on dry cured bacon and eggs before visiting 55 acres of Humphry Repton and Lewis Kennedy designed grounds with orchard, summer house and kitchen gardens. Dip into outdoor theatre, wine tastings, special seasonal dinners… and the river! You can even get married here.

Rooms	8 twin/doubles: £135-£255.
	1 four-poster suite for 2: £210-£230. Singles £120-£240.
Meals	Dinner in the castle, £35. DIY supper, 2-courses, £18.
	Pubs/restaurants 10-minute drive.
Closed	Rarely.

Sammie Coryton
Pentillie Castle,
St Mellion,
Saltash, PL12 6QD
Tel   +44 (0)1579 350044
Email contact@pentillie.co.uk
Web   www.pentillie.co.uk

Entry 46   Map 2

Cumbria

Hawksdale Lodge

Spring heaven! Bowl along blissfully quiet roads while sheep bleat and daffs bob in the breeze. This is a supremely comfortable B&B at any time of the year and your hosts look after you with great charm from their stunning 1810 gentleman farmer's house with pretty garden. Home baking and local produce at breakfast, sumptuously dressed bedrooms with plenty of space and seating, warm and inviting bathrooms with proper windows. The National Park is only six miles away for strenuous walking and cycling, the northern Lakes and fells beckon, Hadrian's wall is near. Return to something homemade and delicious. Lovely.

Rooms	1 double; 1 double with separate bath: £125–£150. Singles £95–£130.
Meals	Packed lunch on request, from £6. Pubs/restaurants less than 1 mile.
Closed	Rarely.

Minimum stay: 2 nights at Easter & New Year.

	Lorraine Russell Hawksdale Lodge, Dalston, Carlisle, CA5 7BX
Mobile	+44 (0)7810 641892
Email	enquiries@hawksdalelodge.co.uk
Web	www.hawksdalelodge.co.uk

Entry 47 Map 11

Cumbria

Wood House

Wood House sits quietly in a sea of green… Reached over stunning mountain passes where sheep cling to the roadsides, it's surrounded by trees – with Crummock Water at the end of the valley. Tony is affable and gives you an elegant drawing room with open fire, art, piano, antiques; a dining room with polished oak floor and china-laden table; comfortably furnished bedrooms with wonderful lake views. Breakfast is a Cumbrian spread with famous sausages, granola, homemade bread; there's dinner too if you want. Wordsworth House nearby, a private woodland path to the lake and Tony can sort canoeing, guided walks, mountain biking and more.

Rooms	1 double, 2 twins: £130. Singles £90.
Meals	Dinner £28.50. Pubs/restaurants 15-minute walk.
Closed	Rarely.

No minimum stay.

	Tony McKenzie Wood House, Buttermere, Cockermouth, CA13 9XA
Tel	+44 (0)1768 770208
Email	wood.house@icloud.com
Web	www.woodhousebuttermere.uk

Entry 48 Map 11

Cumbria

Johnby Hall

You are ensconced in the quieter part of the Lakes and have independence in this Elizabethan manor. Once a fortified Pele tower, it's a fascinating historic house yet very much a lived-in family home with a wonderful atmosphere. The airy suites have a sitting room each with books, children's videos, squashy sofas, pretty fabrics and whitewashed walls. Beds have patchwork quilts, windows have stone mullions and all is peaceful. Henry gives you sturdy breakfasts, and you can join him and Anna for convivial home-grown suppers by a roaring fire in the great hall. Children will have fun: hens and pigs to feed, garden toys galore and woods to roam.

Rooms	1 twin/double, with sitting room; 1 family room for 4, with sitting room: £130. Singles £90. Extra bed/sofabed £20 p.p.p.n. Extra child £15; under 5s free.
Meals	Supper, 2 courses, £22.50. Pub 1 mile.
Closed	Rarely.

	Henry & Anna Howard Johnby Hall, Johnby, Penrith, CA11 0UU
Tel	+44 (0)1768 483257
Email	bookings@johnbyhall.com
Web	www.johnbyhall.co.uk

Entry 49   Map 11

Cumbria

Whitrigg House

There's a warm and woody, solidly inviting feel to Mike & Robbie's Whitrigg House. They live nearby and look after you well: laying on soup for late arrivals, chalking-up the weather and the breakfast menu daily. Ingredients are carefully sourced and much is homemade. Ceramics, paintings and other work by local artists may inspire a gallery or workshop visit; there's a lot of creative energy in the area – excellent eateries too, including the village pub, the George & Dragon. It's easy to break a journey here, and to linger for fabulous hill walking and cycling – there's a bike shed and sauna in the garden – and for simply strolling around pretty villages and lakes; nearby Ullswater is lovely as are the Aira Force waterfalls.

Rooms	2 doubles: £95-£120. 1 single: £65.
Meals	Pubs/restaurants 5-minute walk.
Closed	Rarely.

Please check owners' website for availability before enquiring. Over 12s welcome.

	Mike Taylor Whitrigg House, Clifton, Penrith, CA10 2EE
Tel	+44 (0)1768 895077
Email	info@whitrigghouse.co.uk
Web	www.whitrigghouse.co.uk

Entry 50   Map 11

Cumbria

Robyns Barn

Wow, fabulous views – fells and mountains in every direction including Blencathra, the most climbed fell in the Lakes. Robyns Barn is attached to the main house, and it's all yours. Step into a large, welcoming open-plan space: limewashed walls, big oak table, beams, antique pine, toasty wood-burner and plenty of DVDs, books and games. Inviting bedrooms, upstairs, have sheepskins on wooden floors. Wake when you want – Kathryn leaves a continental breakfast with homemade bread, muesli, fruit, yogurts; there's a farm shop close by serving excellent cooked breakfasts too. The garden has a picnic area, barbecue – and those views!

Rooms	1 double with sitting/dining room & kitchenette, 1 twin (let to same party only): £90-£120.
Meals	Continental breakfast. Supper £20. Pubs/restaurants 1 mile.
Closed	Rarely.

Minimum stay: 2 nights. Children over 8 welcome.

Adrian & Kathryn Vaughan
Robyns Barn,
Lane Head Farm, Troutbeck,
Keswick, Penrith, CA11 0SY
Tel +44 (0)1768 779841
Email robynsbarn@hotmail.co.uk
Web www.robynsbarn.co.uk

Entry 51   Map 11

Cumbria

Greenah

Tucked into the hillside off a narrow lane, this 1750s smallholding is surrounded by fells, so is perfect for walkers. Absolute privacy for friends or family with your own entrance to a beamed, stone-flagged sitting room with a wood-burning stove, and cheery floral curtains. Warm bedrooms have original paintings, good beds, hot water bottles, bathrobes and a sparkling bathroom with a loo with a remarkable view. Malcolm and Marjorie are totally committed to organic food – you get a welcoming pot of tea and cake on arrival and a fabulous breakfast. They'll give you good advice about the local area too. Fell walking is not compulsory!

Rooms	1 double, 1 twin, sharing shower (let to same party only): £96-£100. Singles £60-£65.
Meals	Pubs/restaurants 3 miles.
Closed	30 November – 28 February.

Children over 8 welcome.

Marjorie & Malcolm Emery
Greenah,
Matterdale, Penrith, CA11 0SA
Tel +44 (0)1768 483387
Mobile +44 (0)7767 213667
Email info@greenah.co.uk
Web www.greenah.co.uk

Entry 52   Map 11

Cumbria

Lowthwaite

Leave your worries behind as you head up the lanes to the farmhouse tucked into the fell. Jim, ex-hiking guide, and Danish Tine are charming, helpful and well-travelled. Their barn is dotted with Tanzanian furniture and your peaceful bedrooms are in the view-filled wing. Beds are made of recycled dhow wood, sparkling bathrooms sport organic soaps; the garden room has its own patio. Breakfasts with homemade granola, bread and muffins are delicious – perhaps halloumi with mushrooms, tomatoes and egg or smoked salmon with creamed spinach. Birds galore in the garden, a trickling stream... endless fells to explore too – advice is happily given.

Rooms	2 twin/doubles: £95–£100.
	2 family rooms for 4: £100–£130.
	Singles £65–£73.
Meals	Pubs 2.5 miles.
	Packed lunch £4.50–£7.
Closed	Christmas.

Tine & Jim Boving Foster
Lowthwaite,
Matterdale,
Penrith, CA11 0LE
Tel   +44 (0)1768 482313
Email   info@lowthwaiteullswater.com
Web   www.lowthwaiteullswater.com

Entry 53   Map 11

Cumbria

Crake Trees Manor

At the end of a long drive with panoramic views... a peaceful farm with open doors, tea and cake waiting. It's been in the family for generations; find slate floors, Mike's beautiful green oak furniture, original art, books and beams. Colourful bedrooms have tip-top linen on brass beds; the Peasland suite has space for children, a huge bathroom and a balcony for catching the evening sun. Ruth's breakfasts are delicious: homemade granola and jams, halloumi with thyme-baked tomatoes, local bacon platters. She's passionate about the area too – find out about events, borrow maps, roam woodland and fields, explore Pennines and Lakes.

Rooms	1 double, 1 twin: £95–£110.
	1 suite for 2: £105–£125.
	Singles £60–£80.
Meals	Pubs/Restaurants 10-minute walk.
Closed	Rarely.

Minimum stay: 2 nights at weekends.

Ruth Tuer
Crake Trees Manor,
Crosby Ravensworth, Penrith, CA10 3JG
Tel   +44 (0)1931 715205
Mobile   +44 (0)7968 744305
Email   ruth@craketreesmanor.co.uk
Web   www.craketreesmanor.co.uk

Entry 54   Map 12

Cumbria

Drybeck Hall

In the Yorkshire Dales National Park, looking south to fields, woodland and beck, this Grade II* listed, 1679 farmhouse has blue painted mullion windows and exposed beams. Expect a deeply traditional home with good furniture, open fire and pictures of Anthony's predecessors looking down on you benignly; the family has been in the area for 800 years. Comfortable bedrooms have pretty floral fabrics and oak doors; bathrooms are simple but sparkling. Lulie is relaxed and charming and a good cook: enjoy a full English with free-range eggs in the sunny dining room, and home-grown vegetables and often game for dinner. A genuine slice of history.

Rooms	1 double, 1 twin: £100. Singles £50.
Meals	Dinner, 3 courses, £25. Pub/restaurant 4 miles.
Closed	Rarely.

Lulie & Anthony Hothfield
Drybeck Hall,
Appleby-in-Westmorland, CA16 6TF
Tel   +44 (0)1768 351487
Email lulieant@aol.com
Web   www.drybeckhall.co.uk

Entry 55   Map 12

Cumbria

Lapwings Barn

In the back of most-beautiful-beyond, down narrow lanes, this converted barn is a gorgeous retreat for two – or four. Delightful generous Gillian and Rick give you privacy and an upstairs sitting room with log stove, sofa and a balcony with views. Bedrooms downstairs (separate entrances) are pleasingly rustic with beams and modern stone-tiled bathrooms. Breakfast is delivered: sausages and bacon from their Saddlebacks, eggs from their hens, superb homemade bread and marmalade. Stroll along lowland tracks, watch curlews and lapwings, puff to the top of Whinfell. Ambleside and Beatrix Potter's house are near. One of the best.

Rooms	Barn: 2 twin/doubles & sitting room: £72–£90.
Meals	Packed lunch £5. Dinner £20. Pub/restaurant 3.5 miles.
Closed	Rarely.

Rick & Gillian Rodriguez
Lapwings Barn,
Howestone Barn,
Whinfell, Kendal, LA8 9EQ
Tel   +44 (0)1539 824373
Mobile +44 (0)7901 732379
Email   stay@lapwingsbarn.co.uk
Web   www.lapwingsbarn.co.uk

Entry 56   Map 12

Cumbria

Summerhow House

In four acres of fine landscaping and fun topiary is a large and inviting home of flamboyant wallpapers and shades of aqua, lemon and rose. Stylish but laid-back, grand but unintimidating, both house and hosts are a treat. Bedrooms have gilt frames and marble fireplaces, Molton Brown goodies and garden views, there are two sitting rooms to retreat to and breakfasts to delight you – fruits from the orchard, eggs from Sizergh Castle (John's family home). Two miles from Kendal: hop on the train to the Lakes. Walkers, sailors, skiers, food-lovers, dog-lovers will be charmed... aspiring actors too (talk to Janey!).

Rooms	1 double, 1 twin: £80–£120. Singles £50–£69.
Meals	Pub/restaurant 1.5 miles.
Closed	Occasionally.

Janey & John Hornyold-Strickland
Summerhow House,
Shap Road, Kendal, LA9 6NY
Tel   +44 (0)1539 720763
Mobile +44 (0)7976 345558
Email janeyfothergill@googlemail.com
Web   www.summerhowbedandbreakfast.co.uk

Entry 57   Map 11

Cumbria

Brownber Hall

Peter and Amanda, London escapees keen on cycling and walking, have stylishly restored this big old house, adding contemporary touches and all the comforts. The atmosphere is relaxed and sociable, there's an honesty bar with local craft beers and excellent wines, plenty of space to chill, and heaps of bedrooms with deeply comfortable beds to choose from. The rooms at the front have the views. Breakfast tables have white cloths and wild flower posies; wake to homemade granola, sausages, bacon, sourdough toast and great coffee. Join the Coast to Coast path by foot or bike, hop on the wonderfully scenic Settle to Carlisle railway.

Rooms	4 doubles, 2 twin/doubles: £90–£130. 1 suite for 2: £130–£180. 1 single: £60–£70. Dogs £5. Cot £10. Extra bed £15 per night with breakfast included.
Meals	Dinner for walkers available by arrangement. Pub/restaurants 5 miles.
Closed	Christmas.

Parking on-site. Dog friendly rooms available.

Peter Jaques & Amanda Walker
Brownber Hall,
Newbiggin-on-Lune,
Kirkby Stephen, CA17 4NX
Tel   +44 (0)1539 623208
Mobile +44 (0)7412 504765
Email peter@brownberhall.co.uk
Web   www.brownberhall.co.uk

Entry 58   Map 12

Cumbria

Fellside Studios

Off the beaten tourist track, a piece of paradise in the Troutbeck valley: seclusion, stylishness and breathtaking views. Prepare your own candlelit dinners, rise when the mood takes you, come and go as you please. The flower beds spill with heathers, hens cluck, and there's a decked terrace for continental breakfast in the sun – freshly prepared by your gently hospitable hosts who live in the attached house. In your studio apartment you get oak floors, slate shower rooms, immaculate kitchenettes with designer touches, DVD players, comfy chairs, luxurious towels. Wonderful.

Rooms	1 double, with kitchenette, 1 twin/double, with kitchenette: £80-£100. Singles £50-£60.
Meals	Continental breakfast. Pub/restaurant 0.5 miles.
Closed	Rarely.

Minimum stay: 2 nights.

Monica & Brian Liddell
Fellside Studios,
Troutbeck,
Windermere, LA23 1NN
Tel   +44 (0)1539 434000
Email brian@fellsidestudios.co.uk
Web   www.fellsidestudios.co.uk

Entry 59   Map 11

Cumbria

Gilpin Mill

Come to be seriously spoiled. Down leafy lanes is a pretty white house by a mill pond, framed by pastures and trees. Steve took a year off to build new Gilpin Mill, and Jo looks after their labs and guests – beautifully. In the country farmhouse sitting room oak beams span the ceiling and a slate lintel sits above the log fire. Bedrooms are equally inviting: beds are topped with duck down, luscious bathrooms are warm underfoot. Alongside is a lovely old barn where timber was made into bobbins; in the mill pond is a salmon and trout ladder and a dam, soon to provide power for the grid. And just six cars pass a day!

Rooms	3 twin/doubles: £95-£115. Singles £95-£115.
Meals	Pub 2.5 miles.
Closed	Christmas.

Children over 10 welcome.

Jo & Steve Ainsworth
Gilpin Mill,
Crook,
Windermere, LA8 8LN
Tel   +44 (0)1539 568405
Email info@gilpinmill.co.uk
Web   www.gilpinmill.co.uk

Entry 60   Map 11

Cumbria

The Malabar

Surrounded by stone walls, sheep and Howgill Fells... in the glorious Yorkshire Dales National Park. Well-travelled Fiona and Graham have restored the barn next to their farmhouse into deeply comfortable, smart spaces. Graham was born in India and tea plays a big part here! Arrive to a mound of scones, meringues, triple choc brownies. Sitting and dining rooms are upstairs: high rafters, Indian art, rugs, colourful elephant side tables. Tuck into breakfast at the big communal table: wild boar bacon, venison sausages, vegetarian choices, homemade bread. Sedbergh is a hop; return to a sunny terrace, toasty wood-burners and a wonderfully luxurious bed.

Rooms	3 doubles: £140–£180. 3 suites for 2: £190–£240. Singles £120–£220.
Meals	Afternoon tea included. Pubs/restaurants 2 miles.
Closed	Rarely.

Pets by arrangement.

Fiona Lappin
The Malabar,
Garths, Marthwaite,
Sedbergh, LA10 5ED
Tel   +44 (0)1539 620200
Mobile   +44 (0)7594 550046
Email   info@themalabar.com
Web   www.themalabar.com

Entry 61   Map 12

Cumbria

Viver Water Mill

Dianne and Ian have spent years renovating their attractive Lakeland stone water mill. Mentioned in the Domesday Book, it dates from the 13th century and one of the grinding stones is set in the traditional sitting room. Arrive to afternoon tea next to the fire, or by the summerhouse overlooking the mill stream and pretty valley. Fresh bedrooms have comfy beds and coordinating fabrics. Wake to home-grown fruits, homemade jams and eggs from the hens; Dianne is happy to do supper too. Wander the beautiful garden, visit historic homes and market town Kirkby Lonsdale; great walking and cycling, and close to the A590 so a good Scotland stop-over.

Rooms	1 double; 1 double with separate bathroom: £70–£80.
Meals	Supper £10. Dinner, 2 courses, £17. Pubs/restaurants 3 miles.
Closed	Rarely.

Dianne Woof
Viver Water Mill,
Viver Lane,
Hincaster, LA7 7NF
Tel   +44 (0)15395 61017
Email   info@viverwatermill.co.uk
Web   www.viverwatermill.co.uk

Entry 62   Map 11

Cumbria

Broughton House

Down lanes edged with dry stone walls and hedges, with distant views of the Lakeland mountains... what peace! You feel instantly at home too, in a house full of books and colour. Bedrooms come with a jar of Cate's homemade brownies, a bowl of fruit and a deep mattress: owls hooting you to sleep in one, privacy in the wing, snug simplicity in Ben's Cabin. Wake to fresh juice, pancakes, homemade bread, local bacon and sausages, smoked salmon and scrambled eggs. Puffin the dog, cats Fuss and Bother, a host of hens and a big garden add to the charm. Perfect for cycling, a hop from Windermere and eating out in pretty Cartmel is a treat.

Rooms	2 doubles: £85-£90. 1 cabin for 2 with yurt sitting room: £60-£80. Singles £60.
Meals	Pub 1 mile.
Closed	1 November – 31 January.

Cate Davies
Broughton House,
Field Broughton,
Grange-over-Sands, LA11 6HN
Tel   +44 (0)1539 536439
Email   info@broughtonhousecartmel.co.uk
Web   www.broughtonhousecartmel.co.uk

Entry 63   Map 11

Cumbria

Broadgate

Through stone pillars is a lovely Georgian house with stunning views to the sea. Vivid blue hydrangeas make a startling contrast to its white façade and smooth green lawns. Find large elegant bedrooms with comfortable beds and antique furniture, a cosy sitting room with a wood-burner, and a beautifully laid table in the dining room. Diana, an accomplished cook, treats you to home-produced vegetables and fruits, local sausages, cakes and scones. Her walled garden, surrounded by woodland, is full of old roses, wide borders and places to sit. Head out for castles, gardens, Beatrix Potter's house, Coniston Water sailing and great walks.

Rooms	2 doubles both with separate bath: £95. 2 singles both with separate shower room: £55. Singles £55.
Meals	Dinner, 3 courses, £25. Pub 5 miles.
Closed	Rarely.

Children over 10 welcome.

Diana Lewthwaite
Broadgate,
Millom,
Broughton-in-Furness, LA18 5JZ
Tel   +44 (0)1229 716295
Email   dilewthwaite@bghouse.co.uk
Web   www.broadgate-house.co.uk

Entry 64   Map 11

Derbyshire

Underleigh House

A Derbyshire longhouse in Charlotte Brontë's *Jane Eyre* country built by a man called George Eyre. The position is unbeatable – field, river, hill, sky – but the stars of the show are Philip and Vivienne, dab hands at spoiling guests rotten. There's a big sitting room with maps for walkers, a dining room hall for hearty breakfasts, and tables and chairs scattered about the garden. Back inside, bedrooms vary in size, but all have super beds, goose down duvets and stunning views; a couple have doors onto the garden, the suites have proper sitting rooms. Fantastic walks start from the front door, Castleton Caves are on the doorstep and Chatsworth is close.

Rooms	1 double: £95–£105.
	3 suites for 2: £115–£125.
	Singles £75–£105.
	Extra bed/sofabed £20 p.p.p.n..
Meals	Packed lunches £6.
	Pubs/restaurants 0.5 miles.
Closed	Christmas, New Year,
	1 January – 7 February.

Over 12s welcome.

Philip & Vivienne Taylor
Underleigh House,
Lose Hill Lane, Hope,
Hope Valley, S33 6AF
Tel +44 (0)1433 621372
Email underleigh.house@btconnect.com
Web www.underleighhouse.co.uk

Entry 65   Map 12

Derbyshire

The Lodge at Dale End House

One of those places where you get your own annexe – in this case, the former milking parlour of the listed farmhouse. It certainly has scrubbed up nicely. The ground-floor bedroom has a finely dressed antique bed and magnificent chandelier while the well-equipped kitchen is a boon if you don't fancy venturing out for supper. Friendly, helpful Sarah leaves you a breakfast hamper too, so cook whenever you want – cereals, juice, eggs from her hens, local sausages and bacon, homemade jams. No open fire but cosy underfloor heating warms you after blustery walks. Bring your four-legged friends – canine or equine – to this happy house.

Rooms	1 double with kitchen/dining/sitting room: £100–£125.
Meals	Pubs/restaurants 2.5 miles.
Closed	Never.

Minimum stay: 2 nights & in high season.

Sarah & Paul Summers
The Lodge at Dale End House,
Gratton,
Bakewell, DE45 1LN
Tel +44 (0)1629 650380
Email thebarn@daleendhouse.co.uk
Web www.daleendhouse.co.uk

Entry 66   Map 8

Derbyshire

Old Shoulder of Mutton

The lively village of Winster is mega-pretty; the Old Shoulder of Mutton, once a pub, sits in its middle. Steven and Julie are welcoming and their home is as cosy as can be. Find a warm contemporary and traditional mix, framed clay pipes (found during renovations), a charming drawing room, luxurious bedrooms and snazzy en suite bathrooms. Breakfast is by the wood-burner: feast on eggs Benedict, homemade jam, local bacon and the famous Derbyshire oatcakes. There's a lovely and unexpected garden at the back; Bakewell, with its legendary Monday market and Chatsworth House, is a short drive, and the walking is dreamy.

Rooms	2 doubles, 1 twin/double: £125–£150. Singles £110–£135.
Meals	Pubs in village.
Closed	1 December – 10 March.

Minimum stay: 2 nights. Over 12s welcome.

Steven White
Old Shoulder of Mutton,
West Bank, Winster,
Matlock, DE4 2DQ
Tel: +44 (0)1629 650005
Email: steven@theoldshoulderofmutton.co.uk
Web: www.oldshoulderofmutton.co.uk

Entry 67 Map 8

Derbyshire

Manor Farm

Between two small dales, close to great houses (Chatsworth, Hardwick Hall, Haddon Hall), lies this peaceful cluster of three ancient farms and a church; welcome to the 16th century! Simon and Gilly, warm, delightful and fascinated by the history, have restored the east wing to create big, beamy rooms in the old hayloft and a pretty garden room on the ground floor. Wake to a choice of scrumptious breakfasts with local and organic produce – served in the cavernous Elizabethan kitchen. There's a lovely garden with sweeping views across Derwent Valley and distant hills, walks from the doorstep and the Peak District to explore.

Rooms	3 twin/doubles, 1 twin: £80–£99. Singles £60–£75.
Meals	Pubs 10-minute walk, restaurants 10-minute drive.
Closed	Rarely.

Minimum stay: 2 nights at weekends. Children over 5 welcome.

Simon & Gilly Groom
Manor Farm,
Dethick, Matlock, DE4 5GG
Tel: +44 (0)1629 534302
Mobile: +44 (0)7944 660814
Email: gilly.groom@w3z.co.uk
Web: www.manorfarmdethick.co.uk

Entry 68 Map 8

Derbyshire

Alstonefield Manor

Country manor house definitely, but delightfully understated and cleverly designed to look natural. This family home, sitting in walled gardens, is high in the hills above Dovedale. Local girl Jo spoils you with homemade scones and tea when you arrive, served on the lawns or by the fire in the elegant drawing room. Beautiful bedrooms have antiques, flowers, lovely fabrics, painted floors and garden views; wood panelled bathrooms have showers or a roll top tub. Wake to birdsong – and a candlelit breakfast with local bacon and Staffordshire oatcakes. After a great walk, stroll across the village green for supper at The George. A joy.

Rooms	1 double; 2 doubles both with separate bathroom: £130-£170. Singles £100.
Meals	Pub 100 yds.
Closed	Christmas, 2 January – 26 January.

Minimum stay: 2 nights. Over 12s welcome.

Robert & Jo Wood
Alstonefield Manor,
Alstonefield,
Ashbourne, DE6 2FX
Tel   +44 (0)1335 310393
Email stay@alstonefieldmanor.com
Web   www.alstonefieldmanor.com

Entry 69   Map 8

Derbyshire

The Old Vicarage

Wind through pretty Wetton, park under the big tree and find a front door with a cheery bell and a box of slippers waiting the other side. You're looked after well and the house has a convivial air. Bedrooms have well-dressed beds; the dining room encourages you to linger: flowers, garden views, open fire, books and maps. Nicky gives you lots of breakfast choices including eggs from the hens and homemade jams from her organic plot. There are benches for sitting outside on sunny days, the colourful garden is full of birds and the White Peak is on the doorstep – Nicky, super-friendly and a keen walker, will happily direct you.

Rooms	2 doubles, 1 twin/double: £98-£125. Extra Z-bed £28 per person per night.
Meals	Packed lunch £7.50. Pubs/restaurants 1 mile.
Closed	Never.

Nicola Drummond
The Old Vicarage,
Wetton, Ashbourne, DE6 2AF
Tel   +44 (0)1335 310296
Mobile +44 (0)7854 456678
Email   nicola@oldvicaragewetton.co.uk
Web   www.oldvicaragewetton.co.uk

Entry 70   Map 8

Derbyshire

Hinchley Wood

Glorious Georgian house with the most engaging, friendly hosts: you're in for a treat. The pineapple-topped gateposts are a symbol of hospitality, and you arrive for tea and cake by the fire in the splendid drawing room. Sleep well in elegant bedrooms; beds are topped with good linen, there are interesting books to browse and the views are stunning. Rosemaré's breakfasts are "legendary"— a local, usually organic, spread with her wonderful Staffordshire oat cakes. Pretty villages, historic houses, Nordic walking, riding, fly fishing on the river Dove… the area is dreamy and Cedric is happy to arrange activities.

Rooms	1 double, 1 four-poster: £130–£140.
Meals	Pubs/restaurants 3-minute walk.
Closed	December/January.

Minimum stay: 2 nights at weekends. Children over 10 welcome. Secure lock-up for bikes.

	Cedric & Rosemaré Stevenson Hinchley Wood, Mappleton, Ashbourne, DE6 2AB
Tel	+44 (0)1335 350219
Email	rose-stevenson@hotmail.co.uk

Entry 71   Map 8

Devon

North Walk House

Sea views, brass bedsteads and big rooms at this calm retreat, perfectly positioned above Lynmouth Bay's dramatic seascape – ideal for walkers and foodies. Ian and Sarah welcome you with homemade cake in a cosy guest lounge, and give you light bedrooms with sparkling bathrooms and inviting beds. Enjoy Exmoor's coastal and moor walks, genteel Lynton and Lynmouth; return to log fire and armchairs. Take tea on the terrace, and be tempted by Sarah's fine dinners, seasonal and mostly organic. The Downings are relaxed, engaging hosts, happy to share their enthusiasm for this lovely area. Stay a few days and really unwind.

Rooms	2 doubles, 1 twin/double: £112–£175. Singles £70–£109.
Meals	Dinner, 4 courses, from £27. Pub/restaurant 0.25 miles.
Closed	1 November – 31 March.

Dogs welcome in ground floor room.

	Ian & Sarah Downing North Walk House, North Walk, Lynton, EX35 6HJ
Tel	+44 (0)1598 753372
Email	walk@northwalkhouse.co.uk
Web	www.northwalkhouse.co.uk

Entry 72   Map 2

Devon

Beachborough Country House

Welcome to this gracious 18th-century rectory with stone-flagged floors, lofty windows, wooden shutters and glorious rugs. Viviane is vivacious and spoils you with dinners and breakfasts from the Aga; dine in the elegant dining room before a twinkling fire. Hens cluck, horses whinny but otherwise the peace is deep. Ease any walker's pains away in a steaming roll top tub; lap up country views from big airy bedrooms. There's a games room for kids in the outbuildings and a stream winds through the garden – a delicious three acres of vegetables and roses. Huge fun.

Rooms	2 doubles, 1 twin/double: £90. Singles £65.
Meals	Dinner, 2-3 courses, £22.50-£27.50. Catering for house parties. Pub 3 miles.
Closed	Rarely.

Viviane Clout
Beachborough Country House,
Kentisbury, Barnstaple, EX31 4NH
Tel +44 (0)1271 882487
Mobile +44 (0)7732 947755
Email viviane@beachboroughcountryhouse.co.uk
Web www.beachboroughcountryhouse.co.uk

Entry 73   Map 2

Devon

Coombe Farm

Easy-going, foodie, country-lovers fit right in here. Lisa and Matt, passionate about real food, cook home-grown dinners; charcuterie a speciality. Their fine old Devon long house sits in a green fold of farmland and you're free to wander the garden, chat to the pigs, plunge in the invigorating pool. Inside find a quirky mix of family and brocante finds, a snug sitting room full of art, colourful comfortable rooms and fab bathrooms. Breakfast is a delicious spread of homemade everything: granola, jams, sourdough bread, sausages and bacon from the rare breed pigs. The No 3 cycle route is close by; Exmoor walks and coast are 20 minutes.

Rooms	1 double, 2 twin/doubles: £75-£90.
Meals	Dinner from £25. Restaurants 15 minutes walk.
Closed	Rarely.

Minimum stay: 2 nights at weekends & in high season.

Matthew Eckford
Coombe Farm,
Goodleigh, Barnstaple, EX32 7NB
Tel +44 (0)1271 324919
Mobile +44 (0)7775 941031
Email info@coombefarmgoodleigh.co.uk
Web www.coombefarmgoodleigh.co.uk

Entry 74   Map 2

Devon

Tabor Hill Farm

Sociable Astley has put love into every inch of her farm, from the smart bedrooms to the spick-and-span livery yard. She's just down the hall and will let you tinkle the Bechstein while she scrambles eggs from her own hens for breakfast. Views look south over Exmoor National Park from a neat front garden; you can spend quiet moments here with a book surrounded by friendly dogs and quacking ducks, or potter around the lake. Bring walking boots, and perhaps your horse, and enjoy being well away from it all – the clearest night skies, trails to walk and abundant wildlife to spot from red deer to birds. Drive nine miles to hike across the historic Tarr Steps or 40 minutes to lovely Lynmouth on the coast.

Rooms	2 doubles: £90.
Meals	Dinner £20.
	Pubs/restaurants 2-6 miles.
Closed	Rarely.

Over 14s welcome.

	Astley Shilton Barlow
	Tabor Hill Farm,
	Heasley Mill,
	South Molton, EX36 3LQ
Mobile	+44 (0)7985 577175
Email	enquiries@taborhillfarm.co.uk

Entry 75   Map 2

Devon

South Yeo

Down windy lanes with tall grassy banks and the smell of the sea is a lovely Georgian country house with two walled gardens and barns at the back. You'll fall for this place the moment you arrive, and its owners: Jo runs an interiors business; Mike keeps the cattle and sheep that graze all around. Bedrooms are inviting; the double, overlooking the valley, has a cream French bed, a pretty quilted cover, a claw-foot bath and a little sitting room (adjoining) with TV. There's an elegant drawing room with a real fire too. Delicious breakfasts with home-laid eggs and homemade jams are brought to a snug room that catches the morning sun.

Rooms	1 double, with sitting room;
	1 twin/double with separate bath:
	£80-£105. Singles £75.
Meals	Pub 1.5 miles.
Closed	Rarely.

	Joanne Wade
	South Yeo,
	Yeo Vale, Bideford, EX39 5ES
Tel	+44 (0)1237 451218
Email	stay@southyeo.com
Web	www.southyeo.com

Entry 76   Map 2

Devon

Beara Farmhouse

At the bottom of a sheltered valley with sheep grazing in open fields, find a whitewashed farmhouse lovingly brought back to life from an old near-ruin, by talented Richard and Ann. It's a friendly, unstuffy sort of place where you'll feel at home. Wander the pretty gardens where Ann has laid brick paths and Richard has created a pond, now home to mallards and geese. You're surrounded by open countryside and near enough to the north coast of both counties for days at the beach. Ask for a 6.30am breakfast if you want to catch the ferry to Lundy Island, return to a roaring fire and a glass of wine with maybe a cat at your feet. Richard will be happy to shoot a few arrows with you if you are interested in archery.

Rooms	1 double, 1 twin: £80. Singles by arrangement.
Meals	Pub 1.5 miles.
Closed	20 December – 5 January.

Minimum stay: 2 nights at weekends, bank holidays & high season.

Ann & Richard Dorsett
Beara Farmhouse,
Buckland Brewer,
Bideford, EX39 5EH
Tel   +44 (0)1237 451666
Email   bearafarmhouse@gmail.com
Web   www.bearafarmhouse.co.uk

Entry 77   Map 2

Devon

Hartland Mill

Cathy and James live with Ruby the labrador, in a storybook house on the edge of the world. The welcome couldn't be warmer, your hosts want to make your stay the very best. From the big airy guest sitting room to the candlelit dining room, all is as neat as a new pin. Breakfast has an outstanding menu that changes daily – overnight oats, full English with Cathy's slow roasted herby tomatoes, freshly baked muffins, pancakes, eggs Benedict. No wonder guests don't leave the convivial table for hours. The seclusion is blissful – all you hear is the stream. From the garden you can walk to the coastal path. Hartland Abbey with its bluebell woods and garden is close by too. Cathy will prepare a home-cooked dinner for your return or you can try the Pattard Kitchen, a new favourite in Clovelly; your generous hosts will drop you off.

Rooms	2 doubles, 1 twin/double: £90-£110.
Meals	Dinner, 2 courses, £15. BYO wine. Pubs/restaurants 10 minutes.
Closed	Rarely.

Minimum stay: 2 nights in high season. Over 12s welcome.

Cathy Walker
Hartland Mill,
Hartland,
Bideford, EX39 6DS
Tel   +44 (0)1237 440181
Email   hello@hartlandmill.co.uk
Web   www.hartlandmill.co.uk

Entry 78   Map 1

Devon

The Granary – Borough Farm

Follow the winding road, past Connemara ponies and rare-breed sheep, to a farm that's been here for centuries. Julia's natural warmth, and the Dartmoor views, will soothe ruffled souls. Hop up the granary's exterior steps to your room: white walls and wood floor, curvaceous French bed, sky windows for gazing at glittering stars, and a delicious French antique double-ended bath, basin and loo behind a screen. There's another beautiful bath in a tent (shared with two yurts), and your own garden with a firepit. The communal Loft has a fridge, kettle and toaster, comfy armchairs, church pews and trestle tables for wholesome breakfasts and suppers.

Rooms	1 double: £85–£125.
Meals	Continental breakfast included. Cooked breakfast £8. Dinner, 2 courses, from £12. Pubs/restaurants 4 miles.
Closed	November – February.

Julia Martin
The Granary – Borough Farm,
Kelly,
Lifton, PL16 0HJ
Tel +44 (0)1822 870366
Email contactus@devonyurt.co.uk
Web www.devonyurt.co.uk

Entry 79 Map 2

Devon

Burnville House

Granite gateposts, Georgian house, rhododendrons, beech woods and rolling fields of sheep: that's the setting. But there's more. Beautifully proportioned rooms reveal subtle colours, elegant antiques, squishy sofas and bucolic views, stylish bathrooms are sprinkled with candles, there are sumptuous dinners and pancakes at breakfast. Your hosts left busy jobs in London to settle here, and their place breathes life – space, smiles, energy. Swim, play tennis, walk to Dartmoor from the door, take a trip to Eden or the sea. Or... just gaze at the moors and the church on the Tor and listen to the silence, and the sheep.

Rooms	3 doubles: £85–£95. Singles £65.
Meals	Dinner from £23. Pub 2 miles.
Closed	Rarely.

Victoria Cunningham
Burnville House,
Brentor, Tavistock, PL19 0NE
Tel +44 (0)1822 820443
Mobile +44 (0)7881 583471
Email burnvillef@aol.com
Web www.burnville.co.uk

Entry 80 Map 2

Devon

Cyprian's Cot

A charming 16th-century terraced cottage filled with beams and burnished wood. The old stone fireplace is huge, the grandfather clock ticks, the views are stunning and Shelagh is warm and welcoming. Guests have their own sitting room with a crackling fire; up the narrow stairs and into cosy bedrooms – a small double and a tiny twin. Tasty breakfasts, served in the dining room, include free-range eggs, sausages and bacon from the local farm and garden fruits. Discover the lovely town with its pubs, fine restaurants and interesting shops. With the Dartmoor Way and the Two Moors Way on the doorstep, the walking is wonderful too.

Rooms	1 twin; 1 double with separate bath: £80. Singles £35-£38.
Meals	Pubs/restaurants 4-minute walk.
Closed	Rarely.

Shelagh Weeden
Cyprian's Cot,
47 New Street, Chagford,
Newton Abbot, TQ13 8BB
Tel   +44 (0)1647 432256
Email   shelaghweeden@btinternet.com
Web   www.cyprianscot.co.uk

Entry 81   Map 2

Devon

Brook Farmhouse

Tuck yourself up in the peace and quiet of Paul and Penny's whitewashed, thatched cottage, surrounded by glorious countryside. Inside find your own charming sitting room with a huge inglenook, good antiques, fresh flowers, and comfy sofa and chairs; breakfast here on homemade apple juice, eggs from the owners' hens and delicious local bacon and sausages. Up the ancient spiral stone stairs is your warm, beamed bedroom with smooth linen, chintzy curtains, lots of cushions. You are near Dartmoor and can reach Devon beaches and the north Cornish coast; perfect for hearty walkers, birdwatchers, surfers and picnic-lovers.

Rooms	1 double with separate bathroom: £80-£90. Singles £55-£65.
Meals	Pub 2 miles.
Closed	Rarely.

Paul & Penny Steadman
Brook Farmhouse,
Tedburn St Mary,
Exeter, EX6 6DS
Tel   +44 (0)1647 270042
Email   penny.steadman@btconnect.com
Web   www.brook-farmhouse.co.uk

Entry 82   Map 2

Devon

Clarendon

This large family house has a laid-back atmosphere. Local art and family photos are dotted about and Helen greets you with a cup of tea. Big comfy bedrooms have Dartmoor views, flowers and a sofa. Helen loves to cook, and you wake to a generous breakfast of homemade bread and jams, fruit, home-laid eggs, local sausages and bacon – served in her cheerful conservatory in summer, or by the wood-burner in winter. Stroll to charming Bovey Tracy in a few minutes, visit nearby National Trust estate Parke where the river Dart flows, or head off onto Dartmoor for walking and cycling. You can sit and chat in the pretty back garden by a fire pit under the stars on your return.

Rooms	1 double, 1 twin/double: £80. Extra double bed/sofa bed £20 per person per night.
Meals	Pubs/restaurants 5-minute walk.
Closed	Rarely.

Cot available. Parking on-site.

	Helen Smith
	Clarendon,
	Newton Road,
	Bovey Tracey, TQ13 9BB
Tel	+44 (0)1626 830355
Email	helsiesmith@gmail.com
Web	www.stayatclarendon.com

Entry 83 Map 2

Devon

Cider House

Big mullion windows and contemporary classic interiors at this enchanting former refectory of a medieval abbey. Bryony and Bertie, an endearing young couple, give you stylish bedrooms with roll top tubs and views of garden or valley. Breakfasts are feasts of estate produce – apple juice, honey, rhubarb compotes, eggs, bacon, sausages, just-baked bread – served on white china in the drawing room with stunning views of the gardens. There are 700 acres of woodland to explore and the ruined abbey plus a kitchen garden heaving with soft fruit and vegetables; the framework of old buildings and stone walls are a magical setting.

Rooms	2 doubles: £135–£155. 1 twin/double: £145–£165. 1 four-poster: £160–£185. Singles £125–£170.
Meals	Pub within walking distance
Closed	19 October – 22 March.

Minimum stay: 2 nights. Over 12s welcome.

	Bryony & Bertie Hancock
	Cider House,
	Buckland Abbey,
	Yelverton
Tel	+44 (0)1822 259062
Email	indulge@cider-house.co.uk
Web	www.cider-house.co.uk

Entry 84 Map 2

Devon

Hooppells Torr

Time to unwind – from the tea and cake on arrival, to the reassuring comfort and luxury of the bedrooms, this is the place to exhale and simply relax. The rambling farmhouse, beautifully updated by Jeeva and Simon, has six acres of spectacular grounds for you to explore and even picnic in. From the conservatory you look out over a glorious English country garden straight out of a Merchant Ivory film, while Simon plies you with his Aga-cooked breakfast, featuring the best of what's local and seasonal. Sheltered, sandy Wonwell beach is just a 20-minute meander away, and the cheery local pub is closer still. Your thoughtful hosts have made sure their guest rooms have a private entrance so you can come and go as you please. Pleasingly understated, but not to be underestimated.

Rooms	2 doubles: £145–£155.
Meals	Pubs 10-minute walk.
Closed	Rarely.

Minimum stay: 2 nights at weekends

	Jeeva & Simon Beckett
	Hooppells Torr,
	Kingston,
	Kingsbridge, TQ7 4HA
Mobile	+44 (0)7772 053919
Email	info@hooppellstorr.com
Web	hooppellstorr.com

Entry 85   Map 2

Devon

Keynedon Mill

Welcome to an ancient stone mill, and beautiful rooms in the old miller's house. There's a big friendly kitchen with stone floors and a cheerful red Aga, a beamed dining room with a long polished table, a guest sitting room with a wood-burner, and a pretty garden with a stream running through – picnic, read, enjoy a glass of wine in peaceful corners. Elegant bedrooms have superb beds, antique linen curtains, fresh flowers, morning tea trays and decanters of port. A delicious breakfast of home-baked bread and local produce will set you up for the day: walk the coastal path, discover secluded coves.

Rooms	2 doubles; 1 double, 1 twin both with separate bath/shower: £95–£125. Singles £75–£95. Extra bed/sofabed £30 per person per night.
Meals	Pub 0.5 miles.
Closed	Rarely.

Over 12s welcome.

	Stuart & Jennifer Jebb
	Keynedon Mill,
	Sherford, Kingsbridge, TQ7 2AS
Tel	+44 (0)1548 531485
Mobile	+44 (0)7775 501409
Email	bookings@keynedonmill.co.uk
Web	www.keynedonmill.co.uk

Entry 86   Map 2

Devon

Stokenham House

Lovely Stokenham House gazes at the sea and the bird-rich Slapton Ley. Iona and Paul – an energetic and thoughtful, imaginative couple – have created a super South Hams base: huge chill-out cushions on the lawn, summerhouse in the pretty banked garden, BBQ by the pool. It's grand yet laid-back, with a fine drawing room, big conservatory and a family-friendly feel. Learn to cook or grow veg, invite friends for dinner, host your own party: Iona is a superb cook. The funky large annexe suite is very private; generous bedrooms in the house are decked in vintage fabrics and papers, and have single rooms off.

Rooms	1 twin/double, sharing separate bath with single: £120.1 suite for 2: £140. 1 family room for 4: £140-£210. 1 single: £80. Extra bed/sofabed available at no charge.
Meals	Dinner from £30. Pubs/restaurants 2-minute walk.
Closed	Rarely.

Dogs welcome in downstairs room.

Iona & Paul Jepson
Stokenham House,
Stokenham, Kingsbridge, TQ7 2ST
Tel +44 (0)1548 581257
Mobile +44 (0)7720 443132
Email ionajepson@googlemail.com
Web www.stokenhamhouse.co.uk

Entry 87   Map 2

Devon

Strete Barton House

Contemporary, friendly, exotic and exquisite: French sleigh beds and Asian art, white basins and black chandeliers, and a garden with sofas for the views. So much to love – and best of all, the coastal path outside the door. Your caring hosts live the dream, running immaculate B&B by the sea, in an old manor house at the top of the village. Breakfasts are exuberantly local (village eggs, sausages from Dartmouth, honey from the bay), there's a wood-burner in the sitting room, warm toasty floors and Kevin and Stuart know exactly which beach, walk or pub is the one for you. Heavenly.

Rooms	3 doubles, 1 twin/double; 1 twin/double with separate shower: £105-£155. Cottage: 1 suite for 2 & sitting room: £150-£165.
Meals	Pub/restaurant 50 yds.
Closed	Rarely.

Children over 8 welcome. Dogs welcome in the cottage suite only.

Stuart Litster & Kevin Hooper
Strete Barton House,
Totnes Road, Strete,
Dartmouth, TQ6 0RU
Tel +44 (0)1803 770364
Email info@stretebarton.co.uk
Web www.stretebarton.co.uk

Entry 88   Map 2

Devon

Fingals

Welcome to an institution from our first B&B book. We call it an 'institution' not because it's been going so long that some of the original guests' grandchildren now take their girlfriends, but because it's always been beyond categorisation. Richard and Sheila have moved back into their Queen Anne manor farmhouse and are winding down – but as ever doing it their own way. There are just two double en suite rooms now (one with an attached room, so good for families or for those who say their other half snores!). The old laissez-faire atmosphere remains: art, books, music, honesty bar, games room, gym. Not your run-of-the-mill B&B... but nor are your hosts.

Rooms	1 four-poster: £110–£210.
	1 family room for 4: £170–£225.
	Extra bed/sofabed £15 per person per night.
Meals	Dinner £36. Pub 1 mile; restaurants 6 miles.
Closed	Mid-January to mid-March.

Minimum stay: 2 nights at weekends.

	Richard & Sheila Johnston
	Fingals,
	Dittisham,
	Dartmouth, TQ6 0JA
Tel	+44 (0)1803 722398
Email	info@fingals.co.uk
Web	www.fingals.co.uk

Entry 89   Map 2

Devon

Brooking

A whitewashed, wisteria-clad house in a gorgeous village... tea and cake will be waiting. Alison's is a relaxed and friendly home. You will sleep well in a peaceful, charming bedroom: luxurious linen on a brass bed, floral cushions, a jug of wild flowers on an antique wooden chest. Alison's breakfasts change with the seasons: homemade granola, jams and bread, fruit compotes and tasty cooked choices. The garden is walled, rambling and pretty with a tangle of climbers, a bright wooden summerhouse and places to sit in the sun. Head out for nearby Totnes (bustling and arty), great wood or moorland walks and fun on the river Dart.

Rooms	1 double: £85–£90. Extra room available (let to same party only).
Meals	Soup, bread & local cheeses (price on request). Children's meals available by arrangement. Pubs 2-minute walk.
Closed	Rarely.

Travel cot, high chair, toys and books in house! Babysitting happily available if needed.

	Alison Carlyon
	Brooking,
	Ashprington, TQ9 7UL
Tel	+44 (0)1803 731037
Email	w.carlyon@btinternet.com
Web	www.brooking-ashprington.co.uk

Entry 90   Map 2

Devon

Avenue Cottage

The tree-lined approach is steep and spectacular; the cottage sits in 11 wondrous acres which overlook the River Dart and Sharpham Estate (local vineyard.) Richard is a gifted gardener and happy to guide you round his fascinating garden with its magical woodland trail and enviable range of hydrangeas. Find a quiet spot to read or absorb the tranquility with tea on the terrace. The house itself is comfortable and calm – rooms look over the sweeping valley and garden. The old-fashioned twin room has a balcony and large, recently refurbished bathroom with a walk in shower. The pretty village, vineyard café and pub are a short walk away.

Rooms	1 twin/double; 1 double, sharing shower room with owner: £70–£90. Singles £55–£75.
Meals	Pub 0.25 miles.
Closed	Rarely.

Richard Pitts & David Sykes
Avenue Cottage,
Ashprington, Totnes, TQ9 7UT
Tel   +44 (0)1803 732769
Mobile   +44 (0)7719 147475
Email   richard.pitts@btinternet.com
Web   www.avenuecottage.com

Entry 91   Map 2

Devon

Beacon House

Perched above Brixham's bustling harbour (a scamper downhill for the sprightly) is this pretty Victorian villa and immaculate B&B. Here live Amanda, Nigel and Henry the springer spaniel, happily sharing garden, house and views. In 'Bay View' the bed is positioned so that you wake to the sun as it rises above the headland and shimmers across the bay… but every room is special and each gets the view. Torbay vistas compete with delicious breakfasts brought to small tables (Devon haddock; apricots stewed in tea and orange; local honey; Amanda's take on the old favourite, the 'Full Beacon'). Dartmouth is five miles, the coastal path a few steps.

Rooms	3 doubles, 1 twin/double: £63–£135.
Meals	Pubs/restaurants 5-minute walk.
Closed	Rarely.

Minimum stay: 2 nights at weekends. Guests are welcome to leave their car in the car park till midday on day of departure.

Nigel Makin
Beacon House,
Prospect Steps, South Furzeham Rd,
Brixham, TQ5 8JB
Mobile +44 (0)7768 565656
Email   enquiries@beaconbrixham.co.uk
Web   www.beaconbrixham.co.uk

Entry 92   Map 2

Devon

Bulleigh Barton Manor

Tea and scones will be waiting. Find long, leafy views to wake up to, a pool for lazy summer days, ponds and a big colourful garden with a summerhouse. Liz and Mark have restored their house with care, uncovering beams and lovely bits of old wood and filling it with original art and books. Bedrooms are inviting: sink-into beds, china pieces on white window sills, a pot of garden flowers, local fudge and homemade cake. They are keen on sourcing the best local produce and their host of hens lay your breakfast eggs. Dartmoor and the south coast are at your feet; return to a friendly hello from Zennor the dog by the fire.

Rooms	2 doubles: £86-£135. 1 suite for 2 with kitchenette: £90-£130. Singles £77-£120.
Meals	Pubs/restaurants 0.5 miles.
Closed	Rarely.

Over 16s welcome.

Liz & Mark Lamport
Bulleigh Barton Manor,
Ipplepen,
Newton Abbot, TQ12 5UA
Tel   +44 (0)1803 873311
Email   liz.lamport@btopenworld.com
Web   www.bulleighbartonmanor.co.uk

Entry 93   Map 2

Devon

Hannaford House

An inviting place to stay, with fabulous views across the valley to Haldon Forest. Kay and Simon give you a cosy annexe for two with a wood-burner, well-dressed bed, books and flowers; you have your own sunny courtyard as well with table, chairs and loungers where you can sit with an evening glass of something or your morning coffee. Breakfast is brought over to you; home-produced and tasty, it includes sausage and bacon from the pigs, eggs from the hens, tomatoes in season, homemade bread and jams. Find hammocks in the colourful garden, woods to explore, Exmouth estuary for boating fun and Dartmoor for hearty walks.

Rooms	1 annexe for 2: £85-£90. Singles £70.
Meals	Pub 1.5 miles.
Closed	Rarely.

Kay & Simon Wisker
Hannaford House,
Kennford, Exeter, EX6 7XZ
Tel   +44 (0)1392 833577
Mobile   +44 (0)7752 701182
Email   kay@hannafordhouse.co.uk
Web   www.hannafordhouse.co.uk

Entry 94   Map 2

Devon

The Linhay

This 18th-century thatched cottage sits in its own peaceful valley – with a stream nearby, a pretty orchard and friendly sheep, this is a place for nature lovers. Owners Andrei and Holly live in the main house and they've cleverly converted your three-level, open-plan hideaway. Expect a cosy, natural feel with rocking chairs by a log burner and a balcony looking out over apple and plum trees. Home-cooked breakfasts are brought over whenever you wish: freshly-laid eggs, sausages from the pigs and artisan bread. They'll give you supper too if you want. Borrow wellies and maps and set off over glorious fields, or venture further to village pubs for long, lazy lunches. Wander the garden and sit under the weeping willow; hole up by the fire with a good book.

Rooms	The Linhay Annexe: 1 suite for 2 with kitchenette: £95.
Meals	Homecooked supper for 2, £30. Pubs/restaurants 3 miles.
Closed	Rarely.

Holly Carter & Andrei Szerard
The Linhay,
Brendon Cottage, Copplestone,
Crediton, EX17 5NZ
Tel +44 (0)1363 84286
Email enquiries@smilingsheep.co.uk
Web www.smilingsheep.co.uk

Entry 95   Map 2

Devon

Barnhill House

A grand house and restoration project, complete with turrets and gothic features. Geri and Kevin are art collectors and travellers – find striking pieces in every stylish corner. Bedrooms have lovely linen, antiques, flowers, chocolates… Breakfast includes honey and eggs from the village – eat in the kitchen, dining room or out on the terrace. The gardens are a perfect mix of nature and design; a bridge takes you over the river Exe (go wild swimming), and on to the Exe Valley Way. Exeter is a ten-minute drive. Settle on a velvet sofa by the log-burner – or up in the Ibiza-style snug at the top of the cupola and soak up 360° views.

Rooms	2 doubles; 1 double sharing bathroom (let to same party only): £100–£150.
Meals	Occasional dinner £25. Pub 5-minute walk.
Closed	Rarely.

Geri Carden
Barnhill House,
Brampford Speke,
Exeter, EX5 5HG
Mobile +44 (0)7794 517235
Email gericarden@me.com
Web www.barnhillhouse.com

Entry 96   Map 2

Devon

The Dairy Loft

The beautiful East Devon Way brings you almost to the door of this smart, new B&B for the independent-minded. Up the exterior stair is your bright, colourful studio with cleverly arranged workstation and wet room with double-headed shower. The funky red leather sofa and big bed (or twins) opposite French windows invite lazing, star-gazing, Merlin-spotting. You're free to concoct your own lavish breakfast beneath the Italian lamp whenever you fancy. Oak-floored inside, larch clad out and with kind, interesting owners across the flowered yard who'll advise on all things local, from sea and river fishing to Exe Trail cycling.

Rooms	1 twin/double: £90–£120.
Meals	Pubs/restaurants 2 miles.
Closed	Rarely.

Minimum stay: 2 nights.

Rob & Annie Jones
The Dairy Loft,
Valley Barn, Hawkerland, Colaton
Raleigh, Sidmouth, EX10 0JA
Tel   +44 (0)1395 568411
Email   anniemacjones@me.com
Web   www.thedairyloft.co.uk

Entry 97   Map 2

Devon

Lower Allercombe Farm

Horses in the paddock, roses climbing the walls and no-frills bedrooms at this down-to-earth, friendly B&B. Susie, a retired eventer, will greet you along with her Labrador Tilly. You have your own sitting room with horsey pictures and a cosy wood-burner while Susie lives at the other end of this Devon longhouse. Breakfast is at one long wooden table in the sunny kitchen: home-grown fruit compote with Greek yogurt, homemade bread and granola, garden tomatoes, home-laid eggs, honey from Susie's neighbour, rashers from local award-winning pigs. Walk along the river Otter on pretty trails, bring bikes, take a picnic to the Jurassic coast or head to Dartmoor. Behind the house is a quiet, well-kept garden with a summerhouse where you're welcome to put together your own picnic suppers in the summer.

Rooms	1 double, 1 twin; 1 double with separate bath: £60–£85. Singles £50–£65.
Meals	Pub/restaurant 2 miles.
Closed	Rarely.

Susie Holroyd
Lower Allercombe Farm,
Rockbeare, Exeter, EX5 2HD
Tel   +44 (0)1404 822519
Mobile +44 (0)7980 255107
Email   holroyd.s@gmail.com
Web   www.lowerallercombefarm.co.uk

Entry 98   Map 2

Devon

Larkbeare Grange

Expectations rise as you follow the tree-lined drive to the immaculate Georgian house... to be warmly greeted with homemade cakes. The upkeep is perfect, the feel is chic and the whole place exudes well-being. Sparkling sash windows fill big rooms with light, floors shine and the grandfather clock ticks away the hours. Expect the best: good lighting, goose down duvets, luxurious fabrics and fittings, a fabulous suite for a small family, flexible (and delicious) breakfasts and lovely views from the bedrooms at the front. Charlie, Savoy-trained, and Julia are charming and fun and there are bikes to borrow. Exceptional B&B!

Rooms	2 doubles, 1 twin/double: £115–£145. 1 suite for 4: £175–£195. Singles £90–£125.
Meals	Pub 1.5 miles.
Closed	Rarely.

Minimum stay: 2 nights some weekends.

Charlie & Julia Hutchings
Larkbeare Grange,
Larkbeare, Talaton, Exeter, EX5 2RY
Tel   +44 (0)1404 822069
Mobile   +44 (0)7762 574915
Email   stay@larkbeare.net
Web   www.larkbeare.net

Entry 99   Map 2

Devon

West Colwell Farm

Devon lanes, pheasants, bluebell walks *and* sparkling B&B. The Hayes clearly love what they do; ex-TV producers, they have converted this 18th-century farmhouse and barns into a snug and stylish place to stay. Be charmed by original beams and pine doors, heritage colours and clean lines. Bedrooms are very private and luxurious, two have terraces overlooking the wooded valley and the most cosy is tucked under the roof. Linen is tip-top, showers are huge and breakfasts (Frank's pancakes, lovely bacon, eggs from next door) are totally flexible. A welcoming glass of wine, starry night skies, beaches nearby, peace all around. Bliss.

Rooms	3 doubles: £105. 10% off for 3-4 nights; 15% off for 5-6 nights; 20% off for 7 nights. Singles £85.
Meals	Restaurants 3 miles.
Closed	December – February.

Minimum stay: 2 nights.

Frank & Carol Hayes
West Colwell Farm,
Offwell,
Honiton, EX14 9SL
Tel   +44 (0)1404 831130
Email   stay@westcolwell.co.uk
Web   www.westcolwell.co.uk

Entry 100   Map 2

Devon

Glebe House

Set on a hillside with fabulous views over the Coly valley, this late-Georgian vicarage is now a heart-warming B&B. The views will entice you, the hosts will delight you and the house is filled with interesting things. Chuck and Emma spent many years at sea – he a Master Mariner, she a chef – and have filled these big light rooms with cushions, kilims and treasured family pieces. There's a sitting room for guests, a lovely conservatory with vintage vine, peaceful bedrooms with blissful views and bathrooms that sparkle. All this, two sweet pygmy goats, wildlife beyond the ha-ha and the fabulous coast a hike away.

Rooms	1 double, 1 twin/double: £90. 1 family room for 4: £100-£130. Singles £60.
Meals	Dinner, 3 courses £30. Pubs/restaurants 2.5 miles.
Closed	Christmas & New Year.

Minimum stay: 2 nights July & August weekends & bank holidays.

Emma & Chuck Guest
Glebe House,
Southleigh, Colyton, EX24 6SD
Tel   +44 (0)1404 871276
Mobile   +44 (0)7867 568569
Email   guestsatglebe@gmail.com
Web   www.guestsatglebe.com

Entry 101   Map 2

Devon

Green Dragon House

Head down Castle Hill, dipping from Axminster's market square to the river to this Victorian house. Find a fun, contemporary vibe inside: a wall clad in old pallets here, a row of finely painted bird boxes there; books and flowers abound, and the sleek walk-in shower rooms are a treat. Hospitality here is a two-generation family affair. They make a friendly, talented team. Expect a cracking full English breakfast with French butter and locally sourced everything else. A small, pretty garden begs to be enjoyed; you're positively encouraged to bring home a bottle and quaff it al fresco. This part of town is rich in industrial heritage – next door are the last feather-dyers in the country! The prime place for otter-spotting on the Axe is a minute's walk, the River Cottage Canteen footsteps in the other direction.

Rooms	2 doubles, 1 twin/double: £95-£110. Singles £76-£88.
Meals	Restaurants 5-minute walk.
Closed	Christmas & New Year.

Dianne Bruce
Green Dragon House,
Castle Hill,
Axminster, EX13 5PY
Tel   +44 (0)1297 647182
Email   greendragonaxe@gmail.com
Web   www.greendragonaxe.com

Entry 102   Map 2

Devon

Applebarn Cottage

A tree-lined drive leads to a long white wall, and a gate opening to an explosion of colour – the garden. Come for a deliciously restful place and the nicest, most easy-going hosts; the wisteria-covered 17th-century cottage is full of books, paintings and fresh flowers. Bedrooms – one in an extension that blends in beautifully – are large, traditional, wonderfully comfortable, and the views down the valley are sublime. Patricia trained as a chef and dinners are delicious and great fun. Breakfast, served in a lovely oak-floored dining room, includes honey from the neighbour's bees.

Rooms	2 suites for 2: £78–£83.
Meals	Dinner, 3 courses with aperitif, £28.
Closed	November to mid-March.

Minimum stay: 2 nights.

Patricia & Robert Spencer
Applebarn Cottage,
Bewley Down,
Axminster, EX13 7JX
Tel +44 (0)1460 220873
Email paspenceruk@yahoo.com
Web www.applebarn.wordpress.com

Entry 103 Map 2

Devon

Pounds Farm

A flock of white geese trot across the field, the cottage gardens are a summer-blooming feast of colour and the Blackdown Hills are the green backdrop. Inside is just as good: polished wood, original lithographs, oil paintings, comfy seats by the fire, airy bedrooms in apple-pie order and freshly picked flowers in every room. Enjoy the pool, wander the gorgeous gardens, have breakfast (free-range and delicious) outside in the sun – Diana wants you to feel at home. You're equidistant from Exmoor and the south coast, and you can wander down the hill for supper and a pint in the local. A friendly house with a timeless charm.

Rooms	1 double; 1 double with separate bath; 1 twin/double sharing bathroom with double (let to same party only): £80–£95.
Meals	Pubs/restaurants 10-minute walk.
Closed	Rarely.

Diana Elliott
Pounds Farm,
Hemyock,
Cullompton, EX15 3QS
Email shillingscottage@yahoo.co.uk
Web www.poundsfarm.co.uk

Entry 104 Map 2

Dorset

Wodetone Vineyard

Deep Dorset with patchwork fields, miles of hedgerows, ancient oaks. Arrive at this farmstead with its old barns and rows of vines, and breathe in the peace. Mary and Nigel are relaxed hosts; find a happy mix of antique and retro, splashes of gingham, artworks, family photos, flowers. Solar heats the water; wood fires keep it all toasty. The elegant sitting room has two tables in the window for sunny breakfasts: seasonal fruit, homemade granola and jams, local bacon, good bread. Explore bluebell woods and footpaths, walk the coastal path. Mary has created a wonderful place to stay, and you can book vineyard tours and tastings too.

Rooms	2 doubles: £90–£105. Singles £80–£95.
Meals	Pubs/restaurants 2.5 miles.
Closed	10 October – 12 February.

Minimum stay: 2 nights at weekends in high season

Mary Riddle
Wodetone Vineyard,
Spence Farm,
Wootton Fitzpaine, Bridport, DT6 6DF
Mobile +44 (0)7966 751467
Email   info@vineyardbandb.co.uk
Web   www.vineyardbandb.co.uk

Entry 105   Map 2

Dorset

Greenhill House

There's something timeless about Lyme and the views from the south-facing windows here are spectacular: rolling hills, the town and the bay lie before you. Sara and Ed live on the third floor with the rest of the house given over to guests to come and go as they please. You'll feel very well looked after, from afternoon tea served next to the open fire in the drawing room or in the garden on arrival, to gourmet breakfasts served at an antique table in the formal cream-and-blue dining room. You can wander into town in 15 minutes – explore the many art galleries, look for fossils on the beach or wander along to the historic harbour. There are superb restaurants here too; HIX Oyster & Fish House is a 20-minute walk – you can easily get a taxi back.

Rooms	3 doubles: £150–£165. Singles from £120.
Meals	Pubs/restaurants 1 mile.
Closed	Christmas.

Sara & Ed Hollway
Greenhill House,
Somers Road,
Lyme Regis, DT7 3EX
Tel   +44(0)1297 445497
Email greenhillhousebandb@gmail.com
Web   www.greenhillhousebandb.co.uk

Entry 106   Map 2

Dorset

Old Monmouth

Tudor townhouse with a colourful past – the Duke of Monmouth, Oscar Wilde, a box of love letters found after WWII American soldiers stayed… Tony and Alex have loved discovering the history and bringing this old house back to life. They're a creative, immensely likeable pair and their vintage finds from French trips abound. Bedrooms are romantic with lavender-scented drawers, tea trays, perhaps an antique gilt mirror, Liberty wallpaper or flame-pink cushion. There's a summery breakfast room, wood fires burning bright all winter and orchids in every corner. Walk along The Cobb, explore the coast path; sailing, great restaurants, famous gardens too.

Rooms	4 doubles: £95–£140. Cot available.
Meals	Pubs/restaurants 2-minute walk.
Closed	Christmas, Easter and summer holidays.

Pass to nearest car park provided.

Tony & Alex Kossykh-Bearman
Old Monmouth,
12 Church Street, Lyme Regis, DT7 3BS
Tel   +44 (0)1297 444124
Mobile   +44 (0)7919 858693
Email   oldmonmouth@gmail.com
Web   www.oldmonmouth.com

Entry 107   Map 2

Dorset

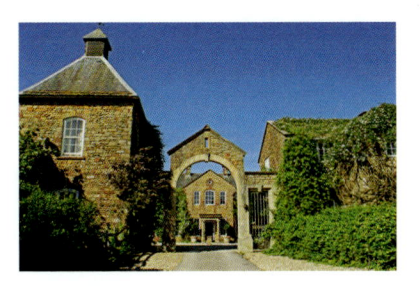

Manor Farm

Pheasants stroll along grassy lanes, kestrels fly overhead and this stunning stone manor house is a delight. Ashley is easy-going and you have your own wing as well as a private courtyard next to the orangery; take a book and sit by the koi ponds. Bedrooms come in comfy country style; the Rose suite with antique linen and pretty wallpaper is charming. The dining room gleams with antiques, silver and flowers; feast on a breakfast of home-laid eggs, homemade jams and local sausages. Climb Eggardon Hill, visit Bridport and Sherborne; Lyme Regis and the Jurassic Coast are a short drive. Friendly lurchers add to the relaxed feel.

Rooms	1 double, 1 twin both with separate bath/shower: £100–£140. 1 suite for 2: £120–£150. Singles £80–£100. Extra bed/sofabed £50 per person per night.
Meals	Pubs within 3 miles.
Closed	Rarely.

Minimum stay: 2 nights. Coarse fishing available on estate lake.

Ashley Stewart
Manor Farm,
West Compton,
Dorchester, DT2 0EY
Tel   +44 (0)1300 320400
Email   ashley@manorfarmwestcompton.com
Web   www.westcomptonmanor.co.uk

Entry 108   Map 3

Dorset

Tudor Cottage

There are gentle walks from this thatched cottage along the Frome valley, and rugged coastal paths nearby. Return to a beautiful sitting room with lots of art and a roaring fire on chilly days – architecture buffs will swoop upon the medieval overmantle and ancient stone archway. Sleep soundly in crisp white linen with thick fabrics at the windows (you are on the road but it's quiet at night); bathrooms are gleaming. Charming Louise can make anybody feel at home and cooks beautiful, multifarious breakfasts from scratch including her own bread and preserves. Fossils abound and you can track down public gardens too.

Rooms	1 double, 1 twin: £90-£105.
Meals	Dinner, 2-3 courses, £23-£28 (autumn and winter only). Pubs/restaurants 2 miles.
Closed	Rarely.

Over 16s welcome.

Louise Clarke
Tudor Cottage,
9 Dorchester Road, Frampton,
Dorchester, DT2 9NB
Tel   +44 (0)1300 320382
Mobile   +44 (0)7970 282151
Email   stay@tudorcottagedorset.co.uk
Web   www.tudorcottagedorset.co.uk

Entry 109   Map 3

Dorset

Manor Farm

You are high up on the chalk hills that fall to the Jurassic Coast. Tessa's family have lived in the flint and stone house since 1860 and it is crammed with history: solid antiques, books galore, pictures, maps and photographs. From all the windows views soar to sheep-dotted hills. Settle by the wood-burner in the dining room for your Aga-cooked breakfast or dinner; in the summer you can eat outside in the garden; cooking is one of Tessa's passions so the food is good! Bedrooms are without frills but clean and comfortable; the bathroom is large and sparkling. Outdoor heaven is yours; find a pet pig called Pork!

Rooms	1 double, 1 twin, sharing bath (let to same party only): £80-£95.
Meals	Dinner, 2-3 courses, from £15. Pub/restaurant 4 miles.
Closed	Rarely.

Tessa Russell
Manor Farm,
Compton Valence,
Dorchester, DT2 9ES
Tel   +44 (0)1308 482227
Mobile   +44 (0)7818 037184 (signal unreliable)
Email   tessa@cvfarms.co.uk
Web   www.manor-farm.uk.com

Entry 110   Map 3

Dorset

The Old Rectory

Hills and meadows surround this lovely old rectory on the river Frome. It's a friendly home, and Nessie is a foodie too – you arrive to a home-baked something with tea, and breakfast comes with homemade bread, granola and jams. Your tranquil suite on the first floor is independent from the happy hub of family life and a perfect hideaway for two. Relax in the peace of your cosy sitting room drinking in the hillside views. Wander through sweeping lawns, grand trees, crumbling walls and a productive veg garden. Bring your racquet if you fancy a spot of tennis. You can hike through water meadows or bike straight from the door into glorious countryside and it's a 20-minute stroll to a good pub (the Fox and Hounds) in Cattistock.

Rooms	1 suite for 3 with living room with sofabed for a child: £100-£120. Extra bed/sofabed £30-£40 per person per night.
Meals	Dinner, 2 courses, £25. Pubs/restaurants 1 mile.
Closed	Christmas, 1 August – 1 September.

Pets by arrangement.

	Nessie Owen The Old Rectory, Chilfrome, Dorchester, DT2 0HA
Mobile	+44 (0)7973 927208
Email	nessieowen@icloud.com

Entry 111   Map 3

Dorset

Fullers Earth

Such an English feel: the village with pub, post office and stores, the rose-filled walled garden with fruit trees beyond, the tranquil church view. This listed house – its late-Georgian frontage added in 1820 – is a treat: flowers and white linen, a lovely sitting room where you settle with tea and cake by the fire, roomy bedrooms with comfortable beds, books and views. At breakfast enjoy perfect compotes and jams from the garden, homemade muesli and local produce. Friendly Ian and Wendy will plan great walks with you in this AONB, the Jurassic coast is 20 minutes away and you can walk to the pub through the garden.

Rooms	1 double; 1 double, sharing bath/shower room with single (let to same party only): £115. Singles £75.
Meals	Pub 5-minute walk.
Closed	Christmas.

Minimum stay: 2 nights at weekends & in high season.

	Wendy Gregory Fullers Earth, Cattistock, Dorchester, DT2 0JL
Tel	+44 (0)1300 320190
Mobile	+44 (0)7792 654543
Email	stay@fullersearth.co.uk
Web	www.fullersearth.co.uk

Entry 112   Map 3

Dorset

Old Forge

Snug in a stream-tickled hamlet, deep in Hardy country, this B&B is as pretty as a painting and wonderfully peaceful. Judy is charming and friendly – this is a happy place, a real country home, a no-rules B&B. The 17th-century farmhouse opposite is where you breakfast: Judy, ex Prue Leith, serves a neighbour's eggs, a friend's sausages and good coffee in an eclectically furnished room with bucolic views to garden, meadows and hills. Walk from the door or head to the Jurassic Coast for more demanding hikes, explore Bridport's vibrant Saturday market or beautiful Sherborne Abbey, discover bronze age forts. Judy is happy to give you a lift to and from the nearby pub.

Rooms	Old Forge: 1 double: £100. Singles £60–£70. Stays of 2+nights: £80–£90.
Meals	Pub 1.5 miles.
Closed	Rarely.

Judy Thompson
Old Forge,
Lower Wraxall Farmhouse,
Lower Wraxall, Dorchester, DT2 0HL
Tel +44 (0)1935 83218
Email judyjthompson@hotmail.co.uk
Web www.lowerwraxall.co.uk

Entry 113   Map 3

Dorset

Urless Farm

In its own beautiful valley, this extended, refurbished 19th-century family house does seriously smart B&B. You'll want to linger over breakfast – local bacon, their hens' eggs, homemade jams, their own tomato sauce – in the light-filled orangery with breathtaking views across rich farmland to the distant Mendips. Luxuriate in traditional bedrooms with antiques and colourful rugs on polished floors; sensors control the lighting in peerless bathrooms with heated floors. Watch for wildlife by the ponds in the large, well-kept grounds. It's a short walk to a good pub and Dorset's delights surround you.

Rooms	2 doubles, 1 twin; 1 double with separate shower: £140. Singles £120.
Meals	Pubs/restaurants 15-minute walk.
Closed	Rarely.

Charlotte Hemsley
Urless Farm,
Corscombe,
Dorchester, DT2 0NP
Tel +44 (0)1935 891528
Email charlie.urless@gmail.com

Entry 114   Map 3

Dorset

Wooden Cabbage House

Leafy lanes and a private drive lead you to Martyn and Susie's beautifully restored hamstone house, hidden in rolling West Dorset. Savour the total peace and stunning valley views in a home full of flowers, fine antiques and paintings. Cosy bedrooms have country-house charm; the suite is dog-friendly. Delicious breakfasts are served in the garden room: homemade muesli and jams, home-grown fruit compote, local eggs, bacon, sausages, smoked trout; French windows open to a productive potager and terraced gardens. Good walks, and the Jurassic coast is 30 minutes; return to sofas by the log fire. Fabulous hosts – nothing is too much trouble.

Rooms	2 doubles, 1 twin/double: £115–£125. 1 suite for 4 (2 singles available for children when needed): £145. Singles £105.
Meals	Pubs/restaurants 3 miles.
Closed	1 November – 12 March.

Children over 6 welcome. Suite: £20 per child per night. Dogs welcome in suite: £10 per dog per night.

Martyn & Susie Lee
Wooden Cabbage House,
East Chelborough,
Dorchester, DT2 0QA
Tel   +44 (0)1935 83362
Email relax@woodencabbage.co.uk
Web   www.woodencabbage.co.uk

Entry 115   Map 3

Dorset

Caundle Barn

Take the pretty route... ramble through rich pasture, tiny hamlets and woodland to reach this attractive 17th-century stone barn. All is spotless, from the oak stairs and galleried landing to the antiques and exquisite curtains; Sarah has blended old and new beautifully. Your bedroom is sunny and sumptuous; the little shower room has scented oils and luxurious towels. Sarah cooks with the seasons and you'll enjoy homemade marmalade, fruits, local eggs, bacon and sausages. Views and walks are sublime, Sherborne is fun, there are gourmet pubs galore and Poppy the Jack Russell adds her charm to this friendly home.

Rooms	1 double: £80–£110. Singles £60.
Meals	Pubs/restaurants 4 miles.
Closed	Rarely.

Sarah Howes
Caundle Barn,
Purse Caundle,
Sherborne, DT9 5DY
Tel   +44 (0)1963 251264
Email howes20@btinternet.com

Entry 116   Map 3

Dorset

Lawn Cottage

In a quiet village in Blackmore Vale, the path to this spacious cottage is lined with tulips and vegetables. Easy-going June is a collector of pretty things; art, antiques and china blend charmingly with soft colours and zingy kilims. Bedrooms are sunny – one is downstairs (en suite) with a private entrance; there's a sweet very comfy shepherd's hut too if you fancy a night under the stars and sunset views. Breakfasts are generous; hut dwellers can come in to the dining room or have a hamper delivered. Visit Sherborne (abbey, castle, smart shops), walk from the gate to Duncliffe Wood. Return to a tiny snug sitting room. Perfect Dorset B&B!

Rooms	1 twin/double; 1 double with separate bathroom: £80-£90. 1 shepherd's hut for 2 (with bathroom in main house): £90. Singles £50. Extra bed/sofabed £20 per person per night.
Meals	Pub/restaurant 1 mile.
Closed	Rarely.

June Watkins
Lawn Cottage,
Stour Row, Shaftesbury, SP7 0QF
Tel   +44 (0)1747 838719
Mobile +44 (0)7809 696218
Email   enquiries@lawncottagedorset.co.uk
Web   www.lawncottagedorset.co.uk

Entry 117   Map 3

Dorset

Lower Fifehead Farm

A passion for cooking here! The dramatic dining room has church pews at an oak refectory table; the log fire will be lit in winter, and you can eat on the terrace in summer. Hearty breakfasts include bacon and sausages from home-reared pigs, devilled mushrooms or eggs Benedict; Jessica makes the bread and preserves, and there's always freshly squeezed orange juice. It's a gorgeous house – it's been in Jasper's family for many years and shines with pretty fabrics, antiques, hand-painted furniture, vintage pieces, rich colours, shelves of books – and seriously comfortable brass beds. Don't miss the candlelit dinners.

Rooms	2 doubles, 1 twin/double: £75-£95. Singles from £55.
Meals	Dinner, 2-3 courses, £20-£30. Pubs/restaurants 2 miles.
Closed	Christmas & New Year.

Minimum stay: 2 nights at weekends.

Jessica Miller
Lower Fifehead Farm,
Fifehead St Quinton,
Sturminster Newton, DT10 2AP
Tel   +44 (0)1258 817335
Email lowerfifeheadfm@gmail.com
Web   www.lowerfifeheadfm.co.uk

Entry 118   Map 3

Dorset

The Old Mill

Ancient willow trees cast shade over stretches of lawn as kingfishers flit from branch to branch. A secret paradise unfurls before you, as through the Mill's gardens the Stour and its tributaries flow, their banks a-shimmer with hostas, irises, day lilies, gunneras and ferns. Find privacy and independence in your own comfortably contemporary bolthole above the detached garage; a chandelier sparkles in the sun, a mini kitchen hides behind louvre doors, and relaxed Caroline brings you a fine continental breakfast. Walk across the water meadows to little Spetisbury for a pint; discover the delights of Brownsea Island and Blandford Forum.

Rooms	1 family room for 2 (self-contained with sofabed & kitchenette): £95 Singles £80, mid-week only. £15 per child per night.
Meals	Continental breakfast. Pub 10-minute walk.
Closed	Rarely.

Minimum stay: 2 nights at weekends during high season & bank holidays. Self-catering by arrangement.

Caroline Ivay
The Old Mill,
Spetisbury, Blandford Forum, DT11 9DF
Tel   +44 (0)1258 456014
Mobile +44 (0)7786 096803
Email c.ivay@btinternet.com
Web   www.theoldmillspetisbury.com

Entry 119   Map 3

Dorset

Crawford House

Below, the river Stour winds through the valley and under the medieval, nine-arched bridge. Above, an Iron Age hill fort; between is Crawford House. Elegant and Georgian, it sits in attractive walled gardens full of roses; inside is pretty too, with an easy, relaxed atmosphere. Bedrooms with period furnishings are homely and warm; one room has four-poster twin beds. The sun streams through the tall windows of the downstairs rooms, and charming oil paintings hang in the dining room. Andrea is fun, and a great host, with lots of local knowledge; there's a gate from the garden on to the North Dorset Trailway – useful for dog walking.

Rooms	1 twin/double; 1 twin with separate bath, 1 twin with separate shower: £75–£80. Singles £40.
Meals	Pub 10-minute walk.
Closed	Rarely.

One night stays available.

Andrea Lea
Crawford House,
Spetisbury,
Blandford Forum, DT11 9DP
Tel   +44 (0)1258 857338
Email andrea.lea888@gmail.com

Entry 120   Map 3

Dorset

Abbots Court House

A refreshingly unfussy place, set in five acres with roaming chickens and pigs and a large kitchen garden. Jez and Niki are the most open and engaging couple and staying here will lift your spirits. Everything about Abbots Court feels warm and soulful. Dine by roaring fires on an outstanding menu of home-grown, very local or freshly foraged ingredients; settle in the snug for romantic pre-dinner drinks; little ones are well looked after too with early suppers, high chairs and a connecting family room. Cosy nights in big beds are followed by breakfasts of homemade breads, chef's porridge and a full cooked spread. Then if you've time to explore, get your wellies on and take a long, lazy walk through stunning countryside.

Rooms	5 doubles: £90-£180.
	1 family room for 4: £90-£180.
	Extra beds available.
Meals	Dinner approx. £28.
	7-course tasting menu, £58.
	Pubs/restaurants 8 miles.
Closed	Occasionally.

Jez Barfoot
Abbots Court House,
East Street,
Winterborne Kingston, DT11 9BH
Email info@abbots-court.co.uk
Web   abbots-court.co.uk

Entry 121   Map 3

Dorset

7 Smithfield Place

Valerie is creative and her home an elegant blend of old and new: tapestries and art, large restored mirrors, antiques and modern pieces in your own sitting room. She's also unstinting with treats, from wine to shortbread, kettle chips and chocolates. And breakfast is equally lavish: fruits and yogurts, excellent coffee, pastries, kedgeree or the full works served outdoors on sunny days. Built in 1880, the house sits on a quiet cul-de-sac off the high street, two miles from Bournemouth town centre with easy public transport. The garden is lit up in spring by blooming camellias and cherry blossom, and the whole house sparkles.

Rooms	1 double: £90-£95.
	Singles £65-£70.
Meals	Packed lunch £15.
	Pub/restaurant 100 yds.
Closed	Christmas.

Valerie Johns
7 Smithfield Place,
Winton, Bournemouth, BH9 2QJ
Tel   +44 (0)1202 520722
Mobile +44 (0)7398 665195
Email   valeriejohns@btinternet.com
Web   www.smithfieldplace.co.uk

Entry 122   Map 3

Dorset

Bering House

Fabulous in every way. Renate's attention to detail reveals a love of running B&B: the fluffy dressing gowns and bathroom treats, the biscuits, fruit and sherry… she and John are welcoming and delightful. Expect pretty sofas, golden bath taps, a gleaming breakfast table, and a big sumptuous suite with views across sparkling Poole harbour to Brownsea Island and the Purbeck Hills. Breakfasts are served on blue and white Spode: exotic fruits with Parma ham; smoked salmon with poached eggs and muffins; kedgeree; smoked haddock gratin; warm figs with Greek yogurt and honey – the choice is superb. An immaculate harbourside retreat.

Rooms	1 twin/double: £80–£90.
	1 suite for 2 with kitchenette: £100–£110. Singles £80–£100.
Meals	Pub 400 yds. Restaurant 500 yds.
Closed	Rarely.

Minimum stay: 2 nights at weekends & in high season. Children over 10 welcome.

Renate & John Wadham
Bering House,
53 Branksea Avenue, Hamworthy,
Poole, BH15 4DP
Tel   +44 (0)1202 673419
Email johnandrenate1@tiscali.co.uk
Web   www.beringhouse.co.uk

Dorset

Lulworth House

Down through hills, wild heaths and pine forests to Lulworth. Carole and John's home is set back from the cove in a peaceful lane; artist and garden designer, their 1980s house is a creative treasure, inside and out. The garden has a tropical feel with banana trees, ferns, deep borders and abundant grapes over a pergola. Inside is a sparkling white canvas dotted with colour: paintings, glass vases, antique desk, old grandfather clock, cubist furniture. Garden bedrooms are delightful – one has a king-size bed and opens to its own terrace. Wake for a generous breakfast served upstairs in the open-plan living space. Walks galore from the door.

Rooms	1 double; 1 double with separate shower room: £95–£130.
Meals	Pubs/restaurants within walking distance.
Closed	Occasionally.

Minimum stay: 2 nights. Over 12s welcome.

John & Carole Bickerton
Lulworth House,
Bindon Road, West Lulworth,
Wareham, BH20 5RU
Tel   +44 (0)1929 406192
Email info@lulworthhousebandb.co.uk
Web   www.lulworthhousebandb.co.uk

Dorset

Marren

On the Dorset coastal path overlooking Weymouth Bay – a blissful spot for Jurassic Coast adventures. The owners have transformed this 1920s house, set in six acres of terraced and wooded garden, and their style reflects their penchant for natural materials and country life. Bedrooms are elegant and comfortable; one has a door onto the garden; from the other you can marvel at the sun setting over the sea. Enjoy superb spreads of farm produce and homemade bread, then head off to the secluded beach below and a turquoise sea swim. There's a sense of slow living here. Leave the low-slung Morgan at home: the track is steep!

Rooms	2 doubles: £95-£135.
Meals	Pub 1 mile.
Closed	Rarely.

Minimum stay: 2 nights at weekends. Over 12s welcome.

Peter Cartwright
Marren,
Holworth, Dorchester, DT2 8NJ
Tel +44 (0)1305 851503
Mobile +44 (0)7957 886399
Email marren@lineone.net
Web www.marren.info

Entry 125   Map 3

Dorset

Old Harbour View

Perch in the bow-fronted window and gaze down on the harbour where the fishing boats dock. What a position – in the heart of Old Weymouth. As for the house, built in 1805, it is uniquely 12 feet wide, yet all is spacious inside, and brimming with light. Imagine stained-glass windows, huge gilt mirrors, fragrant lilies, amusing etchings and posters, sumptuous sofas, and the most delightful hosts. Boat trips, seafood restaurants galore… then it's back home to ivory-white beds in soft-carpeted rooms. Wake to Anna's breads and jams, and locally-smoked haddock: outstanding breakfasts served on lovely china.

Rooms	1 double, 1 twin/double: £98. Singles £80.
Meals	Pubs/restaurants within walking distance.
Closed	Rarely.

Ask about permits for parking, on booking. Minimum stay: 2 nights.

Peter Vincent
Old Harbour View,
12 Trinity Road,
Weymouth, DT4 8TJ
Tel +44 (0)1305 774633
Email info@oldharbourview.co.uk
Web www.oldharbourviewweymouth.co.uk

Entry 126   Map 3

Durham

Burnhopeside Hall

It's peaceful, traditional, pristine, and nothing is too much trouble for Christine. Welcome to a listed Georgian house on a 475-acre estate near Durham, its elegant sitting rooms furnished with pictures and photos, log fires and big sofas, billiards and a baby grand, and great sash windows with garden and woodland views. Resident springer spaniels Max and Barney love all dogs, so bring yours; stroll the magnificent lawns, cycle alongside the river. Breakfast? Eggs from the hens, bacon from the pigs, honey and fruits from the walled garden: a perfect start to the day. Enormous beds, luxurious linen and fresh flowers await your return.

Rooms	6 doubles: £100–£120.
	1 apartment for 6: £100–£150.
	Singles £70–£85.
Meals	Pubs/restaurants 4 miles.
Closed	Rarely.

Christine Hewitt
Burnhopeside Hall,
Durham Road,
Lanchester, DH7 0TL

Tel	+44 (0)1207 520222
Email	harmerchristine@hotmail.com
Web	www.burnhopeside-hall.co.uk

Entry 127   Map 12

Essex

32 The Hythe

The Thames barge in all her glory: the Gibbs' garden runs almost into the river Blackwater where these majestic old craft are moored and the mudflats are a bird watcher's dream. Summer breakfast on the deck – local smoked kippers and free-range eggs – watching the barges sail up the river is a rare treat. Beneath wide limpid skies this sensitively extended fisherman's cottage looks out to 12th-century St Mary's at the back where Kim and Gerry ring the Sunday bells. It's immaculate and comfortable inside, an inspired mix of modern and antique lit by myriad candles, among other romantic touches.

Rooms	2 doubles: £100. Singles £80.
Meals	Pub 100 yds.
Closed	Christmas & Boxing Day.

Over 14s welcome.

Kim & Gerry Gibbs
32 The Hythe,
Maldon, CM9 5HN

Tel	+44 (0)1621 859435
Mobile	+44 (0)7753 135108
Email	gibbsie@live.co.uk
Web	www.thehythemaldon.co.uk

Entry 128   Map 10

Essex

The Old Pottery

Tubs of flowers at the door, Twiglet the dog to pat and a friendly feel throughout. Jacky moved from London to this charming village house and has restored and decorated with natural style: new oak floors, stripped beams, polished antique pieces. Bedrooms have well-dressed beds and thick curtains; the extra little room is just right for a child. Jacky is a good cook, so hop downstairs for a delicious breakfast – the best sausages and bacon or continental with home-baked ham; she's happy to do light suppers, and makes Christmas puds to sell. There are fun events at the Norman motte-and-bailey castle; thriving Long Melford and Clare are close.

Rooms	1 twin/double; 1 double with separate bathroom: £90-£95. 1 single, sharing bathroom with double (let to same party only): £60-£65.
Meals	Light supper from £20. Pubs/restaurants 2-minute walk.
Closed	Rarely.

Children over 8 welcome.

Jacky Short
The Old Pottery,
37 St James Street,
Castle Hedingham,
Halstead, CO9 3EW
Tel +44 (0)1787 582168
Email jackyshort@outlook.com
Web www.hedinghamoldpottery.com

Entry 129   Map 10

Essex

Elmdon Lee

Take the London train to Audley End (55 minutes), and this Georgian farmhouse retreat is just a five-minute drive. It's on top of a hill with farmland all around and has been in the Duke family for over 100 years. Bedrooms all have views of the pretty gardens; there are stairs down to one of the bathrooms. Wake to birdsong and hop down for breakfast next to the Aga in the family kitchen; Kate gives you a full English with local produce (veggie options too). In the evenings, pick up a book and settle by the fire in the guest drawing room. Heaps of history and culture to dip into nearby and walkers can join the Icknield Way, which passes near the house. Back here, book one of Kate's well-being sessions or bushcraft events for children, explore the garden, meadow and bluebell woods.

Rooms	1 double; 1 double with separate bathroom: £80-£105. 1 family room for 4 with separate bathroom: £105-£165. Singles £80-£90.
Meals	Pubs/restaurants 4 miles.
Closed	Rarely.

Minimum stay: 2 nights.

Kate Duke
Elmdon Lee,
Littlebury Green,
Saffron Walden, CB11 4XB
Tel +44 (0)1763 838237
Mobile +44 (0)7813 709593
Email kate.duke@btopenworld.com
Web www.elmdonlee.co.uk

Entry 130   Map 9

Gloucestershire

The Moda House

A fine house and a big B&B, but one that retains a deeply homely feel; Duncan and Jo are hugely well-travelled and have filled it with pictures and artefacts from all over the world. Bedrooms differ (three are in a neat annexe) but all are cosy and well decorated with lovely colours, good fabrics, pocket sprung mattresses and bright bathrooms with thick towels. Breakfast – locally sourced, cooked on the Aga and brought to round tables – sets you up for fabulous walks: you are a mile from the Cotswold Way. Return to a basement sitting room with comfy armchairs and lots of books, and a bustling town full of restaurants and shops.

Rooms	8 doubles: £87–£105. 3 singles: £67–£75.
Meals	Pubs/restaurants within 100 metres.
Closed	Rarely.

Minimum stay: 2 nights over busy weekends; 3 nights during Badminton.

Duncan & Jo MacArthur
The Moda House,
1 High Street,
Chipping Sodbury, BS37 6BA
Tel +44 (0)1454 312135
Email enquiries@modahouse.co.uk
Web www.modahouse.co.uk

Entry 131   Map 3

Gloucestershire

Legg Barn

Ted and Paddy's barn is a surprise. Tucked off the High Street, it has four acres of garden with space for pigs, chickens, veg, sunny seats, trees – and for collie Bill to chase squirrels. The long hall has a quirky line of antique high chairs, and there's a soaring living space beyond with a big wood-burner and comfy sofas; the white theme throughout contrasts with honey-coloured wood and odd splashes of colour. Bedrooms – one up spiral stairs on the sitting room mezzanine – have lovely linen and piles of pillows. Paddy is a good cook – her generous breakfasts often include their own sausages. Walk from the door into the Forest of Dean.

Rooms	1 double; 2 doubles sharing bathroom: £80–£90.
Meals	Restaurant 2-minute walk; pub 10-minute walk.
Closed	Christmas & occasionally.

Paddy Curtis
Legg Barn,
Church Square,
Blakeney, GL15 4DP
Tel +44 (0)1594 510408
Email paddy@leggbarn.co.uk
Web www.leggbarn.co.uk

Entry 132   Map 8

Gloucestershire

Frampton Court

Deep authenticity in this magnificent Grade I-listed house. The manor of Frampton on Severn has been in the Clifford family since the 11th century and although Rollo and Janie look after the estate, it is cooking enthusiast Kim who greets you on their behalf and looks after you. There are exquisite examples of decorative woodwork and, in the hall, a cheerful log fire; perch on the Mouseman fire seat. Bedrooms are traditional with antiques, panelling and long views. Beds have fine linen, one with embroidered Stuart hangings. Stroll around the ornamental canal, soak up the old-master views. An architectural masterpiece.

Rooms	1 double, 1 twin/double, 1 four-poster: £150-£250.
Meals	Dinner from £45. Pub across the green. Restaurant 3 miles.
Closed	Christmas.

Children over 10 welcome.

Kim Hawkins
Frampton Court,
The Green, Frampton on Severn,
Gloucester, GL2 7EX

Tel	+44 (0)1452 740267
Email	framptoncourt@framptoncourtestate.co.uk
Web	www.framptoncourtestate.co.uk/framptoncourthomepage.htm

Entry 133   Map 8

Gloucestershire

The Grange

The largest green in England and this house is at a leafy corner. Rosanne has that happy knack of making you feel at home. Gibraltarian and keen cook too, her breakfasts come with a continental edge — eggs with chorizo, homemade baked beans; her Spanish soup suppers are hearty. The house has stories — ask about Miss Kickler... Family photos, art, quirky monkeys add warmth, the guest sitting room has original wood panelling with the Clifford Crest, inviting bedrooms are all different; there's an indoor pool, gym, playroom, places to read — dogs Spud and Otto keep you company. Walk to Slimbridge, have fun at Frampton's festivals.

Rooms	1 twin/double; 2 doubles both with separate bathroom: £95-£125. 1 single child's room sharing bath with nearby double: £50.
Meals	Soup with bread, £10. Restaurant and 2 pubs 3 miles.
Closed	Rarely.

Rosanne Gaggero-Brodermann
The Grange,
The Green, Frampton on Severn,
Gloucester, GL2 7DX

Tel	+44 (0)1452 740654
Email	rockape@mac.com
Web	www.atthegrange.com

Entry 134   Map 8

Gloucestershire

Hammonds Farm

This old farmhouse snoozes in its own valley a mile out of Stroud. It's been restored from top to toe with lots of original features. The surrounding 100 acres are home to 100 alpacas and a small flock of black sheep. There's a big wood-burner in the guest sitting room, homemade biscuits and little fridges in smart bedrooms, and flowers in every room. Bea serves breakfast in the sunny dining room at separate tables: avocado on sourdough toast, American pancakes, homemade jams, croissants or a full English. After a wander round to see the animals, head out on one of Bea's recommended walks, visit the humming farmers' market in Stroud or Painswicks Rococo Garden (swathes of snowdrops in spring), then have dinner out at one of Nailsworth's starred restaurants.

Rooms	3 doubles, 2 twins: £100. Extra room available, sofabed available.
Meals	Pubs/restaurants 1 mile.
Closed	Rarely.

Over 12s welcome.

Bea Hyde
Hammonds Farm,
Wick Street,
Stroud, GL6 7QN
Mobile +44 (0)7733 101137
Email   hello@hammonds-farm.co.uk
Web   www.hammonds-farm.co.uk

Entry 135   Map 8

Gloucestershire

Woodchester Valley Vineyard Barns

Head up the hill to the vineyard and the Stroud valleys spread out below you. It's an area full of wooded hills, pretty villages, arty events – and inspiring artisans like the Woodchester team. The suites are in a restored barn next to the fields of vines. Each has its own big living room downstairs – watch TV, warm your feet on the underfloor heating or by the gas log-burner. Order a continental basket with crumpets, croissants and granola, and rustle up your breakfast when you want. Admire fabulous views from floor to ceiling windows; sip a Bacchus white or Pinot Rosé on your terrace or balcony after a day's exploring. Taster evenings are on offer and you can book one of their tours, which includes a visit to the winery, learning about the grapes and process and a tasting session. There's a Cellar Door shop too.

Rooms	3 doubles: £120–£165.
Meals	Pubs/restaurants 1.5 miles.
Closed	Never.

Minimum stay: 2 nights at weekends.

Gail Shiner
Woodchester Valley Vineyard Barns,
Upper Atcombe Farm,
Convent Lane, Woodchester,
Stroud, GL5 5HR
Mobile +44 (0)7808 650883
Email   gail@woodchestervalleyvineyard.co.uk
Web   www.woodchestervalleyvineyard.co.uk

Entry 136   Map

Gloucestershire

The Close

Up a hill of pretty Cotswold-stone houses, this large Queen Anne house with handsome sash windows delivers what it promises. Step into a stone-flagged hall with grandfather clock and Georgian oak staircase; take welcoming tea with Karen in the elegant drawing room; then upstairs to three light and airy bedrooms furnished with antiques. Cushioned window seats, generous curtains and views over garden or pretty street add to the restful atmosphere. Karen, is as gracious and relaxed as her house, and serves excellent breakfasts in the polished dining room. An elegantly hospitable base for exploring the Cotswolds.

Rooms	2 doubles, 1 twin: £88-£99. Singles £68-£79.
Meals	Pubs/restaurants 1-minute walk.
Closed	1 January – 28 February.

Minimum stay: 2 nights at weekends.

Karen Champney
The Close,
Well Hill, Minchinhampton,
Stroud, GL6 9JE
Tel   +44 (0)1453 883338
Email theclosebnb@gmail.com
Web   www.theclosebnb.co.uk

Entry 137   Map 8

Gloucestershire

Well Farm

Perhaps it's the gentle, unstuffy attitude of Kate and Edward. Or the great position of the house with its glorious views across the Slad valley. Whichever, you'll feel comforted and invigorated by your stay. It's a real family home and you get both a fresh, pretty bedroom that feels very private and the use of a comfy, book-filled sitting room opening to a flowery courtyard; Kate is an inspired garden designer. Sleep soundly on the softest of pillows, wake to deep countryside peace and the delicious prospect of eggs from their own hens and good bacon. Friendly dogs Jaffa and Dot add to the charm, the area teems with great walks – lovely pubs too.

Rooms	1 twin/double, with sitting room: £95.
Meals	Dinner from £25. Pubs nearby.
Closed	Rarely.

Kate & Edward Gordon Lennox
Well Farm,
Frampton Mansell,
Stroud, GL6 8JB
Tel   +44 (0)1285 760651
Email kategl@btinternet.com
Web   www.well-farm.co.uk

Entry 138   Map 8

Gloucestershire

Lowfield Farm

Another classic old Cotswold house set in pretty countryside, but with unique character thanks to Giles and Amanda who spent many years in California and have now returned to the family home. Your rooms are on the top floor – both newly done up and neat as a pin with thick cream carpets, heavy floral fabrics, windows with views and comfortable chairs (no guest sitting room). Breakfast, a flexible affair, includes full English with eggs from their own hens and is taken at one long mahogany table. Wander a small wood with mown paths, head off for antiques in Tetbury, gardens at Highgrove, polo at Cirencester.

Rooms	1 double, 1 twin/double (let to same party only): £95-£125.
Meals	Pubs/restaurants 2 miles.
Closed	Rarely.

Minimum stay: 2 nights in high season.

Amanda & Giles Preston
Lowfield Farm,
Tetbury, GL8 8AE
Tel   +44 (0)1666 503086
Mobile   +44 (0)7876 385441
Email   amanda.lowfield@gmail.com

Entry 139   Map 3

Gloucestershire

Ashley Barn

On the edge of a hamlet... a beautifully restored, traditional converted barn. Huge doorways and floor to ceiling timber-framed windows let the light flood in. You have your own entrance and can come and go as you please. Your suite has good linen, plump pillows, flowers and views onto the garden; the roomy bathroom is gleaming. Walk through for breakfast by a log fire in the huge dining hall in the main barn: local sausages and bacon, eggs from the hens on pretty Poole pottery; Amanda is happy to cook dinner too. Badminton Horse Trials are a hop, Cirencester too; return for a wander round the rose garden, and a snooze by the fire.

Rooms	1 suite for 2: £100-£120. Singles £85.
Meals	Dinner, 3 courses, £25. Pub/restaurant 5-minute drive.
Closed	Rarely.

Amanda Montgomerie
Ashley Barn,
Ashley, Tetbury, GL8 8SU
Tel   +44 (0)1666 575156
Mobile   +44 (0)7785 505548
Email   amanda@montgomerie.org
Web   www.ashleybarn.co.uk

Entry 140   Map 3

Gloucestershire

Poole Keynes House

This old rectory is a lovely informal place to stay for a group of friends or family. There's an elegant drawing room for tea or drinks, a snug with books and TV and a big garden to wander. Bedrooms have good linen and natural colours; hop up more stairs to the two in the attic; you share a bathroom, and sometimes there's an extra one you can use. Charlie serves Aga-cooked breakfasts in the friendly family kitchen – a large, airy room with garden views and sofas round a wood-burner; she's happy to do suppers and children's teas too. You can join the Thames Path from the village; Westonbirt, Gatcombe, Cheltenham are all nearby.

Rooms	2 doubles, 1 twin/double, sharing bathroom (let to same party only): £90–£110. Children's bunk room for 2: £45. Extra rooms & second bathroom available.
Meals	Dinner, 2 courses, £20. Tea for children available. Pub 2 miles.
Closed	Christmas, New Year & occasionally.

Charlotte & Edwin Case
Poole Keynes House,
Poole Keynes,
Cirencester, GL7 6EG

Tel	+44 (0)1285 771285
Mobile	+44 (0)7767 318782
Email	c_case@hotmail.co.uk

Entry 141   Map 3

Gloucestershire

The Guest House

Your own timber-framed house with masses of light and space, a sunny terrace, and spectacular valley and woodland views... A peaceful secluded place, it's full of books and mementoes of Sue's treks across the world; the large living room has wooden floors, lovely old oak furniture and French windows onto the rose-filled garden. Sue brims with enthusiasm and is a flexible host: breakfast can be over in her kitchen with delicious farm shop sausages and bacon, or continental in yours at a time to suit you. There's a wet room downstairs, and you hop up the stairs to your charming up-in-the-eaves bedroom with oriental rugs and a big comfy bed. Wonderful!

Rooms	1 double, with sitting room & kitchenette: £140–£160.
Meals	Dinner, 2 courses, from £17.50; 3 courses, from £22.50; 4 courses, from £28. Pub 1 mile.
Closed	Christmas.

Minimum stay: 2 nights at weekends Easter – October.

Sue Bathurst
The Guest House,
Manor Cottage, Bagendon,
Cirencester, GL7 7DU

Tel	+44 (0)1285 831417
Email	sue.bathurst@icloud.com
Web	www.cotswoldguesthouse.co.uk

Entry 142   Map 8

Gloucestershire

Calcot Peak House

A treat to stay in such a handsome old house with such relaxed owners – lovely Alex is full of enthusiasm for her B&B enterprise. There's an excellent butcher in Northleach so breakfasts are tip-top, and the bedrooms are a sophisticated mix of traditional and contemporary: Farrow & Ball colours, rich florals, fresh flowers, and fluffy white robes for trots to the bathroom. You also have your own charming drawing room: tartan carpet, pink sofas, family oils. Outside: 19 acres for Dexie the dog and a bench on the hill for the view. Tramp the Salt Way, dine in Cirencester, let the owls hoot you to sleep.

Rooms	1 double, 1 twin, sharing bathroom & drawing room (let to same party only): £95–£110. Children's room available. Singles £75. One-night stay at weekends, £110.
Meals	Pub 2 miles.
Closed	Rarely.

Dogs very welcome to sleep in utility room (comfortable and warm!) but not in bedrooms.

	Tom & Alexandra Pearson Calcot Peak House, Northleach, Cheltenham, GL54 3QB
Tel	+44 (0)1285 721047
Mobile	+44 (0)7738 468798
Email	pearsonalex5@gmail.com

Entry 143 Map 8

Gloucestershire

Clapton Manor

This 16th-century house is as all homes should be: loved and lived-in. And, with three-foot-thick walls, Persian rugs on flagstoned floors, sit-in fireplaces and stone-mullioned windows, it's gorgeous. The garden, enclosed by old stone walls, is full of birdsong and roses. One bedroom has a secret door leading to a duck-egg blue bathroom; the other room, smaller, has a Tudor stone fireplace and wonderful garden views. Unbend in the book-filled sitting room, breakfast by a vast fireplace: homemade bread, award-winning marmalade and eggs from the hens. Karin is vivacious and looks after you beautifully. A charming, down-to-earth place.

Rooms	1 double, 1 twin/double: £125–£130. Singles £110. Extra bed/sofabed £15 per person per night.
Meals	Pub/restaurants within 15-minute drive.
Closed	Rarely.

	Karin & James Bolton Clapton Manor, Clapton-on-the-Hill, GL54 2LG
Tel	+44 (0)1451 810202
Mobile	+44 (0)7967 144416
Email	bandb@claptonmanor.co.uk
Web	www.claptonmanor.co.uk

Entry 144 Map 8

Gloucestershire

Aylworth Manor

Set in a peaceful Cotswolds valley and surrounded by attractive gardens, John and Joanna's gorgeous manor is immaculate. Your hosts have that happy knack of making you feel instantly at home. Find art and family photos, a wood-burner lit on cold nights in a comfy snug and a range of beauty treatments that you can book. Large sunny bedrooms come with garden and valley views, perfect linen on seriously cushy beds, antiques and lavish bathrooms. Wake refreshed for breakfast in the dining room: homemade bread, eggs from the ducks and hens, coffee in a silver pot. The Windrush Way passes the gate at the end of the drive. What a treat!

Rooms	1 double; 1 double, 1 twin/double both with separate bath: £110–£130. Singles £60.
Meals	Pub 1 mile.
Closed	Rarely.

Over 12s welcome.

John & Joanna Ireland
Aylworth Manor,
Naunton, Cheltenham, GL54 3AH

Tel	+44 (0)1451 850850
Mobile	+44 (0)7768 810357
Email	enquiries@aylworthmanor.co.uk
Web	www.aylworthmanor.co.uk

Entry 145   Map 8

Gloucestershire

The Courtyard Studio

This smart first-floor studio, attractive in reclaimed red brick, is reached via its own wrought-iron staircase; you are beautifully private. Find a clever, compact, contemporary space with a light and uncluttered living area, a mini window seat opposite two very comfortable boutiquey beds, fine linen, wicker armchair, and a patio area for balmy days. John and Annette live next door, and you stroll over to their friendly home for a tasty, locally sourced breakfast: artisan bread, homemade jams, marmalade and muesli, a traditional full English. It's a 20-minute easy walk to the centre of Cheltenham and you're a quick canter from the races.

Rooms	Studio: 1 twin: £90.
Meals	Restaurants/pubs within 1 mile.
Closed	Christmas, New Year & 1 January – 27 February.

John & Annette Gill
The Courtyard Studio,
1 The Cleevelands Courtyard,
Cleevelands Drive,
Cheltenham, GL50 4QF

Tel	+44 (0)1242 573125
Mobile	+44 (0)7901 978917
Email	courtyardstudio@aol.com

Entry 146   Map 8

Gloucestershire

Pepper Cottage

Well-travelled Toushy looks after you with warmth – homemade brownies and tea, an elegant drawing room, inviting bedrooms with perfect white linen, and a quiet garden with pretty places to sit in the sun. Her cottage is full of beautiful things: polished antiques, portraits, flowers, lovely old beams. Breakfast is usually in the family room, with doors onto the terrace: eggs and marmalade from friends, fruits, award-winning sausages, continental choices... You're on the edge of the Cotswolds: head out for Bredon Hill walks, Cheltenham's festivals, shops and races, Stow's popular Gypsy Horse Fair. Amiable Raffles the terrier is a treat too.

Rooms	1 double; 1 twin with separate bathroom: £60–£100. Singles £60–£70.
Meals	Pubs/restaurants 10-minute walk.
Closed	Occasionally.

Minimum stay: 2 nights.

Toushy Squires
Pepper Cottage,
Peppercorn Lane, Kemerton,
Tewkesbury, GL20 7JL
Tel   +44 (0)1386 725644
Email   peppercottage1@gmail.com
Web   www.peppercottage.org

Entry 147   Map 8

Gloucestershire

North Farmcote

Step back 50 years, to a solid 19th-century farmhouse high on the escarpment, and views falling away to the west; on a clear day you can see Hay Bluff. A brilliant spot for North Cotswolds' exploration, it is run by charming and gently self-deprecating David – farmer of cereals and sheep, keen walker, good shot. The exploits of his family decorate the walls (racing at Brooklands, hunting in Africa), there's a floral three-piece to sink into, a terrace with outstanding views, and a great pub you can stride to across fields. Bedrooms and bathrooms are old-fashioned, spacious, comfortable and spotless.

Rooms	1 double, 1 twin; 1 twin with separate bath: £100–£110. Singles from £70.
Meals	Pub 2 miles.
Closed	January/February.

David Eayrs
North Farmcote,
Winchcombe,
Cheltenham, GL54 5AU
Tel   +44 (0)1242 602304
Email   davideayrs@yahoo.co.uk
Web   www.northfarmcote.co.uk

Entry 148   Map 8

Gloucestershire

Wren House
Barely two miles from Stow-on-the-Wold, this peaceful house sits charmingly on the edge of a tiny hamlet. It was built before the English Civil War and Kiloran spent two years stylishly renovating it; the results are a joy. Downstairs, light-filled, elegant rooms with glowing rugs on pale Cotswold stone; upstairs, delicious bedrooms, spotless bathrooms and a doorway to duck. Breakfast in the vaulted kitchen is locally sourced and organic, where possible, and the well-planted garden, in which you are encouraged to sit, has far-reaching views. Explore rolling valleys and glorious gardens; Kiloran can advise.

The Old School
So comfortable and filled with understated style is this 1854 Cotswold stone house. Wendy and John are generous, beds are huge, linen is laundered, towels and robes are fluffy. Your own mini fridge is carefully hidden and pretty lamps cast a warm glow. Best of all is the upstairs sitting room: a chic, open-plan space with church style windows letting light flood in and super sofas, good art, lovely fabrics. A wood-burner keeps you toasty, Wendy is a grand cook and all is flexible. A gorgeous, relaxing place to stay – on the A44 but peaceful at night – that positively hums with hospitality. Guests say "even better than home!"

Rooms	1 twin/double; 1 twin/double with separate bath, 1 twin/double with separate bath/shower: £120-£135. Singles £110-£135.	Rooms	3 doubles, 1 twin/double: £130-£160. Singles £120-£135. Extra bed/sofabed £30 per person per night.
Meals	Pubs/restaurants 1 mile.	Meals	Dinner, 3 courses, £32; minimum 4 guests.
Closed	Rarely.	Closed	Rarely.

Minimum stay: 2 nights at weekends & in high season. Over 12s welcome.

	Mrs Kiloran McGrigor Wren House, Donnington, Stow-on-the-Wold, GL56 0XZ		Wendy Veale & John Scott-Lee The Old School, Little Compton, Moreton-in-Marsh, GL56 0SL
Tel	+44 (0)1451 831787	Tel	+44 (0)1608 674588
Mobile	+44 (0)7802 676673	Mobile	+44 (0)7831 098271
Email	enquiries@wrenhouse.net	Email	wendy@theoldschoolbedandbreakfast.com
Web	www.wrenhouse.net	Web	www.theoldschoolbedandbreakfast.com

Entry 149   Map 8

Entry 150   Map 8

Gloucestershire

Trinity House

Meet Zelie: generous, charming, and passionate about the Cotswolds. Off a lane in dreamy Upper Oddington is a smart modern house with a crisp gravel drive and newly planted borders. Inside, a country elegance prevails. Antique furniture shines with care and polish, walls are covered with 20th-century art and splendid sofas front the fire. Bedrooms and bathrooms ooze comfort and joy: one with a private balcony, another with its own terrace, all with village views. But don't snuggle under the goose down for too long: breakfast verges on the sinful and is locally sourced and delicious. Prepare to be thoroughly spoiled!

Rooms	1 double, 2 twin/doubles: £110-£120. Singles £70-£85.
Meals	Pubs within walking distance.
Closed	Rarely.

Zelie Mason
Trinity House,
Upper Oddington,
Moreton-in-Marsh, GL56 0XH
Tel   +44 (0)1451 831284
Mobile +44 (0)7809 429365
Email info@trinityhousebandb.co.uk
Web   www.trinityhousebandb.co.uk

Entry 151   Map 8

Hampshire

Bay Trees

The Isle of Wight and the Needles loom large as you approach Milford on Sea: the beach is shingle, the views are amazing. Mark and Sarah have become dab hands at B&B and welcome you with tea and cake in the conservatory; their award-winning breakfasts with home-laid eggs are delicious too. Warm bedrooms have deeply comfortable beds topped with excellent linen, designer wallpapers, decanters of sherry and gleaming bathrooms with fluffy towels. One room opens to the lush garden: magnolias, weeping willow and pond. With Mark's background in hospitality and Sarah's passion for cooking the service here is second to none.

Rooms	1 double, 1 four-poster: £110-£130. 1 family room for 3: £120-£140. Singles £100.
Meals	Restaurants 100 yds.
Closed	Rarely.

Minimum stay usually: 2 nights at weekends.

Mark & Sarah Clayson
Bay Trees,
8 High Street,
Milford on Sea,
Lymington, SO41 0QD
Tel   +44 (0)1590 642186
Email mark.clayson@btinternet.com
Web   www.baytreebedandbreakfast.co.uk

Entry 152   Map 3

Hampshire

Vinegar Hill Pottery

A sylvan setting, stylish pottery, talented hosts and lively young family. The cobalt blues and rich browns of David's ceramics fill the old stables of a Victorian manor house. Take pottery courses (one day to a long weekend) and be inspired by the warm décor. A narrow staircase spirals up to a modern loft: crisp whites, cathedral ceiling with sunny windows, brilliant shower. The ground-floor garden suite has a patio (with a gorgeous Showman's wagon!), sitting room, painted bed and optional children's beds. Lucy brings a continental breakfast hamper to your room. Stroll to the beach: you can almost touch the Isle of Wight.

Rooms	1 double: £95. 1 suite for 2-4: £100. 1 wagon for 2 available in summer with separate wet room: £85. Singles from £60.
Meals	Continental breakfast. Pub/restaurant 0.25 miles.
Closed	Rarely.

Minimum stay: 2 nights at weekends (April-October); 3 on bank holidays weekends.

Lucy Rogers
Vinegar Hill Pottery,
Vinegar Hill,
Milford on Sea, SO41 0RZ
Tel   +44 (0)1590 642979
Email   info@vinegarhillpottery.co.uk
Web   www.vinegarhillpottery.co.uk

Entry 153   Map 3

Hampshire

Yew Tree House

Philip and Janet's house is artistic and tranquil. The views, the house and the villagers are said to have inspired Dickens, who escaped London for the peace of the valley. The exquisite red brick house was there 200 years before him; the rare dovecote in the next door churchyard, to which you may have the key, 300 years before that. Thoughtful hosts, interesting to talk to, have created a home of understated elegance: a yellow-ochre bedroom with top quality bed linen, cashmere/silk curtains designed by their son, enchanting garden views, flowers in every room, a welcoming log fire. Breakfast with good coffee is delicious too.

Rooms	1 twin/double: £90. Twin by arrangement.
Meals	Pub within 50 yds.
Closed	Rarely.

Philip & Janet Mutton
Yew Tree House,
Broughton, SO20 8AA
Tel   +44 (0)1794 301227
Email   mutton@mypostoffice.co.uk

Entry 154   Map 3

Hampshire

Brymer House

Complete privacy in a B&B is rare. Here you have it, just a 12-minute walk from town, cathedral and water meadows. Relax in your own half of a Victorian townhouse immaculately furnished and decorated, and with a garden to match – all roses and lilac in the spring. Breakfasts are sumptuous, there's a log fire in the guests' sitting room and fresh flowers abound. An 'honesty box' means you may help yourselves to drinks. Bedrooms are small and elegant, with antique mirrors, furniture and bedspreads; bathrooms are warm and spotless. Guy and Fizzy have charmed Special Places guests for many years.

Rooms	1 double, 1 twin: £90–£95. Singles £70–£75. Extra bed/sofabed £25 per person per night.
Meals	Pubs/restaurants nearby.
Closed	Rarely.

Children over 7 welcome.

Guy & Fizzy Warren
Brymer House,
29-30 St Faith's Road, St Cross,
Winchester, SO23 9QD
Tel   +44 (0)1962 867428
Email brymerhouse@aol.com
Web   www.brymerhouse.co.uk

Entry 155   Map 4

Hampshire

Bridge House

A beautifully tended garden, with a paved breakfast area, surrounds this 1920s family home and the Grettons couldn't be more hospitable: tea, cake and good talk on arrival; stacks of local knowledge. Family photos and evidence of Michael's naval career personalise the elegant sitting room, with its open fire and doors onto the garden. Bedrooms – Yellow and Blue – are comfortable, pretty, immaculate, and the double overlooks the garden. Steph's breakfasts are a happy mix of good things homemade and local. The old Watercress Line is nearby, Winchester is a draw and have you been to Jane Austen's Chawton?

Rooms	1 double; 1 twin with separate bath: £100–£115.
Meals	Pubs/restaurants 5-minute drive.
Closed	Rarely.

Stephanie & Michael Gretton
Bridge House,
Chillandham Lane, Martyr Worthy,
Winchester, SO21 1AS
Tel   +44 (0)1962 779379
Email bh@itchenvalleybandb.com
Web   www.itchenvalleybandb.com

Entry 156   Map 4

Hampshire

Tudor House B&B

Julia couldn't be friendlier and you'll feel at home in her Tudor style house in the heart of the village. Inside all is beautifully decorated. The drawing room has comfy sofas and chairs and you can settle by the fire with one of the many books. Julia's design flair works its magic upstairs too. Bedrooms have fine linen, an eclectic collection of art, wide South Down country views and swish bathrooms. Wake to a locally sourced full English breakfast, lighter continental choices or 'Mrs Morgan's Omelettata' — served in the pretty garden on sunny days. Explore Winchester with its cathedral, theatre and festivals.

Rooms	2 doubles sharing bathroom with single: £110.
	1 single sharing bathroom with doubles: £65. Single & double for 2-3 guests, £140-£160. Single & 2 doubles for 3-5 guests, £200-£260.
Meals	Restaurants 4-minute drive.
Closed	Rarely.

Tea and cake is served till 5.30pm.

Julia Morgan
Tudor House B&B,
Ropley,
Alresford, SO24 0DS
Tel   +44 (0)1962 773749
Email info@tudorhouseandb.com
Web   www.tudorhousebandb.com

Entry 157   Map 4

Hampshire

Shafts Farm

The 1960s farmhouse has many weapons in its armoury: a tremendous South Downs thatched-village setting, owners who know every path and trail, comfortable generous bedrooms and a stunning rose garden designed by David Austin Roses (parterres, obelisks, meandering paths). The two bedrooms are fresh in cream, florals and plaids, each with a shower room with heated floors to keep toes toasty. Homemade granola, garden fruit and the full English make a fine start to the day; the airy, cane-furnished conservatory is the place for afternoon tea and a read. Your hosts are both geographers and have created an intriguing display of maps.

Rooms	2 twins: £95. Singles £60.
Meals	Pubs/restaurants 500 yds.
Closed	Rarely.

Quiet village — motorbikes not encouraged!

Rosemary Morrish
Shafts Farm,
West Meon,
Petersfield, GU32 1LU
Tel   +44 (0)1730 829266
Email info@shaftsfarm.co.uk
Web   www.shaftsfarm.co.uk

Entry 158   Map 4

Hampshire

Dunhill Barn

Arrive for Jan's homemade cake and feel quite at home. Her relaxed, rustic house is full of natural tones, quirky pieces, candles and twinkling wood fires. Bedrooms brim with beamy character; there are four in the main barn, which has the odd steep stair and low bit. Breakfast is in the stunning living area – light streams in through big windows while you tuck into home-baked banana muffins, granola, berries, a full cooked spread. If you fancy independence, Cartshed is self-catering with doors opening onto a garden area with BBQ firepit. You're in the heart of South Downs National Park; thriving Petersfield and heaps of good pubs are nearby.

Rooms	Barn: 3 doubles: £100-£120. 1 single: £80. Cartshed – self-catering barn: £150. Parties 2+: additional £20 per person.
Meals	Pubs/restaurants 2-minute walk.
Closed	Christmas & New Year. Self-catering Cartshed November to end March.

Minimum stay: 2 nights at weekends.

Jan Martin
Dunhill Barn,
Steep, Petersfield, GU32 2DP
Tel +44 (0)1730 268179
Mobile +44 (0)7789 002342
Email dunhillbarn@gmail.com
Web www.dunhillbarn.co.uk

Entry 159   Map 4

Herefordshire

The Bridge Inn

Getting here is huge fun. The 16th-century inn (with a pretty garden) and farmhouse sit by the river beneath the Black Hill of Bruce Chatwin fame and willows line the footbridge. Walkers descend, as do local farmers and shooting parties, and Glyn is a great host. Comfy country bedrooms lie in the farmhouse; find antiques, flagstone floors and a dark panelled sitting room below. Breakfast on the best bacon and local eggs in the huge farmhouse kitchen, visit Hay for bookshops, yomp in the Beacons. Return to a piping hot bath then wander down to the pub for a tasty supper and a pint of Butty Bach (small friend) by the wood-burner.

Rooms	1 double, 2 twin/doubles: £95-£110. Hay Festival £165 for 2 per night.
Meals	Lunch £8-£22. Dinner £12-£22.
Closed	Rarely.

Glyn Bufton & Gisela Vargas
The Bridge Inn,
Michaelchurch Escley,
Hereford, HR2 0JW
Tel +44 (0)1981 510646
Email thebridgeinn@hotmail.com
Web www.thebridgeinnmichaelchurch.co.uk

Entry 160   Map 7

Herefordshire

Rock Cottage

Birds, books and beautiful Black Mountain views highlighted by morning sun, turning to an inky black line at dusk; the cottage glows. There's an instant feeling of warmth and friendliness as you step into the snug hall; find rich autumnal colours, old rugs, a big wood-burner and comfy sitting rooms. Local art and photos line the walls, bedrooms have sumptuous beds, perfect linen and garden posies. You eat (very well) en famille at the communal oak table, or out on the pretty terrace. Thoughtful Chris and Sue will take you to hear the dawn chorus and there are food and literary festivals, bookshops and walks galore.

Rooms	2 doubles: £80-£100. Singles £70. Extra bed/sofabed £10 per person per night.
Meals	Packed lunch £6. Dinner, 2-3 courses, £20. Pub/restaurant 4 miles.
Closed	Christmas & New Year.

	Chris & Sue Robinson Rock Cottage, Newton St Margarets, Hereford, HR2 0QW
Tel	+44 (0)1981 510360
Email	robinsrockcottage@googlemail.com
Web	www.rockcottagebandb.co.uk

Entry 161   Map 7

Herefordshire

St Martin's B&B

Rick and Andrea have filled their Georgian townhouse with colour and music. Find maps, etchings, books, flowers and teapots on mantelpieces; Rick's chic-upcycling includes a headboard from old doors. Your cosy bedroom at the top has its own sitting room next door; your friendly Dutch hosts leave you a carafe of port and brimming trolley of nice things; Japanese-style foldaway beds can be set up for a child or extra guests. Breakfast on delicious choices: organic bacon and sausages, veggie and vegan options; Andrea can do high tea of savoury and sweet treats, and dinner too. Hereford Cathedral, swimming pool, park, shops: all a stroll away.

Rooms	1 twin/double with separate shower room: £95.
Meals	Dinner, 3 courses, £20. High tea £20, served in the guests' sitting room. Pubs/restaurants 2-minute walk.
Closed	Rarely.

Minimum stay: 2 nights at weekends. 2 parking spaces available (1 on-street space with a visitors' permit & 1 in private car park across the road).

	Rick & Andrea Noordegraaf-Teeuw St Martin's B&B, 49 St Martin's Street, Hereford, HR2 7RD
Tel	+44 (0)1432 340183
Email	andrea@teacosy.nl

Entry 162   Map 7

Herefordshire

Hall's Mill House

Quiet lanes bring you to this peaceful spot, a stone cottage in a light and open valley. Easy-going Grace welcomes you with a cuppa and scones – by the wood-burner in the snug sitting room or on the garden terrace if the sun's out. Your cosy bedroom has exposed beams and far-reaching all-green views. Drift off to sleep to the sound of the river Arrow bubbling by and wake to birdsong and a big cooked breakfast, with homemade marmalade and honey from nearby hives. Head off for a long walk at Offa's Dyke (just over a mile away), a trip through picturesque Hereford on the Black and White Village Trail or, further afield, a bike ride in the Beacons. The kitchen is the real hub of this house and you can return to a hearty Aga-cooked dinner at a big table with garden views.

Rooms	1 double; 1 double, 1 twin sharing bathroom: £60–£75. Singles £40.
Meals	Dinner from £15. Pub/restaurant 3 miles.
Closed	Christmas.

	Grace Watson Hall's Mill House, Huntington, Kington, HR5 3QA
Tel	+44 (0)1497 831409
Email	hallsmillhouse@hotmail.co.uk
Web	www.hallsmillhouse.co.uk

Entry 163   Map 7

Herefordshire

Wickton Court

At the end of a no-through road, two miles from little Stoke Prior, is a rambling old place steeped in history, a courthouse that dates from the 15th century; ask Sally to show you the wig room! Be welcomed by ducks on the pond, sheep in the field, dogs by the fire, and lovely hosts who make you feel at home. The hallway is flagged, the sitting room panelled, the fireplace huge and often lit; all feels authentic and atmospheric. Visit Hampton Court Castle, antique-browse in Leominster, play golf, walk to the pub. Return to cosseting bedrooms with generous curtains, big bathrooms, wonky floors and ancient beams; one room even has a wood-burner.

Rooms	1 four-poster suite (cot & extra bed available); 1 twin/double with separate bathroom: £95–£120. Singles £85–£95.
Meals	Dinner, 2 courses, £25; 3 courses, £30–£35; non-residents welcome too. Cold platter for late arrivals, £12.50. Pubs/restaurants 5 miles.
Closed	Rarely.

Minimum stay: 2 nights at weekends.

	Sally Kellard Wickton Court, Stoke Prior, Leominster, HR6 0LN
Mobile	+44 (0)7812 602122
Email	sally@wickton.co.uk
Web	www.wickton.co.uk

Entry 164   Map 7

Herefordshire

Staunton House

This handsome Georgian rectory has a traditional, peaceful feel. Step into light, colourful and well-proportioned rooms that brim with family photographs, antiques, china and masses of books. The original oak staircase leads to inviting bedrooms with comfortable beds, pretty fabrics and garden posies; the blue room looks onto garden and pond. Wander through the beautiful garden, drive to Hay or Ludlow, stride across ravishing countryside, play golf near Offa's Dyke; return to Rosie and Richard's lovely home to relax in their drawing room before enjoying a delicious dinner in the elegant dining room. You will be well looked after here.

Rooms	1 double, 1 twin/double: £90-£100. Singles £65-£70.
Meals	Dinner, 3 courses, £30. Pub/restaurant 2.5 miles.
Closed	Rarely.

Pets by arrangement.

	Rosie & Richard Bowen Staunton House, Staunton-on-Arrow, Pembridge, Leominster, HR6 9HR
Tel	+44 (0)1544 388313
Mobile	+44 (0)7780 961994
Email	rosbown@aol.com
Web	www.stauntonhouse.co.uk

Entry 165   Map 7

Herefordshire

Bunns Croft

The timbers of this medieval yeoman's house are quite possibly a thousand years old. Little of the structure has ever been altered and it is sheer delight. Stone floors, rich colours, a piano, books, cosy chairs, friendly dog – all give a homely, lived-in warm feel. Cruck-beamed bedrooms are snugly small, the stairs are steep, and the twin's bathroom has its own sweet fireplace. The countryside is 'pure', too, with 1,500 acres of National Trust land a short hop away. Anita is charming, loves to look after her guests, grows her own fruit and vegetables and makes fabulous dinners. Just mind your head.

Rooms	1 twin; 1 double sharing bathroom with 3 singles (let to same party only): £85-£95. 3 singles sharing bathroom: £43.
Meals	Dinner, 3 courses BYO, £25. Pub 7 miles.
Closed	Rarely.

	Anita Syers-Gibson Bunns Croft, Moreton Eye, Leominster, HR6 0DP
Tel	+44 (0)1568 615836
Email	anitasyersg2@gmail.com

Entry 166   Map 7

Hertfordshire

Number One

It's worth hopping out of bed for Annie's breakfast: luxury continental with raspberry brioche or the full delicious Monty. Her house is a sparkling Aladdin's cave of mirrors, bunches of white twigs with birds atop, candles, cherubs, painted wooden floors, big open fires and generous bunches of roses. Bedrooms are lavishly done; nifty bathrooms have Italian tiles – and more roses! Close to the centre, this good-looking Georgian terrace house featured in Pevsner's guide to Hertfordshire, and the market town is busy with theatre, shops and galleries. Return for a gourmet dinner in the magical courtyard garden – when the sun is shining!

Rooms	2 twin/doubles; 1 double with separate bath/shower: £130-£160.
Meals	Dinner £45 (minimum 6 people). Pubs/restaurants 5-minute walk.
Closed	Rarely.

Over 12s welcome.

Annie Rowley
Number One,
1 Port Hill, Hertford, SG14 1PJ
Tel   +44 (0)1992 587350
Mobile   +44 (0)7770 914070
Email   annie@numberoneporthill.co.uk
Web   www.numberoneporthill.co.uk

Entry 167   Map 9

Isle of Wight

Westbourne House

Watch the yachts go by from this elegant townhouse on the waterfront. A welcoming drink and chat with Richard in the drawing room sets you up well: antiques, oil paintings, a bevy of guitars, family photos – and stunning views. Bedrooms (one downstairs) have WiFi, home-baked biscuits, cosy well-dressed beds. Kate's a marine artist and gives you breakfast looking over the water: lots of choice, homemade marmalade, Bucks Fizz too; if you're an early bird you can help yourself to a continental spread. Between the two main marinas and close to the high street, so shops, bars and restaurants (as well as Southampton ferry) are all a saunter.

Rooms	2 doubles: £110-£140.
Meals	Pubs/restaurants 1-minute walk.
Closed	Rarely.

Over 13s welcome.

Kate Gough
Westbourne House,
43 Birmingham Road,
Cowes, PO31 7BH
Tel   +44 (0)1983 290009
Email   katec56@gmail.com
Web   www.westbournehousecowes.co.uk

Entry 168   Map 4

Isle of Wight

Northcourt

A Jacobean manor in matchless grounds: 15 acres of terraced gardens, exotica and subtropical flowers. The house is magnificent too; huge but a lived-in home with big comfortable guest bedrooms in one of the wings. The formal dining room has separate tables, where delicious homemade bread and jams, garden fruit, honey and local produce are served. There's a snooker table in the library, a chamber organ in the hall and lovely antiques in every room. Groups are welcome and John offers garden tours. The peaceful village is in lovely downland – and you can walk from the garden to the Needles.

Rooms	3 twin/doubles: £82–£110.
Meals	Pub 3-minute walk through gardens.
Closed	Rarely.

Minimum stay: 2 nights at weekends.

John & Christine Harrison
Northcourt,
Shorwell, PO30 3JG
Tel   +44 (0)1983 740415
Mobile   +44 (0)7955 174699
Email   christine@northcourt.info
Web   www.northcourt.info

Entry 169   Map 4

Isle of Wight

Gotten Manor

Miles from the beaten track and bordered by old stone barns, the guest wing of this Saxon house is charmingly simple. Up steep stone steps (you must be nimble!) and through a low doorway find big bedrooms in laid-back rustic, funky French style: beams, limewashed stone, wooden floors, Persian rugs and a sweet window. Sleep on a rosewood bed and bathe by candlelight – in a roll top tub in your room. Friendly, informal Caroline serves breakfast in the old creamery: homemade yogurts, compotes and organic produce. There's a walled garden and a guest living room with cosy wood-burner.

Rooms	2 doubles: £80–£115.
Meals	Pub 1.5 miles.
Closed	Rarely.

Over 12s welcome.

Caroline Gurney-Champion
Gotten Manor,
Gotten Lane, Chale, PO38 2HQ
Tel   +44 (0)1983 551368
Mobile   +44 (0)7746 453398
Email   caroline@gottenmanor.co.uk
Web   www.gottenmanor.co.uk/bed-breakfast

Entry 170   Map 4

Kent

Applebys

You'd have to be made of stone not to fall in love with this beautifully restored 16th-century farmhouse. It oozes history and charm from the inglenook fireplace and opium bed coffee table in the guest sitting/dining room to the wonky oak boards and its three beautifully furnished en suite bedrooms. Jamie, who grew up here, and Karena are well-travelled and relish hosting guests. Breakfast on lashings of tea and coffee, muesli and local preserves or the full works; read the paper in the pretty suntrap garden. Set in gently undulating Wealden countryside this is perfectly placed for stately piles and grand gardens galore.

Rooms	3 doubles: £90. Singles £65.
Meals	Pubs/restaurants 0.5 miles.
Closed	Occasionally.

Parking on-site.

Jamie & Karena Donald
Applebys,
Chiddingstone Causeway,
Tonbridge, TN11 8JH
Tel   +44 (0)1892 871422
Email jamiedonald47@gmail.com
Web   www.applebysbnb.com

Entry 171   Map 5

Kent

Charcott Farmhouse

The 1750s farmhouse is rustic and family orientated, and if you don't come expecting an immaculate environment you will enjoy it here. In the old bake house there's a small sitting room with original beams and bread oven, TV and WiFi; relax in here on cooler days, with cats and a dog to keep you company. On sunny days tea is served in the garden. Bedrooms are pretty and comfy with oriental rugs and antique furniture. Nicholas – a tad eccentric for some – is half French and cooks amazing breakfasts on the Aga, while Ginny's great grandfather (Arnold Hills) founded West Ham football team. Come and go as you please.

Rooms	2 twins; 1 twin with separate bath: £80-£90. Singles £60. Extra bed/sofabed £10 per person per night.
Meals	Pub 5-minute walk.
Closed	22-28 December.

Nicholas & Ginny Morris
Charcott Farmhouse,
Charcott, Tonbridge, TN11 8LG
Tel   +44 (0)1892 870024
Mobile +44 (0)7734 009292
Email   charcottfarmhouse@btinternet.com
Web   www.charcottfarmhouse.com

Entry 172   Map 5

Kent

Ightham

Lord it through electric oak gates to find B&B in your own modern barn. Gardening enthusiast Caroline's house is close but not hugely visible: you're wonderfully independent. Bedrooms on the ground floor are eclectic and appealing, with pine floors, dazzling white walls and slatted wooden blinds for a moody light; the bathroom is big and contemporary with a walk-in shower. Upstairs: an enormous family space for sitting, eating, playing, and glass doors on to a terrace for outdoor fun. Breakfast is delivered: eggs from the hens, pancakes, French toast. Great walks start from the door, and you can stroll to a pub for dinner.

Rooms	1 double, 1 twin, let to same party only: £125. Extra bed/sofabed £25 per person per night.
Meals	Pubs 5-minute walk.
Closed	Rarely.

Minimum stay: 2 nights at weekends & in high season.

Caroline Standish
Ightham,
Hope Farm,
Sandy Lane,
Ightham, Sevenoaks, TN15 9BA
Tel   +44 (0)1732 884359
Email   clstandish@gmail.com
Web   www.ighthambedandbreakfast.co.uk

Entry 173   Map 5

Kent

Reason Hill

Brian and Antonia's 200-acre fruit farm is perched on the edge of the Weald of Kent, with stunning views over orchards and oast houses. The farmhouse has 17th-century origins (low ceilings, wonky floors, stone flags) and a conservatory for sunny breakfasts; colours are soft, antiques gleam, the mood is relaxed. Pretty bedrooms have garden views, TVs and magazines; there's a comfy sitting room too. Come in spring for the blossom, in summer for the fruit and veg from the garden; chickens roam free. The Greensand Way runs along the bottom of the farm, you're close to Sissinghurst Castle and 45 minutes from the Channel Tunnel.

Rooms	1 double, 2 twins: £90-£95. 1 single sharing shower with double (let to same party only): £60.
Meals	Pubs within 1 mile.
Closed	Christmas & New Year.

Brian & Antonia Allfrey
Reason Hill,
Westerhill Road, Coxheath,
Maidstone, ME17 4BT
Tel   +44 (0)1622 743679
Mobile   +44 (0)7775 745580
Email   antonia@allfrey.net
Web   www.reasonhill.co.uk

Entry 174   Map 5

Kent

Merzie Meadows

This lovely ranch-style house has huge windows, pergolas groaning with climbers and a Mediterranean-style swimming pool. Sitting in landscaped gardens, paddocks and woodland there are horses, hens, wild flowers and lots of twittering birds. Pamela gives you a locally sourced breakfast with fruits, organic bread and just-laid eggs. Bedrooms are beautifully dressed with pretty fabrics, handmade mattresses are topped with good linen and goose down pillows; the suite has a sitting area looking onto the garden, a study and a bathroom sleek with Italian marble and plump towels. All is peaceful; garden and nature lovers will adore it here.

Rooms	1 double: £115-£120.
	1 suite for 2-3: £115-£160.
	Singles £98-£100.
	Extra bed/sofabed available £50-£60 per person per night.
Meals	Pub 2.5 miles.
Closed	Mid-December to February.

Minimum stay: 2 nights at weekends April-September.

	Pamela Mumford
	Merzie Meadows,
	Hunton Road, Marden,
	Maidstone, TN12 9SL
Tel	+44 (0)1622 820500
Mobile	+44 (0)7762 713077
Email	merziemeadows@me.com
Web	www.merziemeadows.co.uk

Entry 175   Map 5

Kent

Handley Cross

This peaceful country house sits in six acres of paddock and flowery gardens. You stay in the charming annexe and have your own entrance. There's a large, sunny living space opening to a terrace, with comfy sofas by the wood-burner, a polished table in the window, a pretty painted dresser. Amanda leaves you a generous continental breakfast – cereals, yogurts, local jams, fresh bread, pastries. Wye has vintage and farmers' markets and you can walk from the door on to the North Downs Way. Further afield are Canterbury, Leeds Castle, Sissinghurst and many stately homes. Return to your elegant bedroom upstairs with a king-size twin bed and wide countryside views.

Rooms	1 twin/double: £80-£95.
Meals	Fresh croissants for weekday breakfasts and cooked breakfasts available at weekends.
	Pubs/restaurants 1 mile.
Closed	Rarely.

	Amanda-Jane Amiss
	Handley Cross,
	Wye,
	Ashford, TN25 5DL
Mobile	+44 (0)7796 332078
Email	ajamiss@outlook.com

Entry 176   Map 5

Kent

Hereford Oast

Jack the Jack Russell will meet you, swiftly followed by Suzy who'll bring you tea and cake in the garden: sheer heaven in summer. The 1876 oast house, set back from a country road and gazing over fields, has become the loveliest B&B. Downstairs is the dining room, as unique as it is round. Upstairs is the guest room, sunny, fresh and bright, with a rural view; the small bath has an overhead shower. As for the village – white-clapboard cottages, pubs, fine church – it's the prettiest in Kent. Sausages from Pluckley, homemade jams and good coffee set you up for cultured jaunts: Leeds Castle, Sissinghurst, Great Dixter... all nearby.

Rooms	1 twin/double: £85–£90. Singles £50–£55.
Meals	Pubs 1 mile.
Closed	Rarely.

Minimum stay: 2 nights at weekends.

Suzy Hill
Hereford Oast,
Smarden Bell Road, Smarden,
Ashford, TN27 8PA
Tel   +44 (0)1233 770541
Email suzyhereford@gmail.com
Web   www.herefordoast.co.uk

Entry 177   Map 5

Kent

Romden

Guarded by trees and birds, lording it over meadows and lanes, this rambling 'castle' with its 18th-century tower has a charmingly lived-in feel. Lovely laid-back Miranda and Dominic make you feel at home; help yourself to cereals while they drum up your bacon and eggs, enjoy the flower-filled terrace, play croquet or use their pool and tennis court (by arrangement). Bedrooms, sitting room and hall are decked out with pretty wallpapers, antiques, art, rugs and throws; one of the twins has a tiny shower room; log fires keep things toasty. And if you're hankering after a real castle, Sissinghurst and Leeds are down the road.

Rooms	1 double, 1 twin; 1 twin with separate bath: £70–£100. Singles £55–£75.
Meals	Pubs/restaurants 1.5 miles.
Closed	Rarely.

Miranda Kelly
Romden,
Smarden,
Ashford, TN27 8RA
Tel   +44 (0)1233 770687
Email miranda_kelly@hotmail.com

Entry 177.1   Map 5

Kent

Snoadhill Cottage

You'll feel at home the moment you arrive at Yvette and Philip's friendly cottage. Once a medieval 'hall house', it's awash with huge oak beams. Up steep stairs and past shelves of books find fresh, sunny bedrooms with lovely views. Enjoy a flagstone terrace for summery breakfasts or a fireside spot in the dining room; expect eggs from the hens, homemade jams, kippers perhaps or a full English. You're surrounded by glorious open countryside, walks and cycle rides start from the door and it's just 25 minutes from the Channel Tunnel. Dip in the swimming pond, chat to Rocky the labrador... and wander the blooming gardens.

Rooms	1 double with separate shower, 1 twin with separate bath: £90. Singles £65.
Meals	Pub 1 mile.
Closed	Rarely.

Yvette James
Snoadhill Cottage,
Snoadhill, Bethersden,
Ashford, TN26 3DY
Tel   +44 (0)1233 820245
Email   enquiries@snoadhillcottage.co.uk
Web   www.snoadhillcottage.co.uk

Entry 178   Map 5

Kent

Barclay Farmhouse

Lynn's breakfasts are fabulous: fresh fruit, warm croissants, home-baked breads and a daily changing twist on the traditional English. The weatherboarded guest barn may be in perfect trim but it has a been-here-for-ever feel; you have country-cosy dining tables for breakfast, a patio for summer, a big peaceful garden. Gleaming bedrooms have handmade oak bedheads, chocolates, slippers, discreet fridges, radios, TVs; shower rooms are in perfect order. Couples, honeymooners, garden lovers – many would love it here (but no children: the garden pond is deep). Warm-hearted B&B, and glorious Sissinghurst nearby.

Rooms	Barn: 3 doubles: £95. Singles from £70.
Meals	Pubs/restaurants 1 mile.
Closed	Rarely.

Minimum stay: 2 nights at weekends in high season.

Lynn Ruse
Barclay Farmhouse,
Woolpack Corner,
Biddenden, TN27 8BQ
Tel   +44 (0)1580 292626
Email   info@barclayfarmhouse.co.uk
Web   www.barclayfarmhouse.co.uk

Entry 179   Map 5

Kent

Pullington Barn

Up a private drive and straight in to a vast, beamed expanse of bright light, warm colours, beautiful art and a cheery welcome from Gavin and Anne in their converted barn. There are endless books to choose: settle in the comfy drawing room with its grand piano, or sit in the pretty south-facing garden on a fine day. On the other side, views from the orchard spread over oast houses and church spires. Big bedrooms (one on the ground floor) have good mattresses, coordinated bed linen and feather pillows. You breakfast well on local and homemade produce, served at the travertine table in the dining hall. Lovely walks from the door.

Rooms	1 double, 1 twin: £90-£105. Singles £65-£80.
Meals	Pub/restaurant 0.5 miles.
Closed	Christmas.

Children over 9 welcome, younger ones by arrangement.

Gavin & Anne Wetton
Pullington Barn,
Benenden, TN17 4EH

Tel	+44 (0)1580 240246
Mobile	+44 (0)7849 759929
Email	anne@wetton.com
Web	www.wetton.info/bandb

Entry 180 Map 5

Ramsden Farm

The views across the Wealds are stunning! These former farm buildings have been renovated with flair, and Sally has created a gorgeous, comfortable home. Leisurely, tasty breakfasts are eaten in the huge kitchen by the jaunty lemon Aga; floor to ceiling glass doors open on to a wooden deck: spill outside on warm days. After a hearty walk you can doze in front of a tree-devouring inglenook. Upstairs, lovely sunny bedrooms with more of that view from each, natural colours, tip-top mattresses and the crispest white linen – chocolates too; bathrooms have travertine marble and underfloor heating. Friendly, spoiling and completely peaceful.

Rooms	1 double, 1 twin; 1 double with separate bath: £95-£120. Singles £85-£110.
Meals	Pub 1 mile.
Closed	Rarely.

Sally Harrington
Ramsden Farm,
Dingleden Lane,
Benenden, TN17 4JT

Tel	+44 (0)1580 240203
Email	sally@ramsdenfarmhouse.co.uk
Web	www.ramsdenfarmhouse.co.uk

Entry 181 Map 5

Kent

Beacon Hall House

A family home and Julie truly enjoys having guests. Aga breakfasts are full of delicious homemade, home-grown things; supper too, perhaps cottage pie or Hastings sea bass with veg from the garden. Find sweet herbs on your pillow, home-baked biscuits, flowers and beautiful eclectic furnishings in comfortable bedrooms. Explore seven acres of paddocks, cutting garden and mature elevated terraces, with gorgeous views across rolling Kent and Sussex. Sissinghurst and Great Dixter, castles and pretty villages are close. Return to a sitting room with huge relaxing sofas and fat cushions; Buster and Hetty the spaniels are an added boon.

Rooms	1 double, 2 twin/doubles: £115–£130. Singles £85–£110. Extra bed/sofabed £15–£25 per person per night.
Meals	Supper from £20. Pub within 1 mile.
Closed	Christmas.

Extra bed available in 1 twin/double so can be family room for 3.

	Julie Jex Beacon Hall House, Rolvenden Road, Benenden, TN17 4BU
Tel	+44 (0)1580 240434
Email	jjjex@icloud.com
Web	www.beaconhallhouse.co.uk

Entry 182 Map 5

Kent

Lamberden Cottage

Down a farm track find two 1780 cottages knocked into one, with flagstone floors, a cheery wood-burner in the guest sitting room and welcoming Beverley and Branton. There's a traditional country-cottage feel with pale walls, thick oak beams, soft carpeting and very comfortable bedrooms (two twins adjoin to form the family room); views from all are across the Weald of Kent. Find a private spot in the lovely gardens, sip a sundowner on the terrace, relax in the garden room; hearty breakfasts in the family dining room include home-grown fruits, homemade marmalades and yogurts. Near to Sissinghurst, Great Dixter and many historic places.

Rooms	1 double: £85–£90. 1 family room for 4: £120. Singles from £65.
Meals	Pub 1 mile.
Closed	Christmas & New Year.

	Beverley & Branton Screeton Lamberden Cottage, Rye Road, Sandhurst, Cranbrook, TN18 5PH
Tel	+44 (0)1580 850743
Mobile	+44 (0)7768 462070
Email	thewalledgarden@lamberdencottage.co.uk
Web	www.lamberdencottage.co.uk

Entry 183 Map 5

Kent

The Old Rectory

On a really good day (about once every year) you can see France. But you'll be more than happy to settle for the superb views over Romney Marsh, the Channel in the distance. The big, friendly house, built in 1845, has impeccable, elegant bedrooms and good bathrooms; the large, many-windowed sitting room is full of books, pictures and flowers from the south-facing garden. Marion and David are both charming and can organise transport to the Channel Tunnel for you. It's remarkably peaceful – perfect for walking (right on the Saxon Shore path), cycling and bird watching.

Rooms	1 twin; 1 twin with separate bath/shower: £90. Singles £60.
Meals	Pubs within 4 miles.
Closed	Christmas & New Year.

Children over 10 welcome.

Marion & David Hanbury
The Old Rectory,
Ruckinge,
Ashford, TN26 2PE
Tel +44 (0)1233 732328
Email oldrectory@hotmail.com
Web www.oldrectoryruckinge.co.uk

Entry 184   Map 5

Great Selson Manor

A gem of a restoration in a blooming garden. Graham (film maker) and Yolanda's home is one of the earliest Dutch-influenced buildings in east Kent, and you step inside to wonderful features at every turn: a striking brick hall floor, a Jacobean oak staircase, Graham's artwork, oriental musical instruments, an elegant library. Inviting bedrooms, claw foot baths, and cushiony sofas in the sitting room add to the comfortable vibe. Breakfast includes a neighbour's award-winning apple juice, best-sourced sausages, homemade jams, eggs from the hens. Graham and Yolanda exude cheerfulness and interest – it's a treat to stay with them.

Rooms	2 doubles: £100-£150.
Meals	Continental breakfast available. Pubs/restaurants 2.5 miles away.
Closed	Rarely.

Minimum stay: 2 nights at weekends & in high season.

Graham Johnston
Great Selson Manor,
Selson Lane,
Eastry, Sandwich, CT13 0EF
Mobile +44 (0)7957 160385
Email g.j3@btinternet.com

Entry 185   Map 5

Kent

7 Longport

A delightful, unexpected hideaway bang opposite the site of St Augustine's Abbey and a five-minute walk to the Cathedral. You pass through Ursula and Christopher's elegant Georgian house to emerge in a pretty courtyard, with fig tree and rambling rose, to find your self-contained cottage. Downstairs is a cosy sitting room with pale walls, tiled floors and plenty of books, and a clever, compact wet room with mosaic tiles. Then up steep stairs to a swish bedroom with crisp cotton sheets on a handmade bed and views of the ancient wisteria. You breakfast in the main house or in the courtyard on sunny days. Perfect.

Rooms	Cottage – 1 double with sitting room: £100. Singles £70.
Meals	Restaurants 5-minute walk.
Closed	Rarely.

Ursula & Christopher Wacher
7 Longport,
Canterbury, CT1 1PE
Tel   +44 (0)1227 455367
Email   info@7longport.co.uk
Web   www.7longport.co.uk

Entry 186   Map 5

Kent

Northwood Lodge

Emma is happy to share her friendly home. Bedrooms have pretty beds and rugs on painted floors; the huge guest bathroom is gorgeous: freestanding bath, fluffy towels, scented lotions, a jug of flowers. A delicious breakfast with a dish of the day and homemade jam is served in the big, bright kitchen, or outside in the sun. You can settle in the drawing room for a film/dinner night (book beforehand), and there's another sitting room with heaps of books, open fire and large antique mirrors. Head out for seaside walks, Whitstable Oyster Festival and Faversham with its medieval market place; Canterbury and Margate are a short drive too.

Rooms	2 doubles sharing bathroom: £110. Singles £85.
Meals	Dinner from £25. Dinner and movie from £35. Pubs/restaurants 5 miles.
Closed	Rarely.

Minimum stay: 2 nights at weekends & in high season. Children over 8 welcome.

Emma Clarke
Northwood Lodge,
Bullockstone Road,
Herne Bay, CT6 7NR
Tel   +44 (0)1227 634549
Email   emma@stellarproductions.co.uk

Entry 187   Map 5

Kent

Dadmans

Once the dower house to Lynsted Park, Dadmans sits on the edge of parkland surrounded by orchards, grazing cattle and sheep. Happy hens provide your breakfast eggs and Amanda sources fantastic local produce for dinner, served in the dining room on gleaming mahogany. There's an elegant drawing room with roaring winter fires and a place to catch the evening summer sun; bedrooms have indulgent beds, views and good bathrooms. Large gardens are pretty too with ancient trees, walled areas, a nuttery, herb gardens – and a swing seat for sitting and admiring. Nearby, find plenty of gardens, castles and cathedrals.

Rooms	1 twin/double; 1 double with separate bath: £110. Singles £75.
Meals	Dinner, 4 courses, £35. Supper from £15. Pubs/restaurants 2 miles.
Closed	Rarely.

Children over 4 welcome.

Amanda Strevens
Dadmans,
Lynsted, Sittingbourne, ME9 0JJ
Tel   +44 (0)1795 521293
Mobile +44 (0)7931 153253
Email   amanda.strevens@btopenworld.com
Web   www.dadmans.co.uk

Entry 188   Map 5

Kent

Huntingfield House

This is a joining in sort of place. Children can help feed the hens and meet the ponies, while grown-ups can relax. Roses clamber up the walls of this classic Georgian fronted house in open farmland interspersed with woods and orchards. Emma is a charming mum and runs a busy kitchen. Not only does she produce local sausages at breakfast, drop-scones from the Aga and honey from the bees, but she whips up children's teas and your suppers too – good honest home cooking. Generosity flows, from free bikes for all to umbrellas on wet days to a fire in the drawing room on winter nights. It's a 30-minute walk to the pub in sleepy little Eastling, 40 to stately Belmont House, and a hop in the car to Faversham, Canterbury and Whitstable. Then it's back home to big traditional bedrooms and owls to hoot you to sleep.

Rooms	1 double, 1 twin: £100–£110.
Meals	Supper, 2 courses, £20. Dinner, 3 courses, £30; children £10. Pubs/restaurants 2 miles.
Closed	Christmas & New Year.

Minimum stay: 2 nights.

Emma Norwood
Huntingfield House,
Stalisfield Road, Eastling,
Faversham, ME13 0HT
Tel   +44 (0)1795 892138
Email emma@huntingfieldhouse.co.uk
Web   www.huntingfieldhouse.co.uk

Entry 189   Map 5

Lancashire

Challan Hall

The wind in the trees, the boom of a bittern and birdsong. That's as noisy as it gets. On the edge of the village, delightful Charlotte's former farmhouse overlooks woods and Haweswater Reservoir; deer, squirrels and Leighton Moss Nature Reserve are your neighbours. The Cassons are well-travelled and the house, filled with a colourful collection of mementos, is happily and comfortably traditional. Expect a sofa-strewn sitting room, a smart red and polished-wood dining room and two freshly floral bedrooms (one with a tiny shower room). Morecambe Bay and the Lakes are on the doorstep – come home to lovely views and stunning sunsets.

Rooms	1 twin/double; 1 twin/double with separate bath: £75. 2 nights or more: £70 (Mon-Fri). Singles from £50.
Meals	Dinner, 2 courses, £25. Packed lunch available. Pubs 1 mile.
Closed	Rarely.

Charlotte Casson
Challan Hall,
Silverdale, LA5 0UH
Tel   +44 (0)1524 701054
Mobile   +44 (0)7790 360776
Email   cassons@btopenworld.com
Web   www.challanhall.co.uk

Entry 190   Map 11

Lancashire

Sagar Fold House

In a spectacular setting, a 17th-century dairy and two perfect studios, one up, one down. Private entrances lead to big beamed spaces that marry immaculate efficiency with unusual beauty. A gorgeous Indian door frame serves as the en suite door upstairs, soft colours and contemporary touches lift the spirit, plentiful books and DVDs entertain you and a continental breakfast is supplied – homemade and organic whenever possible. The gardens are amazing with lovely places to sit, a sweet old summer house and an Italian knot garden – very Wolf Hall! Take walks in deeply peaceful countryside; top-notch places to eat are an easy drive.

Rooms	2 studios for 2 each with kitchenette: £90.
Meals	Continental breakfast in fridge. Pubs/restaurants 1-2 miles.
Closed	Rarely.

Helen & John Cook
Sagar Fold House,
Higher Hodder, Clitheroe, BB7 3LW
Tel   +44 (0)1254 826844
Mobile   +44 (0)7850 750709
Email   helencook14@gmail.com
Web   www.sagarfoldhouse.co.uk

Entry 191   Map 12

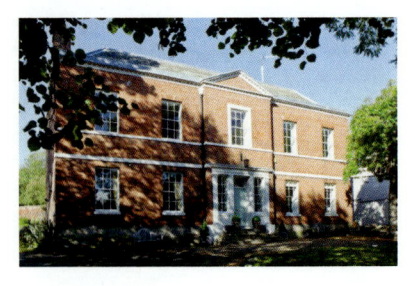

Leicestershire

Breedon Hall

Through high walls find a listed Georgian manor house in an acre of garden, and friendly Charlotte and Charles. Make yourselves at home in the fire-warmed drawing room full of fine furniture, art and furnishings in the richest reds and golds. Charlotte is a smashing cook: homemade granola and marmalade, local eggs, bacon and sausages for breakfast; you can book a three-course dinner too. Bedrooms are painted in soft colours, beds are covered in goose down; bathrooms are immaculate. The old stabling now houses three neat self-catering cottages too. Borrow a bike and discover the glorious countryside right on the cusp of two counties.

Rooms	5 doubles: £80–£150.
Meals	Supper £25. Dinner, 3 courses, £35; only for parties of 4 or more; not Sundays. Pub/restaurant 1-minute walk (closed on Sundays).
Closed	Christmas, New Year, 1–8 July, usually Sundays.

Minimum stay: 2 nights in high season. Contact owner for self-catering prices.

Charlotte Meynell
Breedon Hall,
Main Street, Breedon-on-the-Hill,
Derby, DE73 8AN
Tel   +44 (0)1332 864935
Mobile   +44 (0)7973 105467
Email   charlottemeynell1963@gmail.com
Web   www.breedonhall.co.uk

Entry 192   Map 8

Leicestershire

The Gorse House

Passing cars are less frequent than passing horses — this is a peaceful spot in a pretty village. Lyn and Richard's 17th-century cottage has a feeling of lightness and space; there's a fine collection of paintings and furniture, and oak doors lead from dining room to guest sitting room. Country style bedrooms have green views and are simply done. The garden layout was designed by Bunny Guinness, you can bring your horse (there's plenty of stabling) and it's a stroll to a good pub dinner. The house is filled with laughter, breakfasts with home-grown fruits are tasty and the Cowdells are terrific hosts who love having guests to stay.

Rooms	1 double: £80. 1 family room for 4: £80–£130. Stable: 1 triple with kitchenette: £80–£120. Singles £50.
Meals	Packed lunch £5. Pub 75 yds (closed on Sun eves).
Closed	Rarely.

Pets by arrangement (not in the house).

Lyn & Richard Cowdell
The Gorse House,
33 Main Street, Grimston,
Melton Mowbray, LE14 3BZ
Tel   +44 (0)1664 813537
Mobile   +44 (0)7780 600792
Email   cowdell@gorsehouse.co.uk
Web   www.gorsehouse.co.uk

Entry 193   Map 9

Lincolnshire

The Barn

Surrounded by meadows this 17th-century barn is in a quiet spot in a conservation village. Step in to a light-filled home with old beams and good antiques; a fireplace glows and heated floors keep toes warm. Above the high-raftered main living/dining room is a comfy, good-sized double; two adjoining rooms share a shower and are perfect for family or friends sharing; the single has an antique brass bed. Jane is helpful and friendly, there are endless extras and nothing is too much trouble; her delicious breakfasts and suppers are entirely local or home-grown. Views are to sheep-dotted fields and the village is on a 25-mile cycle trail.

Rooms	1 twin/double; 2 twin/doubles sharing a shower: £60-£80. 1 single with separate bath/shower: £55-£60.
Meals	Supper, 2 courses, £17.50. Dinner, 3 courses, £25. BYO. Pubs in village & 2 miles.
Closed	Rarely.

Pets by arrangement.

Jane Wright
The Barn,
Spring Lane, Folkingham,
Sleaford, NG34 0SJ
Tel   +44 (0)1529 497199
Mobile +44 (0)7876 363292
Email   sjwright@farming.co.uk
Web   www.thebarnspringlane.co.uk

Entry 194   Map 9

Lincolnshire

Lut's B&B

You'd be hard pressed to find as warm as welcome as you will at this 18th-century farmhouse. Set in a rural spot by a livery yard, it's had great care poured into it by lovely Lut and Bruce, who've kept the original features but given it a fresh feel. Bedrooms have well-dressed beds and flowers (hop up to the attic for the single); bathrooms are spotless. Anglo-Belgian breakfasts are plentiful and eaten at one large table. There's plenty to do: historic Lincoln nearby, bikes to borrow and walks from the door. Return to a stroll in the beautiful garden, an inviting sitting room and a tasty veggie meal — make sure to book ahead.

Rooms	1 double; 1 double sharing shower/bathroom with single room (let to same party only): £85-£100. 1 single sharing shower/bathroom (let to same party only): £60.
Meals	Dinner £25. BYO. Pubs/restaurants 2 miles.
Closed	Rarely.

Minimum stay: 2 nights at weekends.

Lut Dierckx
Lut's B&B,
Grange Farm, Mill Lane, North
Hykeham, Lincoln, LN6 9PB
Tel   +44 (0)1522 306215
Mobile +44 (0)7793 034734
Email   lut@lutsbandb.co.uk
Web   lutsbandb.co.uk

Entry 195   Map 9

Lincolnshire

Baumber Park

Lincoln red cows and Longwool sheep surround this attractive rosy-brick farmhouse – once a stud that bred a Derby winner. The old watering pond is now a haven for frogs, newts and toads; birds sing lustily. Maran hens conjure delicious eggs, and charming Clare, a botanist, is hugely knowledgeable about the area. Bedrooms are light and traditional with mahogany furniture; two have heart-stopping views. Guests have their own wisteria-covered entrance, sitting room with an open fire, dining room with local books and the lovely garden to roam. This is good walking, riding and cycling country; seals and rare birds on the coast.

Rooms	2 doubles; 1 twin with separate shower: £72-£85. Singles £45-£70. Extra bed/sofabed £15-£25 per person per night.
Meals	Pubs 1.5 miles.
Closed	Christmas & New Year.

Minimum stay: usually 2 nights at weekends in high season.

Clare Harrison
Baumber Park,
Baumber,
Horncastle, LN9 5NE

Tel	+44 (0)1507 578235
Mobile	+44 (0)7977 722776
Email	mail@baumberpark.com
Web	www.baumberpark.com

Entry 196   Map 9

Lincolnshire

The Grange

Wide open farmland and an award-winning farm on the edge of the Lincolnshire Wolds. This immaculately kept farm has been in the family for generations; Sarah and Jonathan are delightful and make you feel instantly at home. Find acres of farmland and a two-mile farm trail to explore, a trout lake to picnic by and an open fire to warm you in an elegant drawing room with Georgian windows. Sarah gives you delicious homemade cake on arrival and huge Aga breakfasts with home-laid eggs and local produce. Comfortable bedrooms have TVs, tea trays and gleaming bathrooms. Fabulous views stretch to Lincoln Cathedral and the walks are superb.

Rooms	2 doubles: £82-£84. Singles £56-£58.
Meals	Supper from £18. Dinner, 2 courses, from £25. BYO. No evening meals during harvest. Pub/restaurant 1 mile.
Closed	Christmas & New Year.

Sarah & Jonathan Stamp
The Grange,
Torrington Lane,
East Barkwith, LN8 5RY

Tel	+44 (0)1673 858670
Mobile	+44 (0)7951 079474
Email	sarahstamp@myfwi.co.uk
Web	www.thegrange-lincolnshire.co.uk

Entry 197   Map 9

Lincolnshire

Grayingham Lodge

An attractive stone farmhouse surrounded by fields. Jane and Peter's house is a working sheep farm, and you arrive to a welcoming cup from a silver teapot and delicious cake by the fire. If you're peckish later too, there are homemade flapjacks in pretty, very comfortable bedrooms. In the morning, the sideboard holds an impressive spread: homemade marmalade, fruit salad, compote, cereals – and a tasty cooked breakfast to follow. Have a day sightseeing in Lincoln – the Cathedral is magnificent and the castle has a copy of the Magna Carta; explore the Lincolnshire Wolds and coast; head off early for some exciting racing at Blyton Park.

Rooms	3 doubles: £60-£85. Singles £60.
Meals	Pubs/restaurants 3 miles.
Closed	Rarely.

	Jane Summers
	Grayingham Lodge,
	Gainsborough Road,
	Northorpe,
	Gainsborough, DN21 4AN
Tel	+44 (0)1652 648544
Email	janesummers@btinternet.com
Web	www.grayinghamlodge.co.uk

Entry 198   Map 13

Lincolnshire

The Manor House

At the end of a neatly raked gravel drive, a new manor house with wide views and stunning sunsets over the peaceful Trent valley. The Days have farmed in the village since 1898 and look after you with friendly ease. They give you a bedroom in the main house, or an annexe with its own entrance hall and sunny patio; find period furniture, a comfy sofa or two and rural art. The beautiful gardens are awash with roses, ducks on the pond, horses in the paddock. Shooting can be arranged and you can fish for carp in the lake, or play golf nearby; there are music and art festivals, antique fairs and walks in abundance too.

Rooms	1 double: £75-£80. Annexe: 1 twin/double with kitchenette: £75-£80. Singles £55.
Meals	Pub/restaurant 3.5 miles.
Closed	Christmas & New Year.

	Judy Day
	The Manor House,
	Manton, Kirton Lindsey,
	Gainsborough, DN21 4JT
Tel	+44 (0)1652 649508
Mobile	+44 (0)7712 766347
Email	hobbsmanton@gmail.com
Web	www.manorhousebedandbreakfast.co.uk

Entry 199   Map 13

Lincolnshire

The Old Farm House

You will feel at home in this rambling, quirky house – Nicola loves having guests to stay. The house is 300 years old and it's said that Dick Turpin, on the run, once hid in the roof. Read the papers by a winter fire, flop into worn leather chairs, sip an evening glass of wine in the garden, sleep soundly on a fine brass bed. Rooms are named after the men of the extended family – King Henry, George and James – and all are colourful, comfortable and cushioned. There are cycle routes, walks and golf courses galore (Nicola has all the info), racing at Market Rasen, quaint churches to visit and an annual classic car rally.

Rooms	2 doubles: £85. 1 family room for 4: £120 (£90 for 3, £80 for 2). Singles £55.
Meals	Pub 2.5 miles.
Closed	Christmas, New Year & occasionally.

Nicola Clarke
The Old Farm House,
Low Road, Hatcliffe,
Grimsby, DN37 0SH

Tel	+44 (0)1472 824455
Mobile	+44 (0)7818 272523
Email	clarky.hatcliffe@btinternet.com
Web	www.oldfarmhousebandbgrimsby.com

Entry 200   Map 13

London

30 King Henry's Road

Shops, restaurants and sublime views of Primrose Hill are a five-minute stroll from this interesting 1860s house; walls are covered in a lifetime collection of watercolours, drawings and maps. Your room on the top floor has a comfortable brass bed, a sisal floor, fine pieces of furniture, a wall of books, digital TV and a smart new bathroom. Breakfast on homemade bread and jams, bagels, croissants, yogurts and fresh fruit salad in the large kitchen/dining room with a big open fire and garden views. There's open-air theatre in Regent's Park in summer; Carole and Ted know London well and will happily advise.

Rooms	1 double: £120. Singles £115.
Meals	Continental breakfast. Pubs/restaurants 2-minute walk.
Closed	Occasionally.

Carole & Ted Cox
30 King Henry's Road,
Primrose Hill,
London, NW3 3RP

Tel	+44 (0)20 7483 2871
Mobile	+44 (0)7976 389350
Email	carole.l.cox@gmail.com

Entry 201   Map 22

London

The Roost

The pale blue-painted front door sets the tone for this large, lofty and airy home with smart hotel-standard rooms at a fraction of the price. The furniture is excellent: fine family pieces and Liz's handsome finds. There is a conservatory for continental breakfast overlooking the garden, a delightful Parson Russell dog and art everywhere. Liz, a former fashion pattern cutter and dancer, is a natural and lovely hostess. The Roost is brilliantly positioned for whizzing into town, transport links are easy, there is lovely Queen's park, an irresistible bakery, great pubs, restaurants and a farmers' market on Sundays. Marvellous.

Rooms	3 doubles: £95-£135. One night-stay (Monday–Thursday) additional fee £20.
Meals	Continental breakfast. Pubs/restaurants 5-minute walk.
Closed	Rarely.

Minimum stay: 2 nights at weekends.

Liz Crosland
The Roost,
37 Lynton Road, Queen's Park,
London, NW6 6BE
Tel   +44 (0)20 7625 6770
Mobile +44 (0)7967 354477
Email liz@boutiquebandblondon.com
Web   www.boutiquebandblondon.com

Entry 202 · Map 22

London

22 York Street

If you need to be in London but don't much enjoy staying in impersonal hotels then you'll be happy here. It's a homely place with simple, good-sized bedrooms, and two antique-filled sitting rooms where you can help yourself to tea, coffee or a work space with printer. There's a happy vibe at breakfast where owner/curator Michael may join you at the curved oak table; bubbly manageress Ingrid lives in and looks after you impeccably. It's not for minimalists – there's clutter everywhere – but it's amiable, well-priced and in a fantastic spot for tourists. The fabulous Wallace Collection is near, as is Wigmore Hall with lunchtime concerts.

Rooms	5 doubles, 2 twins: £150. 1 family room for 4: £240. 1 triple: £180. 3 singles: £95-£99.
Meals	Continental breakfast included. Pubs/restaurants nearby.
Closed	Never.

Michael & Liz Callis
22 York Street,
London, W1U 6PX
Tel   +44 (0)20 7224 2990
Email mc@22yorkstreet.co.uk
Web   www.22yorkstreet.co.uk

Entry 203 · Map 22

London

1 Peel Street

Pretty, gabled and surprisingly quiet with central London on your doorstep. Fascinating old maps, photos from Susie's world travels, interesting books and objets d'art all create an unusual and elegant feel. The top floor is all yours: the bedroom is full of character, framed by the slanting angles of the roof and soothingly decorated in neutral shades. Breakfast is at a table overlooking the patio or downstairs in the elegant dining room: organic bread, pastries, fruit and excellent coffee. Just a stroll to good tapas, wine bars, Hyde Park and Notting Hill. Hop on a bus or tube to explore further. Guests love it here.

Rooms	1 double with separate bath/shower: £130. Singles £95.
Meals	Continental breakfast. Pubs/restaurants 2-minute walk.
Closed	Occasionally.

Second bedroom with bunk beds available for overflow with the same group.

	Susan Laws 1 Peel Street, Kensington, London, W8 7PA
Tel	+44 (0)20 7792 8361
Mobile	+44 (0)7776 140060
Email	susan@susielaws.co.uk

Entry 204 Map 22

London

101 Abbotsbury Road

The area is one of London's finest and Sunny's family home is a four-minute walk from Holland Park Avenue with interesting cafés, pubs and shops. It's a fuss free and easy place to stay right in the heart of things. Holland Park is one of the loveliest parks in London with formal gardens, woods and wildlife – the Kyoto garden is serene and beautiful. Browse happily in Daunt Books then treat yourself to supper at Marco Pierre White's Belvedere restaurant. Hop on the tube for Kensington High Street, Notting Hill, Portobello Market and Knightsbridge. Relax, unwind, feel free to come and go but do ask Sunny for tips – she's lived here for more than 40 years.

Rooms	1 double sharing bath with single: £110–£120. 1 single: £65–£75.
Meals	Continental breakfast. Pubs/restaurants 5-minute walk.
Closed	Occasionally.

Children over 6 welcome. Tube: Holland Park, 7-minute walk. Off-street parking sometimes available.

	Sunny Murray 101 Abbotsbury Road, Holland Park, London, W14 8EP
Tel	+44 (0)20 7602 0179
Mobile	+44 (0)7768 362562
Email	sunny.murray@gmail.com
Web	www.hollandparkbandb.co.uk

Entry 205 Map 22

London

31 Rowan Road

Terrific value for money in leafy Brook Green. The two studios are fantastic spaces: one under the eaves (comfy twin beds and armchairs, a deep cast-iron bath from which you can gaze at the birds), the other larger and more contemporary in style, on the lower ground floor, with its own wisteria-clad entrance. All independent with a continental breakfast popped in your fridge. Or join in with family life and stay in the little pink bedroom with books and hats, and take breakfast in the pretty conservatory with Vicky and Edmund. A friendly home with flowers, art, photos and a relaxed vibe – Tiger the terrier and a blossoming garden too.

Rooms	1 double with separate bath/shower: £75-£90. 2 studios for 2 both with kitchenette: £95-£130. Singles £75. Extra bed/sofabed £20 per person per night.
Meals	Continental breakfast. Pubs/restaurants 2 minutes.
Closed	Occasionally.

Tube: Hammersmith. Off-street parking £20 a day.

Vicky & Edmund Sixsmith
31 Rowan Road,
Brook Green, Hammersmith,
London, W6 7DT
Tel   +44 (0)20 8748 0930
Mobile   +44 (0)7966 829259
Email   vickysixsmith@me.com
Web   www.abetterwaytostay.co.uk

Entry 206   Map 22

London

37 Trevor Square

A three-minute walk from Hyde Park or Harrods – a fabulous find. The square is peaceful and private, with a well-kept garden in the middle. Margaret is flexible about everything – breakfast and check in times; she will call cabs, arrange collection and really look out for you. A superb full English breakfast is served in the relaxed kitchen/diner; the friendly dachshunds, Jester and Waggy, keep you company. Luxurious bedrooms (one downstairs has an enormous bed and a little patio) have goose down pillows, cashmere duvets, electric blankets and a mini fridge; slip on your robe, listen to some music or watch a DVD – it's all here.

Rooms	1 double; 1 double sharing shower with single (let to same party only): £200. 1 single: £50-£75.
Meals	Restaurants 200 yds.
Closed	Occasionally.

Tube: Knightsbridge. Nearest car park £25 for 24 hrs (closed overnight).

Margaret & Holly Palmer
37 Trevor Square,
Knightsbridge,
London, SW7 1DY
Tel   +44 (0)20 7823 8186
Email   margaret@37trevorsquare.co.uk
Web   www.37trevorsquare.co.uk

Entry 207   Map 22

London

Chelsea Park Garden

A super-central B&B tucked behind the King's Road, just a saunter away from bustling shops and restaurants. Return to a deeply comfortable bedroom up in the eaves with rosebud papered walls, blue and white china bedside lights, plenty of hanging space and views over swaying treetops; a single room is next door and shares the bathroom. There's a guest sitting room (with honesty bar) overlooking the garden and an antique dark wood trestle table for proper breakfasts of bacon, Lincolnshire sausages and eggs how you like them. Suzie, a cook, can rustle up a light supper or a full blown dinner party. Invite friends!

Rooms	1 double with separate bathroom: £140-£170. 1 single (let to same party only): £60. Extra bed/sofabed £40 per child per night.
Meals	Dinner from £20. Restaurants 2-minute walk.
Closed	Christmas, July/August.

Children over 5 welcome.

Suzie Hyman
Chelsea Park Garden,
Chelsea,
London, SW3 6AE
Mobile +44 (0)7885 586181
Email   suziehyman@gmail.com

Entry 208   Map 22

London

15 Delaford Street

A pretty Victorian, terraced Fulham home, inside all is charming and spacious. In a tiny, sun-trapping courtyard you can have continental breakfast in good weather – tropical fruits are a favourite and the coffee is very good; a second miniature garden bursts with life at the back. The bedroom, up a wide spiral staircase, is nicely private on the second floor. Expect perfectly ironed sheets on a comfy bed, a big sofa, TV and books, a sunny bathroom and fluffy white towels. The tennis at Queen's is in June and on your doorstep. Tim and Margot – she's from Melbourne – are fun, friendly and happy to pick you up from the nearest tube.

Rooms	1 double: £100-£105. Sofabed suitable for a child available; extra room too. Singles £80-£85.
Meals	Restaurants nearby.
Closed	Occasionally.

Tube: West Brompton. Parking free eves & weekends; otherwise pay & display. 74 bus to West End nearby.

Margot & Tim Woods
15 Delaford Street,
Fulham,
London, SW6 7LT
Tel   +44 (0)20 7385 9721
Email woodsmargot@hotmail.co.uk

Entry 209   Map 22

London

29 Bronsart Road

Caroline is warm, elegant and her house is comfortable and effortlessly chic with a roof terrace for sundowners (or even a wicked ciggy…). You breakfast on fruit, croissants and cereals at a long wooden table which looks onto an outdoor space inspired by an operatic stage set with a large mirror, trellises, tubs and flowers. Your bedroom, up in the eaves, is a light and airy space with Mary Poppins views and very little traffic noise; and you have your own pretty sitting room with plenty of books. You're bang in the middle of Fulham (Boris bikes to hand) near South Ken museums, Peter Jones, the King's Road.

Rooms	1 double: £110–£130. Singles £110–£135.
Meals	Continental breakfast available. Restaurants 2-minute walk.
Closed	Rarely.

Children over 8 welcome. Parking by permit only 9am-5pm during weekdays; free on Sundays.

Caroline Docker
29 Bronsart Road,
Fulham, London, SW6 6AJ
Tel   +44 (0)20 8616 9595
Mobile   +44 (0)7767 436487
Email   dockercaroline@gmail.com
Web   www.londonfulhambnb.com

Entry 210   Map 22

London

Ara

Jenny and Henry's Belgian Spitz barge was originally used for shipping grain, but they've transformed it single-handedly into an utterly unique home. They're on hand to greet you on arrival, along with Moose, their friendly Newfoundland. There's a wonderful feeling of space, and two rooms at a time are given over to guests unless you're a group. Settle in the guest sitting room by the wood-burner, hop up a ladder into a little wheelhouse library, sunbathe on the two decks and lap up the to-ing and fro-ing of passing boats, herons and cormorants. Jenny loves to cook, so breakfast is a treat: good coffee, croissants, eggs Benedict or a full English – it's a convivial affair at a long table. You can take the river bus into central London and there are plenty of restaurants and shops close by.

Rooms	3 doubles; 1 double with separate wc: £130–£300.
Meals	Pubs/restaurants 2-minute walk.
Closed	Occasionally.

Jennifer Forrester
Ara,
Battersea,
London, SW11 3TN
Mobile   +44 (0)7921 764634
Email   jennifersforrester@gmail.com

Entry 211   Map 22

London

Battersea B&B

Come to retreat from the frenzy of city life. In the 1890 Victorian cottage all is peaceful and calm and Barbara looks after you beautifully. The dining room, with the odd oriental piece from past travels, is where you have your full English breakfast — unusual for London — and across the hall is the elegant sitting room, with gilt-framed mirrors, sumptuous curtains, and a piano which you are welcome to play. Upstairs is a bright, restful bedroom with pretty linen and a cloud of goose down. The large bathroom next door is all yours — fabulous. Nothing has been overlooked and the tiny courtyard garden is a summer oasis.

Rooms	1 double with separate bath & shower: £115. Singles £85. Stays of 2 or more nights: £110 double, £80 single.
Meals	Pubs/restaurants 200 yds.
Closed	Occasionally.

Barbara Graham
Battersea B&B,
Battersea,
London, SW8 3SL
Tel   +44 (0)20 7622 5547
Email batterseabedandbreakfast@gmail.com
Web   www.batterseabandb.co.uk

Entry 212   Map 22

London

Brixton Townhouse

You're separated from busy Brixton Hill by a large communal garden so it's tranquil here, and Anne and Ian give you a whole floor of their house along with an elegant sitting room with a wood-burner. Breakfast is in the garden room — excellent coffee, sourdough toast, homemade jams and fruit compotes. Head off to explore — you'll find lots of maps and guide books in the house or ask your hosts who are locals. The tube is a ten-minute walk, or you can hop on a bus to get there in five. In summer explore the back garden — enormous for London with secret paths, a greenhouse, herb garden, veg patch and fruit trees. Walk out to a huge choice of all kinds of food and some independent shops including Anne and Ian's 'Cornercopia' which sells useful, beautiful and curious things for the home and garden. Guests get 10% discount.

Rooms	3 doubles, sharing 2 bathrooms £90. 1 triple, sharing 2 bathrooms with doubles: £100-£110
Meals	Pubs/restaurants 5-minute walk.
Closed	Christmas.

Minimum stay: 2 nights.

Anne Fairbrother
Brixton Townhouse,
17 Raleigh Gardens,
Brixton,
London, SW2 1AD
Mobile +44 (0)7803 528739
Email   anne.fairbrother@gmail.com

Entry 213   Map 22

London

38 Killieser Avenue

On a quiet leafy street, the Haworths have brought country-house chic to South London. Philip and Winkle have filled their elegant Victorian townhouse with attractive fabrics, sunny colours and treasures from far-flung travels. The house glows, the garden is ravishing with parterre, arbour, brimming borders and secluded seats. Breakfasts are delicious and bedrooms are spacious: fine linen, lambswool throws, waffle robes, the scent of roses. Few people do things with as much natural good humour as Winkle, whose passions are cooking, gardening and garden history. Transport is close and you can be in Victoria in 15 minutes.

Rooms	1 twin: £110–£115.
	1 single with separate bath: £90–£95.
Meals	Dinner £30–£35.
Closed	Occasionally.

Minimum stay: 2 nights at weekends. Free and unrestricted parking on street outside the house.

Winkle Haworth
38 Killieser Avenue,
Streatham Hill,
London, SW2 4NT
Tel   +44 (0)20 8671 4196
Email winklehaworth@hotmail.com
Web   www.thegardenbedandbreakfast.com

Entry 214   Map 22

London

The Coach House

A rare privacy: you have your own coach house, separated from the Notts' home by a stylish terracotta-potted courtyard with Indian sandstone paving and various fruit trees (peach, pear, nectarine). Breakfast in your own sunny kitchen, or let Meena treat you to a full English in hers (she makes great porridge, too). The lovely big attic bedroom has beams, cream curtains, rugs on polished wood floors; the brick-walled ground-floor twin is pleasant and airy; both look over the peaceful garden. Urban but bucolic – just perfect as a romantic retreat, or a family getaway.

Rooms	1 twin with separate shower (same-party bookings only): £125.
	1 family room for 2-3: £190.
	£210 for the whole Coach House.
Meals	Pub/restaurant 200 yds.
Closed	Occasionally.

Minimum stay: 3 nights; 2 nights January & February. Tube: Balham Station to Leicester Square & Oxford Street or train to Victoria.

Meena & Harley Nott
The Coach House,
2 Tunley Road, Balham,
London, SW17 7QJ
Tel   +44 (0)20 8772 1939
Email coachhouse@chslondon.com
Web   www.coachhouse.chslondon.com

Entry 215   Map 22

London

108 Streathbourne Road

It's a handsome house in a conservation area that manages to be both elegant and cosy. The cream-coloured double bedroom has an armchair, a writing desk, pretty curtains and a big comfy walnut bed; the twin is light and airy. The dining room overlooks a secluded terrace and garden and there are newspapers at breakfast. You can eat in – David, who works in the wine trade, always puts a bottle on the table – or out, at one of the trendy new restaurants in Balham. A friendly city base on a quiet, tree-lined street – maximum comfort, delicious food and good value for London. Delightful.

Rooms	1 double, 1 twin: £98–£100. Singles £80–£85.
Meals	Dinner £35. Restaurants 5-minute walk.
Closed	Occasionally.

Over 12s welcome..

	Mary & David Hodges 108 Streathbourne Road, Balham, London, SW17 8QY
Tel	+44 (0)20 8767 6931
Email	davidandmaryhodges@gmail.com
Web	www.southwestlondonbandb.co.uk

Entry 216   Map 22

London

24 Fox Hill

This part of London is full of sky, trees and wildlife; Pissarro captured on canvas the view up the hill in 1870 (the painting is in the National Gallery). There's good stuff everywhere – things hang off walls and peep over the tops of dressers; bedrooms are stunning, with antiques, textiles, paintings and big, firm beds. Sue, a graduate from Chelsea Art College, employs humour and intelligence to put guests at ease and has created a special garden too. Tim often helps with breakfasts: eggs to order, good coffee. Owls hoot at night, woodpeckers wake you in the morning, in this lofty, peaceful retreat.

Rooms	1 twin/double; 1 double, 1 twin sharing shower: £90–£120. Singles £60. Extra bed £30 per person per night; sofabed £50 per night.
Meals	Dinner £35. Pubs/restaurants 5-min walk.
Closed	Rarely.

Train: Crystal Palace. Underground: East London line. Collection possible. Good buses to West End & Westminster. Victoria 20 min by train.

	Sue & Tim Haigh 24 Fox Hill, Crystal Palace, London, SE19 2XE
Tel	+44 (0)20 8768 0059
Email	suehaigh@hotmail.com
Web	www.foxhill-bandb.co.uk

Entry 217   Map 22

London

113 Pepys Road

This Victorian terraced house overlooks the first landscaped park of its kind in south-east London; the pretty garden, designed by David's father, is graced with majestic magnolias. Find a quirky mix of classic British furniture and oriental antiques. Picking up from his Chinese mother Anne, David has now taken on the B&B (helped by his housekeeper) and breakfast can be English or oriental. It's a convivial, lived-in home full of family portraits, batiks and books; the Chinese 'Peony' room downstairs has a huge bed, bamboo blinds, kimonos for the bathroom. A short walk to buses and tubes... and blissfully quiet for London.

Rooms	1 double, 1 twin/double; 1 twin with separate bath: £110. Singles £85.
Meals	Restaurant 0.5 miles.
Closed	Rarely.

David Marten
113 Pepys Road,
New Cross, London, SE14 5SE
Tel +44 (0)20 7639 1060
Email davidmarten@pepysroad.com
Web www.pepysroad.com

Entry 218   Map 22

London

16 St Alfege Passage

The peaceful approach is along the passage between Hawksmoor church and its graveyard, away from Greenwich hubbub. At the end of the lane is a 'cottage' set about with greenery, lamp posts and benches; inside, bold art and antiques – and tea with flapjack awaiting you in an eccentrically furnished (stuffed cat on dentist chair, huge parasol) sitting room. Bedrooms are cosy and colourful, with double beds (not huge) that positively encourage intimacy. Breakfast – delicious – is in the basement, another engagingly furnished room awash with character. Robert, an actor, is easy, funny, chatty – and has created an unusual, attractive place.

Rooms	1 double, 1 four-poster: £110–£150. 1 single: £90.
Meals	Pubs/restaurants 2-minute walk.
Closed	Rarely.

3-min walk from Greenwich train & Docklands Light Railway station or Cutty Sark DLR station. Parking free from 5pm (6pm Sundays) to 9am.

Nicholas Mesure & Robert Gray
16 St Alfege Passage,
Greenwich, London, SE10 9JS
Tel +44 (0)20 8853 4337
Email info@st-alfeges.co.uk
Web www.st-alfeges.co.uk

Entry 219   Map 22

Norfolk

College Farm

Katharine is a natural at making guests feel like friends. Her beautiful farmhouse tucks itself away on the edge of the village and the big friendly kitchen is filled with delicious smells of home baking. Meals are served by the large wood-burner in the grand Jacobean dining room, filled with good antiques, period furnishings and cosy places to sit; food is home-grown, seasonal and local. Sleep well in charming bedrooms with smooth linen, pretty furniture and garden views; bathrooms are small and simple. A fascinating area teeming with pingos, wildlife, old churches… and glorious antique shops.

Rooms	3 twin/doubles: £100-£125. Singles £60.
Meals	Dinner from £20. Pub 1 mile.
Closed	Christmas.

Over 12s welcome.

Katharine Wolstenholme
College Farm,
Thompson, Thetford, IP24 1QG
Tel: +44 (0)1953 483318
Email: info@collegefarmnorfolk.co.uk
Web: www.collegefarmnorfolk.co.uk

Entry 220 Map 10

Norfolk

Manor House Farm

Down country roads lined with flint walls to this beautiful old house next to the church. Step into a home full of flowers, china, antiques, wood fires and books. Bedrooms (one in the main house, two ground floor in the stables) have well-dressed beds; the stables' cosy sitting room opens to the garden. Breakfast is home-grown and delicious: fruit, eggs from the hens, bacon and sausages from their happy pigs – Libby and Robin have won conservation awards for the farm. Masses to do nearby: boat trips, nature reserves, stately homes. Return to glorious gardens with a wisteria-clad summer house; deer and rheas roam the wild corners.

Rooms	1 double: £120-£140. Old Stables: 1 double, 1 twin/double: £120-£140. Singles £70-£75.
Meals	Restaurant 1.5 miles.
Closed	Rarely.

Children over 10 welcome.

Elisabeth Ellis
Manor House Farm,
Wellingham, Fakenham,
King's Lynn, PE32 2TH
Tel: +44 (0)1328 838227
Mobile: +44 (0)7802 579663
Email: libbyelliswellingham@gmail.com
Web: www.manor-house-farm.co.uk

Entry 221 Map 10

Norfolk

Meadow House

A beautifully traditional new-build with handmade oak banisters and period furniture. Step into a large drawing room, where you find a warm, sociable atmosphere with squashy sofas and comfy chairs. Breakfast is served in here or in the conservatory. One bedroom is cosy and chintzy, the other is larger and more neutral; brand-new bathrooms gleam. Amanda looks after you well; she's lived in Norfolk most of her life and is delighted to advise. There are footpaths from the door and plenty to see, starting with Walpole's Houghton Hall, a short walk. A bucolic setting for a profoundly comfortable stay, perfect for country enthusiasts.

Rooms	2 twin/doubles: £70-£85. Singles £40-£50.
Meals	Packed lunch £5-£7. Pub 9-minute walk.
Closed	Rarely.

Amanda Case
Meadow House,
Harpley,
King's Lynn, PE31 6TU
Tel   +44 (0)1485 520240
Mobile   +44 (0)7890 037134
Email   amandacase@amandacase.plus.com
Web   www.meadowhousebandb.co.uk

Entry 222   Map 10

Norfolk

Bagthorpe Hall

Ten minutes from Burnham Market, yet here you are immersed in peaceful countryside. Tid is a pioneer of organic farming and the stunning 700 acres include a woodland snowdrop walk. Gina's passions are music, dance and gardens and she organises open days and concerts for charity. Theirs is a large, elegant house with a fascinating hall mural chronicling their family life; bedrooms – one with a tiny en suite shower room – have big comfy beds and lovely views. Breakfasts are delicious with local sausages and bacon, homemade jams and raspberries from the garden. Birdwatching, cycling and walking are all around.

Rooms	1 double; 1 twin/double with separate shower: £90. Singles £50.
Meals	Pubs/restaurants 2 miles.
Closed	Rarely.

Gina & Tid Morton
Bagthorpe Hall,
Bagthorpe, Bircham,
King's Lynn, PE31 6QY
Tel   +44 (0)1485 578528
Mobile   +44 (0)7979 746591
Email   dgmorton@hotmail.com
Web   www.bagthorpehall.co.uk

Entry 223   Map 10

Norfolk

Heacham House

Rebecca is a dab hand at soft furnishings and creating delicious things. Step in to a home full of pretty fabrics and flowers. All is homemade from the welcoming cake to the granola, potato farls and home-grown roasted tomatoes on brioche; honey, bacon and eggs are sourced from local suppliers, hand-knitted tea cosies and hand-embroidered tablecloths add a thoughtful touch. Immaculate, comfortable bedrooms have all sorts of extra goodies. It's paradise for bird-watchers, you can take a boat trip to spot seals, and it's a short walk to the beach. Norfolk Lavender is minutes away too – buy some pots to take home. Lovely!

Rooms	2 doubles; 1 twin/double with separate bathroom: £95–£105.
Meals	Pubs/restaurants 5-minute walk.
Closed	Christmas & New Year.

Minimum stay: 2 nights. Secure bike storage available.

Rebecca Bradley
Heacham House,
18 Staithe Road,
Heacham,
King's Lynn, PE31 7ED
Tel   +44 (0)1485 579529
Email info@heachamhouse.com
Web   www.heachamhouse.com

Entry 224   Map 9

Norfolk

Troon Cottage

No cottage this! Rather, a large Edwardian terraced house at the far end of town, lovingly renovated, sumptuously furnished and a ten-minute walk from glorious sands. Marian and Barry have been in the antiques business for years, serve brilliant breakfasts, offer you cream teas, and know exactly how to pamper. After a day acquainting yourselves with grand or royal houses (Holkham Hall, Royal Sandringham) and the shops and restaurants of lovely old Hunstanton, what nicer than to come home to a sofa by the wood-burner, a delicious bath scented with lavender and an irresistible king-size bed?

Rooms	2 doubles: £105–£115.
Meals	Pubs/restaurants 5-minute walk.
Closed	October – June.

Marian Sanders
Troon Cottage,
4 Victoria Avenue,
Hunstanton, PE36 6BX
Tel   +44 (0)1485 532918
Mobile +44 (0)7503 276485
Email   marianatmoreau@hotmail.com
Web   www.trooncottage.co.uk

Entry 225   Map 9

Norfolk

The Control Tower

A unique slice of history. This iconic landmark on the former RAF North Creake airfield was built in the 1940s to command 199 and 171 Squadrons. The restoration has been a labour of love and Ni and Claire's attention to detail is remarkable: modernism and Art Deco design in full flow. Be greeted with tea or locally roasted coffee in the art-filled sitting room; sink into goose down in bright bedrooms; enjoy shiny bathrooms with period fittings and lavender soaps. Vegetarian breakfasts are good! House tours include the open roof deck; you can lunch al fresco in the wild flower garden; Wells-next-the-Sea and Blakeney seal trips are close.

Rooms	3 doubles: £110-£130.
	1 suite for 2: £130.
	Extra bed/sofabed £25 per person per night.
Meals	Restaurants 3 miles.
Closed	Rarely.

Claire Nugent & Nigel Morter
The Control Tower,
Bunkers Hill,
Egmere,
Walsingham, NR22 6AZ

Tel	+44 (0)1328 821574
Email	mail@controltowerstays.com
Web	www.controltowerstays.com

Entry 226   Map 10

Norfolk

Green Farm House

This Norfolk farmhouse has been beautifully restored. Choose to stay in the 'Garden Room' wing, or upstairs in the main house – both well-dressed bedrooms have smart bathrooms. Sun streams in through the French windows of the garden room; find books, DVDs, rugs on slate floors, art, pots of flowers and a comfy sofa by the woodburner. The 'Guest Room' has field views and morning sun. Breakfast in the conservatory on local sausages, bacon and eggs, homemade marmalade and muesli – in the pretty, sheltered garden on sunny days. Friendly Lucy can arrange sailing; good for walkers, cyclists and birdwatchers too.

Rooms	1 twin/double: £100-£130.
	Garden Room: 1 double: £100-£130.
Meals	Pub within 2 miles.
Closed	Rarely.

Lucy Jupe
Green Farm House,
Balls Lane, Thursford,
Fakenham, NR21 0BX

Tel	+44 (0)1328 878507
Mobile	+44 (0)7768 542645
Email	ljupe@greenfarmbarns.co.uk
Web	www.greenfarmbarns.co.uk

Entry 227   Map 10

Norfolk

Stable Cottage

Sarah's home is set in the grounds of Heydon, one of Norfolk's finest Elizabethan houses. In the Dutch-gabled stable block, fronted by Cromwell's Oak, is her cottage – fresh, sunny and enchanting. Each room is touched by her warm personality and love of beautiful things: seagrass floors, crisp linen and pretty china; the cosy sitting room is set with tea and biscuits for your arrival. Bedrooms are cottagey and immaculate; bathrooms have baskets of treats. Sarah serves a delicious breakfast with golden eggs from her hens, homemade marmalade and garden fruit. Thursford is close and you're 20 minutes from the coast.

Rooms	2 twin/doubles: £100. Singles £70.
Meals	Pub 1 mile.
Closed	Christmas.

Minimum stay: 2 nights at weekends.

Sarah Bulwer-Long
Stable Cottage,
Heydon,
Norwich, NR11 6RE
Tel   +44 (0)1263 587343
Mobile   +44 (0)7780 998742
Email   sjblong@icloud.com
Web   www.heydon-cottages.co.uk

Entry 228   Map 10

Norfolk

Norfolk Courtyard

Walk straight in through French windows to your own, underfloor-heated room in the courtyard; independence from the main house where friendly Simon and Catherine live. The rooms are decorated in soft colours, mattresses are perfect, cotton sheets are smooth and your handsome bathroom has limestone tiles – all rather luxurious; there's a welcome tea tray and a fridge to cool a bottle too. Continental breakfast is served next door in the old, beamed barn: croissants, Aga pancakes, crumpets, homemade jams, compotes, muesli – and home-laid eggs cooked in an easy egg steamer, very popular! Stunning walks await on the coast.

Rooms	2 doubles, 1 twin/double: £105-£110. Extra bed/sofabed £20-£30 per person per night.
Meals	Continental breakfast. Pub/restaurant 0.5 miles.
Closed	Rarely.

Minimum stay: 2 nights at weekends in high season.

Simon & Catherine Davis
Norfolk Courtyard,
Westfield Farm, Foxley Road,
Foulsham, Dereham, NR20 5RH
Mobile   +44 (0)7969 611510
Email   info@norfolkcourtyard.co.uk
Web   www.norfolkcourtyard.co.uk

Entry 229   Map 10

Norfolk

The Old Rectory

Conservation farmland all around; acres of wild heathland busy with woodpeckers and owls; the coast two miles away. Relax in the big drawing room of this 17th-century rectory and friendly family home, set in mature gardens full of trees. Fiona loves to cook and bakes her bread daily; food is delicious, seasonal and locally sourced, jams are homemade. Comfortable bedrooms have *objets* from diplomatic postings and the suite comes with mahogany furniture and armchairs so you can settle in with a book. Super views, friendly dogs, tennis in the garden and masses of space. If you fancy self-catering then opt for an independent break in the Garden Room.

Rooms	1 double with kitchenette & separate bath/shower: £80–£100. 1 suite for 2: £80–£100. Singles £50.
Meals	Dinner from £25. Pubs 2 miles.
Closed	Rarely.

Peter & Fiona Black
The Old Rectory,
Ridlington, NR28 9NZ
Tel +44 (0)1692 650247
Mobile +44 (0)7774 599911
Email ridlingtonoldrectory@gmail.com
Web www.oldrectorynorthnorfolk.co.uk

Entry 230   Map 10

Norfolk

Primrose Cottage

Karen's a B&B veteran and has thought of everything: peaceful spaces for reading, sweets, fresh flowers on the table. Two bedrooms have views for miles, both with short private staircases and generous tea trays. Breakfasts are hearty: homemade jams, cereals and a full English, served in the quarry-tiled dining room. The big, comfortable sitting room is packed with books, music, games and a TV, so if it pours you can light the wood-burner and batten down the hatches for the day, grab a handful of leaflets from the porch and plan your next outing. The countryside is good for walking and cycling and the coast is close, with Walcott and Happisburgh beaches within two miles and Cromer 30 minutes' drive, or you could mess about on the Broads with boat trips and pub lunches by the water.

Rooms	1 twin/double; 1 double with separate bathroom : £95.
Meals	Pubs 1.5 miles.
Closed	Christmas.

Karen Elliott
Primrose Cottage,
Old Lane,
Walcott, NR12 0PA
Tel +44 (0)7979 982613
Email mkelliott2@aol.com
Web www.primrosecottage-norfolk.co.uk

Entry:231   Map 10

Norfolk

Sloley Hall

A grand and gracious yellow-brick Georgian house with formal gardens, tree-studded parkland and glorious views from every window. It has also been beautifully renovated, with flagstoned floors, Persian rugs, gleaming circular tables and vases of garden-grown flowers. Your hosts are delightful – Barbara and Simon were married here and are easy-going and helpful. A huge light-flooded dining room is perfect for breakfast; the drawing room is comfy and uncluttered with a marble fireplace and long views. Bedrooms are large and elegant with sumptuous bed linen; generous bathrooms glow with warmth.

Rooms	1 double with separate bath, 1 double with separate shower: £80–£90. 1 suite for 2: £90–£100. Singles from £50. Child bed available.
Meals	Pubs/restaurants 2-4 miles.
Closed	Rarely.

Minimum stay: 2 nights in high season.

Barbara Gorton
Sloley Hall,
Sloley, Norwich, NR12 8HA
Tel +44 (0)1692 538582
Mobile +44 (0)7748 152079
Email babsgorton@hotmail.com
Web www.sloleyhall.com

Entry 232   Map 10

Norfolk

Hoveton Hall

A Regency house snoozing in beautiful parkland and gardens. Formal and grand, yet comfortably friendly, Harry and Rachel's home brims with wonderful woodwork, decorated ceilings, art old and new. Their children are keen to play with visiting young ones, there's a lovely collection of hare sculptures up the stairs and the views over the 620 acres are stunning. Airy bedrooms have well-dressed beds, tea trays, biscuits and flowers. Morning sun lights up the panelled library/sitting room where you have breakfast, shelves are crammed with books and there's a large fire to sit by. Explore the estate, head off for beaches and The Broads.

Rooms	1 double: £130. 1 family room for 4: £160.
Meals	Pubs/restaurants 1 mile.
Closed	Rarely.

Minimum stay: 2 nights at weekends & in high season.

Rachel Buxton
Hoveton Hall,
Hoveton Hall Estate,
Hoveton,
Norwich, NR12 8RJ
Tel +44 (0)1603 784297
Email rachel@hovetonhallestate.co.uk
Web www.hovetonhallestate.co.uk

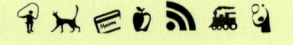

Entry 233   Map 10

Norfolk

The Buttery

Down a farm track, a treasure: your own thatch-and-flint octagonal dairy house perfectly restored by local craftsmen and as snug as can be. You get a jacuzzi bath, a little kitchen and a fridge stocked with delicious bacon and ground coffee so you can breakfast when you want; take it to the sun terrace in good weather. The sitting room is terracotta-tiled and has a music system, a warming fire and a sofabed for those who don't want to tackle the steep wooden stair to the cosy bedroom on the mezzanine. You can play a game of tennis, and walk from the door into peaceful parkland and woods. Lovely!

Rooms	1 double, with sitting room & small kitchen: £90–£110.
Meals	Pub 10-minute walk.
Closed	Rarely.

Minimum stay: 2 nights at weekends.

Deborah Meynell
The Buttery,
Berry Hall,
Honingham,
Norwich, NR9 5AX

Tel	+44 (0)1603 880541
Email	thebuttery@paston.co.uk
Web	www.thebuttery.biz

Entry 234   Map 10

Norfolk

Gothic House

Silver tea and coffee pots and Portmeirion china, pictures and prints from far-flung places, and an unexpected peace in the centre of the city – welcome to Gothic House. The building is listed and Regency and your host, enthusiastic, charming, knows the history. As for breakfast, it is fresh, lavish and locally sourced; in short, a treat. Bedrooms are stylish and spacious with a strong period feel, the double and the two bathrooms on the first floor, and the twin above. Norwich is blessed with culture, character and pubs, and a cathedral with the second tallest spire in England. Fabulous!

Rooms	1 double with separate bathroom, 1 twin with separate bathroom & wc: £105. Singles £75.
Meals	Pubs/restaurants 5-minute walk.
Closed	Rarely.

Parking space available.

Clive Harvey
Gothic House,
King's Head Yard,
42 Magdalen Street,
Norwich, NR3 1JE

Tel	+44 (0)1603 631879
Email	charvey649@aol.com
Web	www.gothic-house-norwich.com

Entry 235   Map 10

Norfolk

Washingford House

Tall octagonal chimney stacks and a Georgian façade give the house a stately air. In fact, it's the friendliest of places to stay and Paris gives you a delicious, locally sourced breakfast including plenty of fresh fruit. The house, originally Tudor, is a delightful mix of old and new. Large light-filled bedrooms have loads of good books and views over the four-acre garden, a favourite haunt for local birds. Bergh Apton is a conservation village seven miles from Norwich and you are in the heart of it; perfect for cycling, boat trips on the Norfolk Broads and the twelve Wherryman's Way circular walks.

Rooms	1 twin/double; 1 twin/double with separate bath & shower: £75-£90. 1 single with separate bath: £40-£60.
Meals	Pubs/restaurants 4-6 miles.
Closed	Christmas.

Paris & Nigel Back
Washingford House,
Cookes Road, Bergh Apton,
Norwich, NR15 1AA

Tel	+44 (0)1508 550924
Mobile	+44 (0)7900 683617
Email	parisb@waitrose.com
Web	www.washingford.com

Entry 236   Map 10

Northamptonshire

Bridge Cottage

A truly peaceful place, yet only a few miles from Peterborough. Sip a glass of wine on the decking down by the Willow Brook; beautiful countryside envelops you, cattle doze, kingfishers flash by and you may see a red kite (borrow some binoculars). Inside find pretty bedrooms with sloping ceilings, the purest cotton sheets and proper blankets; bathrooms are thickly towelled and full of lotions and bubbles. Breakfast is local, scrumptious and served in the friendliest kitchen facing that heavenly view. Walks and cycle rides start from the door; return and settle with a book in the conservatory. A hidden gem, and Judy and Rod are brilliant hosts.

Rooms	1 double, 1 twin; 1 double with separate bath: £92-£98. Singles £65-£75.
Meals	Pub/restaurant 500 yds.
Closed	Christmas.

Pets by arrangement.

Judy Young
Bridge Cottage,
Oundle Road, Woodnewton,
Peterborough, PE8 5EG

Tel	+44 (0)1780 470860
Mobile	+44 (0)7979 644864
Email	enquiries@bridgecottage.net
Web	www.bridgecottage.net

Entry 237   Map 9

Northamptonshire

The Old House

Northamptonshire is the county of spires and squires. And here, on the through-road of this fascinating medieval town, is a listed squire's house – once home to a merchant who traded in the marketplace opposite. Enter the heavy oak door and step back 400 years. William, courteous, hospitable and upgrading with aplomb, is forever tweaking the ambience. Facing the courtyard at the back (furnished for summery breakfasts and aperitifs) are the quietest rooms; all have sumptuous fabrics and wallpapers, dramatic touches and divine beds. Delightfully quirky, spanking new bathrooms with power showers are as special as all the rest.

Rooms	4 doubles, 1 twin/double: £85. Singles £65.
Meals	Pubs/restaurants 150 yds.
Closed	Rarely.

William Evans
The Old House,
5 Market Square,
Higham Ferrers,
Rushden, NN10 8BP

Tel   +44 (0)1933 314006
Email   theoldhousehighamferrers@gmail.com
Web   www.theoldhousehighamferrers.co.uk

Entry 238   Map 9

Northamptonshire

Colledges House

Huge attention to comfort here, and a house full of laughter. Liz clearly derives pleasure from sharing her 300-year-old stone thatched cottage, immaculate garden, conservatory and converted barn with guests. Sumptuous bedrooms have deep mattresses with fine linen, sparkling bathrooms are a good size. The house is full of interesting things: a Jacobean trunk, a Bechstein piano, mirrors and pictures, pretty china, bright fabrics, a beautiful bureau. Cordon Bleu dinners are elegant affairs – and great fun. Stroll around the conservation village of Staverton – delightful.

Rooms	1 double with separate bath: £99. Cottage: 1 double, 1 twin: £99. 1 single: £70. Stays of 3 nights or more: £95 for 2 per night.
Meals	Dinner, 3 courses, £35. Pub 4-minute walk.
Closed	Rarely.

Babes in arms & children over 8 welcome.

Liz Jarrett
Colledges House,
Oakham Lane, Staverton,
Daventry, NN11 6JQ

Tel   +44 (0)1327 702737
Mobile   +44 (0)7710 794112
Email   liz@colledgeshouse.co.uk
Web   www.colledgeshouse.co.uk

Entry 239   Map 8

Northamptonshire

The Vyne

Weighed down by wisteria, this 16th-century cottage rests in a honey-hued conservation village on the cusp of Oxfordshire. Beams and wonky lines abound; rooms are filled with good antiques and eclectic art. The twin overlooking the garden is enchanting, tucked under the rafters, its beds decorated in willow-pattern chintz, its walls glinting with gilded frames; the double has a Georgian four-poster and a sampler-decorated bathroom that's a quick flit next door. Warm and charming, Imogen not only works in publishing but is a contented gardener and Cordon Bleu cook – enjoy supper in her sunny secluded garden.

Rooms	1 twin; 1 four-poster with separate bath: £90-£100. Singles £55-£65.
Meals	Supper £20. Dinner £30. BYO. Pub 2-minute walk.
Closed	Rarely.

Babies welcome.

	Imogen Butler The Vyne, High Street, Eydon, Daventry, NN11 3PP
Tel	+44 (0)1327 264886
Mobile	+44 (0)7974 801475
Email	imogenbutler@outlook.com

Entry 240   Map 8

Northumberland

Post Office House

Claire and ex-chef Simon have converted the old Belford post office with flair. The red pillar box is still in use, jaunty stamp fabrics and post box blinds give you colourful reminders, and the wood-burning stove in the dining room keeps it all cosy. Bedrooms have robes, comfy chairs, brimming trays and espresso machines; morning sun in one, evening rays in the other. Breakfast at one convivial table is a local and home-baked spread: Bamburgh bacon and sausages, Craster kippers, homemade baked beans and marmalade. Pretty garden and heaps to do nearby: unspoilt Northumbrian beaches, Farne Islands, castles, brilliant walks.

Rooms	2 doubles, 1 twin: £89-£99. Singles £79-£89.
Meals	Packed lunch £6. Pub within 5-minute walk & pubs/restaurants 5 miles.
Closed	Christmas.

Minimum stay: 2 nights at weekends and in high season. Over 15s welcome. On-site parking.

	Claire Jarmain Post Office House, 2 Church Street, Belford, NE70 7LS
Tel	+44 (0)1668 219622
Email	enquiries@postofficehouse.com
Web	www.postofficehouse.com

Entry 241   Map 16

Northumberland

Bilton Barns

A solidly good farmhouse B&B whose lifeblood is still farming. The Jacksons know every inch of the surrounding countryside and coast; it's a pretty spot. They farm the 400 acres of mixed arable land that sweeps down to the sea yet always have time for guests. Dorothy creates an easy and sociable atmosphere with welcoming pots of tea and convivial breakfasts – all delicious and locally sourced. Comfortable, smartly done bedrooms have a traditional feel, bathrooms have underfloor heating, the huge conservatory is filled with sofas and chairs and there's an elegant guest sitting room with an open fire and views to the sea.

Rooms	1 double, 1 twin, 1 four-poster: £84–£95. Singles £47.50–£75.
Meals	Packed lunch £4–£6. Pub/restaurant 2 miles.
Closed	Christmas.

Brian & Dorothy Jackson
Bilton Barns,
Alnmouth, Alnwick, NE66 2TB
Tel   +44 (0)1665 830427
Mobile +44 (0)7939 262028
Email dorothy@biltonbarns.com
Web   www.biltonbarns.com

Entry 242   Map 16

Northumberland

Thistleyhaugh

Enid is one of those very special people who lifts your heart with her generosity of spirit, warmth and humour. Her passions are pictures, people and cooking, so you will be fed exceptionally well – breakfasts are delicious and include local farm eggs. Choose any of the four large, lovely bedrooms and stay the week; they are awash with old paintings, silk fabrics and crisp linen. Wake refreshed and nip downstairs, past the log fire, to a laden and sociable table, head off afterwards to find 720 acres of organic farmland and a few million more of the Cheviots beyond. Wonderful hosts, a glorious region, a happy house.

Rooms	3 doubles, 1 twin: £100. Singles from £70. Extra bed/sofabed available £15 per person per night.
Meals	Pub/restaurant 2 miles.
Closed	Christmas, New Year & January.

Henry & Enid Nelless
Thistleyhaugh,
Longhorsley,
Morpeth, NE65 8RG
Tel   +44 (0)1665 570098
Email thistleyhaugh@hotmail.com
Web   www.thistleyhaugh.co.uk

Entry 243   Map 16

Northumberland

Swinburne Castle

Sweep through parkland to find a manor house on an estate with a real sense of history. Parts date back to the 12th century, and your traditionally furnished suite is in an original wing that's over 300 years old. Zoe will warmly greet you on arrival and show you around, but you'll be given a key to come and go as you please. You take breakfast in the formal dining room of the main house – local produce and home-laid eggs – and you're welcome to make use of the garden and tennis court. Walking routes pass by the house and the area is great for cycling. Good pubs and restaurants nearby include the Barrasford Arms, a half hour walk away. It's an easy drive to Hadrian's Wall, as well as the Northumberland National Park, Kielder Water and Forest Park.

Rooms	1 double, 1 twin sharing bathroom: £85.
Meals	Pubs/restaurants 3 miles.
Closed	Christmas & New Year.

Zoe Murphy
Swinburne Castle,
Swinburne,
Hexham, NE48 4DQ
Mobile +44 (0)7786 610542
Email ztrg24@yahoo.co.uk

Entry 244   Map 16

Northumberland

The Hermitage

A magical setting, three miles from Hadrian's Wall, in a house of friendship and comfort. Through ancient woodland, up the drive, over the burn and there it is: big, beautiful and Georgian. Interiors are comfortable country-house, full of warmth and charm; bedrooms, carpeted, spacious and delightful, are furnished with antiques, paintings and superb beds; bathrooms have roll top baths. Outside are lovely lawns, a walled garden, wildlife, and breakfasts on the terrace in summer. Katie – who was born in this house – looks after you brilliantly.

Rooms	1 double, 1 twin; 1 double with separate bath: £85–£90. Singles from £55.
Meals	Pub 2 miles.
Closed	Rarely.

Babes in arms & children over 7 welcome.

Simon & Katie Stewart
The Hermitage,
Swinburne, Hexham, NE48 4DG
Tel +44 (0)1434 681248
Mobile +44 (0)7708 016297
Email katie.stewart@themeet.co.uk

Entry 245   Map 16

Northumberland

Errington House

Carolyn is a superb cook: breakfast on homemade bread, jams and marmalade, eggs from their hens, local sausages and bacon. You eat around the big dining table with other guests. The Dowies' handsome farmhouse and gardens are deeply peaceful and you can make yourself completely at home. Watch birds from a comfortable chair outside, sit and read in your airy bedroom or take a cup of tea to the guest sitting room and throw another log on the fire. You can walk from the house (or drive ten minutes) to Hadrian's Wall. Corbridge and Hexham have plenty of interest for an afternoon out and hum with shops, cafés and restaurants. Bring a group of friends for a walking holiday if you stay between June and October – Lex is hugely knowledgeable about the county.

Rooms	3 twin/doubles: £100–£110. 1 twin/double with separate bathroom: £85–£95. Singles £75–£110.
Meals	Pubs/restaurants 5 miles.
Closed	Christmas & New Year.

Minimum stay: 2 nights at weekends.

Carolyn Dowie
Errington House,
Humshaugh, NE46 4HP
Tel   +44 (0)1434 672389
Email carolyn@erringtonwalks.co.uk
Web   erringtonwalks.co.uk

Entry 246   Map 16

Northumberland

Matfen High House

Bring your boots – and jumpers! You are 25 miles from the border and the walking is a joy. Struan and Jenny are good company, love sporting pursuits and will advise on where to eat locally (and drive you there if needed). The sturdy stone house of 1735 is a lived-in, happily shabby-chic kind of place: the bedrooms have fine fabrics and pictures, bathrooms are well-kept and the drawing room has books and choice pieces. Enjoy local bacon and sausages at breakfast, with Struan's marmalade and bread warm from the oven. The countryside is stunning, Hadrian's Wall and the great castles (Alnwick, Bamburgh) beckon.

Rooms	1 double, 2 twins; 1 double, 1 twin sharing bath: £60–£80. Singles £45.
Meals	Packed lunch £4.50. Restaurant 2 miles.
Closed	Rarely.

Struan & Jenny Wilson
Matfen High House,
Matfen,
Corbridge, NE20 0RG
Tel   +44 (0)1661 886592
Email struan@struan.enterprise-plc.com

Entry 247   Map 12

Northumberland

3 Ada Crescent

Rosemary's end-terrace, Victorian house is in a quiet cul-de-sac, and the serenity of Hexham Abbey is just across the park. Calm and welcoming, it's filled with antiques, books, colourful rugs and paintings. The bedroom is fresh with country colours, handsome family pieces, flowers and books; the airy bathroom has big blue towels and good soaps. Breakfast, including homemade bread and muesli, is super-flexible; relax with newspapers and coffee in the snug, pretty sitting room or in the little south-facing courtyard. Rosemary, warm and cultured, and Garlic the terrier, greet you with homemade cake and encourage you to feel at home.

Rooms	1 twin/double with separate bathroom: £90. Singles £55. Extra room available.
Meals	Pubs/restaurants 10-minute walk.
Closed	Rarely.

Children over 10 welcome.

	Rosemary Stobart 3 Ada Crescent, Hexham, NE46 3DR
Tel	+44 (0)1434 694242
Mobile	+44 (0)7850 375535
Email	rosemary.stobart@btinternet.com

Entry 248   Map 12

Northumberland

Emley Farm

You will be happy here, deep in the rural bliss of Northumberland with its bleating sheep and spectacular views. The Smarts look after you beautifully in their elegant Georgian farmhouse surrounded by a charming garden and on the edge of the village. You have your own comfortable sitting room with open fire, and delicious meals are taken in the handsome dining room; do stay in for dinner – local lobster, fish or game perhaps? Margaret is an accomplished cook. Sleep soundly in your view-filled bedroom under a proper eiderdown and savour the total peace. Hadrian's Wall is near, and the Lakes close enough for a bracing day out.

Rooms	1 suite for 2 with separate bath: £95–£100.
Meals	Dinner on request. Pubs less than a mile away.
Closed	Rarely.

	Margaret Smart Emley Farm, Whitfield, Hexham, NE47 8HB
Tel	+44 (0)1434 345776
Email	margiecook2001@yahoo.co.uk

Entry 249   Map 12

Nottinghamshire

Willoughby House

A tall village house with an air of smart comfort. Step in to a warming log fire, antiques, quirky collections, art and lively colours. Bedrooms have tea, coffee and homemade flapjacks, fine linen and comfy sofas; Harry's and Bobby's are in the main house, Arthur's Stable and Top Barn are over the cobbles in Granary Annexe. Suzannah runs the family fruit farm and turns the produce into jams and juices; she and Marcus make scrumptious breakfasts. Norwell is on the edge of the Dukeries; head out for Sherwood Forest and the famous Major Oak, Lincoln and its cathedral, historic Newark and Southwell. Walk to the village pub for supper.

Rooms	1 twin/double; 1 double with separate bathroom: £120–£130. 1 family room for 4: £250. Annexe: 1 twin/double: £120–£130; 1 suite for 3: £180. Singles £80–£90. Extra beds £60. Dogs £20.
Meals	Pub 3-minute walk.
Closed	Rarely.

Suzannah & Marcus Edwards-Jones
Willoughby House,
Main Street, Norwell,
Newark, NG23 6JN

Tel	+44 (0)1636 636266
Mobile	+44 (0)7780 996981
Email	willoughbyhousebandb@gmail.com
Web	www.willoughbyhousebandb.co.uk

Entry 250   Map 9

Nottinghamshire

Manor Farm House

A 17th-century house with colourful English Civil War connections. There are outdoor activities galore, Nottingham is just 25 minutes and you can walk to a fine pub for dinner. The atmosphere here is of a calm retreat. You can book a holistic massage with Paul or a coaching session with Harriet and her horses. They offer guided walks around the farm and woodlands, and you're welcome to wander in the orchard and large garden. Their home is full of original art and handmade textiles and furniture; bedrooms have dreamily comfortable cashmere mattresses and fabrics from Harriet's travels to India. Breakfasts are inventive and delicious with locally sourced produce, vegan and vegetarian options and perhaps a Middle Eastern slant.

Rooms	1 double, 1 twin/double; 1 double with separate bathroom: £85–£120. Extra bed/sofabed £15 per night.
Meals	Pubs 3-minute walk.
Closed	Rarely.

Minimum stay: 2 nights in high season.

Harriet Hanmer
Manor Farm House,
Bakers Lane,
Colston Bassett, NG12 3FG

Tel	+44 (0)1949 81935
Email	hello@manor-farmhouse.com
Web	www.manor-farmhouse.com

Entry 251   Map 9

Oxfordshire

Fyfield Manor

A fabulous house in Oxfordshire (once owned by the de Montfort family) with water gardens providing a most romantic setting. The Browns have added solar panels, and charming bedrooms in your own part of the house have views, slippers and comfy sofas. From the grand wood-panelled hall enter a beamed dining room with high-backed chairs, brass rubbings, wood-burner and pretty 12th-century arch; breakfast is largely locally sourced with organic bacon and eggs and garden fruit. Oxford Park & Ride is nearby, there's walking from the door and delightful Christine has wangled you a free glass of wine in the local pub if you walk to get there! Superb.

Rooms	1 twin/double: £85–£95. 1 family room for 4 with sofabed & separate bath: £85–£95. Singles £70–£80. £20–£25 extra per person.
Meals	Pubs within 1 mile.
Closed	Rarely.

Children over 10 welcome.

Christine Brown
Fyfield Manor,
Benson,
Wallingford, OX10 6HA
Tel +44 (0)1491 835184
Email chris_fyfield@hotmail.co.uk
Web www.fyfieldmanor.co.uk

Entry 252   Map 8

Oxfordshire

Oxford University

Oxford at your fingertips – at a fair price. In the city's ancient heart are Wadham and Keble; in leafy North Oxford is friendly St Hugh's. Keble's sleeping quarters, functional though a good size, stand in stark contrast to the neo-gothic grandeur of its dining hall – pure Hogwarts! Wadham's hall, 17th century, soaring, is yet more glorious – with top breakfasts. Its student-simple bedrooms are reached via crenellated cloisters and lovely walled gardens; ask for a room facing the beautiful quad. At St Hugh's: three residences (one historic), a student café, 14 acres of romantic gardens and a 15-minute walk into town.

Rooms	52 doubles, 121 twins: £69–£120. 12 family rooms for 3-4: £100–£165. 1052 singles: £35–£93.
Meals	Breakfast included. Keble: occasional supper £22.50. Restaurants 2-15 minutes' walk.
Closed	Mid-Jan to mid-Mar, May/June, Oct/Nov; Christmas. A few rooms available throughout year.

38 colleges in total.

University Rooms
Oxford University,
Oxford
Web www.universityrooms.com/en-GB/city/oxford/home

Entry 253   Map 8

Oxfordshire

Rectory Farm

This big country house has a wonderfully settled, tranquil feel – the family have farmed here for three generations. Find large, light bedrooms, floral and pretty, with bold chintz bed covers, draped dressing tables, thick mattresses and tea trays with delicious chocolate shortbread; all have garden views. Sink into comfortable sofas flanking a huge fireplace in the drawing room, breakfast on local bacon and sausage with free-range eggs, stroll the lovely garden, or grab a rod and try your luck on one of the trout lakes. Elizabeth knows her patch well, walkers can borrow maps and lively market town Chipping Norton is close.

Rooms	1 double, 1 twin/double; 1 twin/double with separate bath: £100-£120. Singles £85-£95.
Meals	Pub/restaurant 1.5 miles.
Closed	December/January.

Elizabeth Colston
Rectory Farm,
Salford, Chipping Norton, OX7 5YY
Tel   +44 (0)1608 643209
Mobile   +44 (0)7866 834208
Email   enquiries@rectoryfarm.info
Web   www.rectoryfarm.info

Entry 254   Map 8

Oxfordshire

The Glove House

Handmade chocolates from Turin (Francesco is Italian) and espresso machines in the bedrooms show proper respect for the important things in life. This handsome Georgian house in the heart of Woodstock combines calm contemporary comfort with warm smiles. The sitting room is panelled in golden oak; the suites, overlooking rooftops at the back, are discreet and delicious. Upholstered headboards, best feather duvets, Cotswolds wool throws, books, magazines and small buttoned armchairs… Enjoy a chilled prosecco by the garden's fountain before venturing out for supper; this lovely old town is awash with treats.

Rooms	1 double: £170-£180. 2 suites for 3: £200-£275. Singles £155-£205.
Meals	Pubs/restaurants nearby.
Closed	Rarely.

Ask about parking. Children over 10 welcome.

Francesco & Caroline Totta
The Glove House,
24 Oxford Street,
Woodstock, OX20 1TS
Tel   +44 (0)1993 813475
Email   info@theglovehouse.co.uk
Web   www.theglovehouse.co.uk

Entry 255   Map 8

Oxfordshire

Green Close

This trim idyllic village abuts Blenheim Park and the parish church is famous for its medieval wall paintings. The Freelands' old stone house sits on the edge of one of the greens. The feel inside is harmonious and airy: high rafters, polished wood, a hall dining room with light streaming through mullioned windows, a winter fire in the lived-in sitting room, simple spotless bedrooms. Your hosts are easy-going, the retriever is smiley and children are welcome. An Aga breakfast will include compote, yogurt, eggs from the hens, homemade bread and good coffee. Woodstock and Oxford are a hop, and you can walk to supper at the pub.

Rooms	2 double; 1 twin with separate bath: £95. Singles £55.
Meals	Pubs/restaurants 75 yds.
Closed	Rarely.

Pets by arrangement.

Caroline Freeland
Green Close,
West End, Combe,
Witney, OX29 8NS

Tel	+44 (0)1993 891223
Email	julian.freeland@btinternet.com
Web	www.greenclose.net

Entry 256   Map 8

Oxfordshire

Star Cottage

Classic Cotswolds – from the cottagey stone walls to the flower-bright garden – and swathes of open countryside for cyclists and walkers. Step inside to hand-sewn fabrics, cute lampshades, country furniture, fresh flowers and calm, pretty bedrooms: Sally delights in details. She and Peter, a plant biologist, love their winding stone-walled garden with its herbs, climbers and medlar tree; its jelly appears at breakfast, alongside smoked haddock and local sausages. The pub (yards away) offers dinner, Burford market town is a ten-minute walk, Cheltenham and Oxford a half-hour drive. Or kind Peter will fetch from the station.

Rooms	1 double: £110–£140. 1 family room for 3: £125–£140. Barn – 1 family room for 3, with kitchen: £125–£140. Singles £70–£80.
Meals	Pubs/restaurants within walking distance.
Closed	Rarely.

Peter & Sally Wyatt
Star Cottage,
Meadow Lane, Fulbrook,
Burford, OX18 4BW

Tel	+44 (0)1993 822032
Email	wyattpeter@btconnect.com
Web	www.burfordbedandbreakfast.co.uk

Entry 257   Map 8

Oxfordshire

The Summerhouse

Jacobean Shipton Court has been carefully preserved by the Arathoon family – flats created, outbuildings restored, gardens kept. You stay in Martin and Pauls's Summerhouse – splendid with antiques and china galore. Bedrooms (one ground floor) have well-dressed beds and immaculate shower rooms; step through a 'Narnia' door (cleverly reclaimed old linen press) into the huge second double. Martin rustles up a generous breakfast and the view from your table is a treat: a 300-foot pond with ducks darting between the lilies. Blenheim and Oxford both an easy drive; drinks by the fire in the richly furnished drawing room on your return.

Rooms	2 doubles: £130-£170. Extra double available. Exclusive use for 3 rooms: £400. Short breaks available, £390-£420 midweek. 6-night stay: £740-£810.
Meals	Pubs 5-minute walk.
Closed	Rarely.

Martin Thomas-Jeffreys
The Summerhouse,
High Street, Shipton-under-Wychwood,
Chipping Norton, OX7 6DG
Mobile +44 (0)7796 615931
Email   martinbandb@hotmail.com
Web   www.shsuw.com

Entry 258 Map 8

Oxfordshire

Corner House at Churchill

Peter and Caroline, London escapees keen on the fine detail, have turned this handsome listed house into an immaculate home. All is beamed and inviting with warm colours, smart furniture, limestone floors, white linen on the refectory table; carbon-neutral too. Bedrooms are in a separate wing and named after local villages; find a headboard clad in tweed, Welsh rugs, plump pillows on comfy beds. Peter cooks you a generous classic breakfast along with compotes, yogurt, smoked salmon, pancakes with fruit. The Cotswolds is foodie heaven; there are literary and music festivals to attend, National Trust gems to visit. It's a treat to stay.

Rooms	2 doubles, 1 twin/double: £90-£120. Singles £90-£105.
Meals	Breakfast served until 10am. Pubs 2-minute walk.
Closed	Rarely.

Minimum stay: 2 nights at weekends.

Caroline & Peter Dunnicliffe
Corner House at Churchill,
Church Road, Churchill,
Chipping Norton, OX7 6NJ
Tel   +44 (0)1608 658432
Email cornerhousepeter@icloud.com
Web   www.cornerhousechurchill.co.uk

Entry 259 Map 8

Oxfordshire

Rectory Farm

Come for the happy relaxed vibe, and Mary Anne's welcome with tea and homemade shortbread. There's a wood-burner in the guest sitting room, and bedrooms have beautiful arched mullion windows. The huge twin with ornate plasterwork overlooks the garden and church, the pretty double is cosier and both have good showers and big fluffy towels. Wake for an excellent Aga breakfast with eggs from the hens, garden and hedgerow compotes, home or locally produced bacon and homemade jams. A herd of Red Ruby Devon cattle are Robert's pride and joy; the family have farmed for generations and you can buy the beef.

Rooms	1 double, 1 twin: £90-£95. Singles £70.
Meals	Pub 2-minute walk.
Closed	Christmas & New Year.

Minimum stay: 2 nights at weekends.

Mary Anne Florey
Rectory Farm,
Northmoor, Witney, OX29 5SX
Tel   +44 (0)1865 300207
Mobile +44 (0)7974 102198
Email   enquiries@visitrectoryfarm.co.uk
Web   www.visitrectoryfarm.co.uk

Entry 260   Map 8

Oxfordshire

Castle Farmhouse

You'll eat well – this is B&B with an award-winning pop-up restaurant! Sparkling Tanya cooks like a dream – try venison loin with pommes Anna and port jus, broccoli and carrots, raspberry meringue pies for pudding. Drinks and canapés are served first, petit fours and coffee afterwards. If you can manage the stairs after all that there are super-comfy beds upstairs with smart white cotton and fat pillows, toe-tickling carpets, linen-covered armchairs and books. Spotless shower rooms have Neal's Yard stuff and thick towels. Breakfast is lavish too, and you're close to Blenheim. Great for sociable foodies who like exploring.

Rooms	2 doubles: £110-£125. Singles £110.
Meals	Home restaurant Knife & Fork, 5 courses, £45 (some Fri & Sat evenings, please enquire). Restaurants 5-minute walk.
Closed	Rarely.

Minimum stay: 2 nights.

Tanya Young
Castle Farmhouse,
Clifton Road, Deddington,
Banbury, Oxford, OX15 0TP
Tel   +44 (0)1869 336954
Email tanya@knifeandfork.pro
Web   www.knifeandforkeatery.co.uk

Entry 261   Map 8

Oxfordshire

Heyford House

Old church and handsome house face each other down a village lane – and then the road runs out. In this timeless Oxfordshire valley, the white gate leads into gardens where pathways weave between borders to a kitchen garden and orchards. The house, warm-hearted and well-proportioned, has been in the family for years; your hosts (he a personal trainer, she a chef) live in one wing. Find contemporary art, bright old rugs and open fires – a happy mix of traditional and new. Bedrooms are handsome and comfortable, with excellent bath and shower rooms; Sonja's breakfasts, served by the Aga, are a treat.

Rooms	2 doubles, 2 twin/doubles: £110–£120. Extra bed/sofabed £30 per person per night.
Meals	Dinner, 2 courses from £20; 3 courses from £27; available for larger parties. Picnic from £10. Enquire for further catering. Pubs/restaurants 4 miles.
Closed	Rarely.

Leo Brooke-Little
Heyford House,
Church Lane, Lower Heyford,
Bicester, OX25 5NZ
Tel +44 (01869 349061
Email info@stayatheyfordhouse.co.uk
Web www.heyfordhouse.org

Entry 262   Map 8

Oxfordshire

Uplands House

Come to be spoiled at this handsome house, built in 1875 for the Earl of Jersey's farm manager. All is elegant and lavishly furnished; expect large light bedrooms, crisp linen, thick towels and vases of flowers. There are long views from the orangery; relax here with a book as the scents of the pretty garden waft by, or have tea and cake in the drawing room. Poppy will make a delicious dinner – a convivial occasion enjoyed with your hosts. Breakfast is Graham's domain – try smoked salmon with scrambled eggs and red caviar. You're well placed for exploring – Moreton-in-Marsh and Stratford are close, Oxford just under an hour.

Rooms	1 double, 1 twin/double, 1 four-poster: £110–£180. Singles £85–£110; 2-night stay Monday to Thursday.
Meals	Dinner, 2-4 courses, £20–£35. Pub 1.25 miles.
Closed	Rarely.

Poppy Cooksey & Graham Paul
Uplands House,
Upton, Banbury, OX15 6HJ
Tel +44 (0)1295 678663
Mobile +44 (0)7836 535538
Email poppy@cotswolds-uplands.co.uk
Web www.cotswolds-uplands.co.uk

Entry 263   Map 8

Rutland

Old Hall Coach House

A rare and special setting; the grounds of the house meet the edge of Rutland Water, with far-reaching lake and church views. There's a terrace with table and chairs, a stunning garden and a croquet lawn. Inside: high ceilings, stone archways, antiques, a log fire to sit by. Comfortable and traditional bedrooms have smart, handsome bathrooms; the twin has glorious views from both windows. Wake for an Aga-cooked spread of home-laid eggs, sausages and homemade marmalade. Rutland is a mini-Cotswolds of stone villages and gentle hills; Georgian Stamford, Burghley House and Belvoir Castle are all near. Cecilie is a well-travelled, interesting host.

Rooms	1 double, 1 twin with separate bath: £95. Singles from £45.
Meals	Dinner £30. Pub/restaurant 5-minute walk.
Closed	Occasionally.

Minimum stay: 2 nights at weekends. Children over 6 welcome.

Cecilie Ingoldby
Old Hall Coach House,
31 Weston Road, Edith Weston,
Oakham, LE15 8HQ

Tel	+44 (0)1780 721504
Mobile	+44 (0)7767 678267
Email	cecilieingoldby@aol.com
Web	www.oldhallcoachhouse.co.uk

Entry 264   Map 9

Rutland

Old Rectory

Jane Austen fans will swoon. This elegant 1740s village house was used as Mr Collins's 'humble abode' by the BBC: you breakfast in the beautiful dining room that was 'Mr Collins's hall', and you can sleep in 'Miss Bennett's bedroom'. Victoria is wonderful – feisty, fun and gregarious – and looks after you beautifully with White Company linen in chintzy old-fashioned bedrooms, a log fire in the drawing room, fruit from the lovely garden, homemade jams and Aga-cooked local bacon and eggs. Guests love it here. You are near to some pleasant market towns and good walking and riding country. Don't forget the smelling salts!

Rooms	1 double, 1 twin: £90. Singles £50.
Meals	Pubs within 3 miles.
Closed	Rarely.

Pets by arrangement.

Victoria Owen
Old Rectory,
Teigh, Oakham, LE15 7RT

Tel	+44 (0)1572 787681
Mobile	+44 (0)7484 600721
Email	torowen@btinternet.com
Web	www.teighbedandbreakfast.co.uk

Entry 265   Map 9

Shropshire

The Isle

History buffs and nature lovers rejoice. You drive through lion-topped stone pillars to a house built in 1682 (then extended) that stands in 800 acres enfolded by the river Severn. Charming Ros and Edward are down-to-earth and hands-on: eggs, bacon, ham, vegetables, and logs, come from the estate. Flop in front of a huge fire in the drawing room, homely with family antiques, big rug, magazines strewn on large tables. Peaceful bedrooms are large and light with pocket-sprung memory mattresses and snazzy upmarket bathrooms. Walk, fish, ride (there's a livery stable on site) and lap up the views – they're sublime.

Rooms	3 doubles, 1 twin: £80–£100. 1 family room for 4: £90–£145. Singles £50–£70.
Meals	Packed lunch £5. Dinner £15–£20. Pub/restaurant 4.3 miles.
Closed	Rarely.

Ros & Edward Tate
The Isle,
Bicton,
Shrewsbury, SY3 8EE
Mobile +44 (0)7776 257286
Email   ros@isleestate.co.uk
Web   www.the-isle-estate.co.uk

Entry 266   Map 7

Shropshire

Hardwick House

On a quiet street in the heart of Shrewsbury, this fine Georgian house has been in Lucy's family for generations. The dining room (oak panelling, a huge fireplace) is a lovely space to breakfast on locally sourced produce and homemade bread; vases of garden flowers are dotted all around this cheerful family home. Bedrooms are traditional and comfortable with pretty china tea cup and old-fashioned bathrooms. The walled garden is fabulous; take tea in an 18th-century summerhouse. Birthplace of Darwin, this is a fascinating historic town; walk to the abbey, castle, theatre, festivals and great shops. Lucy is delightful.

Rooms	2 twin/doubles (one with adjoining room can form large suite): £90–£100. Singles £65–£75.
Meals	Pubs/restaurants 150 yds.
Closed	Christmas & New Year.

Luggage can be stored after check out on request.

Lucy Whitaker
Hardwick House,
12 St John's Hill,
Shrewsbury, SY1 1JJ
Tel   +44 (0)1743 350165
Email   gilesandlucy@btinternet.com
Web   www.hardwickhouseshrewsbury.co.uk

Entry 267   Map 7

Shropshire

Brimford House

Beautifully tucked under Breidden Hill, farm and Georgian farmhouse have been in the Dawson family for four generations. Views stretch all the way to the Severn; the simple garden does not try to compete. Spotless bedrooms have flowers, and pretty china for morning tea; there's a half-tester with rope-twist columns, a twin with Victorian wrought-iron bedsteads, a double with a brass bed, a big bathroom with a roll top bath. Liz serves you farm eggs and homemade preserves at breakfast, and there's a pub just down the road for dinner. Sheep and cattle outdoors, a lovely black lab in, and wildlife walks from the door. Good value.

Rooms	2 doubles, 1 twin: £80-£90. Singles £50-£60. Extra bed/sofabed £20 per person per night.
Meals	Packed lunch £4.50. Pub 3-minute walk.
Closed	Rarely.

Pets by arrangement.

Liz Dawson
Brimford House,
Criggion, Shrewsbury, SY5 9AU
Tel   +44 (0)1938 570235
Mobile   +44 (0)7801 100848
Email   info@brimford.co.uk
Web   www.brimford.co.uk

Entry 268   Map 7

Shropshire

Whitton Hall

Down a long private drive with fields on either side is a lovely 18th-century farmhouse, elegant but not intimidating, with a sense of timelessness. A large open hallway and a cosy sitting room where tea and a drinks tray are provided are peaceful spaces for relaxing with a book. You breakfast in the dining room, on local muesli, bread, marmalades and jams, milk from their Jersey cows, soft fruit from their garden, sausages and bacon from down the road. Peaceful, light and large bedrooms in an adjacent wing have modern bathrooms, country house furniture and long views to glorious gardens. Unwind in the peace.

Rooms	1 double with separate bath, 1 twin/double with separate shower: £100-£110. 1 family room for 4 with separate bath: £110-£140. Singles £70.
Meals	Supper in dining room £25; 4+ guests. Cold supper tray in room or garden, £10-£15. Pub 10-min drive.
Closed	Christmas, New Year & Easter.

Children over 10 welcome. Self-catering available.

Christopher & Gill Halliday
& Kate Boscawen
Whitton Hall,
Westbury, Shrewsbury, SY5 9RD
Tel   +44 (0)1743 884270
Mobile   +44 (0)7974 689629
Email   kate@whittonhall.com
Web   www.whittonhall.co.uk

Entry 269   Map 7

Shropshire

North Farm

Peaceful green Shropshire and a stunning garden surround this classic white farmhouse. Chickens, ducks and geese are happily dotted about and the veg patch blooms. Tess and family look after you well. Bedrooms have flowery fabrics, tip-top linen, Lloyd Loom chairs and pretty tea trays. Wake for a delicious breakfast served on Portmeirion china: homemade marmalade, compotes, eggs from the hens, bacon and sausages from home-reared pigs. Lots to do close by: historic Shrewsbury, Ironbridge, Ludlow, Powis Castle – and the walks are a treat. Settle by the log-burner on your return: books to browse, a glass of wine... lovely.

Rooms	1 double, 1 twin; 1 double with separate bath: from £95. Singles £60-£65. Extra bed/sofabed from £95 per person per night.
Meals	Pubs/restaurants 4-minute drive.
Closed	Rarely.

Tess Bromley
North Farm,
Eaton Mascot, Cross Houses,
Shrewsbury, SY5 6HF
Tel   +44 (0)1743 761031
Mobile   +44 (0)7956 817705
Email   tessbromley@ymail.com
Web   www.northfarm.co.uk

Entry 270   Map 7

Shropshire

5 Wilmore Street

Clare delights in making her home glow. Passionate about interior décor, she's designed an immaculate house crammed with creative touches and Georgian elegance; inviting sitting and breakfast rooms have comfy sofas, a wood-burner and refectory tables. An experienced cook too, so expect good breakfasts and dinners: homemade treats, eggs from a friend's hens, fish from the market. Soak in a slipper bath; sleep in a charming bedroom – both have armchairs, hand-painted antiques and pictures; church bells keep time. The historic town is rich in timbered buildings, monastic ruins, arty festivals and award-winning independent shops.

Rooms	2 doubles: £110. Singles £85.
Meals	Lunch & dinner by arrangement. Pubs/restaurants 5-minute walk.
Closed	Rarely.

Richard & Clare Wozniak
5 Wilmore Street,
Much Wenlock, TF13 6HR
Tel   +44 (0)1952 727268
Mobile   +44 (0)7530 779568
Email   5wilmorestreet@gmail.com
Web   www.5wilmorestreet.co.uk

Entry 271   Map 7

Shropshire

Davenport House

The mile-long drive follows an escarpment, falling away beneath you with big rural views, to reach this impressive Georgian house. Well-kept lawns, water lily pond, fields of grazing cattle, ancient trees stretching into the distance... Lizzie and Joe have bags of energy and have refurbished until all is gleaming. Find a pretty sitting room with open fire and doors out to the garden; an elegant dining room where generous continental breakfasts are served; and a grand staircase leading to four luxurious bedrooms with tip-top bathrooms. Bridgnorth is an intriguing town, AONB Shropshire Hills are on the doorstep. Special wedding venue too.

Rooms	3 doubles: £140.
	1 suite for 2: £175-£250.
Meals	Continental breakfast.
	Pub/restaurant 20-minute walk.
Closed	Christmas & New Year.

Joseph Adams
Davenport House,
Worfield, Bridgnorth, WV15 5LE
Tel   +44 (0)1746 716021
Mobile +44 (0)7586 325551
Email twentyfivegroup@gmail.com
Web   www.davenporthouse.co.uk

Entry 272   Map 8

Shropshire

The Old Rectory

With its own spring water, horses, dogs and slow pace this Georgian rectory is comfortable country living at its best. Izzy and Andy are charming and interesting and give you scones and tea by the fire in a drawing room full of family photos, plump sofas and books. Elegant bedrooms have fluffy hot water bottles; smart bathrooms have scented lotions in pretty bottles, robes and slippers. Candlelit dinner will often be fish or game with garden vegetables; breakfast is local and leisurely with homemade granola and jams. There's a bootroom for muddy feet and paws, stabling and seven acres to roam.

Rooms	1 double, 1 twin/double; 1 double with separate bathroom: £85-£125. Singles £70-£110.
Meals	Dinner, 3 courses with coffee, drinks & canapés, £35. Supper tray (soup & sandwich) £10. Pubs 1.25-4 miles.
Closed	Rarely.

Pets welcome, sleeping in bootroom.

Isabel Barnard
The Old Rectory,
Wheathill, Ludlow, Bridgnorth,
WV16 6QT
Tel   +44 (0)1746 787209
Email enquiries@theoldrectorywheathill.com
Web   www.theoldrectorywheathill.com

Entry 273   Map 7

Shropshire

Timberstone Bed & Breakfast

The house is young and engaging – as are Tracey and Alex, new generation B&Bers. Come for charming bedrooms – two snug under the eaves, two in the smart oak-floored extension – roll top baths, pretty fabrics, thick white cotton, beams galore... and reflexology or a sauna in the garden studios. Tracey, once in catering, is a reflexologist. In the warm guest sitting/dining room find art, books, comfortable sofas and glass doors onto the terrace. Breakfasts are special with croissants and local eggs and bacon; dinners are delicious too, or you can head off to Ludlow and its clutch of Michelin stars.

Rooms	2 doubles; 1 double, with sofabed: £70–£110. 1 family room for 4: £110–£120. Summerhouse – 1 double (Summer only): £70–£110. Singles £75–£98.
Meals	Dinner, 3 courses, £25. Pubs/restaurants 5 miles.
Closed	Rarely.

Pets by arrangement.

Tracey Baylis & Alex Read
Timberstone Bed & Breakfast,
Clee Stanton, Ludlow, SY8 3EL

Tel	+44 (0)1584 823519
Mobile	+44 (0)7905 967263
Email	timberstone1@hotmail.com
Web	www.timberstoneludlow.co.uk

Entry 274   Map 7

Shropshire

Cleeton Court

Rare peace: a tiny lane leads to this part 14th-century farmhouse, immersed in the countryside with views over meadows and heathland. You have your own entrance, and the use of the pretty drawing room, elegantly comfortable with sofas and a log fire. Beamed bedrooms are delightfully furnished, one with a magnificent, chintzy four-poster and a vast bathroom; recline in the cast-iron bath with a glass of wine, gaze on views from the window as you soak. Bring your boots: the walking is superb, and charming Ros gives you a smashing, locally sourced breakfast to get you going.

Rooms	1 twin/double, 1 four-poster: £90–£100. 3 nights or more: 10% discount. Singles £70.
Meals	Pubs/restaurants 1.5-4 miles.
Closed	Christmas & New Year.

Rosamond Woodward
Cleeton Court,
Cleeton St Mary, Ludlow, DY14 0QZ

Tel	+44 (0)1584 823379
Mobile	+44 (0)7778 903136
Email	roswoodward1@gmail.com
Web	www.cleetoncourt.co.uk

Entry 275   Map 7

Shropshire

35 Lower Broad Street

You're almost at the bottom of the town, near the river and the bridge. Elaine's terraced Georgian cottage is spotless and cosy; her office doubles as a sitting area for guests with leather armchairs, TV and a desk space for workaholics. Upstairs are two good-sized doubles with a country crisp feel, king-size beds and a pretty blue and white bathroom. Walkers, shoppers, antique- and book-hunters can fill up on a superb breakfast of homemade potato scones, black pudding, organic eggs and good coffee before striding out to explore. This is excellent value, comfortable B&B and can be enjoyed without a car.

Rooms	1 double with sitting room & separate bathroom; 1 double sharing bathroom (let to same party only): £75. Singles £60.
Meals	Pubs/restaurants 100 yds.
Closed	Rarely.

Elaine Downs
35 Lower Broad Street,
Ludlow, SY8 1PH
Tel +44 (0)1584 876912
Mobile +44 (0)7970 151010
Email sande.downs@gmail.com

Entry 276   Map 7

Shropshire

Walford Court

Come for a break from clock-watching and a spot of Shropshire air. Large bedrooms delight with the comfiest mattresses on king-size beds, scented candles, antiques, books, games and double-end roll top baths – one under a west facing window. Debbie and Craig's Aga-cooked breakfasts have won awards and include eggs from 'the ladies of the orchard'. Wander through the apple, plum and pear trees, find a motte and bailey, strike out for a long, leafy hike. Craig and Debbie are thoughtful and hugely keen on wildlife (you get binoculars) and this is the perfect place to bring a special person – and a bottle of champagne.

Rooms	1 double; 2 doubles each with sitting room: £95-£105. Extra bed/sofabed £30 per person per night.
Meals	Room platter of local pâté, cheeses, ham & homemade pickles & chutney. Packed lunch. Pubs/restaurants 1-3 miles.
Closed	Christmas & Boxing Day.

Minimum stay: 2 nights.

Debbie & Craig Fraser
Walford Court,
Walford, Leintwardine,
Ludlow, SY7 0JT
Tel +44 (0)1547 540570
Email info@romanticbreak.com
Web www.romanticbreak.com

Entry 277   Map 7

Shropshire

Hopton House

Karen looks after you very well – she's such an expert on B&B she runs courses on how to do it. And how to do it beautifully: unwind in this fresh converted granary with old beams, high ceilings and a sun-filled dining/sitting room overlooking the hills. You sleep over in the barn: choose between two bedrooms – one up, one down – each with its own entrance. Find beautifully dressed beds, silent fridges, good lighting, homemade cakes. Bathrooms have deep baths (and showers) – from one you can lie back and gaze at the stars. Karen's breakfasts promise Ludlow sausages, home-laid eggs, fine jams and homemade marmalade.

Rooms	Barn – 2 doubles: £125-£135. Check owner's website for availability calendar & booking engine.
Meals	Restaurant 3 miles.
Closed	19-27 December.

Minimum stay: 2 nights. Over 16s welcome.

Karen Thorne
Hopton House,
Hopton Heath,
Craven Arms, SY7 0QD
Tel   +44 (0)1547 530885
Email   info@shropshirebreakfast.co.uk
Web   www.shropshirebreakfast.co.uk

Entry 278   Map 7

Somerset

Taggart House

Past the church, up through the pretty village, to Andrew and Rachel's relaxed eco-friendly house. Through your own doorway, find a smart bedroom with tip-top linen, TV, a basket of books, French windows onto patios – perfect for an evening glass of wine – and a sleek bathroom with thick white towels. Wake for bacon and sausages from the Potting Shed Farm Shop, eggy bread, local jams. Walton Brook runs through the garden, a visiting pair of ducks can be spotted on the pond, and you can walk through ancient woodland to join the coastal path to Clevedon. Close to Portishead and only 25 minutes from Bristol. A leafy retreat.

Rooms	1 double, 1 twin/double: £99-£110.
Meals	Pubs/restaurants within 2 miles.
Closed	Rarely.

Andrew & Rachel Francis
Taggart House,
Walton Street, Walton-in-Gordano,
Clevedon, BS21 7AP
Tel   +44 (0)1275 316970
Email   rachel@taggarthouse.co.uk
Web   www.taggarthouse.co.uk

Entry 279   Map 3

Somerset

Stonebridge

A country house with scrumptious food, charming hosts and croquet on the lawn. Liz and Richard give you scones and tea, and your own independent wing of their listed house. You have two pretty bedrooms (one up, one down) with country furniture and super bathrooms. In winter, a wood-burner keeps your little sitting room cosy; in summer, laze in a sea of flowers. You feast on local eggs and homemade bread and jams for breakfast; Liz cooks memorable dinners too with home-grown veg. Just off the village road, it's close to Bristol airport, Wells – and the M5, so the perfect pit-stop if you're on your way to Devon or Cornwall.

Rooms	1 double, 1 twin/double: £90–£100. Singles £70–£80.
Meals	Dinner, 2 courses, £28; 3 courses, £33. Pub 2 miles.
Closed	Rarely.

Children over 2 welcome.

Richard & Liz Annesley
Stonebridge,
Wolvershill Road,
Banwell, BS29 6DR
Tel   +44 (0)1934 822549
Email liz.annesley@talktalk.net
Web   www.stonebridgebandb.co.uk

Entry 280   Map 3

Somerset

Burrington Farm

High in the Mendips, Ros and Barry's 15th-century longhouse is blissfully rural, yet Bristol, Bath and Wells are close. Their wonderful house glows: rugs and flagstones, books, burnished beams, paintings and fine old furniture. Guests have a cosy sitting room and bedrooms are charming; you'll need to be nimble to negotiate ancient steps and stairs. For those who prefer a bit more privacy there's a lovely family room in a separate green oak barn – stunningly converted and with views over the enchanting garden. Wake for a locally sourced breakfast round a big table. A friendly, relaxed and special place.

Rooms	1 double; 1 double, 1 twin, sharing bath (let to same party only): £85–£120. Barn – 1 family room for 4: £100–£120. Singles £65.
Meals	Pub 10-minute walk.
Closed	Christmas.

Barry & Ros Smith
Burrington Farm,
Frys Lane, Burrington, BS40 7AD
Tel   +44 (0)1761 462127
Mobile +44 (0)7825 237144
Email bookings@burringtonfarm.co.uk
Web   unwindatburringtonfarm.co.uk

Entry 281   Map 3

Somerset

Coombe Lodge Farm House

Charming Jenny and her energetic Jack Russell Titch welcome you with tea and homemade cake. You'll be looked after well in this big, comfortable Victorian house with its huge open fire, antiques in every room, ancestral oil paintings and contemporary art. Inviting bedrooms overlook the gardens; breakfast is at one convivial table and is as locally sourced and organic as possible. If it's sunny you can find your own spot to sit among mature trees, plants and shrubs with views to Blagdon Lake – tawny owls, woodpeckers and birds of prey can often be seen. Bristol and Bath are close, you can walk into the hills or down to the lake. Treat yourself to dinner at The Ethicurean in Wrington, The Seymour Arms in Blagdon or the Michelin-starred Pony & Trap near Chew Magna.

Rooms	2 doubles; 1 twin with separate bathroom: £95–£120.
Meals	Pubs/restaurants 10-minute walk.
Closed	Rarely.

Pets by arrangement.

	Jenny Marks
	Coombe Lodge Farm House,
	Bourne Lane,
	Blagdon, BS40 7RF
Tel	+44 (0)1761 462793
Email	jennifer.marks10@me.com

Entry 282   Map 3

Somerset

The Old Vicarage

The vicarage sits at the foot of Jack and Jill's hill in a sleepy Mendip village. Both bedrooms have goose down comfort: one has an antique French bed and limestone wet room; the sunny blue room upstairs has a freestanding roll top. Your hosts are informal and friendly and their home exudes charm: a medieval stone floor in the hall, old flagstones, carpets designed by Lizzy, flowers, wood-burners and a pretty kitchen. Hens potter, carp laze in the canal pond; breakfast when you want on a full English, garden compotes and delicious coffee. National Trust gems and splendid walking on the Colliers Way will keep you busy.

Rooms	1 double with sitting room; 1 four-poster with separate wc: £100–£110.
Meals	Pub 100 yds.
Closed	Rarely.

Minimum stay: 2 nights.

	Elizabeth Ashard
	The Old Vicarage,
	Church Street, Kilmersdon,
	Radstock, BA3 5TA
Tel	+44 (0)1761 436926
Email	lizzyashard@gmail.com
Web	www.theoldvicaragesomerset.com

Entry 283   Map 3

Somerset

The Ammerdown Centre

If you want to write undisturbed, enrol on one of the courses or escape and meditate, this is just the ticket. It's incredibly peaceful. Helpful, friendly staff welcome you at reception; functional communal spaces include a bar, TV lounge and library. Simple en suite bedrooms are clean as a whistle; the trio of rooms across the courtyard are bigger. Breakfast is continental, lunches are generous, suppers light. You can enjoy the beautiful gardens, swim in the pool in summer, ponder in the all faiths chapel, read by pots of geraniums, walk in woodland. It's not luxurious or typically homely but we admire the ethos of this place.

Rooms	8 doubles, 16 twins & 3 twins (limited mobility): £94.
	1 family room for 4: £188.
	16 singles (most en suite): £47.
Meals	Lunch £14. Dinner £14.
	Pubs/restaurants 5 miles.
Closed	27 December – 1 January.

Lucy Jefferyes
The Ammerdown Centre,
Ammerdown Park,
Radstock, BA3 5SW
Tel +44 (0)1761 433709
Email bookings@ammerdown.org
Web www.ammerdown.org

Entry 284   Map 3

Somerset

Park Farm House

Sink into deep well-being here at Katherine's beautiful old Bath stone house with mullion windows. There are bracing walks from the door, a swimming pool and tennis court to make use of, Frome is close for a bit of culture or shopping and there are good pubs and restaurants nearby. Come back to a drawing room with an open fire for chilly evenings and plenty of books and games, bedrooms with squishy pillows and bright white linen, warm bathrooms, soft towels. Breakfast on homemade granola, bacon and sausages from down the road; there are fresh flowers from the garden on the table and always plenty of Italian coffee.

Rooms	1 double; 1 double with separate bathroom: £95-£115.
Meals	Pubs/restaurants 1 mile.
Closed	Christmas, New Year & Easter.

Over 12s welcome.

Katherine Dabell
Park Farm House,
Lullington, Frome, BA11 2PF
Tel +44 (0)1373 831402
Mobile +44 (0)7775 520032
Email k@dabell.net
Web www.parkfarm-house.co.uk

Entry 285   Map 3

Somerset

Swallow Barn

Views sweep over hills from this eco-friendly barn conversion – join the Macmillan Way from the garden. You have your own entrance to a wing of Penny and Paul's home; each warm bedroom has its own sunny spot outside too. Find tip-top linen on big luxurious beds, espresso machines, Roberts radios and homemade shortbread, Smart TVs (with Sky) and comfy seating; swish wet rooms have huge shower heads and Somerset Lavender soaps. Penny brings a delicious continental breakfast to your room – you can take it out to the stunning wild flower meadow in summer. Bath, Frome and Wells are all a hop away: arty haunts, markets and theatre beckon.

Rooms	2 doubles: £115-£125.
Meals	Pub 5-minute walk.
Closed	Rarely.

Minimum stay: 2 nights.

Penny Reynolds
Swallow Barn,
The Cross, Buckland Dinham,
Frome, BA11 2QS
Mobile +44 (0)7967 003261/(0)7790 586085
Email   paulpennyreynolds@hotmail.com
Web   www.swallowbarnfrome.com

Entry 286   Map 3

Somerset

Old Reading Room

Mells is a treasure with its medieval centre and liberal sprinkling of charming cottages; you'll find Vicky and John's attractive house down a track in the quiet wooded valley. It's a home with a friendly feel: books, art, pots of flowers, intriguing finds from family travels, comfy sofas around the wood-burner. Beds are wrapped in fine cotton and colourful quilts; sweet bathrooms have scented candles. Come down for breakfast in the kitchen – homemade bread, eggs from happy hens – delivered by a friend on a pony! Sunny cottage garden, walks from the door, a five-minute drive to Babington House… and entertaining hosts.

Rooms	2 doubles: £95.
Meals	Pubs/restaurants 5-minute walk.
Closed	Rarely.

Vicky & John Macdonald
Old Reading Room,
Mells,
Frome, BA11 3QA
Tel   +44 (0)1373 813487
Email johnmacdonaldm@gmail.com

Entry 287   Map 3

Somerset

Penny's Mill

The old part of Nunney village, with its small pretty streets, has a shop, a café and Rosie's gorgeous old stone millhouse down in the river valley. You are greeted warmly with tea and biscuits at a large wooden table in the kitchen, or in the drawing room upstairs with family photos, paintings and a big window looking over the millpond. Sunny bedrooms painted in gentle blues and greens have a mix of antique and modern furniture; bathrooms have Molton Brown soaps and white fluffy towels. Rosie's fine breakfasts set you up for a stroll in the woodland, a short walk to Nunney Castle, or a yomp further afield.

Rooms	1 double; 1 twin/double with living room: £95. 1 family room for 4 with living room: £165.
Meals	Pub 300 yds.
Closed	Christmas, New Year.

Minimum stay: 2 nights at weekends & in high season.

Rosie Davies
Penny's Mill,
Horn Street, Nunney,
Frome, BA11 4NP

Tel	+44 (0)1373 836210
Email	stay@pennysmill.com
Web	www.stayatpennysmill.com

Entry 288   Map 3

Somerset

Broadgrove House

Head down the long, private lane and arrive at Sarah's peaceful 17th-century stone house with its pretty walled cottage garden and views to Alfred's Tower and Longleat. Inside is just as special. Beams, flagstones and inglenook fireplaces have been sensitively restored; rugs, pictures, comfy sofas and polished antiques add warmth and serenity. The twin, at the end of the house, has a little shower room and its own sitting room. Breakfast on homemade and farmers' market produce before exploring Stourhead, Wells, Glastonbury. Sarah, engaging, well-travelled and a great cook, looks after you warmly.

Rooms	1 double with separate bath; 1 twin with sitting room: £90-£100. Singles £70-£75.
Meals	Pub/restaurant 1 mile.
Closed	Christmas.

Children by arrangement. Minimum stay: 2 nights at weekends in summer. Dogs welcome in twin room (own door into garden).

Sarah Voller
Broadgrove House,
Leighton,
Frome, BA11 4PP

Tel	+44 (0)1373 836296
Mobile	+44 (0)7775 918388
Email	broadgrove836@tiscali.co.uk
Web	www.broadgrovehouse.co.uk

Entry 289   Map 3

Somerset

Hillview Cottage

Catherine is a wonderful host: warm-spirited, cultured and humorous. She knows the area well, and is happy to show you around Wells Cathedral – she's an official guide. This is a comfy tea-and-cakes family home with rugs on wooden floors and antique quilts. Bedrooms have a French feel, the bathroom an armchair for chatting and there's a friendly sitting room with an open fire. The stunning vaulted breakfast room has huge beams, an old Welsh dresser with hand painted mugs, a cheerful red Aga, a wood-burner to sit by and glorious views; breakfasts are superb. Guests love it here; excellent value too.

Rooms	1 twin/double, 1 twin, sharing bath (let to same party only): £80–£90. Singles £50–£55.
Meals	Pubs 5-minute walk.
Closed	Rarely.

Michael & Catherine Hay
Hillview Cottage,
Paradise Lane,
Croscombe, Wells, BA5 3RN
Tel   +44 (0)1749 343526
Mobile   +44 (0)7801 666146
Email   cathyhay@yahoo.co.uk
Web   www.hillviewcottage.me.uk

Entry 290   Map 3

Somerset

Middle Farm Cottage

David's grandmother bought these two cottages in the 50s. He (ex-TV) and Julie (a professional singer) have hurled themselves into village life, spruced up the whole place and thrown open their door to guests. You'll be well looked after: breakfast at a pretty walnut table on homemade bread, jams and marmalade, a full Welsh of local bacon, sausages and eggs, good strong coffee. They sometimes do kitchen supper, or it's a short walk to a good pub in the next village. Bedrooms are traditional, peaceful and comfortable – the garden room has its own little outdoor space. Walk to Wells across the fields, get the bus back!

Rooms	1 twin/double; 2 doubles sharing bathroom (let to same party only): £85. Singles £50.
Meals	Family supper £17. Pubs/restaurants 12-minute walk.
Closed	31 March – 2 April.

Well-behaved dogs welcome in the Garden Room.

David & Julie Costley-White
Middle Farm Cottage,
Riverside,
Dinder,
Wells, BA5 3PL
Tel   +44 (0)1749 672120
Email david@costley-white.com

Entry 291   Map 3

Somerset

Coach House

Take a glass of wine to your private courtyard and absorb the peace; or picnic in the gardens. In the hamlet of Dulcote, a mile from Wells, is your own two-storey, two-bedroom coach house flooded with light, full of character and the latest mod cons. Downstairs, a black and white zebra theme; upstairs, white walls, crisp linen, high beams, a glimpse of Wells Cathedral and views that reach to the Mendips. Friendly Chumba the dog greets you and your (well-behaved) waggy friend. Karen leaves eggs from her hens and other goodies in your fridge so you can breakfast in your jim-jams. A delightful B&B for nature lovers and dog-walkers.

Rooms	Annexe – 1 double, 1 twin/double, sharing sitting/dining room, sofabeds & kitchen (let to same party only): £100–£110. Singles £90.
Meals	Pubs within 2 miles.
Closed	Rarely.

Minimum stay: 2 nights. Over 12s welcome. Pets by arrangement.

Karen Smallwood
Coach House,
Little Fountains,
Dulcote, Wells, BA5 3NU
Tel   +44 (0)1749 678777
Mobile   +44 (0)7789 778880
Email   stay@littlefountains.co.uk
Web   www.littlefountains.co.uk

Entry 292   Map 3

Somerset

Mount Pleasant Farm

This whitewashed cottage is full of surprises. Daisy has restored it using reclaimed everything – the quirkier the better: painted or gold-leafed pieces, polished boards, beautiful bedheads and Indian banister, clever clothes hooks... Bedrooms, all differently styled, have well-dressed beds and fantastic bathrooms. The breakfast room has separate tables that can be put together for friends, a snug sofa by the wood-burner, artworks – and pottery for sale; it opens to a sunny terrace. Daisy loves to cook: homemade granola, bread, jams, local bacon, eggs from her parents' smallholding, cakes. Cheddar and Glastonbury are 20 minutes.

Rooms	4 doubles: £95–£115.
Meals	Pubs/restaurants 4-minute walk.
Closed	Christmas, New Year.

Daisy Nicolaou
Mount Pleasant Farm,
Chapel Allerton,
Axbridge, BS26 2PP
Tel   +44 (0)1934 710285
Email   mountpleasantfarmsomerset@gmail.com
Web   www.mountpleasantbnb.com

Entry 293   Map 3

Somerset

Upper Crannel Farm Barn

Your views, across sheep and the lush Somerset Levels, reach to both Glastonbury and Wells; birds wing across a vast, silent sky. Phoebe has created a magical place: up you climb to the first floor of the barn, into a huge sitting room with a vast medieval painted fireplace. Each room is a work of art, with stacks of it on the walls – the kitchen is handsome and has all you need, bedrooms are generous and richly clad (there are extra rooms available too). Breakfast will be left for you to cook when you want, you can walk across fields to climb Glastonbury Tor, and Wells is just five miles. This house is a treat, and Phoebe is too.

Rooms	2 doubles with sitting room & kitchen (let to same party only): £150. Singles £90. Second bedroom, same party, £80.
Meals	Pubs/restaurants 2.5 miles.
Closed	Rarely.

Minimum stay: 2 nights.

Phoebe Judah
Upper Crannel Farm Barn,
Glastonbury, BA6 9AD
Tel   +44 (0)1458 831758
Email   phoebeannejudah@gmail.com

Entry 294   Map 3

Somerset

Keepers Cottage

Restored stable, hayloft and cottage… take your pick from imaginatively restored spaces. Oak-beamed bedrooms have well-dressed beds, sofas, reclamation finds, books and biscuits; 'Hayloft' has a wood-burner; 'Paddock' and 'Orchard' can interconnect for a family. Amble over to the friendly kitchen in the main house for breakfast: homemade granola, organic porridge, all sorts of cooked choices – pop your menu-sheet in the 'bread bin' by the back door in the evening; Emma will bring over a continental breakfast to your room if preferred. Sunny sitting spots in the garden, a scramble up Glastonbury Tor, a stroll to a good supper at the pub…

Rooms	3 doubles: £105-£125. Singles £90-£100. Extra bed/sofabed £30 per person per night.
Meals	Pop-up restaurant, 5 courses, £37 (usually 3rd Sat in month). Pubs/restaurants 10-minute walk.
Closed	Christmas.

Children over 10 welcome.

Emma Taylor
Keepers Cottage,
Wood Lane, Butleigh,
Glastonbury, BA6 8TR
Tel   +44 (0)1458 851103
Email   info@keeperssomerset.com
Web   www.keeperssomerset.com

Entry 295   Map 3

Somerset

High House Bruton

A home full of antiques, lovely old wooden floors, colourful rugs, log fires and good art. An easy place to stay and Olivia, ex-London chef, gives you comfortable, peaceful bedrooms with robes, flowers, homemade biscuits and elderflower cordial; bathrooms with big drench showers are a treat too. Guests love the breakfasts! It's served in the big, airy sitting/dining room by the window. Olivia bakes her own bread and drop scones and changes the cooked choice each day. A great base for exploring arty Bruton, visiting the schools (there are three), walking, cycling; Glastonbury, Wells and heaps of National Trust houses are nearby.

Rooms	1 double, 1 twin/double: £80. Extra bed/sofabed £15 per person per night.
Meals	Pubs/restaurants 2-minute walk.
Closed	Rarely.

Minimum stay: 2 nights in high season. Parking on High Street: 2 hours (8am-6pm). Free car park within walking distance.

	Olivia Stewart-Cox High House Bruton, 73 High Street, Bruton, BA10 0AL
Tel	+44 (0)1749 813015
Mobile	+44 (0)7590 817644
Email	olivia@highhousebruton.com
Web	www.highhousebruton.co.uk

Entry 296   Map 3

Somerset

Ansford Park Cottage

An old farmworker's house, modernised and freshly spruced, stands proud in verdant countryside. Long views from the clipped garden drift into the distance; warm Sue (plus cute Jack Russells) greets you. You sleep in the extension to the front of the house; one bedroom has valley views, the other has views over the Mendips. Both have comfy beds, books, homely touches and peacefulness. Breakfast is a leisurely affair of local bacon and eggs. Tramp off on an inspiring walk – Leland trail, Macmillan Way – you're spoilt for choice. Escape London by train (95 minutes) – collection from the station can be arranged.

Rooms	1 twin/double; 1 twin/double with separate bath: £70-£85. Singles £70.
Meals	Dinner £25. Packed lunch £5. Pub/restaurant 1 mile.
Closed	Christmas & rarely.

	Susan Begg Ansford Park Cottage, Ansford Park, Maggs Lane, Castle Cary, BA7 7JJ
Tel	+44 (0)1963 351066
Email	nigelbegg@lineone.net
Web	www.ansfordparkcottage.co.uk

Entry 297   Map 3

Somerset

Yarlington House

A mellow Georgian manor surrounded by impressive parkland, romantic rose gardens, apple tree pergola and laburnum walk. Your hosts are friendly and flexible artists with an eye for quirky detail; Carolyn's embroideries are everywhere, and there's something to astound at every turn: fine copies of 18th-century wallpapers, elegant antiques, statues with hats atop and tremendous art. Traditional bedrooms with glorious garden views and proper 50s bathrooms have a faded charm. Enjoy a full English breakfast, grape juice from the glasshouse vines, log fires and lovely local walks. Surprising, unique.

Rooms	1 double; 2 doubles each with separate bath: £150.
	1 family room for 4 with separate bath: £150-£210. Singles £75.
Meals	Pubs/restaurants within 0.5 miles.
Closed	25 July – 23 August.

Heated swimming pool in the summer.

Carolyn & Charles de Salis
Yarlington House,
Yarlington,
Wincanton, BA9 8DY
Tel +44 (0)1963 440344
Email carolyn.desalis@yarlingtonhouse.com
Web www.yarlingtonhouse.com

Entry 298   Map 3

Somerset

Studio Farrows

Artsy folk will love it here and those wanting to unleash their creativity can take a course, from drawing and painting to book binding and glass blowing. Or, you can simply relax in this quirky, peaceful studio hidden in the garden of artists Paul and Tracey. They give you a big space with giant wood-burner, books, and eclectic art and furniture (including an Anglia!); bedrooms are colourful, bathrooms sleek. Continental breakfasts are gorgeous, with home-grown fruit and artisan bread. Sit out on the veranda, light the fire baskets, gaze at the stars… Bliss. You can even arrange to swim in a nearby private pool set in a walled garden.

Rooms	2 doubles with sitting room & kitchen: £130. Singles £65.
Meals	Continental breakfast. Pub 3 miles.
Closed	Rarely.

Pets by arrangement.

Tracey Baker
Studio Farrows,
Aller,
Langport, TA10 0QW
Tel +44 (0)1458 252599
Email tracey@studiofarrows.com
Web www.studiofarrows.com

Entry 299   Map 3

Somerset

Blackmore Farm

Come for atmosphere and architecture: the Grade I-listed manor-farmhouse is remarkable. Medieval stone, soaring beams, four-posters, ecclesiastical windows, giant logs blazing in the Great Hall. Ann and Ian look after guests and busy dairy farm with equal enthusiasm. Furnishings are rich, bedrooms are large and the oak-panelled suite (with secret stairway) takes up an entire floor. The stable rooms are simpler. Aga breakfasts with local sausages and jams are eaten at the long polished table in the Hall. Don't miss the excellent farm shop – there's a café too with cakes, drinks and produce from the area.

Rooms	2 four-posters: £120-£130.
	1 suite for 2 (sitting room & bathroom up steep stairs): £120-£130.
	Cider Press – 1 double, 1 twin: £120-£130. Singles £75-£85.
Meals	Occasional dinner from £27 (large parties only).
	Pubs/restaurants 5-minute walk.
Closed	Rarely.

Ann Dyer
Blackmore Farm,
Cannington,
Bridgwater, TA5 2NE
Tel   +44 (0)1278 653442
Email dyerfarm@aol.com
Web   www.blackmorefarm.co.uk

Entry 300   Map 2

Somerset

Westleigh Farm

The farmhouse is in its own peaceful valley. Step inside to find an eclectic collection of vintage finds; a snooker room; a guest sitting room with sofas by the wood-burner and board games; bedrooms with big comfy beds, colourful linen and flowers. You eat in the cosy red dining hall at a long candlelit table: perfect poached eggs from the hens, homemade granola, fresh fruit for breakfast, perhaps homemade pâté and local lamb for dinner. Kerstin grows lavender in the fields and you can buy her deliciously scented soaps and creams too. Space for bikes, walks into the Quantocks from the door, and the coast is just 30 minutes away.

Rooms	2 doubles: £110. Singles £75.
Meals	Dinner, 2-3 courses, £25-£30.
	Packed lunch £10. Pub 3 miles.
Closed	Rarely.

Kerstin Sharpe
Westleigh Farm,
Broomfield,
Bridgwater, TA5 2EH
Tel   +44 (0)1823 240041
Email bookings@westleighfarm.com
Web   www.westleighfarm.com

Entry 301   Map 2

Somerset

Witheridge Farm

Head down the lane to this Exmoor farmhouse snoozing in the Exe valley. It's a home with a heart – Jackie and Michael have created a friendly, relaxed vibe and are past masters at restoring houses. Find window seats in every room, pots of flowers, beautiful fabrics and art. The sitting room is snug with comfy chairs by the wood-burner; bedrooms and bathrooms are inviting: good white linen, big towels, robes and views over the garden and hills. Tuck into an Aga breakfast round the polished table in the beamed dining room, simple suppers too. Characterful ponies add to the happy feel, there's a suntrap terrace and you can walk from the door onto Exmoor.

Rooms	1 twin/double; 1 double, 1 twin sharing bathroom (let to same party only): £60–£90. Singles £80.
Meals	Supper £20. Pubs/restaurants 1.5 miles.
Closed	Rarely.

Pets by arrangement.

Michael & Jackie Archer
Witheridge Farm,
Winsford, Dulverton, TA22 9JY
Tel +44 (0)1643 851895
Mobile +44 (0)7779 749668
Email jacksarcher@hotmail.co.uk
Web www.witheridgefarmexmoorbandb.co.uk

Entry 302   Map 2

Somerset

Bashfords Farmhouse

A feeling of warmth and happiness pervades this exquisite 17th-century farmhouse in the Quantock Hills. The Ritchies love doing B&B – even after over 20 years! – and interiors have a homely feel with well-framed prints, natural fabrics, comfortable sofas, and a sitting room with inglenook, sofas and books. Bedrooms are pretty, fresh and large and look over the cobbled courtyard or open fields. Charles and Jane couldn't be nicer, know about local walks (the Macmillan Way runs by) and love to cook: local meat and game, tarte tatin, homemade bread and jams. A delightful garden rambles up the hill; the pub is just a minute away.

Rooms	1 twin/double; 1 double with separate shower; 1 twin/double with separate bath: £90. Singles £55.
Meals	Dinner £27.50. Supper £22.50. Pub 75 yds.
Closed	Rarely.

Charles & Jane Ritchie
Bashfords Farmhouse,
West Bagborough,
Taunton, TA4 3EF
Tel +44 (0)1823 432015
Email info@bashfordsfarmhouse.co.uk
Web www.bashfordsfarmhouse.co.uk

Entry 303   Map 2

Somerset

Maunsel House

There's so much to blurt out it's tricky to start. Let's begin with eccentric owner Ben, Seventh Baronet, who has restored the family pile and is (incidentally) looking for the perfect provider of an heir. Beware, you must jump through hoops! The house is packed with history, furniture, guns, swords, stuffed animals, hats, surprises, nudes in the loos, books, board games and roaring fires. It's completely bonkers and huge fun and you must immediately get together a group and flock here for winter shenanigans. Couples alone will probably end up in one of the annexe rooms – perfectly comfortable, but not as mind-boggling.

Rooms	13 doubles, 4 twin/doubles, 2 twins: £120-£400.
Meals	Pubs/restaurants 5 miles. Dinners for groups available on request.
Closed	Rarely.

Open for B&B October to April. April to October – try your luck!

Ben Slade
Maunsel House,
North Newton,
Taunton, TA7 0BU
Tel   +44 (0)1278 661076
Email   info@maunselhouse.co.uk
Web   maunselhouse.co.uk

Entry 304   Map 2

Somerset

Brook Farm

The front door is open for your arrival… Step into the rich red hallway of this traditional Georgian-fronted farmhouse, and find cosy corners for reading, period prints, polished wood, and open fires in the winter. Maria gives you breakfast in a sunny dining/sitting room, where doors open out to the patio and garden beyond; the guest sitting room is snug with comfy sofas and plenty of books. Sink into luxurious beds in immaculate bedrooms; TVs are smart, WiFi is on tap, bathrooms gleam and views are green and peaceful. The Somerset Levels surround you, Glastonbury and Wells are close and there's a good pub in the village too.

Rooms	1 double, 1 twin/double: £90-£105. Singles £75-£85.
Meals	Pubs/restaurants 1.2 miles.
Closed	Rarely.

Over 12s welcome.

Maria Laing
Brook Farm,
Newport Road,
North Curry, Taunton, TA3 6DJ
Tel   +44 (0)1823 491124
Email   maria.follett@hotmail.co.uk
Web   www.brookfarmbb.com

Entry 305   Map 2

Somerset

Brewers Cottage

David and Rosie are relaxed hosts and everything slows down the moment you open the gate. If you enjoy your own space, spread out in the annexe with a wet room or find upstairs bedrooms white and fresh with lavender and Rosie's paintings. Breakfast in the neat cottage dining room or al fresco: honey from the bees plus anything you ask for, David might go foraging or catch a trout for supper; bring your own wine and wander the garden with a glass — masses of colour, rare trees, ample veg patch where five types of tomato grow! Cider tasting is just up the road, Barrington Court and market town Ilminster are close.

Rooms	1 double; 1 double with separate bathroom: from £90. 1 annexe for 2 with wet room: from £95. Extra twin available sharing bathroom (let to same party only). Supplement charged for single night bookings.
Meals	Dinner, 3 courses with coffee, from £29.50. BYO. Pubs/restaurants 1 mile.
Closed	Occasionally.

David & Rosie Darrah
Brewers Cottage,
Isle Brewers, Taunton, TA3 6QL
Tel   +44 (0)1460 282900
Email brewerscottagebandb@gmail.com
Web   www.bedandbreakfastat
       brewerscottage.com

Entry 306   Map 3

Somerset

Frog Street Farmhouse

Through a pastoral landscape, past green paddocks and fine thoroughbreds, to a beautiful longhouse set in pretty secluded gardens surrounded by 130 acres. Its heart dates back to 1436 and its renovation is remarkable, highlighting beamed ceilings, Jacobean panelling and open fireplaces. Louise and David, brimful of enthusiasm for both house and visitors, give you four exquisite bedrooms in French country style, one with its own sitting room — very romantic. You're bang in between the north and the south coasts — after a happy day exploring, return to great leather sofas and a wood-burning stove. Guests love it here!

Rooms	3 doubles: £81–£130. 1 family room for 4: £108–£180.
Meals	Pub 1.3 miles.
Closed	3 November – 9 February.

Minimum stay: 2 nights at weekends.

Louise & David Farrance
Frog Street Farmhouse,
Hatch Beauchamp,
Taunton, TA3 6AF
Tel   +44 (0)1823 481883
Mobile +44 (0)7811 700789
Email   frogstreet@hotmail.com
Web   www.frogstreet.co.uk

Entry 307   Map 2

Somerset

Wellies

Set just back from the main road with the church next door this ivy-covered vicarage is the ultimate lure for grown-up sybarites – but children are equally welcome. You'll be greeted by a roaring wood-burner then home baking before being shown to your room full of treats – it's so much more than a stopover place. You breakfast in what is a sunny tea room and popular Sunday brunch spot in summer: Trina's homemade pastries and granola, local bacon and sausages, locally-roasted coffee and anything else you desire. Afterwards, if you've time, Bill can arrange a smörgåsbord of sporting things to do. Watch a falconry display, set off on a gentle walk through countryside, drive to the Blackdown Hills for something more challenging or stroll for a pint at the Queens Arms in Pitminster. Trina or Bill will give you a lift if they're free.

Rooms	4 doubles: £115-£230. Extra beds available in 2 rooms.
Meals	Tea room, Saturday & Sunday 10am-4pm, seves brunch, lunch & tea. Pubs/restaurants 10-minute drive.
Closed	Never.

William Hosie
Wellies,
Old Vicarage, Mill Lane, Corfe,
Taunton, TA3 7AQ
Tel   +44 (0)1823 420050
Email   bill.hosie@btinternet.com
Web   www.welliessomerset.com

Entry 308   Map 2

Somerset

Causeway Cottage

Robert and Lesley are ex-restaurateurs, so guests heap praise on their food, most of which is sourced from a local butcher and fishmonger; charming Lesley is an author, runs cookery courses and once taught at Prue Leith's. This is the perfect, pretty Somerset cottage, with an apple orchard and views to the church across a cottage garden and a field. The bedrooms are light, restful and have a country-style simplicity with their green check bedspreads, white walls and antique pine furniture; guests have their own comfortable sitting room. Easy access to the M5 yet with a rural feel. Very special.

Rooms	1 double, 1 twin: £90. Singles £70.
Meals	Supper from £35. Pub/restaurant 0.75 miles.
Closed	Christmas.

Children over 10 welcome.

Lesley & Robert Orr
Causeway Cottage,
West Buckland, Taunton, TA21 9JZ
Tel   +44 (0)1823 663458
Mobile   +44 (0)7703 412827
Email   orrs@causewaycottage.co.uk
Web   www.causewaycottage.co.uk

Entry 309   Map 2

Somerset

Cider Barn

Set back from the lane is a newly converted and refurbished barn. Step in to find fine old proportions, heated oak floors and heaps of character. Louise's stunning living quarters lie privately below on the ground floor, spread under the beams and bedrooms. One opens to the courtyard, and all are airy and peaceful with modern fabrics and cream walls. There's a sunny guest sitting room leading onto the garden, and delightful Louise, a great cook, serves breakfast at a long table by the wood-burner. You can walk through fields to the river or hills, stroll to the pub for supper – and alternative therapies can be arranged locally.

Rooms	1 double, 1 twin/double: £90-£95. Singles £70-£75.
Meals	Pub 1 mile.
Closed	Rarely.

Pets by arrangement.

Louise Bancroft
Cider Barn,
Runnington,
Wellington, TA21 0QW
Tel +44 (0)1823 665533
Email louisegaddon@btinternet.com
Web www.runningtonciderbarn.co.uk

Entry 310   Map 2

Somerset

Cothay Manor

A truly magical place. Step through the Gatehouse and into the ancient manor and marvel at the history, the atmosphere, the beauty. From the soaring Great Hall, richly furnished Winter Parlour and panelled dining room to the colourful Gold Room and bedrooms – all is fascinating. Find an eclectic mix of period pieces, stained glass, art, remarkable 15th-century wall paintings… Soak up the past by wood fires; browse interesting books; fall in love with the gorgeous garden with its 200-yard yew walk, water features and romantic garden rooms. Breakfast includes artisan bread, homemade marmalade and eggs from the hens.

Rooms	1 double; 1 twin with separate bathroom: £110-£145.
Meals	Pubs/restaurants 2.5 miles drive.
Closed	Christmas, New Year, Easter.

Over 12s welcome. Garden & house tours; plants for sale; small café; garden fair for nurserymen in summer; antiques fairs.

Mary-Anne Robb
Cothay Manor,
Greenham,
Wellington, TA21 0JR
Tel +44 (0)1823 672283
Email cothaymanor@btinternet.com
Web www.cothaymanor.co.uk

Entry 311   Map 2

Somerset

Brook House

A relaxed home with no rules; arrive to tasty cake and tea or a tipple, settle in the sitting room by one of the wood-burners, chat in the kitchen, wander mown paths in the garden. The sunny open-plan kitchen/living room is the heart of the house; Becky is a keen cook so food is good, local, homemade; Crumpet, one of the terriers, snoozes by the Aga. Quiet, comfy bedrooms have tip-top linen, painted furniture, pots of flowers, garden views; the larger twin has a sofa by tall windows. Next door Cider Mill has a farm shop, museum and tea rooms, the walks are great, the Jurassic coast is a short drive. A friendly place, a treat to stay.

Rooms	1 double, 1 twin/double: £95–£105. Singles £70–£80.
Meals	Dinner, 3 courses, from £20. Pub 3 miles.
Closed	Occasionally.

Over 12s welcome.

Becky Jam
Brook House,
Dowlish Wake, Ilminster, TA19 0NY
Tel +44 (0)1460 250860
Mobile +44 (0)7841 594342
Email becky@brookhousesomerset.com
Web www.brookhousesomerset.com

Entry 312   Map 3

Somerset

Fairways

The food, the views – amazing! Tim is a passionate cook, and he and Sarah want you to enjoy their friendly open house. Settle in with tea and Tim's high-rise scones and look out over Seaborough Hill. Their 1960s bungalow is immaculate: white walls, gleaming oak floors, toasty wood-burner and French windows onto the garden. Perfect bedrooms have inviting beds and pots of sweet peas; bathrooms sparkle. Pad through to breakfast in the airy sitting/dining room – or out on the sunny deck: eggs from across the valley, smoked salmon, homemade bread, granola and jams; dinner is equally good with organic local veg and charcuterie. A treat!

Rooms	2 doubles: £110. Singles £95.
Meals	Dinner, 3 courses with tea/coffee, £30. BYO. Pub/restaurant 3 miles.
Closed	1 November – 28 February.

Minimum stay: 2 nights at weekends. Over 16s welcome.

Sarah & Tim Dommett
Fairways,
Hewish Lane,
Crewkerne, TA18 8RN
Tel +44 (0)1460 271093
Mobile +44 (0)7768 753045
Email info@fairwaysbandb.co.uk
Web www.fairwaysbandb.co.uk

Entry 313   Map 3

Staffordshire

Manor House Farm

A working rare-breed farm in an area of great beauty, a Jacobean farmhouse with oodles of history. Behind mullioned windows is a glorious interior crammed with curios and family pieces, panelled walls and wonky floors... hurl a log on the fire and watch it roar. Rooms with views have four-posters; one bathroom flaunts rich red antique fabrics. Chris and Margaret are passionate hosts who serve perfect breakfasts (eggs from their hens, sausages and bacon from their pigs and home-grown tomatoes) and give you the run of a garden resplendent with plants, vistas, tennis, croquet, two springer spaniels and one purring cat. Heaven.

Staffordshire

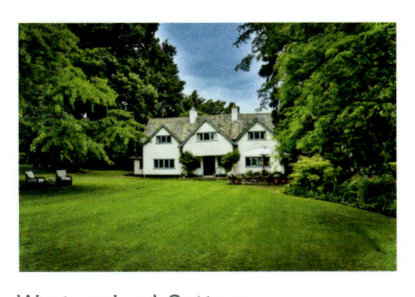

Westmorland Cottage

The pretty village has hanging baskets decorating shops and riverside, and Tim and Caroline's house was built in the arboretum of Oswald Mosley's former family seat. Comfy sitting rooms have heaps of books, art, a log fire; bedrooms (one in the studio) have tip-top linen, garden views and shortbread. Wake for a generous Aga breakfast: homemade granola, Tim's bread, local bacon – or continental with croissants. You're on the edge of the Peak District National Park – head out for walks, cycling, National Trust houses galore. Return to the stunning garden for afternoon tea and cake: unusual trees, Italianate pond, sunny spots...

Rooms	1 double, 2 four-posters: £72–£80. 1 family room for 4 (four-poster): £80–£100.		Rooms	1 double; 1 double with separate bathroom: £75–£85. 1 studio for 2: £95. Singles £65.
Meals	Pub/restaurant 1.5 miles.		Meals	Pubs/restaurants 5-minute walk.
Closed	Christmas.		Closed	Rarely.

Minimum stay: 2 nights at weekends during high season.

Chris & Margaret Ball
Manor House Farm,
Prestwood, Denstone,
Uttoxeter, ST14 5DD
Tel   +44 (0)1889 590415
Mobile   +44 (0)7976 767629
Email   cmball@manorhousefarm.co.uk
Web   www.manorhousefarm.co.uk

Caroline Bucknall
Westmorland Cottage,
Hall Grounds, Rolleston-on-Dove,
Burton-on-Trent, DE13 9BS
Tel   +44 (0)1283 813336
Mobile   +44 (0)7814 849211
Email   bucknalltandc@gmail.com
Web   www.westmorlandcottage.co.uk

Entry 314   Map 8

Entry 315   Map 8

Suffolk

Church Farmhouse

This Elizabethan farmhouse is by the ancient thatched church in a little hamlet close to Southwold. Minsmere RSPB bird sanctuary, Snape Maltings and the coast are nearby for lovely days out. Sarah, characterful, well-travelled and entertaining, is an excellent cook, so breakfast will be a treat with bowls of fruit, Suffolk bacon and free-range eggs; occasional candle-lit dinners are worth staying in for, too. Bedrooms have supremely comfy beds well-dressed in pure cotton. Although there is no sitting room, you can enjoy tea and cake and linger in the garden, there are flowers in every room and books galore.

Rooms	1 double, 1 twin/double; 1 double with separate bath: £105–£115. Singles £80.
Meals	Dinner £28. Pubs/restaurants within 4 miles.
Closed	Christmas.

Over 12s welcome.

Sarah Lentaigne
Church Farmhouse,
Uggeshall,
Southwold, NR34 8BD
Tel   +44 (0)1502 578532
Mobile +44 (0)7748 801418
Email   sarahlentaigne@btinternet.com
Web   www.churchfarmhousesuffolk.co.uk

Entry 316   Map 10

Suffolk

Camomile Cottage

Aly and Tim's 16th-century longhouse is a feast of old beams, kilims, antiques and art. They give you homemade cake on arrival; relax in the garden or the guest lounge, kick off your shoes and enjoy a glass of wine by the log fire. Beamed bedrooms have period furnishings, goose down duvets, luxury linen, flowers and handmade chocolates; bathrooms have Molton Brown toiletries. Aly will also bring you tea in bed! Breakfast is in the garden room: cornbread toast, eggs from the hens, croissants and all sorts of cooked choices. Eye is an attractive old market town; Southwold, Bury St Edmunds and Snape Maltings are all close.

Rooms	2 doubles: £99–£110. Singles £85.
Meals	Pubs/restaurants 0.5 miles.
Closed	Rarely.

Minimum stay: 2 nights at weekends.

Aly Kahane
Camomile Cottage,
Brome Avenue,
Eye, IP23 7HW
Tel   +44 (0)1379 873528
Email aly@camomilecottage.co.uk
Web   www.camomilecottage.co.uk

Entry 317   Map 10

Suffolk

Oak Tree Farm

A magnificent ancient oak tree stands guard over this 300-year old Georgian-fronted farmhouse. John and Julian love all things Art Nouveau/Art Deco and their home is filled with pieces from those periods, including china with masses of different patterns; fine books galore too, and peaceful bedrooms with smart white linen. Breakfast is a moveable feast: in the conservatory in summer, or by the fire in the dining room in winter; the bird feeders get moved too so you're kept amused while you tuck in! You can wander the five-acre garden and meadows, pretty Yoxford village has antique shops to browse, and Snape Maltings is a hop.

Rooms	3 twin/doubles: £90. Singles £70.
Meals	Pubs/restaurants 5-minute walk.
Closed	1 November – 28 February.

Minimum stay: 2 nights at weekends.

Julian Lock & John McMinn
Oak Tree Farm,
Little Street, Yoxford,
Saxmundham, IP17 3JN
Tel   +44 (0)1728 668651
Mobile   +44 (0)7969 459261
Email   oaktreefarmyoxford@gmail.com
Web   www.oaktreefarmyoxford.co.uk

Entry 318   Map 10

Suffolk

Trustans Barn

Ancient oak beams have been carefully kept in this smart Suffolk barn conversion. It's a family affair here: friendly sisters Sally and Rosie give you contemporary bedrooms with artistic touches, king-sized beds, sleek bathrooms and drench showers. Breakfast is served at two scrubbed pine tables in the airy slate-floored breakfast room; a big blackboard lists tasty choices – everything from home-laid eggs and local sausages to home-grown tomatoes and muesli. Masses to do nearby: Snape Maltings music, wonderful old churches, summer festivals, the Heritage coast... A great place for a peaceful holiday with a group of friends.

Rooms	5 doubles, 1 twin/double: £100–£130.
Meals	Pubs less than a mile away.
Closed	Christmas.

Minimum stay: 2 nights in high season.

Sally Prime
Trustans Barn,
Westleton Road,
Darsham,
Saxmundham, IP17 3BP
Tel   +44 (0)1728 668684
Email   sallyandrosie@trustansbarn.co.uk
Web   www.trustansbarn.co.uk

Entry 319   Map 10

Suffolk

Willow Tree Cottage

Seductively near RSPB Minsmere, medieval castles and the glorious Heritage coast. The evening sun pours into the back of this contemporary cottage with butter yellow walls; you are on the edge of the village but all is quiet with an orchard behind and a bird-filled garden for tea and cake. No sitting room, but easy chairs in your pretty bedroom face views. Caroline is a good cook and breakfast is delicious (try her kedgeree and homemade jams). Snape Maltings for music, Southwold for the famous pier, Aldeburgh with its shingle beach, boats, fun shops and good places to eat – all are close by. Holly the labrador adds to the charm.

Rooms	1 double: £80-£85. Singles £50-£60.
Meals	Pub/restaurant 1.5 miles.
Closed	Rarely.

Minimum stay: 2 nights at weekends.

Caroline Youngson
Willow Tree Cottage,
3 Belvedere Close, Kelsale,
Saxmundham, IP17 2RS

Tel	+44 (0)1728 602161
Mobile	+44 (0)7747 624139
Email	cy@willowtreecottage.me.uk
Web	www.willowtreecottage.me.uk

Entry 320   Map 10

Suffolk

Church House

A short hop from riverside Woodbridge and musical Snape Maltings, between a conservation churchyard and a history-rich field, is something different and unusual: a customised house of gentle colours and textures, home to an architect and a designer. From the hand-carved oak porch to the lovely wildlife garden, there's a feeling of warmth and delight. Under the eaves: two jewel-bright and comfortable bedrooms full of books and fresh flowers. In the kitchen: a big farmhouse table laid for breakfasts with homemade bread (locally ground flour from the family farm), granola and marmalade. And, a short walk away, an excellent village pub.

Rooms	1 twin/double; 1 twin/double with separate bath/shower: £80-£85. Singles from £65.
Meals	Pub 1 mile.
Closed	Rarely.

Minimum stay: 2 nights at weekends. Children over 6 welcome.

Sally & Richard Pirkis
Church House,
Clopton,
Woodbridge, IP13 6QB

Tel	+44 (0)1473 735350
Email	sallypirkis@gmail.com
Web	www.churchhousebandbsuffolk.co.uk

Entry 321   Map 10

Suffolk

Holbecks House

Up the drive through parkland studded with ancient trees and step into the flagstoned hall of this 18th–century house. Find gracious rooms, soft colours, Persian rugs, antiques, hunting prints and books to browse. Perry is delightful and looks after you well; settle into big peaceful bedrooms with good beds, chocolates and long rural views. Just beyond the market town of Hadleigh, the house snoozes on a hill with acres of garden, orchard, croquet lawn, rose walk and pond. Explore Constable Country, visit the Munnings Art Museum in Dedham, Gainsborough House in Sudbury and the cathedral city of Bury St Edmunds.

Suffolk

The Old Rectory

A handsome house surrounded by large gardens and sheep-dotted fields. Maggie's home is filled with beautiful things: old family china, prints, portraits, blue and white decorated lamps, polished wood – a piano you can play too. Bedrooms are peaceful and pretty; 'Rose' is reached up a few steps. Breakfast is well worth waking up for: granola, compote, homemade jams, honey from their bees, sausages and bacon from their pigs; sourcing local food is a passion and Maggie loves to cook, so dinner will be equally good. Set off for Constable country, charming old wool town Lavenham, antiques in Long Melford, the coast… it's a fascinating spot.

Rooms	1 double, 1 twin/double; 1 double with separate bath: £110. Singles £90.
Meals	Pubs/restaurants 0.5 miles.
Closed	Christmas.

Minimum stay: 2 nights at weekends.

Perry Coysh
Holbecks House,
Holbecks Lane, Hadleigh,
Ipswich, IP7 5PE

Tel	+44 (0)1473 823211
Mobile	+44 (0)7875 167771
Email	perry.coysh@gmail.com
Web	www.holbecks.com

Entry 322 Map 10

Rooms	1 twin/double; 1 double with separate bathroom: £100-£125. Extra bed/sofabed £25 per person per night. 1-night bookings accepted on Saturdays; 2+ nights including Saturday: 25% discount.
Meals	Dinner, 2-3 courses with wine, £20-£30. Pubs/restaurants 2 miles.
Closed	Rarely.

Maggie Lawrence
The Old Rectory,
Kettlebaston,
Ipswich, IP7 7QD

Tel	+44 (0)1449 740400
Email	theoldrectorykettlebaston@gmail.com
Web	www.theoldrectorykettlebaston.co.uk

Entry 323 Map 10

Suffolk

The Old Vicarage

Up the avenue of fine white horse chestnut trees to find just what you'd expect from an old vicarage: a Pembroke table in the flagstoned hall, a refectory table sporting copies of *The Field*, a piano guests can play, silver pheasants, winter log fires in the breakfast and drawing rooms and homemade cake on arrival. The house is magnificent, with huge rooms and passageways. Comfy beds are dressed in old-fashioned counterpanes; the twin has stunning far-reaching views. Weave your way through the branches of the huge copper beech to Jane's colourful garden; she grows her own vegetables, keeps hens, makes jams and cooks delicious breakfasts.

Rooms	1 twin/double, 1 twin each with separate bathroom: £80–£90. Extra single room available (let to same party only). Singles £50.
Meals	Packed lunch £6. Pub 1 mile.
Closed	Christmas.

Children over 7 welcome.

	Jane Sheppard The Old Vicarage, Great Thurlow, Newmarket, CB9 7LE
Tel	+44 (0)1440 783209
Mobile	+44 (0)7887 717429
Email	s.j.sheppard@hotmail.co.uk
Web	www.thurlowvicarage.co.uk

Entry 324 Map 9

Suffolk

The Old Stable

A rural ramble brings you to a flint and brick bolthole – tucked into the courtyard of the main house. Joanna has restored her stables with a blend of old and new: beams, lime washed walls, rustic window sills, modern log-burner, swish new bathrooms. Bedrooms ('Hayloft' up, 'Coach House' down) are fresh and comfy – one has a double sofabed for extra guests. Wide French windows in the big dining/sitting room open to the pool – have a dip on summer mornings; dahlias and roses fill the garden. Joanna brings over breakfast: homemade jams, honey from their bees, a full English spread. Walk from the door; hop on a bike and discover nearby Bury.

Rooms	1 twin/double; 1 twin with separate bathroom: £90–£115. Extra bed/sofabed £25 per person per night.
Meals	Occasional supper from £15. Packed lunch £7.50. Pubs/restaurants within 3 miles.
Closed	Occasionally.

Over 13s welcome.

	Joanna Mayer The Old Stable, Cattishall Farmhouse, Great Barton, Bury St Edmunds, IP31 2QT
Tel	+44 (0)1284 787340
Mobile	+44 (0)7738 936496
Email	joannamayer42@googlemail.com
Web	www.theoldstablebandb.co.uk

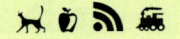

Entry 325 Map 10

Surrey

Swallow Barn

A converted squash court, coach house and stables, once belonging to next-door's manor, have become a home of old-fashioned charm. Full of family memories, and run very well by Joan, this B&B is excellently placed for Windsor, Wisley, Brooklands and Hampton Court; close to both airports too. Lovely trees in the garden, fields and woods beyond, a paddock and a swimming pool… total tranquillity, and you can walk to the pub. None of the bedrooms is huge but the beds are firm, the garden views are pretty and the downstairs double has its own sitting room. Breakfasts are both generous and scrumptious.

Rooms	1 double with sitting room; 1 twin with separate shower: £90-£100. Apple Store – 1 twin with separate shower: £90-£100. Singles £65.
Meals	Pub/restaurant 0.75 miles.
Closed	Rarely.

Children over 8 welcome.

Joan Carey
Swallow Barn,
Milford Green, Chobham,
Woking, GU24 8AU
Tel   +44 (0)1276 856030
Mobile +44 (0)7768 972904
Email info@swallow-barn.co.uk
Web   www.swallow-barn.co.uk

Entry 326   Map 4

Surrey

Broadway Barn

If you love art, gardening and good food, you'll love Mindi and her brilliant conversion of a pretty brick Regency barn on Ripley High Street. You sleep in comfy bedrooms styled with creativity: a painting from a Parisian laundrette, ceramic lamps with bird motifs, leather chests as tables. You relax in a long, light, mirrored conservatory with glazed terrace doors, and are free to wander around the charming walled garden. You breakfast deliciously on local eggs and home-baked treats – Mindi makes five different breads! Minutes from Guildford and Wisley's RHS garden, the village has a Michelin-starred restaurant, cafés and pubs.

Rooms	4 doubles: £120.
Meals	Restaurant next door.
Closed	Rarely.

Mindi McLean
Broadway Barn,
High Street, Ripley,
Woking, GU23 6AQ
Tel   +44 (0)1483 223200
Email mindi@broadwaybarn.com
Web   www.broadwaybarn.com

Entry 327   Map 4

Surrey

South Lodge

The beautiful Surrey Hills surround this smart home overlooking the village green. Joanna's house gets the sun all day and has a country chic feel. She looks after you well, and gives you tea and cake on arrival, cosy, pretty bedrooms in the eaves and locally sourced and homemade treats at breakfast. Her catering business is run from the house so there are always people coming and going – this is a fun place to stay with a lovely friendly feel. Hop next door for a tasty supper at The Grumpy Mole (popular so you need to book). Near Dorking, and handy for Gatwick, too – it's a 15-minute drive.

Rooms	3 doubles; 1 twin with separate bath: £100–£125. Singles £95.
Meals	Evening meal with wine from £35. Pub next door.
Closed	Christmas.

Joanna Rowlands
South Lodge,
Brockham Green, Brockham,
Betchworth, RH3 7JS
Tel   +44 (0)1737 843883
Email bookings@brockhambandb.com
Web   www.brockhambandb.com

Entry 328   Map 4

Surrey

Blackbrook House

Arriving at this elegant Victorian home surrounded by immaculate lawn, woodland, paddocks and a swing hanging from a huge conifer, you immediately want to explore. Emma and Rae are easy-going, and want you to unwind and feel at home. Bedrooms are spacious and smart with floral fabrics, deep pocket sprung mattresses and good linen; bathrooms are tip-top. Breakfast is a delicious spread: free-range eggs from next door, local bacon and sausages, freshly squeezed apple juice from the orchard. Admire the rose garden, enjoy a game of tennis, head out into the Surrey Hills. Return to a snug sitting room with TV and lots of books. Bliss.

Rooms	1 double: £95–£100. 1 suite for 2: £105–£115. Singles from £60.
Meals	Pub 0.5 miles.
Closed	Christmas & New Year.

Emma & Rae Burdon
Blackbrook House,
Blackbrook, Dorking, RH5 4DS
Tel   +44 (0)1306 888898
Mobile +44 (0)7880 723512
Email   blackbrookbb@btinternet.com
Web   www.surreybandb.co.uk

Entry 329   Map 4

Surrey

The Venison House

Drive through Surrey parkland grazed by rare breed cattle to reach this bijou hideaway. The circular cottage topped with a terracotta turret is quite unlike any other B&B you're likely to visit. It's set into a corner of Alison's lovely walled garden, with oval windows overlooking the park. Step through the sage green door into a country-chic bedroom with monogrammed pillows and crisp linen. Along a corridor leading to the sparkling shower room, there's a double-fronted cupboard concealing an immaculate kitchen. Alison provides homemade bread, marmalade, bacon, tomatoes and eggs, so guests can make a delicious, DIY breakfast.

Rooms	1 double with separate bathroom & kitchenette: £120-£150.
Meals	Pubs/restaurants 2 miles.
Closed	Rarely.

Alison Bird
The Venison House,
Garden Cottage, Park Hatch, Loxhill,
Godalming, GU8 4BL
Tel   +44 (0)1483 200410
Mobile +44 (0)7768 745765
Email agmbird@gmail.com

Entry 330   Map 4

Surrey

The Dovecote at Greenaway

An enchanting cottage in an idyllic corner of Chiddingfold. People return time and again — for the house (1545), the garden blooming with flowers, vegetables, hens and dovecote, the glowing interiors, and Sheila and John. The sitting room is inviting with rich colours, flowers, beams and a roaring log fire; the turning oak staircase leads to bedrooms that are cosy and sumptuous at the same time, and bathrooms with deep roll top tubs and a pretty armchair. Breakfast is a spread with homemade bread and home-grown tomatoes. Gorgeous countryside, walks on the Greensand Way… who would guess London and the airports were so close?

Rooms	1 double; 1 double, 1 twin, sharing bathroom: £115-£135. Singles £95, except weekends. Mid-week prices negotiable.
Meals	Pubs 300 yds.
Closed	Rarely.

Pets by arrangement.

Sheila & John Marsh
The Dovecote at Greenaway,
Pickhurst Road,
Chiddingfold, GU8 4TS
Tel   +44 (0)1428 682920
Email info@bedandbreakfastchiddingfold.co.uk
Web   www.bedandbreakfastchiddingfold.co.uk

Entry 331   Map 4

Sussex

Benefold Farmhouse Barn

This 16th-century barn has been renovated with flair by creative hosts. They live in the farmhouse, and the barn is all yours. The living space is open-plan with masses of beautiful beams, sofas by the wood-burner, dining area and well-equipped kitchen. Bedrooms (one down, one mezzanine) are inviting with more honey-coloured wood, natural tones, well-dressed beds and pots of flowers; the double has a striking freestanding bath in the room. Clarissa provides all you need for breakfast – rustle it up when you want. Easy for Goodwood events, Chichester, Arundel; walk the South Downs Way, browse antique shops, spend a day on the beach.

Rooms	1 double, 1 twin (let to same party only): £150-£200.
Meals	Pubs/restaurants 2 miles.
Closed	Rarely.

Minimum stay: 2 nights. Stabling for horses by arrangement. Children over 7 welcome.

| | Clarissa Langdon
Benefold Farmhouse Barn,
Petworth, GU28 9NX |
|---|---|
| Tel | +44 (0)7796 990660 |
| Email | clarissalangdon@hotmail.com |

Entry 332   Map 4

Sussex

Rother Cottage

Katherine is engaging and creative and her house has an informal, lived-in feel. Find an eclectic mix of furniture, vases overflowing with garden flowers, beams galore, a winter wood fire and a sunny open-plan dining/sitting room where you have breakfast. Up the steep, crooked stair to your own wing of the house: a simple bedroom with a hand-sewn Indian throw on a comfy bed; the bathroom is basic and back downstairs. The colourful garden has views over the South Downs. Goodwood racecourse is close, Glyndebourne an hour; it's a fabulous area for rambling, cycling, visiting Sussex villages, and there are heaps of pubs for supper.

Rooms	1 double with separate bath: £95.
1 single: £85.
Meals	Pubs/restaurants 3 miles.
Closed	Christmas, New Year & Easter.

Minimum stay: usually 2 nights.

| | Katherine Wyld
Rother Cottage,
245 Ambersham Green,
Midhurst, GU29 0BX |
|---|---|
| Tel | +44 (0)1798 861365 |
| Mobile | +44 (0)7984 427762 |
| Email | cusackcouture@yahoo.co.uk |

Entry 333   Map 4

Sussex

Lordington House

Croquet on the lawn in summer, big log fires and woolly jumpers in winter, brilliant food all year round. On a sunny slope of the Ems Valley, life ticks by peacefully as it has always done... The house is vast and impressive, a lime avenue links the much-loved garden with the AONB beyond and friendly guard dog Shep looks on. The 17th-century staircase is a glory, the décor is engagingly old-fashioned: Edwardian beds with firm mattresses and floral covers, carpeted Sixties-style bathrooms, toile wallpaper on wardrobe doors. A privilege to stay in a house of this age and character!

Rooms	1 double; 1 twin/double with separate bath/shower; 1 double, sharing bath/shower with single: £115–£145. 1 single sharing bath/shower with double: £57–£72. Extra bed/sofabed £20–£25 per person per night.
Meals	Packed lunch from £6. Pub 1 mile.
Closed	Rarely.

Mr & Mrs Hamilton
Lordington House,
Lordington,
Chichester, PO18 9DX
Tel +44 (0)1243 375862
Email hamiltonjanda@btinternet.com

Entry 334   Map 4

Sussex

Crows Hall Farm

The Renwicks are tremendous hosts. Their wonderful flagstone-halled farmhouse in the South Downs National Park is great for walking and cycling and close to Goodwood. Amanda's style is simple and cottagey. Bedrooms are reached by their own staircase; find open brickwork and a big handmade bed in the main one; fantastic views of the walled garden and beyond in the second. In between, the bathroom is fab and fun, with flamingos, freestanding bath and shower (all yours, or shared with your own party). Breakfasts are local, flexible feasts on the terrace or in the quirky rustic kitchen by the wood-burner — comfy sofas here too. Marvellous!

Rooms	2 doubles sharing bathroom (let to same party only): £110.
Meals	Pubs 1.5 miles.
Closed	Rarely.

Goodwood event prices on request.

Amanda Renwick
Crows Hall Farm,
Chilgrove Road, Lavant,
Chichester, PO18 9HP
Mobile +44 (0)7801 296192
Email amanda@crowshall.com
Web www.crowshallbandb.com

Entry 335   Map 4

Sussex

Seabeach House

Sitting sleepily behind its white gate this pretty stone cottage is surrounded by the Sussex Downs National Park. Throughout Francesca's friendly home her love of folk art, rich oils, antiques and hand-painted pieces adds zest. Comfy cottagey bedrooms are on the ground floor; wake to a delicious breakfast of locally sourced sausages and eggs, garden tomatoes, homemade jams and croissants and brioche. Explore garden and fields, admire wide views from a pretty terrace and chat to Popeye the dog. Heaps to do round about: theatre and sailing in Chichester, the castle in Arundel, and events galore at Goodwood.

Rooms	Annexe – 1 double, 1 twin, sharing bath (let to same party only): £95–£150.
Meals	Pub 1 mile.
Closed	Rarely.

Francesca Emmet
Seabeach House,
Selhurst Park, Halnaker,
Chichester, PO18 0LX
Tel +44 (0)1243 537944
Email francescaemmet@hotmail.co.uk
Web www.bandbatseabeachhouse.co.uk

Entry 336   Map 4

Sussex

The Old Manor House

Wild flowers in jugs, old wooden floors and beams, pretty cottagey curtains: Judy's manor house near Chichester has bags of character and she is friendly and kind. Originally constructed round a big central fireplace, the rooms are all refreshingly simple allowing features to shine. Sunny bedrooms up steep stairs have seagrass flooring, limed furniture, gentle colours and warm bathrooms. Enjoy delicious breakfasts by the wood-burner in the dining room: fresh fruit smoothies and an organic full English. Great for horse racing, castle visiting, sailing, theatre and festivals; fantastic walks on the South Downs, too. Lovely.

Rooms	2 doubles: £95.
Meals	Pub/restaurant 500 yds.
Closed	Christmas, New Year.

Minimum stay: 2 nights.

Judy Wolstenholme
The Old Manor House,
Westergate Street, Westergate,
Chichester, PO20 3QZ
Tel +44 (0)1243 544489
Email judy@veryoldmanorhouse.com
Web veryoldmanorhouse.com

Entry 337   Map 4

Sussex

The Jointure Studios

A thriving village with an arty heritage. In the centre is your apartment above a lovely big gallery/hall — with piano and wood-burning stove. Find a happy mix of antique and new, a quiet comfy bedroom with leafy views and a cosy sitting room with a kitchen area. Shirley leaves you homemade cakes and breakfast things, and each morning brings over a tray of fruits, yogurt, local artisan bread and eggs for you to cook how you wish. The Ditchling Museum of Art + Craft is inspiring, South Downs National Park is your stomping ground, Brighton and Glyndebourne are close. Return and rustle up supper, or stroll down the road to a good pub.

Rooms	1 twin/double (apartment with sitting room and kitchen): £115-£125. Singles £100.
Meals	Pubs/restaurants 1-minute walk.
Closed	Rarely.

Minimum stay: 2 nights at weekends, May — September

Shirley Crowther
The Jointure Studios,
11 South Street,
Ditchling, BN6 8UQ

Tel	+44 (0)1273 841244
Email	thejointurestudios@gmail.com
Web	www.jointurestudiosbandb.co.uk

Entry 338   Map 4

Sussex

The Beeches

Pull the shiny brass bell and step into a wide, welcoming hall. Bedrooms are inviting too with goose down quilts and pillows, striking art and flowers; the guest sitting room below has French windows opening to the garden, more art and comfortable character. Sandy's breakfast by the Aga is a home-produced and local spread, and you eat in a sunny room with pottery on the dresser and an old clock ticking away. Make time to explore the interest-filled garden; there's a willow house by one of the ponds where you can sip wine on summer eves. Find great walks from the door, vineyards and gardens to visit, and Brighton within easy reach.

Rooms	1 double; 1 double with separate shower room: £115-£140.
Meals	Pubs/restaurants 4 miles.
Closed	Rarely.

Sandy Coppen
The Beeches,
Church Road, Barcombe,
Lewes, BN8 5TS

Tel	+44 (0)1273 401339
Email	sand@thebeechesbarcombe.com
Web	www.thebeechesbarcombe.com

Entry 339   Map 4

Sussex

Little Norlington Barn

A convivial home with homemade cake at the ready and a fire to settle by – Sandra loves having visitors. She gives you two rooms in the house, and an independent apartment with kitchen and living space downstairs opening to a patio, fresh white bedroom above; beds are snugly topped with goose down, bathrooms have soft towels and slippers. Wake for a generous breakfast with homemade organic bread and good coffee in the dining room; Milking Parlour guests have a continental basket brought over. Glyndebourne is a few minutes' drive, there are masses of great gardens and festivals to dip into and the coast is within easy reach.

Rooms	2 doubles: £120-£150.
	1 apartment for 2: £120-£150.
	Sofabed available.
Meals	Pubs/restaurants 1 mile.
Closed	Rarely.

Minimum stay: 2 nights at weekends; 2 nights in Milking Parlour.

Sandra Clement
Little Norlington Barn,
Norlington Lane, Ringmer,
Lewes, BN8 5SG
Tel   +44 (0)1273 813321
Email   stay@littlenorlingtonbarn.co.uk
Web   www.littlenorlingtonbarn.co.uk

Entry 340   Map 4

Sussex

Netherwood Lodge

The scent of fresh flowers and a smattering of chintz over calm uncluttered interiors will please you. Engaging Margaret is a mine of local knowledge and offers you peaceful, cosy, ground-floor bedrooms beautifully dressed with wool carpets, designer interlined curtains, luxurious bed linens and gloriously comfortable beds. Enjoy an award-winning breakfast overlooking the garden (it's stunning); all is homemade or locally sourced. Then set off to discover this beautiful corner of East Sussex – ideal for walking, visiting National Trust houses and gardens and, of course, Glyndebourne.

Rooms	1 twin; 1 double with separate bath: £130-£145.
Meals	Pub/restaurant 0.75 miles.
Closed	Rarely.

Minimum stay: 2 nights on weekdays. Over 16s welcome.

Margaret Clarke
Netherwood Lodge,
Muddles Green, Chiddingly, Lewes,
BN8 6HS
Tel   +44 (0)1825 872512
Email   netherwoodlodge@hotmail.com
Web   www.netherwoodlodge.co.uk

Entry 341   Map 5

Sussex

Old Whyly

Breakfast in a light-filled, chinoiserie dining room – there's an effortless elegance to this manor house, once home to one of King Charles's Cavaliers. Bedrooms are atmospheric, one in French style. The treats continue outside with a beautiful flower garden annually replenished with 5,000 tulips, a lake and orchard, a swimming pool and a tennis court – fabulous. Dine under the pergola in summer: food is a passion and Sarah's menus are adventurous with a modern slant. Glyndebourne is close so make a party of it and take a divine 'pink' hamper, with blankets or a table and chairs included. Sheer bliss.

Rooms	2 twin/doubles; 1 double with separate shower; 1 twin/double with separate bath: £98-£150. Singles by arrangement.
Meals	Dinner, 3 courses, £38. Hampers £40. Pub/restaurant 0.5 miles.
Closed	Rarely.

Sarah Burgoyne
Old Whyly,
London Road,
East Hoathly, BN8 6EL
Tel +44 (0)1825 840216
Email stay@oldwhyly.co.uk
Web www.oldwhyly.co.uk

Entry 342 Map 5

Sussex

Starnash Farmhouse

Come to relax and recharge, perhaps write or paint. Vicky and David love having guests and creating delicious meals from local and home-grown produce; their farmhouse table overlooks the garden, or you can eat outside in the orchard or on the terrace. Bedrooms (one downstairs) are named after birds and have pretty fabrics and garden flowers; hop up more stairs to the attic twin (mind your head in the shower room!). Brighton and Glyndebourne are close; walk the South Downs Way, explore the coast, book one of Vicky's writer retreats or winter workshops. David is making a shepherd's hut so you'll soon be able to sleep under the stars too.

Rooms	3 doubles; 1 twin with separate bathroom: £100-£130. Cot £15; z-bed £25.
Meals	Dinner, 2-3 courses, £20-25. Pubs/restaurants 1 mile.
Closed	Christmas.

Vicky Radtke
Starnash Farmhouse,
Coldharbour Road, Upper Dicker,
Hailsham, BN27 3PY
Tel +44 (0)1323 841138
Mobile +44 (0)7876 255792
Email starnashfarmhouse@gmail.com
Web www.starnashbedandbreakfast.co.uk

Entry 343 Map 5

Sussex

Ocklynge Manor

On top of a peaceful hill, a short stroll from Eastbourne, find tip-top B&B in an 18th-century house with an interesting history – ask Wendy! Now it is her home, and you will be treated to home-baked bread, delicious tea time cakes and scrummy jams – on fine days you can take it outside. Creamy carpeted, bright and sunny bedrooms, all with views over the lovely walled garden, create a mood of relaxed indulgence and are full of thoughtful touches: dressing gowns, DVDs, your own fridge. Breakfasts are superb: this is a very spoiling, nurturing place.

Rooms	1 twin; 1 double with separate shower: £100-£120. 1 suite for 3: £120-£130. Singles £60-£110.
Meals	Pub 5-minute walk.
Closed	Rarely.

Please see owner's website for availability.

Wendy Dugdill
Ocklynge Manor,
Mill Road,
Eastbourne, BN21 2PG
Tel   +44 (0)1323 734121
Mobile +44 (0)7979 627172
Email   ocklyngemanor@hotmail.com
Web   www.ocklyngemanor.co.uk

Entry 344   Map 5

Sussex

The Cloudesley

One mile from the sea, a remarkable house full of beautiful things. Shahriar – photographer, holistic therapist, Chelsea gold-medal winner – has created an artistic bolthole: books, African masks, an honesty bar, chic bedrooms and two sitting rooms that double as art galleries. You are looked after with great kindness. Shahriar has a couple of treatment rooms where, in cahoots with local therapists, he offers massage, shiatsu and reiki. You breakfast on exotic fruits, Armagnac omelettes, or the full cooked works – on a bamboo terrace in summer. Don't miss Derek Jarman's cottage at Dungeness or St Clement's for great food.

Rooms	3 doubles, 2 twin/doubles: £75-£135. Extra bed £25.
Meals	Pubs/restaurants 5-minute drive.
Closed	Rarely.

Minimum stay: 2 nights at weekends. Children over 6 welcome. Whole house available.

Shahriar Mazandi
The Cloudesley,
7 Cloudesley Road,
St Leonards-on-Sea, TN37 6JN
Mobile +44 (0)7507 000148
Email   s.mazandi@gmail.com
Web   www.thecloudesley.co.uk

Entry 345   Map 5

Sussex

King John's Lodge

Deep in the High Weald, down a maze of country lanes, is an enchanting 1650s house in eight acres of heaven: Jill's pride and joy. Inside: oak beams, stone fireplaces, big sofas, and a Jacobean dining room with leaded glass windows, fine setting for a perfect English breakfast. Wing chairs, floral fabrics, dressers with china bowls: the country-house feel extends to the comfortable, carpeted bedrooms. Discover Sissinghurst, Great Dixter, Rye… return to sweeping lawns, wild gardens, ancient apple trees, a woodland walk (spot Titania and Oberon) and a delightful nursery and tea room run by Jill's son.

Rooms	2 doubles, 1 twin: £95–£105. 1 family room for 3: £130–£150. Singles from £75.
Meals	Dinner, 3 courses, £30 (minimum 4). Pubs/restaurants 2.5 miles.
Closed	Rarely.

Minimum stay: 2 nights at weekends & in high season. Broadband unreliable – please ring if you don't get a reply straightaway.

Jill Cunningham
King John's Lodge,
Sheepstreet Lane,
Etchingham, TN19 7AZ
Tel +44 (0)1580 819232
Email kingjohnslodge@aol.com

Entry 346   Map 5

Sussex

Bewl Rookery

This 16th-century house has been in Carol's family for generations. She and Mark have rejuvenated the well-loved, attractive old home; find ancient beams, wonky floors and deeply comfortable bedrooms with flowers, antiques and gleaming bathrooms. Breakfast is in the large, sunny garden room: fruit, homemade marmalade, a full English with local and home-grown produce. Head out for walks from the door, great gardens, Bewl Water sports. Return to a garden bordered by rhododendrons and admire the Weald of Kent views from the Bamboozle, as the roosting rooks chatter in the trees; walk along country footpaths to a good pub for dinner.

Rooms	2 twin/doubles; 1 double sharing bathroom with a twin/double: £100–£110.
Meals	Pubs/restaurants 1 mile.
Closed	Rarely.

Minimum stay: 2 nights in high season. Children over 10 welcome.

Carol Ballett
Bewl Rookery,
The Colleens, Cousley Wood,
Wadhurst, TN5 6HE
Tel +44 (0)1892 782482
Mobile +44 (0)7704 196520
Email carol@bewlrookery.co.uk
Web www.bewlrookery.co.uk

Entry 347   Map 5

Warwickshire

Little Bridge Cottage

Your own snug contemporary bolthole. The open-plan living space has a washed oak floor, patchwork armchair, doors to a patio, and a nifty kitchen area. Hop upstairs to a sunny bedroom; shower rooms (wet room down, en suite up) are smart. Karen gives you home-baked cookies, and a breakfast of homemade granola, smoked salmon or full English – brought through from the main house. Walk, cycle, have yoga arranged; Birmingham is a few minutes by train. A Sami hut adds to the fun: book it as an extra sitting room, for children to sleep in, and to cook supper over the fire – Karen brings a basket of salad, Aga potatoes and marinated steaks... wonderful!

Rooms	1 triple with single sofabed: £125. Extra bed/sofabed £25 per person per night.
Meals	Hut supper £25 (DIY). Pubs/restaurants 3 miles.
Closed	Occasionally & Christmas.

Hut where you can cook your own supper; space for 2 children to sleep

Karen Morris
Little Bridge Cottage,
Lea Marston,
Sutton Coldfield, B76 0BN

Tel	+44 (0)1675 470020
Mobile	+44 (0)7411 473791
Email	littlebridgecottage@gmail.com
Web	www.littlebridgecottage.co.uk

Entry 348   Map 8

Warwickshire

Park Farm House

Fronted by a circular drive, the warm red-brick farmhouse is listed and old – it dates from 1655. Linda is friendly and welcoming, a genuine B&B pro, giving you an immaculate guest sitting room filled with pretty family pieces. The bedrooms sport comfortable mattresses, mahogany or brass beds, blankets on request, bathrobes, flowers and magazines; bathrooms are traditional but spotless. A haven of rest from the motorway (morning hum only) this is in the heart of a working farm yet hugely convenient for Birmingham, Warwick, Stratford and Coventry. You may get their own beef at dinner and the vegetables are home-grown.

Rooms	1 double, 1 twin: £79–£82. Singles from £48.
Meals	Dinner, 3 courses, from £25. Supper £19. Pub/restaurant 1.5 miles.
Closed	Rarely.

Linda Grindal
Park Farm House,
Spring Road,
Barnacle Shilton,
Coventry, CV7 9LG

Tel	+44 (0)2476 612628
Email	richgrinfarm@btconnect.com
Web	www.parkfarmguesthouse.co.uk

Entry 349   Map 8

Warwickshire

Shrewley Pools Farm

A charming, eccentric home and fabulous for families, with space to play and animals to see: sheep, bantams and pigs. A fragrant, romantic garden with a blossoming orchard and a fascinating house (1640), all low ceilings, aged floors and steep stairs. Timbered passages lead to large, pretty, sunny bedrooms (all with electric blankets) with leaded windows and polished wooden floors and a family room with everything needed for a baby. In a farmhouse dining room Cathy serves sausages, bacon, and eggs from the farm, can do gluten-free breakfasts and is happy to do teas for children. Buy a day ticket and fish in the lake.

Rooms	1 twin: £55–£75. 1 family room for 4: £60–£110. Singles £55–£65. Extra bed/sofabed £20–£30 per person per night. Cot available.
Meals	Packed lunch £7. Child's high tea £7. Pub/restaurant 1.5 miles.
Closed	Christmas.

Cathy Dodd
Shrewley Pools Farm,
Five Ways Road, Haseley,
Warwick, CV35 7HB
Tel   +44 (0)1926 484315
Mobile   +44 (0)7818 280681
Email   cathydodd@hotmail.co.uk
Web   www.shrewleypoolsfarm.co.uk

Entry 350   Map 8

Warwickshire

Austons Down

A fine modern country house with splendid views of the rural Vale of Arden. Your hosts are generous and chatty and look after you well. Their comfortable and relaxed family home has an elegant, light-filled sitting room complete with antiques, fabulous marquetry and open fire; bedrooms are fresh and traditional, bathrooms immaculate. Breakfast on homemade bread, compotes, a continental spread or full English. Admire Jacob sheep on the farm, relax in the terraced gardens. Plenty to visit nearby too: Warwick Castle, Stratford, National Trust properties, classic car museums... and the Monarch's Way is on the doorstep.

Rooms	1 double, 2 twin/doubles: £90–£160. Singles £60–£140. Extra bed/sofabed £15–£25 per person per night.
Meals	Pubs/restaurants 5-minute drive.
Closed	Rarely.

Minimum stay: 2 nights at weekends.

Lucy Horner
Austons Down,
Saddlebow Lane,
Claverdon, CV35 8PQ
Tel   +44 (0)1926 842068
Mobile   +44 (0)7767 657352
Email   lmh@austonsdown.com
Web   www.austonsdown.com

Entry 351   Map 8

Warwickshire

Marston House

A generous feel pervades this lovely family home; Kim's big friendly kitchen is the hub of the house. She and John are easy-going and kind and there's no standing on ceremony. Feel welcomed with tea on arrival, delicious breakfasts, oodles of interesting facts about what to do in the area. The house, with solar electricity, is big and sunny; old rugs cover parquet floors, soft sofas tumble with cushions, sash windows look onto the smart garden packed with birds and borders. Bedrooms are roomy, traditional and supremely comfortable. A special, peaceful place with a big heart, great walks from the door and Silverstone a short hop.

Rooms	1 twin/double with separate bath; 1 twin/double with separate shower: £95–£115. Singles £80.
Meals	Pubs 10-minute drive. Supper, 3 courses from £30. Dinner £35 (min. 4).
Closed	Rarely.

Electric bikes available to rent.

Kim & John Mahon
Marston House,
Byfield Road, Priors Marston,
Southam, CV47 7RP
Tel +44 (0)1327 260297
Mobile +44 (0)7813 831028
Email kim@mahonand.co.uk
Web www.ivabestbandb.co.uk

Entry 352 Map 8

Warwickshire

Sequoia House

A riverside stroll along the old tramway path brings you to the centre of Stratford. Step into the handsome hallway of this impeccable Victorian house to find high ceilings, deep bays, generous landings and a homely sitting room. The Evanses downsized from the hotel they used to run here, and are happy to treat just a few guests: trouser presses (yes!) and piles of towels mingle with fine old furniture in immaculate bedrooms; two have Swan Theatre views. Hotel touches, a lovely warm welcome, Jean's cake on arrival and homemade preserves at breakfast. Park off road – or leave the car at home.

Rooms	4 doubles: £125–£135. 1 single: £95–£110.
Meals	Pub/restaurant 100 yds.
Closed	Christmas & New Year.

Minimum stay: 2 nights at weekends.

Jean & Philip Evans
Sequoia House,
51 Shipston Road,
Stratford-upon-Avon, CV37 7LN
Tel +44 (0)1789 268852
Mobile +44 (0)7833 727914
Email info@sequoia-house.co.uk
Web www.sequoia-house.co.uk

Entry 353 Map 8

Warwickshire

Cross o' th' Hill Farm

Stratford is a 12-minute walk by footpath across a field, and from the veranda you can see the church where Shakespeare is buried. The farm predates medieval Stratford with later additions to the house in 1860, though it has an earlier Georgian feel. All is chic, spacious and full of light with deco chandeliers, floor to ceiling sash windows, large uncluttered bedrooms and contemporary bathrooms. Wake to bird song, play the baby grand piano, enjoy croquet on the lawn and picnic in the gardens and orchards. Decima grew up here; she and David are charming hosts and passionate about art and architecture.

Rooms	2 doubles; 1 double with separate bath/shower: £110. Singles £75.
Meals	Pubs/restaurants 15-minute walk.
Closed	Easter, 31 October – 1 May.

Minimum stay: 2 nights.

Decima Noble
Cross o' th' Hill Farm,
Clifford Lane,
Stratford-upon-Avon, CV37 8HP
Tel +44 (0)1789 204738
Mobile +44 (0)7973 971067
Email decimanoble@hotmail.com
Web www.cross-o-th-hill-farm.com

Entry 354   Map 8

Warwickshire

Grove Farm

Down quiet lanes to the house that Charlie was born in – her young family are the third generation to live here. Bright bedrooms up in the eaves have oak beams, gingham armchairs and comfy beds; small bathrooms, recently revamped. Hop down for homelaid eggs, homemade bread, sausages, bacon and black pudding from down the road – outside when the sun shines, or by the fire in the dining room. Children will love it: dogs, rabbits, hens all happy to have a pat; a swing, log cabin, dens and Flappy the cockerel too. Roses and gangs of cheerful hollyhocks dot the gardens, you can roam the woodland and owls hoot you to sleep. Charming.

Rooms	2 doubles: £85-£90. 1 family room for 5: £120-£180. Singles £60.
Meals	Pubs/restaurants 1.5 miles.
Closed	Rarely.

Charlie Coldicott
Grove Farm,
Stratford Road,
Ettington,
Stratford-upon-Avon, CV37 7NX
Mobile +44 (0)7774 776682
Email grovefarmbb@btconnect.com

Entry 355   Map 8

Warwickshire

Stamford Hall

Soft hills and lines of poplars bring you to the high, pretty red-brick Georgian house with a smart hornbeam hedge. James, whose art decorates the walls, and Alice look after you impeccably but without fuss. You have a generous sitting room overlooking the garden, with gleaming furniture, early estate and garden etchings, and pastel blue sofas. Peaceful bedrooms are on the second floor and both have charm: soft wool tartan rugs on comfy beds, calming colours, attractive fabrics, restful outlooks. Wake to a delicious full English breakfast; walk it off in open countryside or a day out exploring Stratford.

Rooms	1 double, 1 twin: £85. Singles £60.
Meals	Pub 1 mile.
Closed	Christmas & occasionally.

James & Alice Kerr
Stamford Hall,
Fosse Way, Ettington,
Stratford-upon-Avon, CV37 7PA
Tel   +44 (0)1789 740239
Email   stamfordhall@gmail.com
Web   www.stamfordhall.co.uk

Entry 356   Map 8

Warwickshire

The Old Manor House

An attractive 16th-century manor house with peaceful landscaped gardens sweeping down to the river Stour. The beamed double has oak furniture and a big bathroom; the fresh twin rooms (one in a private wing) are simply lovely. There is a large and elegant drawing and dining room for visitors to share, with antiques, contemporary art and an open fire. Jane prepares first-class breakfasts, and in warm weather you can have tea on the terrace: enjoy the pots of tulips in spring, old scented roses in summer, the meadow land beyond. A comfortable, lived-in family house with Stratford and the theatre close by. Guests love it here.

Rooms	1 double, 2 twin/doubles, each with separate bathroom: £95. Singles £75.
Meals	Dinner, 3 courses, from £35. Restaurants nearby.
Closed	22 December – 1 March.

Minimum stay: 2 nights at weekends after Easter.

Jane Pusey
The Old Manor House,
Halford,
Shipston-on-Stour, CV36 5BT
Tel   +44 (0)1789 740264
Mobile   +44 (0)7786 467916
Email   oldmanorhalford@btinternet.com
Web   www.oldmanor-halford.co.uk

Entry 357   Map 8

Warwickshire

Salford Farm House

Beautiful within, handsome without. Thanks to subtle colours, oak beams and lovely old pieces, Jane has achieved a seductive combination of comfort and style. A flagstoned hallway and an old rocking horse, ticking clocks, beeswax, fresh flowers: this house is well-loved. Jane was a ballet dancer, green-fingered Richard is MD of nearby Hillers, an award-winning fruit farm, café and shop – you may expect meat and game from the Ragley Estate and delicious fruits in season. Bedrooms have a soft, warm elegance and flat-screen TVs, bathrooms are spotless and welcoming, views are to garden or fields. Wholly delightful.

Rooms	2 twin/doubles: £100. Singles £75.
Meals	Dinner £30. Restaurant 2.5 miles.
Closed	Rarely.

Jane & Richard Beach
Salford Farm House,
Salford Priors,
Evesham, WR11 8XN
Tel   +44 (0)1386 870000
Mobile   +44 (0)7798 820713
Email   salfordfarmhouse@aol.com
Web   www.salfordfarmhouse.co.uk

Entry 358   Map 8

Wiltshire

Bullocks Horn Cottage

Up a country lane is this hidden-away house which the delightful Legges have turned into a haven of peace. Liz loves fabrics and flowers and mixes them with flair, Colin has painted a mural for the conservatory, bright with plants and wicker sofa. Sunny bedrooms are traditional and colourful with lovely views; the sitting room has a log fire, fine antiques, big comfy sofas, and the garden is so special it's appeared in magazines. Home-grown organic veg and herbs and local seasonal food make an appearance at dinner which, on balmy nights, you may eat under the arbour, covered in climbing roses and jasmine.

Rooms	1 twin; 1 twin/double with separate shower: £95. Singles £62.50.
Meals	Dinner £25-£30. BYO. Pub 1.5 miles.
Closed	Christmas.

Children over 10 welcome.

Colin & Liz Legge
Bullocks Horn Cottage,
Charlton,
Malmesbury, SN16 9DZ
Tel   +44 (0)1666 577600
Email   bullockshorn@clara.co.uk
Web   www.bullockshorn.co.uk

Entry 359   Map 3

Wiltshire

Manor Farm

Farmyard heaven in the Cotswolds. A 17th-century farmhouse in 550 arable acres; horses in the paddock, dozing dogs in the yard, tumbling blooms outside the door and a perfectly tended village, with duck pond, a short walk. Beautiful bedrooms are softly lit, with muted colours, plump goose down pillows and the crispest linen. Breakfast in front of the fire is a banquet of delights, tea among the roses is a treat, thanks to charming, welcoming Victoria; she will arrange a table for dinner at the pub too. This is the postcard England of dreams, with Castle Combe, Lacock, grand walking and gardens to visit.

Rooms	2 doubles, 1 twin: £100-£110. Singles £55-£65.
Meals	Pub 1 mile.
Closed	Christmas.

Over 12s welcome.

Victoria Lippiatt-Onslow
Manor Farm,
Alderton, Chippenham, SN14 6NL
Tel   +44 (0)1666 840271
Mobile +44 (0)7721 415824
Email victoria.lippiatt@btinternet.com
Web   www.themanorfarm.co.uk

Entry 360   Map 3

Wiltshire

Bridges Court

You're in the heart of the village with its small shop, friendly pub and the Melvilles' lovely 18th-century farmhouse. It's a comfortable, relaxed home; dogs wander, horses whinny, and there's a beautiful garden to wander with a Kiftsgate rose and a swimming pool for sunny days. On the second floor, off a corridor filled with paintings, are three florally inspired bedrooms: comfortable, bright and spacious with views to the village green. Breakfast leisurely on all things local at the long table in a dining room filled with silver and china. There's a pleasant guests' sitting room to relax in too.

Rooms	1 double, 1 twin; 1 double with separate bath: £90. Singles £65. Discount for stays of 3 nights or more, excluding Badminton w/e.
Meals	Pub in village.
Closed	Rarely.

Fiona Melville
Bridges Court,
Luckington, SN14 6NT
Tel   +44 (0)1666 840215
Mobile +44 (0)7711 816839
Email fionamelville2003@yahoo.co.uk
Web   www.bridgescourt.co.uk

Entry 361   Map 3

Wiltshire

Fisherman's House

Swing off the village road to find the prettiest 1810 house, and vivacious Heather who has filled her home with garden flowers, good art and a real eye for design and colour. The welcoming sitting room has lots of plumped up sofas and a roaring fire on chilly days; in summer you'll want tea in the fecund garden which swoops down to the river – a huge draw for birds, maybe even a kingfisher. Bedrooms have pretty wallpapers, fresh ginghams and chintzes, interesting books, impeccable bathrooms. Wake to freshly-squeezed orange juice, scrambled eggs and homemade marmalade. Avebury is a 20-minute drive and Rick Stein's in Marlborough just two miles.

Rooms	1 double; 1 twin with separate bath: £100. 1 single: £55. Stays of 2+ nights £90.
Meals	Pubs/restaurants 4-minute walk.
Closed	Rarely.

Fly fishing can be arranged.

	Heather Coulter Fisherman's House, Mildenhall, Marlborough, SN8 2LZ
Tel	+44 (0)1672 515390
Mobile	+44 (0)7785 225363
Email	heathercoulter610@btinternet.com
Web	www.fishermanshouse.co.uk

Entry 362   Map 3

Wiltshire

Scarwood

A honeysuckle-clad house looking down the Kennet valley. Mike and Louise's home has a friendly vibe; he speaks French and they have stories to tell of their travels. Discover walls of books, a tribal rug on a chair, kilims, African pieces, a magnificent gold-framed patriarchal portrait above a wood-burner. Bedrooms have art, flowers and fine linen; one has a charming old Indian banister as the bedhead. Breakfast is in the sunny, open-plan kitchen: honey from the farm next door, local Ramsbury sausages. Savernake Forest is on the doorstep – heaven for walking and foraging; Marlborough has an annual jazz festival; Avebury stone circle is nearby.

Rooms	1 double; 1 twin/double with separate bathroom: £50-£90. Singles £50-£55.
Meals	Pubs/restaurants 2.5 miles.
Closed	Christmas.

	Louise McNeilage Scarwood, Mildenhall, Marlborough, SN8 2NG
Tel	+44 (0)1672 515707
Mobile	+44 (0)7867 977761
Email	louisedeb@hotmail.co.uk
Web	www.scarwood.co.uk

Entry 363   Map 3

Wiltshire

Oaklands

A spacious townhouse, south-facing garden, two dear dogs and lovely old Silver Cross pram sitting under the stairs. No wonder this delightful, 1880s house has been in the family forever. It was the first house in Warminster to have a bathroom; these have multiplied since and now it's a comfortable home filled with fine antiques and attractive furnishings. Andrew and Carolyn, relaxed and charming, serve delicious breakfasts in the large conservatory. Bedrooms are inviting: beds are topped with fine linen, and you have views over churchyard, lawns and trees; bathrooms sparkle — one has a big walk-in shower. Restaurants are a stroll.

Rooms	1 double: £70. 1 double, 1 twin sharing bathroom (let to same party only): from £85. (Double and twin together: £110.) Singles £55.
Meals	Pub/restaurant 0.5 miles.
Closed	Christmas & occasionally.

Carolyn & Andrew Lewis
Oaklands,
88 Boreham Road,
Warminster, BA12 9JW

Tel	+44 (0)1985 300564
Mobile	+44 (0)7702 587533
Email	apl1944@yahoo.co.uk
Web	www.stayatoaklands.co.uk

Entry 364   Map 3

Wiltshire

Deverill End

Colourful gardens surround this comfortable house, and fantastic views of the Wiltshire downs, Wylye valley and a tall steeple stretch as far as the eye can see. Sim and Joy are well-travelled and friendly; their sunny sitting room, warmed by a wood-burner, is full of books, art and African treasures. Comfortable bedrooms are all downstairs: soft colours, posies of flowers, little shower rooms. In the kitchen or dining room is where you feast on a breakfast of eggs and fruits from the garden, homemade jams and home-grown tomatoes in season — they used to grow 300 acres of them in Africa! Bath and Salisbury are an easy hop.

Rooms	2 doubles, 1 twin: £80. Singles £60-£80.
Meals	Pub 5-minute walk.
Closed	Rarely.

Children over 10 welcome.

Joy Greathead
Deverill End,
Sutton Veny,
Warminster, BA12 7BY

Tel	+44 (0)1985 840356
Email	deverillend@gmail.com
Web	www.deverillend.co.uk

Entry 365   Map 3

Wiltshire

Milton Farm

You'll feel immediately at home when you walk into James and Debs' farmhouse. Built 15 years ago, with beautifully mellow Chilmark stone, yet it looks as if it's been here for much longer. Your airy bedroom has flowers, books, tea, coffee and biscuits; lie in the deeply comfortable bed and soak up stunning countryside views. There's an extra room for children. Breakfast is served by the window in the sitting room; more flowers and cheerful pottery decorate the table. Visit Stourhead, Stonehenge, arty Bruton; the Jurassic coast is just 50 minutes. Return to a huge squashy sofa by the fire, plenty of books and magazines to browse.

Rooms	1 double with separate bathroom: £80. Extra bed available.
Meals	Pubs/restaurants 3 miles.
Closed	Rarely.

James Hyde
Milton Farm,
East Knoyle,
Salisbury, SP3 6BG
Tel   +44 (0)1747 830686
Email   jameshyde27@gmail.com

Entry 366   Map 3

Wiltshire

Dowtys

A beautiful country house with fabulous views over the Nadder valley. Peaceful, private, stylish bedrooms (one on the ground floor with its own sitting room) have original beams, antiques and supremely comfy Vi-Spring beds; bathrooms are perfect. The sunny guest sitting room has a contemporary feel, with its wood-burner and sliding doors to the well-tended garden. Enjoy a delicious breakfast in the dining room, or out on the terrace, sit beneath the espaliered limes in the lovely garden, dip into the National Trust woods. Footpaths start from the gate and your charming hosts will help you with all your plans.

Rooms	1 ground-floor double with sitting room; 1 twin with separate bath/shower: £90–£100. 1 suite for 5: £90–£180. Singles from £65.
Meals	Packed lunch from £7. Pub 0.25 miles.
Closed	Rarely.

Di & Willi Verdon-Smith
Dowtys,
Dowtys Lane,
Dinton, Salisbury, SP3 5ES
Tel   +44 (0)1722 716886
Email   dowtys.bb@gmail.com
Web   www.dowtysbedandbreakfast.co.uk

Entry 367   Map 3

Wiltshire

19 Glenmore Road

An elegant house and a surprising find on the edge of this busy city. Tim (Canadian) and Biddy are a creative pair. Guests have their own sunny yellow sitting room, bedrooms are inviting and you'll find art, antiques, flowers and Tim's photos and beautiful handmade furniture throughout. Breakfast is jam-packed: seasonal fruit from the allotment, greenhouse tomatoes, homemade muesli and marmalade, local market produce – out on the terrace if sunny; the garden is a picture of bluebells in spring. The Cathedral has the tallest spire in the country, Stonehenge is nearby and there are festivals to be enjoyed throughout the year.

Rooms	1 double; 1 twin/double with separate bathroom: £90. Singles £75.
Meals	Pubs/restaurants 20-minute walk.
Closed	Christmas & New Year.

Children over 10 welcome.

Biddy Walker & Tim Chadsey
19 Glenmore Road,
Salisbury, SP1 3HF
Tel +44 (0)1722 412077
Mobile +44 (0)7957 823643
Email tchadsey@uwclub.net
Web www.no19bandbsalisbury.com

Entry 368   Map 3

Wiltshire

The Garden Cottage

You'll love the Woodford Valley and this thatched cottage at the edge of the village. It has long views, stacks of character and traditionally decorated rooms: a ground floor twin with roll top bathroom and two cosy doubles upstairs that share a bathroom. Fabrics are flowered, headboards upholstered, mattresses top quality. Or choose to snuggle up by the wood-burner in a charming shepherd's hut and sleep out under the stars – one has a king-sized bed. Breakfast in the kitchen, or pretty garden, on Annie's homemade bread and good things local. Head out to explore Avebury and Stonehenge.

Rooms	1 twin with separate bathroom; 2 doubles sharing bathroom (let to same party only): £90. 2 shepherd's huts for 2 each with shower, sink and loo: £90.
Meals	Pub 0.5 miles.
Closed	Occasionally.

Cash or cheque accepted. Arrivals before 4pm.

Annie Arkwright
The Garden Cottage,
Upper Woodford,
Salisbury, SP4 6PA
Tel +44 (0)1722 782447
Email annie747@btinternet.com

Entry 369   Map 3

Wiltshire

The Mill House

In a tranquil village next to the river is a house surrounded by water meadows and a wilderness garden. Roses ramble, marsh orchids bloom and butterflies shimmer in this 12-acre labour of love. Michael's home, a time-worn 18th-century miller's house, is packed with country clutter – porcelain, foxes' brushes, ancestral photographs above the fire – while bedrooms are quaint, flowery and old-fashioned with firm comfy beds. Breakfasts are served at small tables in the pretty dining room. Visit nearby Stonehenge, wander round historic Salisbury; return to sunny seats in the garden and watch the river Till go by.

Rooms	3 doubles: £100. 1 family room for 4: £100-£140. Singles £75-£80.
Meals	Pub 5-minute walk.
Closed	Rarely.

Children over 7 welcome.

Michael Mertens
The Mill House,
Berwick St James,
Salisbury, SP3 4TS
Tel   +44 (0)1722 790331 (and fax)
Email   m.mertens@btinternet.com
Web   www.millhouse.org.uk

Entry 370   Map 3

Worcestershire

Huntlands Farm

Deep in the rural shires Lucy (who runs inspiring upholstery courses) and Stephen give you delightful B&B on a working farm. They've lovingly coaxed this 15th-century house back to life: huge rooms, two with four-posters, are hugely comfortable with patterned rugs on wide floorboards, reclaimed wardrobes and views over the orchard or farm. You get roll top tubs to wallow in, fluffy towels and local soaps. Breakfast in the convivial dining room on eggs from the hens, sausages from the pigs and homemade preserves. There's dinner too, roasts and stews or traditional Caribbean fare. The Malvern showground is nearby.

Rooms	2 doubles, 1 twin/double: £85-£100. 1 suite for 2: £100-£105. 1 family room for 4 with sofabed & separate bathroom (price for 2 adults & 2 children): £70-£95.
Meals	Dinner, 3 courses, £24.50. Pubs/restaurants 0.5 miles.
Closed	Rarely.

Minimum stay: 2 nights. Children over 10 welcome.

Lucy Brodie
Huntlands Farm,
Gaines Road, Whitbourne,
Worcester, WR6 5RD
Tel   +44 (0)1886 821955
Mobile +44 (0)7828 286360
Email   lucy@huntlandsfarm.co.uk
Web   www.huntlandsfarm.co.uk

Entry 371   Map 8

Worcestershire

Old Country Farm & The Lighthouse

Ella's passion for this tranquil place – and conservation of its wildlife – is infectious. She's keen on home-grown and local food too so breakfast is delicious. Dating from the 1400s, the farm is a delightful rambling medley: russet stone and colour-washed brick, huge convivial round table by the Aga, rugs on polished floors. The sitting room has wood-burner, piano and books, and you sleep soundly in pretty, cottagey bedrooms: lovely linen, garden flowers. In winter you stay in The Lighthouse, down the lane: an inspired green-oak retreat with soaring beams, snug library, comfy downstairs bedrooms and roses in the garden. Magical.

Rooms	1 double; 2 doubles both with separate shower: £65–£90. Singles £40–£55.
Meals	Pubs/restaurants 3 miles.
Closed	Rarely.

Minimum stay: 2 nights.

Ella Grace Quincy
Old Country Farm & The Lighthouse,
Mathon,
Malvern, WR13 5PS
Tel   +44 (0)1886 880867
Email ella@oldcountryhouse.co.uk
Web   www.oldcountryhouse.co.uk

Entry 372   Map 8

Worcestershire

The Birches

Thoughtful Katharine is attentive; Edward puts you at ease humming a jolly tune. Come and go as you please from this self-contained annexe, spotless and contemporary. French windows lead to a pretty terrace, then to a charming garden opening to fields and views of the Malverns. Though the house is easily accessible, the tranquillity is sublime; plenty of spots to sit and ponder the view back to the timber-framed house. Hens pottering on the lawn lay eggs for breakfast, served – in your room – with local bacon and sausages, and bread from the baker. Wander further for abundant leafy walks and lovely Regency Malvern.

Rooms	Annexe – 1 double: £90. Singles £70.
Meals	Pub/restaurant 0.3 miles.
Closed	Rarely.

Katharine Litchfield
The Birches,
Birts Street, Birtsmorton,
Malvern, WR13 6AW
Tel   +44 (0)1684 833821
Mobile +44 (0)7875 458441
Email katharine-thebirches@hotmail.co.uk
Web   www.the-birchesbedandbreakfast.co.uk

Entry 373   Map 8

Yorkshire

Union Place

A listed Adam Georgian townhouse – elegance epitomised. Lofty well-proportioned rooms with polished floors and cornices and fireplaces intact are delightfully dotted with sophisticated, quirky *objets*: bead-and-embroidery lampshades and chandeliers, bone china, a small mirrored Indian ceramic child's dress – and your urbane host Richard's accomplished paintings. Bedrooms, one painted duck egg blue, one green with floral wallpaper, are beautiful, with lots of lace and fine linen; the claw-foot roll top in the shared bathroom cuts a dash. Breakfast is unbeatable… then it's off to explore the North Yorkshire Moors. Superb.

Rooms	2 doubles sharing bath, extra wc available: £80.
Meals	Pubs/restaurants within walking distance.
Closed	Christmas.

Pets by arrangement.

	Richard & Jane Pottas
	Union Place,
	9 Upgang Lane,
	Whitby, YO21 3DT
Tel	+44 (0)1947 605501
Email	pottas1@btinternet.com
Web	www.unionplacewhitby.co.uk

Entry 374   Map 13

Yorkshire

20 St Hilda's Terrace

Little back lanes, an old gate, a secret walled garden and a large bay-windowed Georgian house. You're bang in the heart of Whitby yet the feel is very peaceful with airy rooms, flowers, botanical fabrics, elegant antiques, original art – and a Blüthner piano to play. Your pretty bedroom is reached up a graceful staircase; find high ceilings, a plump bed and views through sash windows. Your breakfast is continental and you can have it in the drawing room, the garden on fine days, or in bed if you're feeling lazy. Stroll to the beach for wild walks, explore the Yorkshire Moors or the shops in town – returning will be a pleasure.

Rooms	1 double with separate bath/shower: £80.
Meals	Continental breakfast. Pubs/restaurants 0.3 miles.
Closed	Rarely.

	Pip Baines
	20 St Hilda's Terrace,
	Whitby, YO21 3AE
Tel	+44 (0)1947 602435
Email	marylouisa@talktalk.net

Entry 375   Map 13

Yorkshire

Nineteen

You'll be fascinated ambling round Whitby with its cobbled streets, independent shops and deliciously dark literary links – there's a great beach and Rick Stein recommended fish and chips too. Return to the prettiest terrace in town where the first floor is yours, the beds are for conking out in extreme comfort and light streams in through sash windows with shutters intact. Peter and Lucy have good taste, original art and exquisite antiques so everywhere you look there's something beautiful. Breakfast is hidden in your own mini fridge: bread from Bothams, jams, yogurts and proper ground coffee. Walkers can tramp straight onto the moors.

Rooms	2 doubles each with separate bathroom: £70-£90.
Meals	Pubs/restaurants 3-minute walk.
Closed	24-26 December.

Minimum stay: 2 nights.

Lucy Weller & Peter Trickett
Nineteen,
19 St Hilda's Terrace,
Whitby, YO21 3AE
Tel   +44 (0)1947 606385
Email   info@19sthildas.uk
Web   www.19sthildas.uk

Entry 376   Map 13

Yorkshire

Thorpe Hall

Arrive and listen: nothing, bar the wind in the trees and the odd seagull. The eye gathers glimmering sea and mighty headland, the final edge of the moors… are there still smugglers? This old listed house smells of polish and flowers, the drawing room breathes history. Angelique is a delight and has furnished it all, including TV-free bedrooms (one downstairs), with an eclectic mix of old and new; wonky walls and creaky floors add to the atmospheric feel. She's hung contemporary art on ancient walls and made a veg patch with young Phoebe. David helps out with simple breakfast when he's not globetrotting. The very opposite of stuffy.

Rooms	3 doubles, 1 twin; 3 doubles, sharing bath & shower rooms: £75-£90. Singles £70-£80. Extra bed/sofabed £15 per person per night.
Meals	Pubs 1 mile.
Closed	Usually Christmas & January.

Minimum stay: 2 nights. Pets by arrangement.

Angelique Russell
Thorpe Hall,
Middlewood Lane, Fylingthorpe,
Whitby, YO22 4TT
Tel   +44 (0)1947 880667
Email   thorpehall@gmail.com
Web   www.thorpe-hall.co.uk

Entry 377   Map 13

Yorkshire

The Farmhouse

Chris and Clare own and run a Swiss ski chalet and their traditional farmhouse has that vibe: friendly, communal, open-house. Find glowing lamps, Persian rugs, wood fires and squashy sofas. Sleep well in good beds: airy Garden Room, Pigeon Loft with double-ended bath, cosy Rebellion Room, sleekly simple Potting Shed tucked in the garden. Breakfast is in the yellow ochre dining room: homemade everything, Whitby kippers, copious coffee. The garden has views over heathered hills; you're in the heart of the North York Moors; Whitby and the coast are close. Return for a four-course dinner – a sociable affair with local produce.

Rooms	2 doubles: £115–£120. 1 suite for 2: £135–£140. 1 annexe for 2 with kitchen: £165. Singles £90–£125.
Meals	Dinner £25–£45, Fridays & Saturdays (rest of week by arrangement). Pubs/restaurants 10-minute walk.
Closed	January – March.

Minimum stay: 2 nights; 3 nights in the annexe. Over 16s welcome.

Chris & Clare Carr
The Farmhouse,
Orchard Farm, Orchard Lane,
Goathland, Whitby, YO22 5JX
Tel   +44 (0)1947 896391
Email enquiries@thefarmhouseyorkshire.co.uk
Web   www.thefarmhouseyorkshire.co.uk

Entry 378   Map 13

Yorkshire

The Wold Cottage

Drive through mature trees, and a proper entrance with signs, to a listed Georgian manor house in 300 glorious acres; tea awaits in the guest sitting room. The graceful dining room has heartlifting views across the landscaped gardens, and there are many original features: fan-lights, high ceilings, broad staircases. Bedrooms are sumptuous, traditional, with lots of thoughtful extras: chocolates, biscuits, monogrammed waffle robes. You are warmed by straw bale heating, and the food is local and delicious. An award-winning breakfast sets you up for a day of discovery: visit RSPB Bempton Cliffs, and the Wolds that have inspired David Hockney.

Rooms	2 doubles, 2 twins: £100–£130. Barn – 1 double: £100–£130. Barn – 1 family room: £100–£165. Singles £60–£75.
Meals	Supper £28. Wine from £15.
Closed	Rarely.

Minimum stay: 2 nights at weekends.

Derek & Katrina Gray
The Wold Cottage,
Wold Newton, Driffield, YO25 3HL
Tel   +44 (0)1262 470696
Mobile +44 (0)7811 203336
Email   katrina@woldcottage.com
Web   www.woldcottage.com

Entry 379   Map 13

Yorkshire

Village Farm

Tucked behind houses and shops, this was once the village farm with land stretching to the coast. Now the one-storey buildings overlooking a courtyard are large bedrooms in gorgeous colours with luxurious touches. Chrysta, who moved from London, is living her dream and looks after you well: baths are deep, beds crisply comfortable, heating is underfoot. Delicious breakfasts are served at wooden tables in a cheerful light room and if you don't want to venture out you can have supper on a tray – homemade bread, cheese and fruit. Stride the cliffs, watch birds at Flamborough Head or make for Spurn Point – remote and lovely.

Rooms	1 double, 1 twin/double: £85. 1 family room for 4: £100. Singles £65.
Meals	Supper £8.50 per person. Pubs/restaurants 3 miles.
Closed	Rarely.

Chrysta Newman
Village Farm,
Back Street, Skipsea,
Driffield, YO25 8SW

Tel   +44 (0)1262 468479
Email info@villagefarmskipsea.co.uk
Web   www.villagefarmskipsea.co.uk

Entry 380   Map 13

Yorkshire

Dowthorpe Hall

Caroline is lovely, cooking is her passion and she trawls the county for the best; fish and seafood from Hornsea, Dexter beef, game from the local shoot; her fruits and veg are home-grown. All is served in a sumptuous Georgian dining room by flickering candlelight, after which you retire to a comfortable drawing room; this is a marvellously elegant, and happy, house. Sleep peacefully on a luxurious mattress, wake to the aroma of bacon, sausages, eggs and home-baked bread. There are acres of gorgeous garden to roam – orchards, pathways, potager and pond – and a trio of historic houses to visit.

Rooms	1 twin/double; 1 double with separate bathroom: £100-£110. Singles £70.
Meals	Dinner £25. Pubs 0.25-5 miles.
Closed	Rarely.

John & Caroline Holtby
Dowthorpe Hall,
Skirlaugh,
Hull, HU11 5AE

Tel   +44 (0)1964 562235
Email john.holtby@farming.co.uk
Web   www.dowthorpehall.com

Entry 381   Map 13

Yorkshire

Thurst House Farm

This solid Pennine farmhouse, its stone mullion windows denoting 17th-century origins, is English to the core. Your warm, gracious hosts give guests a cosy and carpeted sitting room with an open fire in winter and shelves of books to browse; bedrooms are equally generous, with inviting, very comfortable brass beds, lovely antique linen and fresh flowers. The garden has masses of roses, sunny places to sit, a hammock to snooze in and beautiful views. Tuck into homemade bread, marmalade and jams at breakfast, and good traditional English dinners, too – just the thing for walkers who've trekked the Calderdale or the Pennine Way.

Rooms	1 double: £80.
	1 family room for 4: £80-£160.
	Singles by arrangement.
	No charge for children under 4.
Meals	Dinner, 4 courses, £25. BYO.
	Packed lunch £5.
	Restaurants within 0.5 miles.
Closed	Christmas.

David & Judith Marriott
Thurst House Farm,
Soyland, Ripponden,
Sowerby Bridge, HX6 4NN

Tel	+44 (0)1422 822820
Mobile	+44 (0)7759 619043
Email	judith@thursthousefarm.co.uk
Web	www.thursthousefarm.co.uk

Entry 382   Map 12

Yorkshire

Ponden Hall

A house brimming with atmosphere and said to be the inspiration for *Wuthering Heights*. Julie's knowledge of the history is impressive and she offers tours of her fascinating home. Arrive for tea and home-baked cake and soak up the mullion windows, huge flagstones, period pieces and original paintings. Bedrooms have just the right balance of luxury and individuality: an amazing box bed, rocking horse, raftered ceilings – and log stoves in two. A full Yorkshire breakfast is served in the magnificent main hall. Walk the Pennine Way, hop on a steam train at Keighley; Haworth is close too – for all things Brontë and interesting, independent shops.

Rooms	2 doubles: £95-£180.
	1 family room for 4
	(1 four-poster & 2 singles): £160.
Meals	Pubs/restaurants 10-minute walk.
Closed	24-30 December.

Julie Akhurst
Ponden Hall,
Ponden Lane, Stanbury,
Haworth, Keighley, BD22 0HR

Tel	+44 (0)1535 648608
Email	stay@ponden.force9.co.uk
Web	www.ponden-hall.co.uk

Entry 383   Map 12

Yorkshire

Ponden House

Bump your way up the farm track to Brenda's sturdy house, high on the Pennine Way. The spring water makes wonderful tea, the ginger scones are delicious and the house hums with interest and artistic touches. Comfy sofas are jollied up with throws, there are homespun rugs and hangings, paintings, plants and a piano. Feed the hens, plonk your boots by the Aga, chat with your lovely hostess as she turns out fab home cooking; food is a passion. Bedrooms are exuberant, comfortable and cosy, it's great for walkers and there's a hot tub under the stars (bookable in advance). Good value with a relaxed, homely feel.

Rooms	2 doubles; 1 twin with separate bath (occasionally sharing bathroom with family): £75-£85. Singles £50.
Meals	Dinner, 3 courses, £18. BYO. Packed lunch £6. Pub/restaurant 1 mile.
Closed	Rarely.

Brenda Taylor
Ponden House,
Stanbury,
Haworth, BD22 0HR
Tel +44 (0)1535 644154
Email brenda.taylor@pondenhouse.co.uk
Web www.pondenhouse.co.uk

Entry 384   Map 12

Yorkshire

Cold Cotes

Sue and Mark give you relaxation, delicious breakfasts and a dollop of contemporary chic in their 1890s farmhouse on the edge of the Yorkshire Dales. There's a sitting room with stacks of books, squashy sofas, maps, and a separate library for those who want to escape in a book. Smart bedrooms have sitting areas with garden views; those in the barn are just as swish and comfortable. Outside find a beautiful woodland walk, impressive sweeping borders and a cobblestone walk along a stream. The fruit and veg garden provides abundant produce; a little lawned area is surrounded by cherry trees and has a perfect seating area.

Rooms	3 twin/doubles: £89-£109. 4 suites for 2: £99. Singles £75.
Meals	Cold platters and snacks available. Pub/restaurant 2 miles.
Closed	Mid-December to end of February.

Minimum stay: 2 nights.

Sue Bailey & Mark Dyson
Cold Cotes,
Felliscliffe, Harrogate, HG3 2LW
Tel +44 (0)1423 770937
Mobile +44 (0)7970 713334
Email info@coldcotes.com
Web www.coldcotes.com

Entry 385   Map 12

Yorkshire

The Old Vicarage

South Stainley is a small village, with pub, church and this fine vicarage, six miles from Ripon, ten from Harrogate. Come for the races, the Dales… Sleep peacefully in a charming room up under the eaves. Julia has decorated her guest room unfussily, tucked in a sofa and added an antique wardrobe and blanket chest. The bathroom's really smart and big, with separate shower and bath. Linger over your Aga breakfast – full English, scrambled eggs, smoked salmon – in the lofty new garden room with leafy views, pastel colours, original art. You're welcome to use the swimming pool and tennis court, and you can walk to the pub for dinner.

Rooms	1 double: £75–£125.
Meals	Pubs/restaurants 5-minute walk.
Closed	Rarely.

Julia Roe
The Old Vicarage,
South Stainley, Harrogate, HG3 3NE
Tel   +44 (0)1423 770216
Mobile +44 (0)7956 154786
Email   info@oldvicarageharrogate.co.uk
Web   www.oldvicarageharrogate.co.uk

Entry 386   Map 12

Yorkshire

The Hayloft

A single track runs down to this mellow stone farmhouse, which has been in the family for hundreds of years. You stay in the Hayloft at the far end: stone floors heated underfoot, old beams, sofas by the wood-burner, modern kitchen and your own charming walled garden. Up the curved stairs to the mezzanine bedroom with its vintage quilt on a cast-iron bed, and bathroom with free-standing bath and monsoon shower. Fiona leaves you a first-morning breakfast hamper of local produce and also vouchers for fantastic cooked breakfasts in the village's Old School Café. The garden gate leads onto a footpath; Hebden, with pub as well as café, is a short walk.

Rooms	1 annexe for 2: £90–£120.
Meals	Pubs/restaurants 1 mile.
Closed	Rarely.

Minimum stay: 2 nights; 3 nights in high season.

Fiona Hoole
The Hayloft,
Hole Bottom Farm, Hebden,
Skipton, BD23 5DL
Tel   +44 (0)1756 752369
Email   fiona@jerryandbens.co.uk
Web   www.yorkshirebolthole.co.uk

Entry 387   Map 12

Yorkshire

Lane House

Pam and art restorer Richard are chatty and friendly – they love having guests, and are happy to advise on trips. Their converted barn has an artistic vibe throughout. The big, attractive open-plan living space has a galleried landing above; airy bedrooms have soaring beams, striking light fittings, colourful throws; bathrooms are smart. Pam likes to cook so you're in for a treat: tuck in to local produce, eggs from the hens, homemade granola, breads and jams; delicious, perhaps Lebanese or Moroccan, dishes for dinner too. The 50 acres are yours to wander: farmland, woods, a beck – and there's a four-mile Heritage Trail to Bentham.

Rooms	2 doubles: £89-£100. Singles £70. Extra bed/sofabed available £30 per person per night.
Meals	Dinner £15. BYO. Pubs/restaurants 0.5 miles.
Closed	Christmas.

Minimum stay: 2 nights at weekends.

Pam Zahler
Lane House,
Fowgill, High Bentham,
Lancaster, LA2 7AH
Tel   +44 (0)15242 61998
Email pamzahler@hotmail.com
Web   www.lanehouseandcottage.co.uk

Entry 388   Map 12

Yorkshire

Ellerbeck House

Walk from the door of this beautifully restored country house, or head west to the Lakes, east to the Dales, north to Scotland. Period rooms display exquisite antiques and Harriet's artistic touch: sofas and curtains in dark pink and cream, Persian rugs on shiny oak floors, marble fireplaces, stained glass in the stairwell, huge sash windows overlooking the lawn. One window holds the breakfast table – full Cumbrian, at flexible times. Outside, a courtyard for sitting out with the birds and the breeze. It's all so pretty, as is this bucolic – yet accessible – spot near Kirkby Lonsdale, Settle, and Kendal of Mint Cake fame.

Rooms	1 double: £90. Singles £45-£55.
Meals	Pubs/restaurants 2 miles.
Closed	Rarely.

Harriet Sharp
Ellerbeck House,
Westhouse, Ingleton,
Carnforth, LA6 3NH
Tel   +44 (0)15242 41872
Email harrietnsharp@gmail.com
Web   www.ellerbeckhouse.co.uk

Entry 389   Map 12

Yorkshire

Low Mill

Off the village green this handsome historic mill in the Dales keeps many of its original features. The huge beamed guest sitting room has a roaring fire, and the old waterwheel is working! Friendly relaxed Neil and Jane have restored their home, then filled it with interesting art, quirky sculpture, flowers and vintage gems. Bedrooms have tip-top linen and luxurious throws; bathrooms are fabulous. Eat well at separate tables on all things local and home-grown: bacon, pancakes, homemade bread; and for dinner, perhaps Yorkshire ham or herby lamb. The pretty riverside garden is perfect for chilling with a glass of wine.

Rooms	2 doubles: £110-£180. 1 suite for 2: £130-£180. Singles £82-£128.
Meals	Dinner, 2-3 courses, £20-£25. Pubs 5-minute drive.
Closed	Rarely.

Pets by arrangement.

Neil McNair
Low Mill,
Bainbridge,
Leyburn, DL8 3EF

Tel	+44 (0)1969 650553
Email	lowmillguesthouse@gmail.com
Web	www.lowmillguesthouse.co.uk

Entry 390   Map 12

Yorkshire

Stow House

Past ancient stone walls and fields of lambs you reach sleepy Aysgarth and this dignified rectory. Step inside to find – Shoreditch pizzazz! Sarah and Phil have swapped the world of London advertising for a dream house in the Dales; she does cocktails, he does breakfasts and their take on Victoriana is inspiring. Floors, banisters and sash windows have been restored, stairs carpeted in plush red, sofas covered in zinging velvet. Bathrooms are wow, bedrooms are soothing and the papier-mâché hare's head above the bar says it all. A stroll down the hill are the Aysgarth Falls, beloved of Ruskin, Wordsworth and Turner.

Rooms	6 doubles: £110-£175. 1 family room for 3: £175. Extra bed/sofabed £10-£20 per person per night.
Meals	Pubs/restaurants 5-minute walk.
Closed	Rarely.

Minimum stay: 2 nights at weekends.

Sarah & Phil Bucknall
Stow House,
Aysgarth,
Leyburn, DL8 3SR

Tel	+44 (0)1969 663635
Email	info@stowhouse.co.uk
Web	www.stowhouse.co.uk

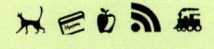

Entry 391   Map 12

Yorkshire

Manor House

It's the handsomest house in the village. Annie – warm, intelligent, fun – invites you in to elegant interiors, artfully cluttered. Tall shuttered windows and a big open fire, candles in sconces, heaps of flowers, charming fabrics: a genuinely relaxing family home. Bedrooms are a treat, one with green views on two sides and a bathroom with a French country feel; fittings are vintage but spotless. Breakfast is good too: eggs from the hens, local chipolatas and bacon. Stride the Dales, bring bikes (secure lock-up, drying room and outdoor hose), discover Georgian Richmond, a hop away; return to a delicious simple supper with garden veg.

Rooms	1 double; 1 twin/double with separate bath: £120.
Meals	Supper, 2 courses, £25–£30. BYO. Pub within 3 miles.
Closed	Christmas.

Annabel Burchnall
Manor House,
Middle Street,
Gayles,
Richmond, DL11 7JF
Tel   +44 (0)1833 621578
Email   annieburchnall@hotmail.com

Entry 392   Map 12

Yorkshire

The Garden Suite

Step from the terrace into a house full of creativity and colour. All on one floor, find cosy places to sit and relax in your deeply comfortable suite. Colin and Wendy (both keen gardeners) are warm souls. Their breakfasts and candlelit dinners include home-grown produce (strawberries, figs, raspberries, veg…) and they're keen for you to feel at home. Outside is a stunning creation of perfect potagers, pathways and pots of lavender, wildflower meadows, secret areas and wisteria-clad walls; there's a summer house too, while Indian Runner ducks, chickens, friendly spaniel and eccentric pigs, Esmerelda and Finlay, add to the relaxed vibe.

Rooms	1 suite for 2: £110. Extra bed/sofabed £25–£40 per person per night.
Meals	Dinner £25–£30. BYO. Pubs/restaurants 20-minute walk.
Closed	Christmas.

Over 12s welcome.

Colin & Wendy Gerrard
The Garden Suite, The Granary, Craggs Lane Farm Steadings, Tunstall, Richmond, DL10 7RB
Tel   +44 (0)1748 832586
Mobile   +44 (0)7596 409632
Email   craggslane@msn.com
Web   www.craggslane.com

Entry 393   Map 12

Yorkshire

The Grange

Through glorious Dales to the pretty village green, where you have a wing of this attractive, old stone house to yourselves. Step into an airy space with original oak beams, comfy sofa, Persian rug and books. Antique and contemporary pieces blend, the bed is clad in pure cotton, the simple shower room has fluffy towels, and there's a kitchen area for rustling up snacks. Your hosts are delightful: Sam has his cabinet making business in the outbuildings; Georgina (professional cook) brings over locally sourced breakfasts and hearty suppers: eggs from the hens, homemade marmalade, smoked salmon… lasagne, crumbles. A friendly place.

Rooms	1 double with sitting and kitchen area: £85. Singles £75.
Meals	Dinner, 2-3 courses, £30-£40. Light supper £15. Restaurant 75 yds.
Closed	Rarely.

Georgina Anderson
The Grange,
East Witton,
Leyburn, DL8 4SL

Mobile +44 (0)7957 144467
Email georgina@thegrangebedandbreakfast.co.uk
Web www.thegrangebedandbreakfast.co.uk

Entry 394   Map 12

Yorkshire

Firs Farm

The landscape is rural and rolling, the lanes are narrow and quiet, and Healey is pretty-as-a-picture: mellow York stone, smart gardens and immaculate paintwork on every house. Richard and Sarah, relaxed and genial, offer homemade cakes and coffee when you arrive and the cosy feel of their home makes you feel instantly at ease. Enjoy a sitting room with an open fire and fabulous fabrics, fresh and cottagey bedrooms with spotted upholstered windows seats, and vases of flowers in every corner. There are great views from the lovely walled garden, acres to roam, wonderful walking, and tip-top towns to visit all around.

Rooms	2 doubles; 1 twin/double with separate bath/shower: £85-£110. Singles £65-£75. Extra bed/sofabed £10-£30 per person per night.
Meals	Packed lunch £7. Pubs/restaurants 1 mile.
Closed	Christmas & New Year.

Children over 10 welcome.

Richard & Sarah Townsend
Firs Farm,
Healey,
Ripon, HG4 4LH

Tel +44 (0)1765 688910
Email sarah@firsfarmbandb.co.uk
Web www.firsfarmbandb.co.uk

Entry 395   Map 12

Yorkshire

Laverton Hall

The hall is a beauty, even on a dull day, and the village is a dream. Half an hour from Harrogate find space, beauty, history (it's 400 years old), three walled gardens and comfort in great measure: beloved antiques, a rocking horse in the hall, feather pillows, thick white towels. Sumptuous breakfasts include seasonal fruit salad, croissants, cereals and a full English spread. The sunny guest sitting room is elegant and charming, the cream and white twin and the snug little single have long views to the river. The area is rich with abbeys and great houses, and then there are the glorious Dales to be explored.

Rooms	1 twin/double: £100. 1 single: £70.
Meals	Pubs/restaurants 2 miles.
Closed	Christmas.

Rachel Wilson
Laverton Hall,
Laverton, Ripon, HG4 3SX
Tel +44 (0)1765 650274
Mobile +44 (0)7711 086385
Email rachel.k.wilson@hotmail.co.uk
Web www.lavertonhall.co.uk

Entry 396   Map 12

Yorkshire

Mallard Grange

Perfect farmhouse B&B. Hens, cats, sheepdogs wander the garden, an ancient apple tree leans against the wall, guests unwind and feel part of the family. Enter the rambling, deep-shuttered 16th-century farmhouse, cosy with well-loved family pieces, and feel at peace with the world. Breakfast is generous – homemade muffins, poached pears with cinnamon, a sizzling full Monty. A winding steep stair leads to big, friendly bedrooms, two cheerful others await in the converted 18th-century smithy, and Maggie's enthusiasm for this glorious area is as genuine as her love of doing B&B. It's a gem!

Rooms	2 twin/doubles: £85-£125. Old Blacksmith's Shop & Carthouse – 2 twin/doubles on ground floor: £85-£125. Singles £85-£110.
Meals	Pubs/restaurants 10-minute drive.
Closed	Christmas & New Year.

Over 12s welcome.

Maggie Johnson
Mallard Grange,
Aldfield, Ripon, HG4 3BE
Tel +44 (0)1765 620242
Mobile +44 (0)7720 295918
Email maggie@mallardgrange.co.uk
Web www.mallardgrange.co.uk

Entry 397   Map 12

Yorkshire

Carlton House

Quietly tucked into a corner of the sedate green, a short stride from the pub, lies a stylishly renovated 18th-century farmhouse. The old wash house, tractor shed and stable have become airy, chic, characterful rooms with beams and fabulous bathrooms. In summer, pull up a chair in a pretty yard with hanging baskets or find a tranquil spot in the charmingly secret garden. The dining room with open fire is a delight, so linger over a breakfast of delicious local produce, then set off for market towns, dales and moors. There's a big-hearted family feel here – Denise's oat and raisin crunchies and soda bread are to die for! Lovely.

Rooms	Outbuildings – 2 doubles, 1 twin/double: £65-£85. Singles £55-£65. Extra bed/sofabed £20-£30 per person per night.
Meals	Pub/restaurant 2-minute walk.
Closed	Rarely.

Denise & David Mason
Carlton House,
Sandhutton,
Thirsk, YO7 4RW
Tel   +44 (0)1845 587381
Email   info@carltonbarns.co.uk
Web   www.carltonbarns.co.uk

Entry 398   Map 12

Yorkshire

Cundall Lodge Farm

Ancient chestnuts, crunchy drive, sheep grazing, hens free-ranging. This four-square Georgian farmhouse could be straight out of Central Casting. Smart, traditional rooms have damask sofas, comfy armchairs, bright wallpapers and views to Sutton Bank's White Horse or the river Swale – and tea and oven-fresh cakes welcome you. Spotless bedrooms are inviting: pretty fabrics, antiques, flowers, Roberts radios. This is a working farm and the breakfast table groans with eggs from the hens, homemade jams and local bacon. The garden and river walks guarantee peace, and David and Caroline are generous and delightful.

Rooms	1 double, 2 twin/doubles: £90-£110.
Meals	Packed lunch £7. Pubs/restaurants 2 miles.
Closed	Christmas & New Year.

Over 14s welcome.

Caroline Barker
Cundall Lodge Farm,
Cundall, York, YO61 2RN
Tel   +44 (0)1423 360203
Mobile   +44 (0)7773 494260
Email   enquiries@cundall-lodgefarm.co.uk
Web   www.cundall-lodgefarm.co.uk

Entry 399   Map 12

Yorkshire

The Mount House

A dollop of stylish fun in the rolling Howardian Hills (AONB), Nick and Kathryn's redesigned village house is light, airy and filled with gorgeous things – good antiques, heaps of photographs, splashy modern art and flowers. The ground-floor twin with white cast-iron beds has its own cosy book-filled sitting room; the sunny upstairs double has views across roof tops to open countryside. Continental breakfasts are a treat, in the garden if it's fine, and Kathryn – an excellent cook – will spoil you at dinner too if you wish. Discover Castle Howard, Nunnington Hall, old market towns and great walking on the doorstep; only 20 minutes from York too.

Rooms	1 double; 1 double with separate bath; 1 twin with sitting room: £90–£140. Singles £75–£100.
Meals	Continental breakfast. Dinner, 3-4 courses, £30–£40. BYO.
Closed	Rarely.

Minimum stay: 2 nights.

	Kathryn Hill The Mount House, Terrington, York, YO60 6QB
Tel	+44 (0)1653 648206
Mobile	+44 (0)7780 536917
Email	mount.house@clayfox.co.uk
Web	www.howardianhillsbandb.co.uk

Entry 400   Map 13

Yorkshire

Shallowdale House

Phillip and Anton have a true affection for their guests so you will be treated royally. Sumptuous bedrooms dazzle in yellows, blues and limes, acres of curtains frame wide views over the Howardian Hills, bathrooms are immaculate. You breakfast on the absolute best: fresh fruit compotes, dry-cured bacon or Whitby kippers, homemade rolls and marmalade. Admire the amazing garden, then walk off in any direction straight from the house. Return to a cosily elegant drawing room with a fire in winter, and an enticing library. Dinner is a real treat – coffee and chocolates before you crawl up to bed? Bliss.

Rooms	2 twin/doubles; 1 double with separate bath/shower: £130–£165. Singles £100–£125.
Meals	Dinner, 4 courses, £45. Pub 0.5 miles.
Closed	Christmas & New Year.

Minimum stay: 2 nights at weekends. Over 12s welcome.

	Anton van der Horst & Phillip Gill Shallowdale House, West End, Ampleforth, YO62 4DY
Tel	+44 (0)1439 788325
Email	stay@shallowdalehouse.co.uk
Web	www.shallowdalehouse.co.uk

Entry 401   Map 12

Channel Islands

Guernsey

Seabreeze

Maggie's house – the most southern on Guernsey – comes with enormous sea views: Herm and Sark glistening in the water under a vast sky, framed by a pretty front garden. The breakfast terrace is hard to beat. Find sofas in the conservatory, entertaining stories from Maggie and Francis, fabulous walks, a beach for picnics. The house started life as HQ for French pilots in WWI; these days warm, rustic interiors make for a great island base. It's not grand, just very welcoming with rooms that hit the spot: bathrobes, super showers, fresh flowers. Use the bikes (or hire locally) then spin up the lane to a top island restaurant. Brilliant.

Rooms	2 twin/doubles: £80-£125. 1 studio for 2 with kitchenette: £125-£150. Singles £50-£85.
Meals	Pubs/restaurants 500 yds & 0.5 miles.
Closed	Rarely.

Self-catering available in studio.

	Maggie Talbot-Cull
	Seabreeze,
	La Moye Lane, Route de Jerbourg,
	St Martin, GY4 6BN
Tel	+44 (0)1481 237929
Email	seabreeze-guernsey@mail.com
Web	www.guernseybandb.com

Entry 402 Map 4

Scotland

Photo: Crookston House, entry 425

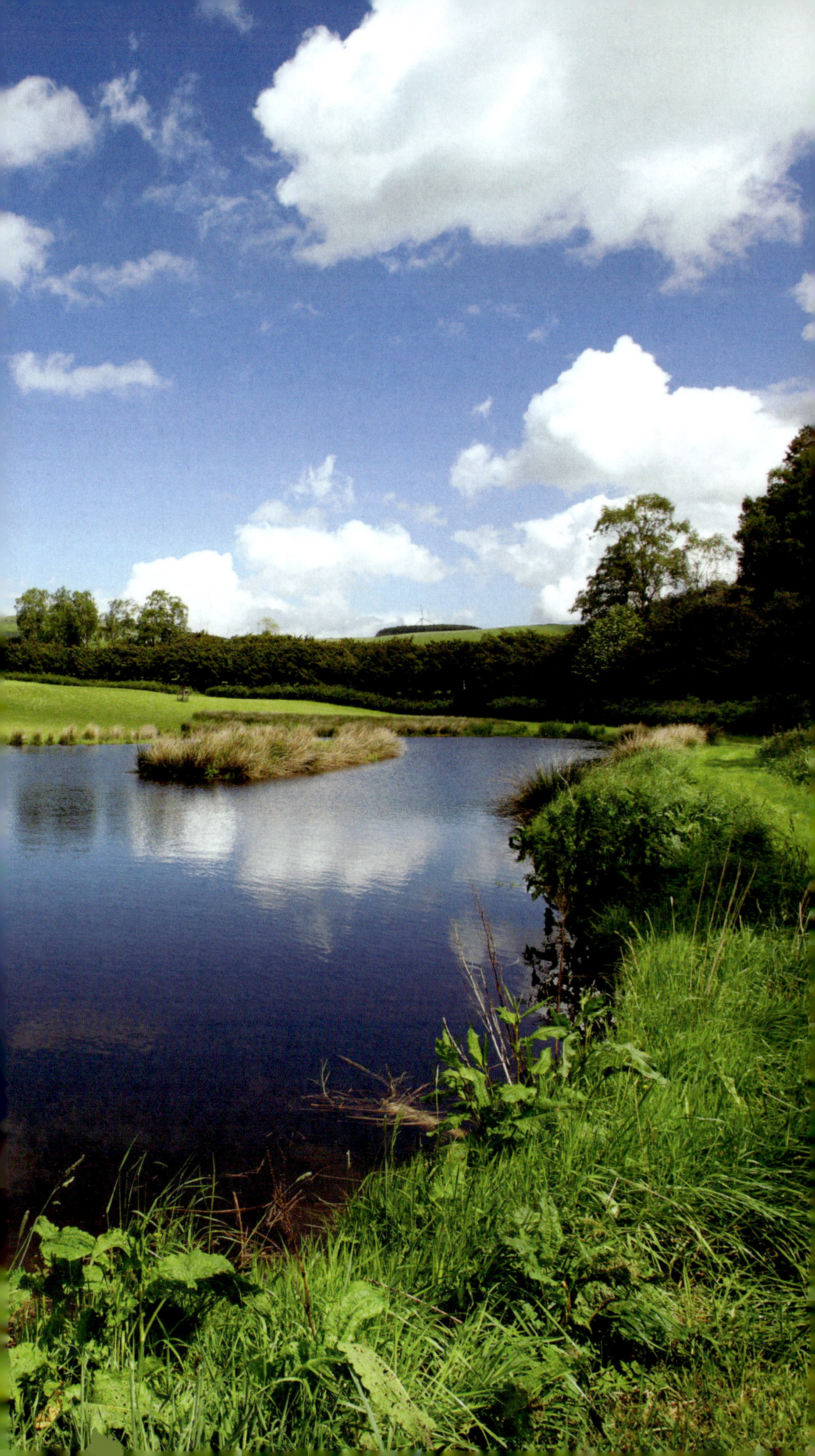

Aberdeenshire

Lynturk Home Farm

The stunning drawing room, with pier-glass mirror, baby grand and enveloping sofas, is reason enough to come; the food, served in a candlelit deep-sage dining room, is delicious too, with produce from the farm. A home full of life where you're treated as friends – your hosts are delightful, helped along by a very personable Jack Russell. It's peaceful, too, on the Aberdeenshire Castle Trail. The handsome farmhouse has been in the family since 1762 and you can roam the rolling 300 acres. Inside: flowers, polished furniture, Persian rugs, family portraits and supremely comfortable bedrooms with fine linen. "A blissful haven," says a guest.

Rooms	1 double, 2 twin/doubles: £100. Singles £60.
Meals	Dinner, 4 courses, £30. Pub 1 mile.
Closed	Rarely.

Pets by arrangement.

John & Veronica Evans-Freke
Lynturk Home Farm,
Alford, AB33 8HU
Tel   +44 (0)1975 562504
Mobile   +44 (0)7773 389793
Email   lynturk@hotmail.com

Entry 403   Map 19

Angus

Newtonmill House

The house and grounds are in perfect order; the owners are warm, charming and discreet. This is a little-known part of Scotland, with glens and gardens to discover; fishing villages, golf courses and deserted beaches, too. Return to a cup of tea in the sitting room or summerhouse, a wander in the lovely walled garden, and a marvellous supper of local produce; Rose grows interesting varieties of potato and her hens' eggs make a great hollandaise! Upstairs are crisp sheets, soft blankets, feather pillows, flowers, homemade fruit cake and warm sparkling bathrooms with thick towels. Let this home envelop you in its warm embrace.

Rooms	1 twin; 1 double with separate bath: £75-£130. Singles £70-£80.
Meals	Dinner £30-£36. BYO. Packed lunch £10. Pub 3 miles.
Closed	Rarely.

Rose & Stephen Rickman
Newtonmill House,
Brechin, DD9 7PZ
Tel   +44 (0)1356 622533
Mobile   +44 (0)7793 169482
Email   rrickman@srickman.co.uk
Web   www.newtonmillhouse.co.uk

Entry 404   Map 19

Argyll & Bute

Callachally House

By the small fishing river at the mouth of the Glen, settled into its own wooded grounds, is a big Scottish farmhouse (once a drovers' inn) where on a still summer night you can hear the lapping of the sea. A fine, traditional, cultured place, it's been in Ian's family since time began and overflows with colour and character. Bedrooms share bathrooms and each is a gem: old polished floors topped with bright rugs, chalky blue walls hung with paintings; you might hear sheepdogs barking at night. Wake to a fine breakfast (Ian loves to cook), head off down winding roads with views of islands and mountains, return to sprawling armchairs by the log fire.

Rooms	3 doubles sharing 2 bathrooms: £90. Adjoining twin also available. Singles £75.
Meals	Restaurants 2 miles away.
Closed	December – March.

	Ian Mazur
	Callachally House,
	Glenforsa, Aros,
	Isle of Mull, PA72 6JN
Mobile	+44 (0)7887 950276
Email	ianmazur@icloud.com
Web	www.largeholidayhousemull.co.uk

Entry 405   Map 17

Argyll & Bute

Melfort House

A truly seductive combination of a wild landscape of ancient woods and hidden glens with rivers that tumble to a blue sea and a big, beautiful house with views straight down the loch. The whole place glows with polished antiques, oak floors, exquisite fabrics, prints and paintings. And Yvonne and Matthew are brilliant at looking after you – whether you're super-active, or not – their fabulous Scottish food is a treat. Bedrooms have soft plaids, superb views and handmade chocolates; bathrooms have huge towels and locally made soaps. Sally forth with boots or bikes, return to a dram by the log fire. Don't book too short a stay!

Rooms	2 twin/doubles: £120–£130. 1 suite for 2: £140. Singles £80. Extra bed/sofabed £20 per person per night.
Meals	Dinner, 4 courses, from £37. Packed lunch £10. Pub/restaurant 400 yds.
Closed	Rarely.

	Yvonne & Matthew Anderson
	Melfort House,
	Kilmelford, Oban, PA34 4XD
Tel	+44 (0)1852 200326
Mobile	+44 (0)7795 438106
Email	relax@melforthouse.co.uk
Web	www.melforthouse.co.uk

Entry 406   Map 17

Argyll & Bute

Glenmore

A pleasingly idiosyncratic traditional country house with no need to stand on ceremony. Built in the 1800s but with 1930s additions setting the style, find solid oak doors and floors, red-pine panelling, Art Deco pieces and a unique carved staircase. Alasdair's family has been here for 150 years and many family antiques remain. One of the huge bedrooms can be arranged as a suite to include a single room and a sofabed; bath and basins are chunky 30s style with chrome plumbing. From the organic garden and the house there are magnificent views of Loch Melfort with its bobbing boats; you're free to come and go as you please.

Rooms	1 double with separate bath/shower: £89–£100. 1 family room for 5: £105–£170. Singles £55–£70. Extra bed/sofabed £15–£25 per person per night.
Meals	Pub 0.5 miles, restaurant 1.5 miles.
Closed	Christmas & New Year.

Melissa & Alasdair Oatts
Glenmore,
Kilmelford, Oban, PA34 4XA
Tel   +44 (0)1852 200314
Mobile   +44 (0)7786 340468
Email   oatts.glenmore22@btinternet.com
Web   www.glenmorecountryhouse.co.uk

Entry 407   Map 14

Argyll & Bute

Winterton

A remote and rugged setting with much comfort indoors. Stephanie and Adrian are a creative, well-travelled pair and their house is packed with warmth and interest, including local art for sale. Be welcomed by home cooking, sink into the views from the sun lounge, sleep soundly in luxurious, very quiet bedrooms. Breakfasts with a delicious twist will set you up for a wonderful day walking in the footsteps of the first Scots through this fascinating history-steeped landscape. Explore the beach, sea loch and woods, discover 'Britain's most beautiful short cut by sea' and from there sail to the Corryvreckan.

Rooms	2 doubles: £105–£120.
Meals	Pubs/restaurants 5 miles. Dinner, 3 courses, from £32.
Closed	Christmas & New Year.

Minimum stay: 2 nights. Parking on-site.

Stephanie Schwind-Parsons
Winterton,
Crinan Ferry,
Lochgilphead, PA31 8QH
Tel   +44 (0)1546 510567
Email   stephanie@crinanferry.co.uk
Web   www.crinanferry.co.uk

Entry 408   Map 17

Ayrshire

Alton Albany Farm

Discover Ayrshire… pine forests, hills and wild beauty. Alasdair and Andrea (sculptor and garden photographer) are generous hosts who love having you to stay – your visit starts with tea, coffee and cake. There's an arty vibe with their work on display; the dining room brims with garden books and games; large bedrooms have cosy lamps and more books. Big breakfasts by a log fire are a treat, perhaps with haggis, garden fruit, homemade bread; hearty dinners too. Rich in wildlife and orchids the garden has a rambling charm, the salmon-filled river Stinchar runs past and dogs are welcome – resident Daisy, Clover and Tansy are friendly.

Rooms	1 double; 1 double, 1 twin, sharing bath (let to same party only): £85-£115. Singles £75-£115.
Meals	Dinner £15. Pubs/restaurants 10-12 miles.
Closed	Rarely.

Retreats & guided experiences available.

Andrea & Alasdair Currie
Alton Albany Farm,
Barr, Girvan, KA26 0TL
Tel   +44 (0)1465 861148
Mobile   +44 (0)7881 908764
Email   alasdair@gardenexposures.co.uk
Web   www.altonalbanyfarm.com

Entry 409   Map 14

Dumfries & Galloway

Chipperkyle

This beautiful Scottish-Georgian family home has not a hint of formality, and sociable Willie puts you at your ease. Your sitting and dining rooms connect through a large arch; find gloriously comfy sofas, family pictures, rugs on wooden floors, masses of books and a constant log fire. Upstairs: good linen, striped walls, armchairs and windows with views – this wonderful house just gets better and better. There are 200 acres, dogs, cats, donkeys and hens – children can collect the eggs and go on tractor rides. The countryside is magnificent, beaches fabulous and this is a classified dark sky area. A house full of flowers and warmth.

Rooms	1 double, 1 twin with separate bath/shower: £115. 10% off for 3 nights or more. Discounts for children. Singles £75. Cot available.
Meals	Supper, 4 courses, £25. Pub 3 miles.
Closed	Rarely.

Willie Dickson
Chipperkyle,
Kirkpatrick Durham,
Castle Douglas, DG7 3EY
Tel   +44 (0)1556 650223
Mobile   +44 (0)7917 610008
Email   willie@chipperkyle.co.uk
Web   www.chipperkyle.co.uk

Entry 410   Map 11

Edinburgh

2 Cambridge Street
(The Dynamite Club)

A mischievous humour, tinged with historical and cultural references, alerts you to the specialness of this place, a ground-floor B&B in the lee of Edinburgh Castle, in the heart of theatre land. Find fin-de-siècle Scotland, with darkly striking colours on walls, antiques aplenty, and a captivating attention to detail. There are interactive art installations that sing and play, a line of old theatre seats up on the wall, photos and 'objets' serving startling and original purposes. Erlend and Hélène are delightful and free-spirited; Erlend, a quietly spoken (but don't be fooled) Shetlander, serves a breakfast to remember.

Rooms	2 doubles: £100–£160. Singles £90–£110.
Meals	Pubs/restaurants 1-minute walk.
Closed	Christmas.

	Erlend & Hélène Clouston 2 Cambridge Street (The Dynamite Club), Edinburgh, EH1 2DY
Tel	+44 (0)131 478 0005
Email	erlendclouston@gmail.com
Web	www.wwwonderful.net

Entry 411   Map 15

Edinburgh

7 Gloucester Place

It's restful here. Those who want to explore Edinburgh's treasures are close to the Royal Mile, Botanical Gardens, museums, galleries and theatres, traditional and innovative restaurants and live music from the concert halls and pubs. Memorably good breakfasts (often accompanied by classical music or jazz) at the convivial dining table include freshly-squeezed orange juice, homemade jams and full Scottish if you like. Naomi is relaxed and happy to chat to you about the local music and art scene, or to leave you in peace. Up the cantilevered staircase in walnut and mahogany, below a hand-painted cupola find restful bedrooms full of finds from travels to far-flung places. One faces the street but they are both quiet at night.

Rooms	1 double; 1 double with separate bath: £100–£140. There is a one week's cancellation policy. Singles £80.
Meals	Pubs/restaurants 5-minute walk.
Closed	Christmas, New Year & rarely.

Italian and French spoken.

	Naomi Jennings 7 Gloucester Place, Edinburgh, EH3 6EE
Mobile	+44 (0)7803 168106
Email	naomijennings@hotmail.com
Web	www.stayinginscotland.com

Entry 412   Map 15

Edinburgh

14 Hart Street

The brightly lit Georgian house has a smart front of polished brass and glossy paint. The warm raspberry hall is lined with art, and the graceful dining room is just as inviting: decanters on the sideboard, period furniture, glowing lamps, and a welcoming home-baked something. Fresh bright bedrooms are elegant and comfortable with whisky and wine on a tray and smart, sparkling bathrooms. Wake for breakfast at a beautifully polished table, with plenty of coffee, newspapers and chat; James and Angela are easy to talk to and love having guests to stay. Perfect for a peaceful city break, and Princes Street is a five-minute walk.

Rooms	2 doubles, 1 twin/double: £95–£170.
Meals	Restaurants 10-minute walk.
Closed	Rarely.

James & Angela Wilson
14 Hart Street,
Edinburgh, EH1 3RN
Tel   +44 (0)131 557 6826
Mobile   +44 (0)7795 203414
Email   hartst.edin@gmail.com
Web   www.14hartst.com

Entry 413   Map 15

Edinburgh

Two Hillside Crescent

Leave your worries behind as you enter this exquisitely restored Georgian townhouse. All is peaceful, spacious and light, with an upbeat contemporary feel. Bedrooms are on the first and second floors: imagine sleek modern furniture, big beds, superb mattresses, clouds of goose down, crisp linen, and immaculate bathrooms with organic toiletries and lashings of hot water. Over a superb breakfast your charming hosts will help you get the most out of your stay. Calton Hill is across the road for the best views of the city, and you're a stroll from the start of the Royal Mile. Wonderful.

Rooms	5 twin/doubles: £125–£165. Singles from £95.
Meals	Pubs/restaurants across the road.
Closed	Rarely.

Elaine Adams
Two Hillside Crescent,
Edinburgh, EH7 5DY
Tel   +44 (0)131 556 4871
Email info@twohillsidecrescent.com
Web   www.twohillsidecrescent.com

Entry 414   Map 15

Edinburgh

Millers64

Who could fail to relax here after a busy day? The bedrooms are comfortable and contemporary, the hosts are knowledgeable and friendly, and the breakfasts are stupendous (jam and marmalade courtesy of Louise and Shona's mum), served gourmet style at the big table. This elegant terraced villa is reached via Leith Walk, a wide busy thoroughfare that gets you to Edinburgh's hub in 20 minutes on foot; Leith's waterfront is an easy half mile. Victorian stained glass and cornices mix with a serene eastern theme (note the stylish pewter sinks from Thailand) and the quietest room is at the back.

Rooms	1 double: £110–£160.
	1 suite for 2: £120–£180.
	Singles from £80.
Meals	Pubs/restaurants 0.5 miles.
Closed	Never.

Minimum stay: 2 nights at weekends; 3 in high season; 4 nights Edinburgh Festival & New Year. Over 12s welcome. Free on-street parking, but can be hard to find a space.

Louise Clelland
Millers64,
64 Pilrig Street,
Edinburgh, EH6 5AS
Tel +44 (0)131 454 3666
Email louise@millers64.com
Web www.millers64.com

Entry 415   Map 15

Edinburgh

Claremont House

This handsome Victorian mansion stands in the widest residential street in Edinburgh, a 20-minute walk from Holyrood Park and a quick bus ride into the centre. For peacefulness and views you could not be better placed. Start the day with breakfast in the morning room: cooked or continental, it's one of the best. End the day with a stroll in the big peaceful garden. Here, everything is a treat, from the log fires lit at the first chill to the decanters of whisky replenished every day. All thanks to your hostess, warm-hearted, generous Gill. Catch the bus from the end of the road into the centre for booming cannons, the castle with its Crown Jewels, the medieval Old Town, Botanic Gardens and a myriad of restaurants. Return to delicious chocolates in your large, luxurious room.

Rooms	1 double, 1 twin/double: £120-180.
Meals	Pubs/restaurants 5-minute walk.
Closed	November – January.

Minimum stay: 2 nights.

Gillian Hunter
Claremont House,
3 South Lauder Road,
Edinburgh, EH9 2LL
Tel +44 (0)7885 411209
Email claremonthouse3@gmail.com

Entry 416   Map 15

Glasgow

64 Partickhill Road

Be greeted by three free-range hens and Gertie the terrier on arrival at this relaxed family home. It's in the bustling West End but the road is peaceful and there's a lovely big garden. Caroline and Hugh are lovers of the arts: the house is full of pictures, vintage finds and books. There are wood floors, rugs, a fire in the comfy sitting room and your bedroom is bright and spacious. Tuck into a delicious breakfast, in the conservatory, of good croissants, organic bacon and sausages, homemade bread and jams. Easy for the underground, trendy cafés and delis, museums, theatres and the university. A city treat.

Rooms	1 double: £85-£95. Extra twin available.
Meals	Packed lunch available. Pubs/restaurant 0.25 miles.
Closed	Occasionally.

Caroline Anderson
64 Partickhill Road,
Glasgow, G11 5NB
Tel   +44 (0)141 339 1946
Mobile +44 (0)7962 144509
Email carolineanderson64@gmail.com

Entry 417   Map 15

Highland

The Old Ferryman's House

This 200-year-old former ferryman's house is small, homely and well lived-in. Mountain views, the river Spey close by and a garden with a tray of tea and homemade treats… Plants tumble from whisky barrels and pots and there are woodpeckers and otters to spy. The sitting room is cosy with the wood-burner and brimming with books. Elizabeth, a keen traveller who has lived in the Sudan, cooks delicious, imaginative meals: eggs from her hens, homemade bread and preserves, heather honey and sometimes herbs and veg from the garden. There's no TV – no need here: it's an unmatched spot for explorers and nature lovers. Good value too.

Rooms	1 double, 1 twin/double, sharing 1 bath and 2 wcs: £80. 1 single, sharing 1 bath and 2 wcs: £40.
Meals	Dinner, 3 courses, £25. BYO. Packed lunch £7.50.
Closed	Occasionally in winter.

Elizabeth Matthews
The Old Ferryman's House,
Boat of Garten, PH24 3BY
Tel   +44 (0)1479 831370
Email tofhbbnw@gmail.com

Entry 418   Map 18

Highland

Craigiewood

The best of both worlds: Highland remoteness (red kites, wild goats) and Inverness just four miles away. The landscape surrounding this elegant cottage exudes a sense of ancient mystery… woodpeckers, deer, glorious roses all round. Araminta is a delightful host and her home has a lovely family feel; bedrooms are old-fashioned and cosy; the drawing room is snug with stove and books. Gavin almost built the house single-handed, planting a glorious garden here, and many throughout Scotland – his special touch remains. Meander up through rowan trees to a view point, sit and enjoy the peace. Inverewe, Attadale and Cawdor – all on the doorstep.

Rooms	2 twins: £90-£100. Singles £50-£65.
Meals	Pub 2 miles.
Closed	Christmas & New Year.

Minimum stay: 2 nights in high season.

Araminta Dallmeyer
Craigiewood,
North Kessock, Inverness, IV1 3XG

Tel	+44 (0)1463 731628
Mobile	+44 (0)7831 733699
Email	minty@craigiewood.co.uk
Web	www.craigiewood.co.uk

Entry 419 Map 18

Highland

The Peatcutter's Croft

Some say there's more beauty in a mile on the west coast than in the rest of the world put together – vast skies, soaring mountains, shimmering water, barely a soul in sight. Pauline and Seori left London to give their family the freedom to roam. Now they have a colourful cast of companions: sheep, hens, ducks, rabbits – all live here. In the adjoining byre: country simplicity, a Norwegian wood-burner, colour, texture and style. Sea eagles patrol the skies, porpoises bask in the loch, red deer come to eat the garden. This, coupled with Pauline's home cooking, makes it very hard to leave. Dogs and children are very welcome.

Rooms	1 apartment for 2, with mezzanine for 2 children: £80-£110. Singles £60-£80.
Meals	Dinner, 3 courses, £30. BYO. Pub/restaurant 30 miles.
Closed	Christmas.

Pets by arrangement.

Seori & Pauline Burnett
The Peatcutter's Croft,
Croft 12, Badrallach, Dundonnell
Garve, Ullapool, IV23 2QP

Tel	+44 (0)1854 633797
Email	info@peatcutterscroft.com
Web	www.peatcutterscroft.com

Entry 420 Map 17

Isle of Skye

The Cottage Stein

John and Fiona are warm and welcoming – you'll feel at home straight away. They've renovated their 200-year-old crofter's cottage with love and contemporary style, the views from bedrooms and guest sitting room are astonishing and a short walk takes you to the edge of the loch. Wake to breakfast in the cosy dining room – continental and cooked options, including full Scottish and lighter and sweeter choices, are all served with John's delicious homemade bread. Heaps to do nearby: boat trips, art galleries, Dunvegan castle and great walks. Supper is easy: it's a stroll to Skye's oldest inn and a fabulous restaurant – both right on the water.

Rooms	1 double, 1 twin/double: £125–£140. Singles £100–£115.
Meals	Pubs/restaurants 1-minute walk.
Closed	December – February.

Minimum stay: 2 nights in high season. Over 12s welcome.

John & Fiona Middleton
The Cottage Stein,
Stein, Waternish, IV55 8GA
Tel   +44 (0)1470 592734
Mobile   +44 (0)7742 193901
Email   stay@thecottagestein.co.uk
Web   www.thecottagestein.co.uk

Entry 421   Map 17 + 20

Isle of Skye

Greenwood Barn

The only thing that compares with the extraordinary views here is the care Christine takes of her guests. From tea and cake when you arrive to a sumptuous full Scottish breakfast replete with local goodies, you're in safe hands. This modern wood-frame house is almost carbon neutral but there's nothing Spartan about it – your bright, airy ground floor bedroom has underfloor heating and a pristine shower room. The private sitting room will take your breath away – full height windows display astonishing vistas of mountains and sea. For help and advice on where to go, Christine has all the answers. One day here is not enough.

Rooms	1 double: £130–£150.
Meals	Pubs/restaurants 3 miles.
Closed	1 November – 26 March.

Christine Jenkins
Greenwood Barn,
Duisdalemore,
Isleornsay, IV43 8QX
Tel   +44 (0)1471 833460
Email   christine@greenwoodbarnskye.co.uk
Web   www.greenwoodbarnskye.co.uk

Entry 422   Map 17 + 20

Lanarkshire

The Lint Mill

Rolling countryside, fields of sheep and a rushing river surround this peaceful converted mill. You have your own light, roomy wing with sitting room, separate entrance and garden so you'll feel nicely private. Your hosts' passion for living off the land is inspiring – meet their rare breeds of sheep, pigs and hens whose meat and eggs will end up on your plate, along with fruit and vegetables from the big kitchen garden. Peacocks wander and the dogs, Golden Guernsey goats and geese are all part of life on this smallholding. You are very well looked after. As well as tea and cake in the conservatory and tasty breakfasts Colin will prepare a lunch platter if you don't want to go out, a packed lunch for day trips and seasonal dinner with a bit of notice. Stay all day if you want or wander two miles to the pub.

Rooms	1 double, with sitting room & conservatory: £90-£135. Singles £60. Dinner, B&B £70 p.p.. Extra bed/sofabed £45 p.p.p.n.
Meals	Dinner, 3 courses, £25. Supper, 2 courses, £20. Platter for 2 £18. Packed lunch £6. Restaurants 9 miles.
Closed	Rarely.

Please see owners' website for availability.

Colin & Deborah Richardson-Webb
The Lint Mill,
Carnwath, Lanark, ML11 8LY
Tel   +44 (0)1555 840042
Mobile +44 (0)7966 164742
Email   info@thelintmill.co.uk
Web   www.thelintmill.co.uk

Entry 423   Map 15

Lanarkshire

Cormiston Farm

Wend your way through the soft hills of the Clyde Valley to a Georgian farmhouse in 26 acres of farmland and mature garden. Richard's a keen cook and produce from the walled garden takes centre stage. Wonderful to retire to quiet, spacious rooms with bucolic views, stunning beds and rich fabrics; characterful Art Deco bathrooms, too. Richard is happy to do children's teas, then you can tuck the nippers up in bunks and slip back for a snifter in front of the log fire in the sitting room. It's home from home, and licensed, too! There's untamed landscape to explore – and the children will love the friendly alpacas, hens and horses.

Rooms	2 doubles, each with separate bath: £96.
Meals	Dinner, 4 courses, £25-£30. Supper, 2 courses, £20. Pub 2 miles.
Closed	Rarely.

Richard Philipps
Cormiston Farm,
Cormiston Road,
Biggar, ML12 6NS
Tel   +44 (0)1899 221507
Email info@cormistonfarm.com
Web   www.cormistonfarm.com

Entry 424   Map 15

Midlothian

Crookston House

Scots Baronial grandeur complete with turrets, balustrades, ancestral portraits and impressive entrance... yet a family home with life and warmth. Engaging hosts welcome you with tea and a homemade something. A splendid staircase leads to huge traditional bedrooms with antiques, art and cosy gowns. Watch the wild birds tucking in as you breakfast too, on home-laid eggs and local treats. The 47 acres have swathes of snowdrops in spring and colour all year. Georgina and Malcolm know the area well; heaps to do: river Tweed fishing, walks, mountain bike trails. Return to a toasty, red sitting room with comfy sofas, log fire and lots of interesting books.

Rooms	1 double, 1 twin; 1 double with separate shower room: £95–£135.
Meals	Pubs/restaurants 11 miles.
Closed	Rarely.

Minimum stay: 2 nights in August. Children over 4 welcome. Pets by arrangement.

Georgina Leslie
Crookston House,
Heriot, EH38 5YS
Tel +44 (0)1875 835661
Email georgina@crookstonhouse.com
Web www.crookstonhouse.com

Entry 425 Map 15

Moray

Westfield House

Sweep up the drive to the grand home of an illustrious family: Macleans have lived here since 1862, and there are 500 peaceful acres of farmland. Veronica cooks sublimely; a proper Scottish breakfast and dinner served at a long candelabrau'd table, with vegetables from the garden. A winter fire crackles in the guest sitting room, old-fashioned bedrooms are inviting (biscuits, books, lovely views), the peace is deep. The coast is close and the walking is splendid. Stride out on walks straight from the doorstep, the Moray Firth, with Spey Bay's pod of dolphins, is less than 30 minutes away, or head to Elgin (ten minutes) for a whisky trail around the local distilleries and cathedral ruins. You can borrow bikes here and explore the quiet coastal roads.

Rooms	1 twin; 1 twin with separate bath & shower: £100. 1 single with separate bath: £55. Extra bed/sofabed £20 per person per night.
Meals	Supper, 2 courses, £20. Pub 3 miles.
Closed	Rarely.

Veronica Maclean
Westfield House,
Elgin, IV30 8XL
Tel +44 (0)1343 547308
Email veronica.maclean@yahoo.co.uk
Web www.westfieldhouseelgin.co.uk

Entry 426 Map 19

Perth & Kinross

Cuil an Duin

Rhododendrons form a brilliant guard of honour to escort you to the front door, and you arrive to tea and scones in the drawing room. Admire mountain views, head off into woodland, roam the gardens, chat to the horses – the 20 acres are stunning. Inside is just as good: elegant rooms, Persian rugs, modern art, flowers, a gleaming Bechstein; sunny bedrooms are luxuriously comforting. Happy hens foraging in the fields lay your breakfast eggs, artisan shops provide the trimmings. Sally and David are charming, Flora the Labrador and Chloe the cat stay behind the kitchen door until given the all clear, and there are outdoor pursuits galore.

Rooms	1 double, 1 twin/double; 1 double with separate bath: £130-£150. Singles £115-£135.
Meals	Pubs/restaurant 1.5 miles.
Closed	Rarely.

Minimum stay: 2 nights. Over 12s welcome.

Sally Keay & David Royce
Cuil an Duin,
Ballinluig,
Pitlochry, PH9 0NN
Tel +44 (0)1796 482807
Email enquiries@cuil-an-duin.com
Web www.cuil-an-duin.com

Entry 427   Map 15 + 18

Perth & Kinross

Essendy House

Down a tree-lined drive blazing with colour, Tess and John's charming country house is surrounded by lochs, castles and serenity. Inside is cosy and comfortable with wood fires, flowers, Tess's striking murals and trompe l'oeil and an unusual collection of family artefacts. Traditional bedrooms have good linen and views of Dunsinane Hill. Enjoy continental breakfasts with homemade bread and jams, perhaps scrambled eggs and smoked salmon, served in the dining room or under the vines in the conservatory; suppers too. There's a suntrap terrace, and you can walk in Macbeth's Birnam Wood, play golf, ski, fish and admire swooping ospreys.

Rooms	1 double, 1 twin: £110. Singles £55.
Meals	Continental breakfast. Packed lunch £5. Supper, 2 courses, £25. Pub/restaurant 2 miles.
Closed	Christmas & New Year; February/March.

John Monteith
Essendy House,
Blairgowrie, PH10 6QY
Tel +44 (0)1250 884260
Mobile +44 (0)7841 121538
Email johnmonteith@hotmail.com
Web www.essendy.org

Entry 428   Map 15 +18

Perth & Kinross

Old Kippenross

What a setting! Old Kippenross rests in 150 peaceful acres of gorgeous park and woodland overlooking the river Allan – spot red squirrels and deer, herons, dippers and otters. The 15th-century house has a Georgian addition and an air of elegance and great courtesy, with its rustic white-vaulted basement, and dining and sitting rooms strewn with soft sofas and Persian rugs. Sash-windowed bedrooms are deeply comfortable, warm bathrooms are stuffed with towels. Susan and Patrick (an expert on birds of prey) are welcoming, the food is good and there's a croquet lawn in the walled garden.

Rooms	1 double, 1 twin/double (adjoining single room, let to same party only): £108–£112. Singles £69–£71.
Meals	Dinner £30. BYO. Pub 1.5 miles.
Closed	Rarely.

Children over 10 welcome. Dogs by arrangement only.

Susan & Patrick Stirling-Aird
Old Kippenross,
Kippenross,
Dunblane, FK15 0LQ
Tel   +44 (0)1786 824048
Email kippenross@hotmail.com

Entry 429   Map 15

Scottish Borders

Eastfield House

Throw back the duvet and revel in the view from your room across the fields to the Cheviot Hills. Full breakfasts are served at the mahogany dining table. Bilingual French-Belgian Francis loves to cook and also produces sumptuous dinners, while florist Camilla fills the house with fragrant displays. Walk, cycle, fish (local guest permits available), discover castles, abbeys and glorious beaches less than an hour away. Slump in front of the fire, read a book in the conservatory, then retire to elegant rooms with comfy beds, chequered headboards and pretty fabrics. Bathrooms are sparkling, fresh and hung with eye-catching pictures.

Rooms	1 double; 1 double with separate bathroom: £100–£125.
Meals	Dinner £10–£50. Pubs/restaurants 5-minute drive.
Closed	Rarely.

Well behaved children & pets welcome.

Francis & Camilla Raeymaekers
Eastfield House,
Greenlaw, TD10 6YJ
Tel   +44 (0)1361 810750
Mobile +44 (0)7788 560326
Email raeymaekers@aol.com

Entry 430   Map 16

Scottish Borders

Fauhope House

Near to Melrose Abbey and the glorious St Cuthbert's Walk, this solid 1890s house is immersed in bucolic bliss. Views soar to the Eildon Hills through wide windows with squashy seats; all is luxurious, elegant, fire-lit and serene with an eclectic mix of art. Bedrooms are warm with deeply coloured walls, pale tartan blankets and soft velvet and linen; bathrooms are modern and pristine. Breakfast is served with smiles at a flower-laden table and overlooking those purple hills. A short walk through the blooming garden and over a footbridge takes you to the interesting town of Melrose, with shops, restaurants and its own theatre.

Rooms	3 twin/doubles: £140-£160. Singles £98.
Meals	Pub/restaurant 0.5 miles.
Closed	Rarely.

Ian & Sheila Robson
Fauhope House,
Gattonside, Melrose, TD6 9LU

Tel   +44 (0)1896 823184
Mobile +44 (0)7816 346768
Email info@fauhopehouse.com
Web   www.fauhopehouse.com

Entry 431   Map 15

Scottish Borders

Singdean

Twist through woodlands to this remote retreat high in the hills away from the hustle and bustle. Your cosy Alpine-style suite has its own entrance in a glorious off-grid cottage with solar panels and its own fresh spring water. Take a deep breath out, light the candles, laze in the hot tub and look up at the stars... romantics will be happy and a mountain feast of a breakfast is delivered through a secret door each morning. Head out into glorious countryside with a picnic or hop in the car to find good places to eat within a 20-minute drive. Browse Christa and Del's Alpine Lifestyle shop, or venture down to Hawick (15 miles) for cashmere – though awe-inspiring walks and wildlife are on your doorstep, and Kielder Water and Forest Park, with its astronomical observatory, is less than ten miles away.

Rooms	1 suite for 2: £170.
Meals	Packed lunch included by prior arrangement (voluntary contribution to the Landscaping fund). Pub 6 miles.
Closed	Rarely.

Christa & Del Dobson
Singdean,
Newcastleton, TD9 0SP

Tel   +44 (0)1450 860622
Email hello@singdean.co.uk
Web   www.singdean.co.uk

Entry 432   Map 16

Stirling

Powis House

A sprawling 18th-century mansion with the volcanic Ochil Hills as a stunning backdrop and a colourful entrance hall of antlers and stuffed animals. Country style bedrooms invite with polished old floors, tartan throws, garden views and original bathrooms. You have a huge dining room with warming woodburner, a guest lounge on the first floor, a sunny stone-flagged patio with places to sit and acres of estate with a woodland walk to explore. Colin and Jane are caring and interesting; Colin is a keen cook and has ghost stories galore to share. Historical Stirling is close: castle, university, festival and more.

Rooms	2 doubles, 1 twin: £110. Singles £75.
Meals	Pub/restaurant 3 miles.
Closed	1 November – 1 April.

Jane & Colin Kilgour
Powis House,
Stirling, FK9 5PS
Tel   +44 (0)1786 460231
Email colinkilgour1@gmail.com
Web   www.powishouse.co.uk

Entry 433   Map 15

Stirling

Cardross

Dodge the lazy sheep on the long drive to arrive (eventually!) at a sweep of gravel and lovely old Cardross in a gorgeous setting. Bang on the enormous ancient door and either Archie or Nicola (plus labradors and lively Jack Russells) will usher you in. And what a delight it is; come here for a blast of Scottish history! Traditional big bedrooms have airiness, long views, antiques, wooden shutters, towelling robes and good linen; one bathroom has a cast-iron period bath. The drawing room is vast, the house is filled with warm character, the Orr Ewings can tell you all the history.

Rooms	1 twin; 1 twin with separate bath: £110-£120. Singles £70-£75.
Meals	Occasional dinner £35. Pubs/restaurants 3-6 miles.
Closed	Christmas & New Year.

Over 14s welcome.

Sir Archie & Lady Orr Ewing
Cardross,
Port of Menteith,
Kippen, FK8 3JY
Tel   +44 (0)1877 385223
Email enquiries@cardrossestate.com
Web   www.cardrossestate.com

Entry 434   Map 15

Photo: Winterton, entry 408

Western Isles

Pairc an t-Srath

Richard and Lena's lovely home overlooks the beach at Borve – another absurdly beautiful Harris view. Inside, smart simplicity abounds: wooden floors, white walls, a peat fire, colourful art. Airy bedrooms fit the mood perfectly: trim carpets, chunky wood beds, Harris tweed throws, excellent shower rooms (there's a bathroom, too, if you want a soak). Richard crofts, Lena cooks, perhaps homemade soup, venison casserole, wet chocolate cake with raspberries. Views from the dining room tumble down hill, so expect to linger over breakfast. You'll spot otters in the loch, while the standing stones at Callanish are unmissable.

Rooms	2 doubles, 1 twin: £104-£108. 1 single: £52-£54.
Meals	Dinner, 3 courses, £37. Restaurant 3 miles, pub 7 miles.
Closed	Christmas & New Year.

Lena & Richard MacLennan
Pairc an t-Srath,
Borve,
Isle of Harris, HS3 3HT

Tel	+44 (0)1859 550386
Email	info@paircant-srath.co.uk
Web	www.paircant-srath.co.uk

Entry 435 Map 20

Wales

Photo: The Slate Shed at Graig Wen, entry 443

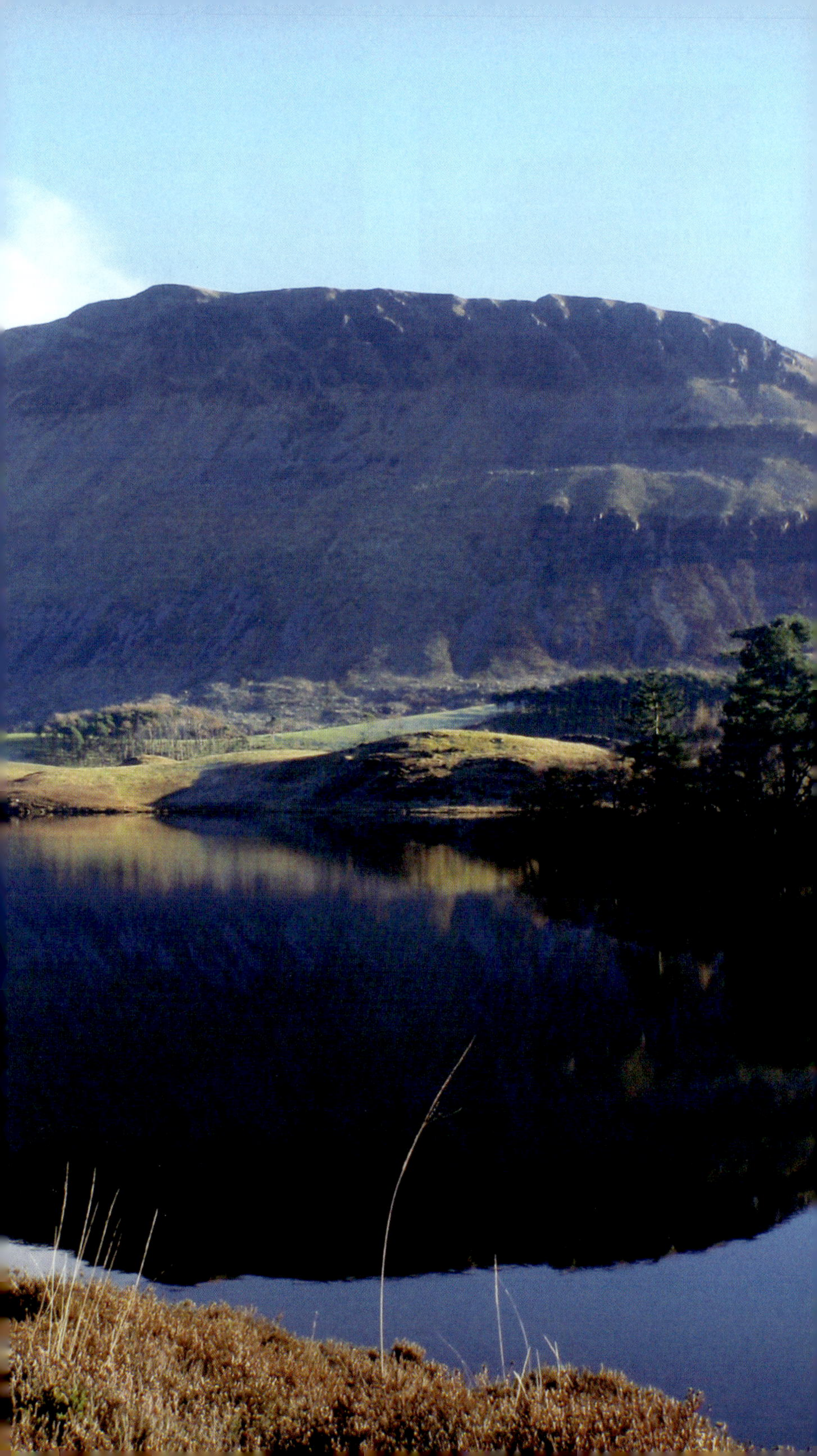

Carmarthenshire

The Glynhir Estate

This 1600s country house stands on the edge of the Black Mountain. Outside: a two-acre kitchen garden, space to wander and brigade of patrolling chickens, ducks and peacocks. Inside, the house has spurned the urge to take itself too seriously and remains decidedly lived in. Find William Morris wallpaper in the dining room, lemon trees in the conservatory, old cabinets stuffed with interesting things in the sitting room and a medley of market finds surprising you at every corner. Bedrooms are big and comfy, bathrooms excellent. Katy's cooking is good too: home-grown, tasty. Head out for fantastic walks, fishing, Aberglasney Gardens.

Rooms	3 doubles: £75. 1 family room for 3 (suitable for 2 adults & 1-2 children under 12): £100-£115. Singles £45.
Meals	Dinner from £19.50. Pubs/restaurants 2 miles.
Closed	November – March.

Katy Jenkins
The Glynhir Estate,
Glynhir Road, Llandybie,
Ammanford, SA18 2TD
Tel   +44 (0)1269 850438
Mobile   +44 (0)7810 864458
Email   enquiries@theglynhirestate.com
Web   www.theglynhirestate.com

Entry 436   Map 7

Carmarthenshire

Mount Pleasant Farm

Wake to circling red kites with a breathtaking backdrop of the Black Mountain. Every room has wonderful views, and Sue and Nick are warm and delightful hosts. Food is a passion here and you'll enjoy homemade bread and jams, deep yellow eggs, organic veg and local lamb and pork; vegetarians are spoiled too – Sue is a brilliant cook. After dinner there's snooker, a log fire, a cosy sofa; then a seriously comfy bed in a room with a lovely country-house feel. There are excellent walks in the valley, fly fishing on the Towy, Llyn y Fan Fach in the Brecon Beacons National Park; Aberglasney and the Botanic Gardens are nearby too.

Rooms	1 twin/double; 1 twin/double, 1 twin sharing bath (let to same party only): £70-£80.
Meals	Dinner, 3 courses with wine, £20. Pub/restaurant 3 miles.
Closed	Christmas.

Over 12s welcome. 1.5 hours from Pembroke Dock.

Sue & Nick Thompson
Mount Pleasant Farm,
Llanwrda, SA19 8AN
Tel   +44 (0)1550 777537
Email   nick@rivarevival.co.uk

Entry 437   Map 7

Conwy

Pengwern Country House

The steeply wooded Conwy valley snakes down to this stone and slate property set back from the road in Snowdonia National Park, and the walks are wonderful. Inside has an upbeat traditional feel: a large sitting room with tall bay windows and pictures by the Betws-y-Coed artists who once lived here. Settle with a book by the wood-burner; Gwawr and Ian are naturally friendly and treat guests as friends. Bedrooms have rough plastered walls, colourful fabrics and super bathrooms; one comes with a double-ended roll top tub and views of Lledr Valley. Breakfast on fruits, herb rösti, soda bread – superb.

Rooms	1 double, 1 twin/double, 1 four-poster: £75-£95.
Meals	Packed lunch £5.50. Pubs/restaurants within 1.5 miles.
Closed	Christmas & New Year.

Minimum stay: 2 nights.

	Gwawr & Ian Mowatt Pengwern Country House, Allt Dinas, Betws-y-Coed, LL24 0HF
Tel	+44 (0)1690 710480
Email	gwawr.pengwern@btopenworld.com
Web	www.snowdoniaaccommodation.co.uk

Entry 438   Map 7

Flintshire

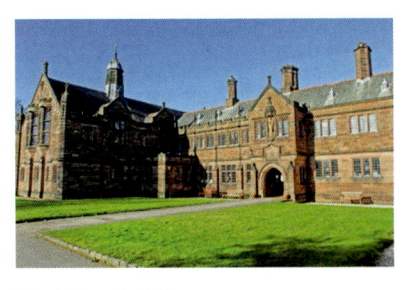

Gladstone's Library

If this glorious, unusual, historic and stunning place fails you as a retreat, then look deep within yourself. You have 150,000 books, silence, space, convivial company if you need it, Theatre Clwyd and Chester but 15 minutes away. Eucharist is held every weekday, delicious local food is there for you in the bistro, an open fire and sofas in the Gladstone room. The staff are lovely, the mood sheer old-fashioned decency. It is a Roberts radio, rather than a TV, place. Bedrooms are warm, simple and unpretentious. Come for as long as you need to recover from this mad world. It will, for all adults, feel like a privilege.

Rooms	14 doubles, 3 twins: £90-£100. 7 singles: £66-£77. Hairdryers, Roberts radios and WiFi in all rooms.
Meals	Restaurant on site.
Closed	Christmas & New Year.

Reception 8.30-5pm. Check in from 2pm, check out 10am; you are welcome to use the facilities and library once you have checked out. If arriving after 5pm please do let us know in advance.

	Gladstone's Library, Church Lane, Hawarden, Deeside, CH5 3DF
Tel	+44 (0)1244 532350
Email	enquiries@gladlib.org
Web	www.gladstoneslibrary.org

Entry 439   Map 7

Flintshire

Tower

A grand yet wonderfully relaxed and friendly country house on the Welsh borders. Overlooking a lake and first mentioned in 1465, Tower has been in owner John's family for hundreds of years, and he is more than happy to share his knowledge on its extensive, fascinating history. Breakfast is served at one long polished table in the impressive dining room, bedrooms are elegant with high ceilings, antiques, portraits and masses of space; the garden is perfect for a stroll. Head out to historic Chester, climb Snowdon or explore lively Mold with its umpteen places to eat. Return to relax by the fire in the drawing room.

Rooms	2 doubles, 1 twin; 1 double with separate bathroom: £90-£125. Singles £75. Extra beds available.
Meals	Restaurants 0.5 miles.
Closed	Rarely.

Parking on-site.

John Wynne-Eyton
Tower,
Nercwys Road,
Mold, CH7 4EW
Mobile +44 (0)7964 008772
Email info@tower.wales
Web www.tower.wales

Entry 440   Map 7

Gwynedd

Y Goeden Eirin

A little gem tucked between the sea and the mountains, an education in Welsh culture, and a great place to explore wild Snowdonia, the Llyn peninsula and the dramatic Yr Eifl mountains. Inside presents a cosy picture: Welsh-language and English books share the shelves, paintings by contemporary Welsh artists enliven the walls, an arty 70s décor mingles with sturdy Welsh oak in the bedrooms – the one in the house best – and all bathrooms are super. Wonderful food is served alongside the Bechstein in the beamed dining room – the welcoming, thoughtful Eluned has created an unusually delightful space.

Rooms	2 doubles £90-£100. 1 twin £90. Singles £65-70.
Meals	Packed lunch available. Pub/restaurant 3 miles.
Closed	Christmas, New Year & occasionally.

Eluned Rowlands
Y Goeden Eirin,
Dolydd,
Caernarfon, LL54 7EF
Tel +44 (0)1286 830942
Email eluned.rowlands@tiscali.co.uk
Web www.ygoedeneirin.co.uk

Entry 441   Map 6

Gwynedd

Coes Faen Lodge

Effortless simplicity is the key to this new spa B&B. A glass and rock entrance, a hallway suffused with light: this Victorian lodge on the edge of Mawddach Estuary has been stunningly, meticulously revived. Bedrooms are cocoons of sleek opulence, bathrooms are rich in slate and stone, and detailing §is sublime: mood lighting, hands-free technology, pearlescent tiles that reflect the light. Choose a sauna smelling of cedar or a rooftop hot tub and terrace… Richard and Sara have Welsh roots and love both place and landscape. Acres of woodland garden await behind; breakfasts and dinners are original and exquisite.

Rooms	6 doubles: £135–£240.
Meals	Dinner from £35.
	Pubs/restaurants 0.5 miles.
Closed	Rarely.

Richard & Sara Parry-Jones
Coes Faen Lodge,
Coes Faen,
Abermaw, LL42 1TE
Tel +44 (0)1341 281632
Email richard@coesfaen.com
Web www.coesfaen.com

Entry 442 Map 7

Gwynedd

The Slate Shed at Graig Wen

Sarah and conservationist John spent months travelling in a camper looking for their own special place and found this lovely old Welsh slate cutting mill… captivated by acres of wild woods and stunning views. You'll feel at ease as soon as you step into their eclectic modern home with its reclaimed slate and wood, cosy wood-burners, books, games, snug bedrooms (one downstairs) and superb bathrooms. Breakfast communally on local eggs and sausages, honey from the mountainside, homemade bread and granola. Hike or bike the Mawddach Trail, climb Cadair Idris, wonder at the views… and John's chocolate brownies.

Rooms	4 doubles, 1 twin/double: £80–£130.
	Singles £65.
Meals	Packed lunch £6.50. Pub 5 miles.
Closed	5 November – 14 February.

Minimum stay: 2 nights at weekends & in high season. Children over 10 welcome.

Sarah Heyworth
The Slate Shed at Graig Wen,
Arthog, LL39 1YP
Tel +44 (0)1341 250482
Email hello@graigwen.co.uk
Web www.slateshed.co.uk

Entry 443 Map 7

Monmouthshire

Upper Red House

Head down the lane into deepest Monmouthshire and the meadows, orchards and woodland of Teona's organic farm. There are six ponds and miles of bushy hedges; bees, ponies, peafowl and wild flowers flourish. The 17th-century house, restored from dereliction, has lovely views, flagstones and oak, limewashed walls and a magical feel. Up steep stairs are rustic bedrooms with beams, lots of books, no TV; the attic rooms get the best views of all. Bathrooms are simple, one has a huge old roll top tub. After a good vegetarian breakfast at the long kitchen table take a farm tour, explore Offa's Dyke or the Wye Valley – and enjoy the silence.

Rooms	1 double; 1 double sharing bath with singles (let to same party only): £80-£95. 2 singles sharing bath with double (let to same party only): £35-£45.
Meals	Vegetarian packed lunch £8. Pubs/restaurants 3.5 miles.
Closed	Rarely.

Teona Dorrien-Smith
Upper Red House,
Llanfihangel-Ystern-Llewern,
Monmouth, NP25 5HL
Tel   +44 (0)1600 780501
Email   upperredhouse@mac.com
Web   www.upperredhouse.co.uk

Entry 444   Map 7

Monmouthshire

Penpergwm Lodge

A rambling Edwardian house... Margot and Maud, resident pug and terrier, make a characterful welcoming party and you step into a warmly painted hall with old rugs on wooden boards. Simon and Catriona give you tea and biscuits in a sunny, lived-in sitting room: heaps of books, family bits and pieces, squashy sofa by the fire. Breakfast is served here, or round the long table in the dining room. Bedrooms are time-worn trad with embroidered covers and chintz; bathrooms are a skip across the landing. Enjoy the beautiful garden with parterre, potager, orchard and brick follies, bring a jumper in winter and don't mind the worn corners... a charming home.

Rooms	2 twins each with separate bath: £85. Singles £55.
Meals	Pub 2 miles.
Closed	Rarely.

Catriona Boyle
Penpergwm Lodge,
Penpergwm,
Abergavenny, NP7 9AS
Tel   +44 (0)1873 840208
Email   boyle@penpergwm.co.uk
Web   www.penplants.com

Entry 445   Map 7

Monmouthshire

Allt-y-bela

It's a rare treat to come here. This beautiful medieval farmhouse sits in its own secret valley and is reached down a narrow lane. Built between 1420 and 1599, Allt-y-bela is now perfectly presented for the 21st century. You'll find conviviality and warmth, soaring beams, period furniture and an enormous log fire. Bedrooms soothe with limewashed walls, fabulous beds, no TV and stunning art. There's a super farmhouse kitchen for delicious and social eating, or the table might be set outside in the sun: homemade everything, beautifully cooked. Peace, privacy and an amazing garden in deep yet accessible countryside. Exceptional.

Rooms	2 doubles: £200. Stays of 2 nights or more, £150.
Meals	Farmhouse supper £30. Pubs/restaurants 3 miles.
Closed	Rarely.

William Collinson & Arne Maynard
Allt-y-bela,
Llangwm Ucha,
Usk, NP15 1EZ
Mobile +44 (0)7892 403103
Email   alltybela@icloud.com
Web   www.alltybela.co.uk

Entry 446   Map 7

Pembrokeshire

Pembrokeshire Farm B&B

Down a beautiful lane flanked by moss-covered walls, two miles from Narberth, is an old fortified longhouse in 25 rolling acres – pristine, peaceful and cosy. Here live three dogs, three donkeys, cats, hens and friendly hosts Rayner and Carol. There's a real fire and books aplenty, equine paintings and fantastic art, and big gorgeous gardens with croquet, a lake and a boat to mess about in. The décor is traditional, the bed linen immaculate, the bathrooms are spanking new and the views to the Preseli Hills gorgeous. Narbeth's restaurants are good but Carol's cooking is fabulous.

Rooms	1 double; 1 double with separate bathroom: £100-£110.
Meals	Dinner, 3 courses, from £35. Pubs/restaurants 2 miles.
Closed	Rarely.

Over 14s welcome.

Rayner & Carol Peett
Pembrokeshire Farm B&B,
Caermaenau Fawr,
Clynderwen, SA66 7HB
Tel   +44 (0)1834 860338
Mobile +44 (0)7796 615332
Email   info@pembrokeshirefarmbandb.co.uk
Web   www.pembrokeshirefarmbandb.co.uk

Entry 447   Map 6

Pembrokeshire

Cresselly House

Imagine staying at the Georgian mansion of an old country friend – that's what it's like to stay at Cresselly. Step into a sunny square hall with a sweeping stair and the ancestors on the walls. Beeswax and lavender scent the air, cosy bedrooms are as grandly traditional as can be, new bathrooms sparkle and views swoop over the park. For breakfast or dinner (if requested) you can seat yourself at the fine Georgian mahogany dining table, gleaming from many decades of polishing. The walking and riding are glorious, and there's impressive stabling for your horse: this is the heartland of the South Pembrokeshire Hunt.

Rooms	3 doubles, 1 twin: £120-£180.
Meals	Dinner, 2 courses, £25-£55. Pub 1 mile.
Closed	Rarely.

Over 16s welcome.

Hugh Harrison-Allen
Cresselly House,
Cresselly,
Kilgetty, SA68 0SP
Tel   +44 (0)1646 651992
Email info@cresselly.com
Web   www.cresselly.com

Entry 448   Map 6

Pembrokeshire

Cresswell House

On a peaceful and pretty tidal river creek between Narberth and Tenby, this Georgian Quay Master's house is heaven for walkers, bird watchers and lovers of a good pub – there's one just down the road. Guests have a separate entrance to cosy, modern-rustic style, third-floor rooms: Welsh blankets, good white linen, pristine stone-tiled bathrooms, sofas, DVDs, coffee machines, a shared fridge. Philip and Rhian's love of art is evident (as is their friendly, lively lurcher!); they make jams and bread for relaxed, full-Welsh breakfasts and happily advise on what to do. An easy-going place – great nearby beaches too.

Rooms	1 double, 1 twin/double: £90.
Meals	Pubs/restaurants 5-minute drive.
Closed	Rarely.

Minimum stay: 2 nights.

Philip Wight & Rhian Davies
Cresswell House,
Cresswell Quay,
Kilgetty, SA68 0TE
Tel   +44 (0)1646 651435
Email rhian@cresswellhouse.co.uk
Web   www.cresswellhouse.co.uk

Entry 449   Map 6

Pembrokeshire

Knowles Farm House

The Cleddau estuary winds its way around this organic farm – its lush grasses feed the cows that produce milk for the renowned Rachel's yogurt. Your hosts love the land, are committed to its conservation and let you come and go as you please; picnic in the garden, wander the bluebell woods, discover a pond; dogs like it too. You have your own entrance to old-fashioned, lived-in pretty bedrooms with comfy beds, simple bathrooms, glorious views and an eclectic selection of books to browse. Breakfast and supper are fully organic or very local: delicious! If Gini is busy with the farm there are terrific river pubs that serve dinner.

Rooms	2 doubles, 1 twin with separate bath: £80-£98. Singles £55-£60.
Meals	Supper from £12. Dinner, 4 courses, £22, (not in school holidays). Packed lunch £6. Pub 1.5 miles; restaurant 3 miles.
Closed	Rarely.

Minimum stay: 2 nights. Pets by arrangement.

	Virginia Lort Phillips Knowles Farm House, Knowles Farm, Lawrenny, SA68 0PX
Tel	+44 (0)1834 891221
Mobile	+44 (0)7815 208772
Email	ginilp@lawrenny.org.uk
Web	www.knowlesfarmhouse.com

Entry 450 Map 6

Pembrokeshire

Awelon

Family house with wonderful views of Manorbier beach. Katherine's home has a relaxed feel with Scandinavian furniture, wide French windows, books, games – and two friendly spaniels. She gives you a guest sitting room, small cosy bedrooms with Welsh blankets, sparkling shower rooms; tea trays too with homemade cake. Breakfast is at a polished table looking over the Pembrokeshire Coast Path: homemade muesli, award-winning bacon, veggy choices... most locally sourced and all delicious. Enjoy a tipple on the terrace with the beautiful garden beyond (designed by Andy Sturgeon, RHS Show Garden); stroll to the popular village pub for supper.

Rooms	1 double; 1 twin with separate bath/shower: £75-£85. Singles £50-£65.
Meals	Pubs/restaurants 5-minute walk.
Closed	31 October – 22 February.

	Katherine Henderson Bowen Awelon, Pembroke Road, Manorbier, Tenby, SA70 7SX
Tel	+44 (0)1834 871587
Email	katherine@manorbierbedandbreakfast.co.uk
Web	www.manorbierbedandbreakfast.co.uk

Entry 451 Map 6

Pembrokeshire

Cefn-y-Dre Country House

Geoff and Gaye want your stay to go without a hitch, and they're proud of the rich history of their house. Solid, handsome and 500 years old, Cefn-y-Dre is on the fringe of the Pembrokeshire Coast National Park with views to the Preseli Hills. The sitting room is set aside for guests, notable for its striking red chairs used during Prince Charles' investiture in 1969 – quite a talking point! Geoff is a great cook who takes pleasure in using local produce and home-grown veg from the large garden; not so long ago he trained at Ballymaloe. St David's, with its ancient cathedral, is nearby, as are some of Britain's finest beaches.

Rooms	1 double, 1 twin/double; 1 double with separate bath/shower: £99–£109. Singles £70–79.
Meals	Dinner, 3 courses, £26.50. Pubs/restaurants 2 miles.
Closed	Rarely.

Gaye Williams & Geoff Stickler
Cefn-y-Dre Country House,
Fishguard, SA65 9QS
Tel +44 (0)1348 875663
Email welcome@cefnydre.co.uk
Web www.cefnydre.co.uk

Entry 452   Map 6

Pembrokeshire

The Old Vicarage

A breath of fresh air close to the beautiful Pembrokeshire Coastal Path. Energetic young owners have completely redecorated their new home and it feels bright, uncluttered, easy-going. Welsh blankets, Edwardian tiling, glass and fireplaces blend their charm with stripped boards, simple blinds, painted and bistro-style furniture. Chalkboards tell you what's for breakfast, and supper – Meg's a good cook and sources as locally as possible. Beds are wide and deep, views are peacefully green. Walk to Newport or St Dogmaels, catch the Poppit Rocket back and watch the sun set over the distant sea. The old vicar would surely approve!

Rooms	4 doubles: £100. Singles £85–£90. Extra bed/sofabed £25 per person per night.
Meals	Dinner £10–£20. Pubs/restaurants 3.5 miles.
Closed	Rarely.

Minimum stay: 2 nights at weekends.

Megan van Soest
The Old Vicarage,
Moylegrove, Cardigan, SA43 3BN
Tel +44 (0)1239 881711
Email stay@theoldvicbedandbreakfast.co.uk
Web www.oldvicaragemoylegrove.co.uk

Entry 453   Map 6

Powys

Ty'r Chanter

Warmth, colour, children and activity: this house is huge fun. Tiggy welcomes you like family; help collect eggs, feed the lambs, drop your shoes by the fire. The farmhouse and barn are stylishly relaxed; deep sofas, tartan throws, heaps of books, long convivial table; views to the Brecon Beacons and Black Mountains are inspiring. Bedrooms are soft, simple sanctuaries with Jo Malone bathroom treats. The children's room zings with murals; toys, kids' sitting room, sandpit – it's child heaven. Walk, fish, canoe, book-browse in Hay or stroll the estate. Homemade cakes and whisky to help yourself to: fine hospitality and Tiggy is wonderful.

Rooms	3 doubles: £100. 1 twin (children's room with separate bath/shower): £20 per child. Singles £55.
Meals	Packed lunch £8. Pub 1 mile.
Closed	Rarely.

Tiggy Pettifer
Ty'r Chanter,
Gliffaes, Crickhowell, NP8 1RL
Tel   +44 (0)1874 731144
Mobile +44 (0)7802 387004
Email tiggy@tyrchanter.com
Web   www.tyrchanter.com

Entry 454   Map 7

Powys

The Old Store House

If a tidy house gives you pleasure, read no further. Peter has filled his home mostly with books, but chickens and swans might wander in too. Things are moved out of the way rather than put away, there are no hard and fast breakfast times and guests are welcome to use the kitchen. Bedrooms are large, light and comfortable with sofas and armchairs; two have wood fires and the room at the top has exterior stone steps and a door that stays open all summer – fledgling swallows might sit on the beam between flying practices. The sitting room is cosy with sofas and a big fire, the lived-in conservatory looks across the valley… come and go as you please.

Rooms	3 doubles, 1 twin: £90. Singles £45.
Meals	Packed lunch £4. Pub/restaurant 0.75 miles.
Closed	Rarely.

Peter Evans
The Old Store House,
Llanfrynach,
Brecon, LD3 7LJ
Tel   +44 (0)1874 665499
Email oldstorehouse@btconnect.com
Web   www.theoldstorehouse.co.uk

Entry 455   Map 7

Powys

Ty Newydd

They live on the canal and own a canoe: hire it for the day and pootle down to the pub, or walk your socks off in the Brecon Beacons. Friendly, generous Rachel and Sid swapped London for Llanfrynach and have breathed new life into the old farmhouse and outbuildings. Bedrooms are ultra comfy (those at the top have vaulted beams), bathrooms are spotless, views are gorgeous. The Taff Trail meets the tow path at the bottom of the garden, there's a tip-top boot dryer for when you get back, and you wake to feasts of local and Fair Trade produce, brought to small tables with a lovely big smile.

Rooms	3 doubles, 1 twin/double: £80. Singles £65. Extra bed/sofabed £15 per person per night.
Meals	Pubs/restaurants 2 miles.
Closed	Rarely.

Minimum stay: 2 nights (Fri-Sun in high season).

Rachel Griffiths
Ty Newydd,
Llanfrynach,
Brecon, LD3 7LJ
Tel +44 (0)1874 665797
Email info@tynewyddholidays.com
Web www.tynewyddholidays.com

Entry 456   Map 7

Powys

Hafod Y Garreg

A unique opportunity to stay in the oldest house in Wales — a fascinating, 1402 cruck-framed hall house, built for Henry IV as a hunting lodge. Informal Annie and John have filled it with a charming mix of Venetian mirrors, Indian rugs, pewter plates, rich fabrics and oak pieces. Dine by candlelight in the romantic dining room — all sorts of delicious dishes; tuck into a big breakfast in the sweet conservatory. Bedrooms are luxuriously comfortable with embroidered linen, quirky lamps, nifty bathrooms. Reach this relaxed retreat by a bumpy track up across gated fields crowded with chickens, cats... a peaceful, special place.

Rooms	2 doubles: £97. Singles £93.
Meals	Dinner, 3 courses, £28. BYO. Pubs/restaurants 2.5 miles.
Closed	Christmas.

Annie & John McKay
Hafod Y Garreg,
Erwood,
Builth Wells, LD2 3TQ
Tel +44 (0)1982 560400
Email johnanniehafod@gmail.com
Web www.hafodygarreg.co.uk

Entry 457   Map 7

Powys

Rhedyn

Come here if you need to remember how to relax. Such an unassuming, little place, but with real character and soul: great comfort too. Find exposed walls in the bedrooms, funky lighting, pocket sprung mattresses, lovely books to read, and calm colours; bathrooms are modern and delightfully quirky. But the real stars of this show are Muiread and Ciaran: warm, enthusiastic and engaging, with a passion for good local food and a desire for more self-sufficiency – pigs and bees are planned next. This is a totally tranquil place, with agreeable walks through the Irfon valley, and bog snorkelling too!

Rooms	3 doubles: £100. Singles £90. Dinner, B&B £85 per person.
Meals	Dinner, 3 courses, £35. Packed lunch £7.50. Pub/restaurant 1 mile.
Closed	Rarely.

Pets by arrangement.

	Muiread & Ciaran O'Connell Rhedyn, Cilmery, Builth Wells, LD2 3LH
Tel	+44 (0)1982 551944
Email	info@rhedynguesthouse.co.uk
Web	www.rhedynguesthouse.co.uk

Entry 458 Map 7

Powys

Eithinog Hall

On the outside, a conventional mellow Georgian country house – sash windows, big trees in mature gardens, vistas of wood and river. Then, step in to an interior you wouldn't have anticipated – a contemporary feast of art, decoration, vivid colour, sculptures... Sisters Laura and Jane match the energy of their house – along with Jane's husband Mark, they're hugely enthusiastic about having guests to stay. Enjoy the views from huge bedrooms; wake for breakfasts with local produce and homemade bread and jams. Great walks and bike rides start from the door, take yourself fly fishing in their two miles of river Banwy, the coast is 50 minutes.

Rooms	3 doubles: £120-£140.
Meals	Pubs/restaurants 10-minute walk. Dinner offered by arrangement.
Closed	Rarely.

Minimum stay: 2 nights.

	Laura Hill Eithinog Hall, Eithinog Lane, Cyfronydd, Welshpool, SY21 9ED
Tel	+44 (0)1938 811200
Email	getaroom@eithinoghall.co.uk
Web	www.eithinoghall.co.uk

Entry 459 Map 7

Wrexham

Worthenbury Manor

Welcome to one half of a Grade II listed country house on the Wales/Shropshire border. Ian and Elizabeth look after you wonderfully well. The guest sitting room is warmed by a log fire in winter; the dining room has ancient polished panelling. Choose between two comfortable bedrooms, one Georgian style, one Jacobean, both with rich drapes, chandeliers and antique four-posters; luxurious bathrooms have baths big enough for two. Breakfast on the best of local and home produce; their award-winning marmalade is for sale too! Enjoy a wildlife-friendly garden filled with birds, explore the Welsh Marches; Powis Castle and Erddig are nearby.

Rooms	1 four-poster; 1 four-poster with separate bathroom: £92-£115. Singles £65-£80.
Meals	Supper by arrangement £14.50. BYO drinks. Pub/restaurant 2.5 miles.
Closed	Christmas & New Year.

Elizabeth & Ian Taylor
Worthenbury Manor,
Worthenbury, LL13 0AW
Tel   +44 (0)1948 770342
Email   enquiries@worthenburymanor.co.uk
Web   www.worthenburymanor.co.uk

Entry 460   Map 7

Wheelchair-accessible
At least one bedroom & bathroom accessible for wheelchair users. Please phone for details.

England
Birmingham 10
Bristol 11
Cornwall 46
Cumbria 63
Derbyshire 68
Devon 73 • 74 • 87
Gloucestershire 142 • 151
Kent 173 • 179
Leicestershire 193
Norfolk 221
Shropshire 278
Somerset 282 • 284 • 290 • 299 • 300 • 313
Suffolk 319
Surrey 326
Sussex 332 • 341
Yorkshire 379 • 380 • 398

Channel Islands
Guernsey 402

Scotland
Edinburgh 411
Isle of Skye 422
Western Isles 435

Wales
Flintshire 439
Gwynedd 442 • 443

Children of all ages welcome
These owners have told us that they welcome children of all ages. Please note cots and highchairs may not necessarily be available.

England
Bath & N.E. Somerset 3 • 5
Bedfordshire 6
Berkshire 9
Birmingham 10
Bristol 12
Buckinghamshire 15
Cambridgeshire 20
Cheshire 23 • 24
Cornwall 27 • 28 • 30 • 35 • 38 • 41 • 42 • 45 • 46
Cumbria 47 • 48 • 49 • 53 • 54 • 55 • 56 • 58 • 61
Derbyshire 66 • 70
Devon 73 • 74 • 80 • 82 • 83 • 87 • 89 • 90 • 98 • 99 • 101 • 104
Dorset 107 • 110 • 111 • 112 • 117 • 118 • 119 • 120 • 121
Durham 127
Essex 130
Gloucestershire 132 • 134 • 139 • 140 • 141 • 143 • 144 • 147
Hampshire 152 • 153 • 157 • 159
Herefordshire 160 • 161 • 162 • 164 • 165
Isle of Wight 169
Kent 171 • 172 • 173 • 174 • 176 • 177 • 177.1 • 178 • 182 • 183 • 189
Leicestershire 192 • 193
Lincolnshire 194 • 195 • 196 •
London 201 • 203 • 206 •

207 • 211 • 215 • 217 • 218 • 219
Norfolk 226 • 228 • 229 • 230 • 232 • 233 • 236
Northamptonshire 237
Northumberland 242 • 243 • 244 • 247 • 249
Nottinghamshire 250
Oxfordshire 256 • 257 • 262 • 263
Rutland 265
Shropshire 266 • 267 • 268 • 270 • 272 • 274 • 275 • 276
Somerset 281 • 282 • 284 • 288 • 290 • 291 • 296 • 298 • 299 • 300 • 302 • 307 • 308 • 310
Suffolk 322 • 323
Surrey 328 • 331
Sussex 333 • 334 • 335 • 336 • 339 • 342 • 346
Warwickshire 348 • 350 • 352 • 355 • 358
Wiltshire 361 • 364 • 366 • 367 • 369
Worcestershire 373 •
Yorkshire 374 • 376 • 377 • 379 • 380 • 382 • 383 • 384 • 388 • 389 • 391 • 396 • 398

Scotland

Aberdeenshire 403
Angus 404
Argyll & Bute 405 • 406 • 407
Ayrshire 409
Dumfries & Galloway 410
Edinburgh 411 • 413
Glasgow 417
Highland 418 • 420
Lanarkshire 423 • 424
Moray 426
Perth & Kinross 428
Scottish Borders 430 • 431
Stirling 433
Western Isles 435

Wales

Carmarthenshire 436
Monmouthshire 444 • 445 • 446
Pembrokeshire 450 • 451 • 452 • 453
Powys 454 • 455
Wrexham 460

Pets welcome

Please let the owner know if you want to bring pets.

England

Bath & N.E. Somerset 1 • 3
Bedfordshire 7
Cheshire 24
Cornwall 27 • 39
Cumbria 49 • 55 • 57 • 58 • 61 • 63
Derbyshire 66
Devon 72 • 73 • 74 • 75 • 80 • 81 • 83 • 87 • 88 • 89 • 93 • 96 • 98 • 101 • 103
Dorset 108 • 110 • 113 • 115 • 117 • 118 • 120
Durham 127
Gloucestershire 132 • 134 • 137 • 139 • 142 • 143 • 148
Herefordshire 162 • 164
Leicestershire 192
Lincolnshire 196
London 206 • 211 • 217 •
Norfolk 225 • 228 • 230 • 231
Northumberland 244 • 246 • 247 • 249

Nottinghamshire 250
Oxfordshire 258 • 263
Shropshire 266 • 269 • 273 • 275 • 278
Somerset 280 • 289 • 290 • 291 • 294 • 297 • 308
Suffolk 318 • 322
Sussex 334 • 335 • 340 • 342
Warwickshire 348 • 352 • 357
Wiltshire 361 • 362 • 369
Yorkshire 376 • 380 • 382 • 384 • 391 • 394 • 396

Scotland
Angus 404
Argyll & Bute 405 • 407
Ayrshire 409
Edinburgh 411
Glasgow 417
Highland 418
Perth & Kinross 428
Scottish Borders 431 • 432
Western Isles 435

Wales
Gwynedd 442 • 443
Monmouthshire 444 • 445 • 446
Pembrokeshire 453
Powys 454 • 455 • 456

Credit cards accepted
These owners have told us that they accept credit cards, most commonly Visa and MasterCard.

England
Bath & N.E. Somerset 2
Bedfordshire 6
Birmingham 10

Buckinghamshire 15
Cambridgeshire 16 • 17 • 18 • 21
Cheshire 24
Cornwall 25 • 26 • 29 • 32 • 34 • 35 • 36 • 39 • 41 • 44 • 45 • 46
Cumbria 47 • 48 • 49 • 50 • 53 • 54 • 58 • 60 • 61 • 63
Derbyshire 67 • 68 •
Devon 72 • 74 • 78 • 79 • 85 • 88 • 89 • 92 • 93 • 96 • 99 • 100 • 102
Dorset 105 • 107 • 109 • 115 • 121 • 124 • 126
Durham 127
Gloucestershire 131 • 133 • 135 • 137 • 139 • 144 • 145 • 147 • 150 • 151
Hampshire 152 • 153 • 157 •
Herefordshire 160 • 164
Hertfordshire 167
Isle of Wight 168 • 169
Kent 171 • 179 • 185 • 188
Leicestershire 192
Lincolnshire 194 • 195 • 197 • 198
London 203 • 215 • 218 • 219
Norfolk 220 • 226 • 229 • 233
Northamptonshire 237 • 238 • 239
Northumberland 241 • 242 • 243 • 246
Nottinghamshire 250 •
Oxfordshire 252 • 253 • 255 • 257 • 258 • 260 • 262 • 263
Shropshire 268 • 270 • 273 • 274 • 277 • 278
Somerset 279 • 280 • 284 • 288 • 293 • 300 • 301 • 303 • 305 • 307 • 308 • 313
Staffordshire 314

Quick reference indices

Suffolk 317 • 319 • 322 • 323 • 325
Surrey 327 • 328 • 331
Sussex 335 • 337 • 338 • 340 • 343 • 345
Warwickshire 348 • 351 • 357
Wiltshire 368
Worcestershire 371
Yorkshire 378 • 379 • 380 • 381 • 385 • 390 • 391 • 395 • 397 • 399 • 401

Scotland
Aberdeenshire 403
Argyll & Bute 406 • 407
Dumfries & Galloway 410
Edinburgh 414
Highland 419 • 420
Isle of Skye 421 • 422
Lanarkshire 424
Midlothian 425
Perth & Kinross 427
Scottish Borders 431 • 432
Stirling 433 • 434
Western Isles 435

Wales
Carmarthenshire 436
Conwy 438
Flintshire 439 • 440
Gwynedd 442 • 443
Pembrokeshire 447 • 448 • 451 • 452 • 453
Powys 458 • 459
Wrexham 460

Special Places to Stay series

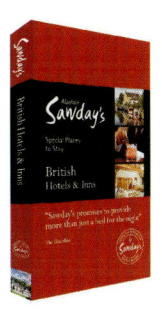

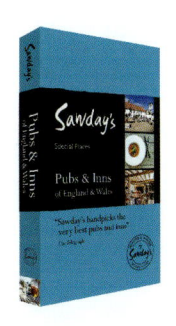

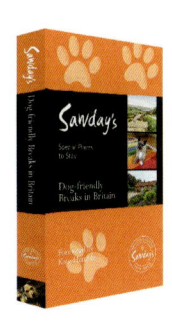

Alastair Sawday has been publishing books for over 20 years, finding Special Places to Stay in Britain and abroad. All our properties are inspected by us and are chosen for their charm and individuality. And there are many more to explore on our perennially popular website: www.sawdays.co.uk. You can buy any of our books at a reader discount of 25%* on the RRP.

List of titles:	RRP	Discount price
British Bed & Breakfast	£15.99	£11.99
British Hotels and Inns	£15.99	£11.99
Pubs & Inns of England & Wales	£15.99	£11.99
Dog-friendly Breaks in Britain	£14.99	£11.24
French Bed & Breakfast	£15.99	£11.99
French Châteaux & Hotels	£15.99	£11.99
Italy	£15.99	£11.99

*postage and packaging is added to each order

How to order:
To order call: **+44 (0)117 204 7810**

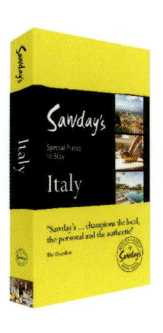

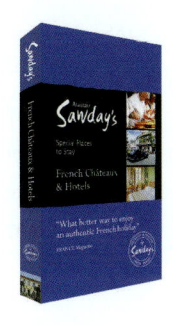

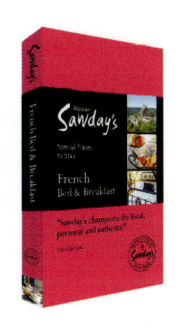

Index by property name

1 Peel Street	204	Alton Albany Farm	409
101 Abbotsbury Road	205	Ansford Park Cottage	297
108 Streathbourne Road	216	Antonia's Pearls, The Studio	44
113 Pepys Road	218	Applebarn Cottage	103
14 Hart Street	413	Applebys	171
15 Delaford Street	209	Ara	211
16 St Alfege Passage	219	Ashley Barn	140
19 Glenmore Road	368	Austons Down	351
2 Cambridge Street	411	Avenue Cottage	91
20 St Hilda's Terrace	375	Awelon	451
22 York Street	203	Aylworth Manor	145
24 Fox Hill	217	Bagthorpe Hall	223
29 Bronsart Road	210	Barclay Farmhouse	179
3 Ada Crescent	248	Barnhill House	96
30 King Henry's Road	201	Bashfords Farmhouse	303
31 Rowan Road	206	Battersea B&B	212
32 The Hythe	128	Baumber Park	196
35 Lower Broad Street	276	Bay House	38
37 Trevor Square	207	Bay Trees	152
38 Killieser Avenue	214	Beachborough Country House	73
5 Chapel Street	18	Beacon Hall House	182
5 Wilmore Street	271	Beacon House	92
64 Partickhill Road	417	Beara Farmhouse	77
7 Gloucester Place	412	Benefold Farmhouse Barn	332
7 Longport	186	Bering House	123
7 Smithfield Place	122	Bewl Rookery	347
9 Princes Buildings	12	Bilton Barns	242
Abbots Court House	121	Blackbrook House	329
Allt-y-bela	446	Blackmore Farm	300
Alstonefield Manor	69	Bosvathick	41

Breedon Hall	192	Caundle Barn	116
Brewers Cottage	306	Causeway Cottage	309
Bridge Cottage	237	Cefn-y-Dre Country House	452
Bridge House	156	Challan Hall	190
Bridges Court	361	Charcott Farmhouse	172
Brimford House	268	Chelsea Park Garden	208
Brixton Townhouse	213	Chipperkyle	410
Broadgate	64	Church Farmhouse	316
Broadgrove House	289	Church House	321
Broadway Barn	327	Cider Barn	310
Brook Farm	305	Cider House	84
Brook Farmhouse	82	Clapton Manor	144
Brook House	312	Claremont House	416
Brooking	90	Clarendon	83
Broughton House	63	Cleeton Court	275
Brownber Hall	58	Coach House	292
Brymer House	155	Coes Faen Lodge	442
Bulleigh Barton Manor	93	Cold Cotes	385
Bullocks Horn Cottage	359	Colledges House	239
Bunns Croft	166	College Farm	220
Burnhopeside Hall	127	Coombe Farm	74
Burnville House	80	Coombe Lodge Farm House	282
Burrington Farm	281	Cormiston Farm	424
Calcot Peak House	143	Corner House at Churchill	259
Callachally House	405	Cothay Manor	311
Cambridge University	16	Cove Cottage	33
Camomile Cottage	317	Crafts Hill Barn	19
Cardross	434	Craigiewood	419
Carlton House	398	Crake Trees Manor	54
Castle Farmhouse	261	Crawford House	120

Cresselly House	448	Forge Cottage Barn	7
Cresswell House	449	Frampton Court	133
Crookston House	425	Frog Street Farmhouse	307
Cross o' th' Hill Farm	354	Fullers Earth	112
Crows Hall Farm	335	Fyfield Manor	252
Cuil an Duin	427	Gilpin Mill	60
Cundall Lodge Farm	399	Gladstone's Library	439
Cyprian's Cot	81	Glebe House	101
Dadmans	188	Glenmore	407
Davenport House	272	Goss Moor	22
Deverill End	365	Gothic House	235
Dowthorpe Hall	381	Gotten Manor	170
Dowtys	367	Grayingham Lodge	198
Drybeck Hall	55	Great Selson Manor	185
Duke House	17	Green Close	256
Dunhill Barn	159	Green Dragon House	102
Eastfield House	430	Green Farm House	227
Ednovean Farm	36	Greenah	52
Eithinog Hall	459	Greenhill House	106
Ellerbeck House	389	Greenwood Barn	422
Elmdon Lee	130	Grosvenor Villa	1
Emley Farm	249	Grove Farm	355
Errington House	246	Hafod Y Garreg	457
Essendy House	428	Hall's Mill House	163
Fairways	313	Halzephron House	37
Fauhope House	431	Hammonds Farm	135
Fellside Studios	59	Handley Cross	176
Fingals	89	Hannaford House	94
Firs Farm	395	Hardwick House	267
Fisherman's House	362	Harlington Manor	6

Hartland Mill	78	Little Bridge Cottage	348
Hawksdale Lodge	47	Little Norlington Barn	340
Hay Barton	43	Long Acre Farm	9
Heacham House	224	Long Crendon Manor	15
Hereford Oast	177	Lordington House	334
Heyford House	262	Low Mill	390
High House Bruton	296	Lower Allercombe Farm	98
Higher Lank Farm	28	Lower Fifehead Farm	118
Hillview Cottage	290	Lowfield Farm	139
Hinchley Wood	71	Lowthwaite	53
Holbecks House	322	Lulworth House	124
Hooppells Torr	85	Lut's B&B	195
Hopton House	278	Lynturk Home Farm	403
House at Gwinear	31	Mallard Grange	397
Hoveton Hall	233	Manor Farm House	251
Huntingfield House	189	Manor Farm, Chippenham	360
Huntlands Farm	371	Manor Farm, Compton Valence	110
Ightham	173	Manor Farm, Matlock	68
Johnby Hall	49	Manor Farm, West Compton	108
Keepers Cottage	295	Manor House	392
Keynedon Mill	86	Manor House Farm, King's Lynn	221
King John's Lodge	346	Manor House Farm, Uttoxeter	314
Knowles Farm House	450	Marren	125
Lamberden Cottage	183	Marston House	352
Lane House	388	Matfen High House	247
Lapwings Barn	56	Maunsel House	304
Larkbeare Grange	99	Meadow House	222
Laverton Hall	396	Melfort House	406
Lawn Cottage	117	Merzie Meadows	175
Legg Barn	132	Middle Farm Cottage	291

Millers64	415	Oxford University	253
Milton Farm	366	Pairc an t-Srath	435
Monks Walk	8	Park Farm House, Coventry	349
Mount Pleasant Farm, Axbridge	293	Park Farm House, Frome	285
Mount Pleasant Farm, Llanwrda	437	Peacocks Fine B&B	21
Mulsford Cottage	24	Pembrokeshire Farm B&B	447
Myrtle Cottage	30	Pengwern Country House	438
Netherwood Lodge	341	Penny's Mill	288
Newtonmill House	404	Penpergwm Lodge	445
Nineteen	376	Pentillie Castle	46
Norfolk Courtyard	229	Pepper Cottage	147
North Farm	270	Pitfour House	4
North Farmcote	148	Ponden Hall	383
North Walk House	72	Ponden House	384
Northcourt	169	Poole Keynes House	141
Northwood Lodge	187	Post Office House	241
Number One	167	Pounds Farm	104
Oak Tree Farm	318	Powis House	433
Oaklands	364	Primrose Cottage	231
Ocklynge Manor	344	Pullington Barn	180
Old Country Farm & The Lighthouse	372	Ramsden Farm	181
Old Forge	113	Reason Hill	174
Old Hall Coach House	264	Rectory Farm, Chipping Norton	254
Old Harbour View	126	Rectory Farm, Witney	260
Old Kippenross	429	Reeves Barn	5
Old Monmouth	107	Rhedyn	458
Old Reading Room	287	Robyns Barn	51
Old Rectory	265	Rock Cottage	161
Old Shoulder of Mutton	67	Romden	177.1
Old Whyly	342	Rother Cottage	333

Sagar Fold House	191		Swinburne Castle	244
Salford Farm House	358		Tabor Hill Farm	75
Scarwood	363		Taggart House	279
Seabeach House	336		The Ammerdown Centre	284
Seabreeze	402		The Barn	194
Sequoia House	353		The Beeches	339
Shafts Farm	158		The Birches	373
Shallowdale House	401		The Bridge Inn	160
Shrewley Pools Farm	350		The Bristol Wing	11
Singdean	432		The Buttery	234
Sir Walter Elliot's House	2		The Close	137
Sloley Hall	232		The Cloudesley	345
Snoadhill Cottage	178		The Coach House	215
South Lodge	328		The Control Tower	226
South Yeo	76		The Corn Mill	27
Springfield House	20		The Cottage Stein	421
St Martin's B&B	162		The Courtyard Studio	146
Stable Cottage	228		The Dairy Loft	97
Stamford Hall	356		The Dovecote at Greenaway	331
Star Cottage	257		The Farmhouse	378
Starnash Farmhouse	343		The Firs	32
Staunton House	165		The Garden Cottage	369
Stokenham House	87		The Garden Suite	393
Stonebridge	280		The Glove House	255
Stow House	391		The Glynhir Estate	436
Strete Barton House	88		The Gorse House	193
Studio Farrows	299		The Granary - Borough Farm	79
Summerhow House	57		The Grange, East Barkwith	197
Swallow Barn, Frome	286		The Grange, Frampton on Severn	134
Swallow Barn, Woking	326		The Grange, Leyburn	394

The Guest House	142	The Old Store House	455
The Hayloft	387	The Old Vicarage, Ashbourne	70
The Hen House	39	The Old Vicarage, Cardigan	453
The Hermitage	245	The Old Vicarage, Harrogate	386
The Isle	266	The Old Vicarage, Newmarket	324
The Jointure Studios	338	The Old Vicarage, Radstock	283
The Linhay	95	The Peatcutter's Croft	420
The Lint Mill	423	The Power House	3
The Lodge at Dale End House	66	The Roost	202
The Malabar	61	The Slate Shed at Graig Wen	443
The Manor House	199	The Summerhouse	258
The Mill House	370	The Venison House	330
The Moda House	131	The Vyne	240
The Mount House	400	The Wold Cottage	379
The Old Farm House	200	Thistleyhaugh	243
The Old Ferryman's House	418	Thorpe Hall	377
The Old House	238	Thurst House Farm	382
The Old Manor House	337	Timberstone Bed & Breakfast	274
The Old Manor House	357	Tower	440
The Old Mill	119	Tredudwell Manor	45
The Old Parsonage	26	Trerose Manor	40
The Old Pilchard Works	34	Trevigue	25
The Old Pottery	129	Trevilla House	42
The Old Rectory, Ashford	184	Trewornan Manor	29
The Old Rectory, Dorchester	111	Trinity House	151
The Old Rectory, Ipswich	323	Troon Cottage	225
The Old Rectory, Ludlow	273	Trustans Barn	319
The Old Rectory, Ridlington	230	Trustwood	23
The Old School	150	Tudor Cottage	109
The Old Stable	325	Tudor House B&B	157

Two Hillside Crescent	414
Ty Newydd	456
Ty'r Chanter	454
Underleigh House	65
Union Place	374
Uplands House	263
Upper Crannel Farm Barn	294
Upper Red House	444
Urless Farm	114
Venton Vean	35
Victoria Park Rooms	13
Village Farm	380
Vinegar Hill Pottery	153
Viver Water Mill	62
Walford Court	277
Washingford House	236
Well Farm	138
Wellies	308
West Colwell Farm	100
Westbourne House	168
Westfield House	426
Westleigh Farm	301
Westmorland Cottage	315
Whitrigg House	50
Whitton Hall	269
Wickton Court	164
Willoughby House	250
Willow Tree Cottage	320
Winterton	408
Witheridge Farm	302
Wodetone Vineyard	105
Wood House	48
Woodbrooke	10
Woodchester Valley Vineyard Barns	136
Wooden Cabbage House	115
Worthenbury Manor	460
Wren House	149
Y Goeden Eirin	441
Yarlington House	298
Yew Tree House	154

Photo: Calcot Peak House, entry 143

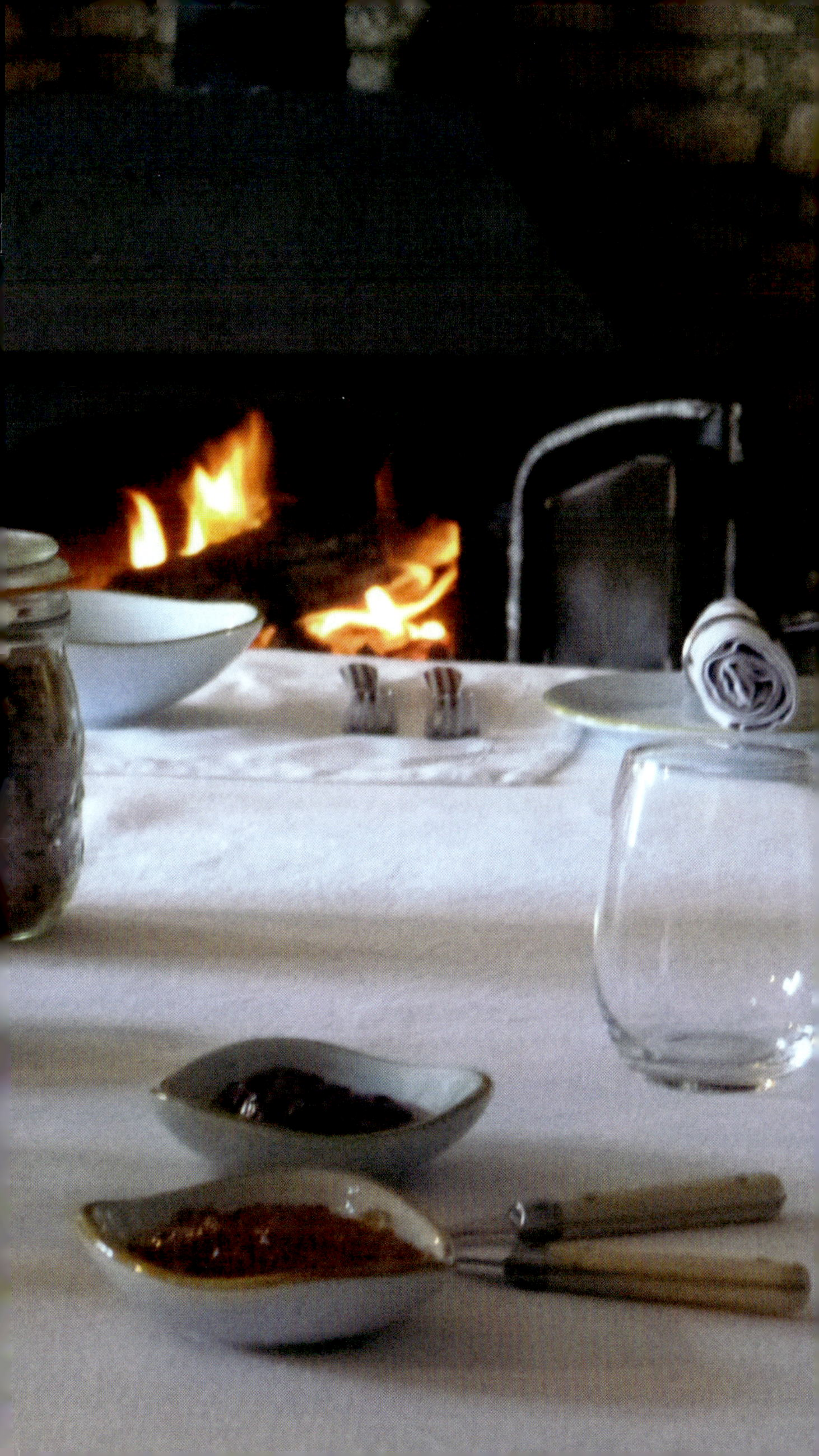

INSPECTED & SELECTED
Sawday's
CANOPY
& STARS
SPECIAL PLACES

A beautiful COLLECTION

Hand-picked collection of amazing places to stay in the great outdoors. From treehouses to cabins, wagons, boats & more across the UK and Europe.

canopyandstars.co.uk

Index by town

Abergavenny	445	Bodmin	27, 28
Abermaw	442	Boscastle	26
Alford	403	Bournemouth	122
Alnwick	242	Bovey Tracey	83
Alresford	157	Brampford Speke	96
Ammanford	436	Brechin	404
Ampleforth	401	Brecon	455, 456
Arthog	443	Bridgnorth	272
Ashbourne	69-71	Bridgwater	300, 301
Ashford	176-178, 184	Bridport	105
Axbridge	293	Bristol	11-13
Axminster	102, 103	Brixham	92
Aylesbury	15	Broughton	154
Bakewell	66	Broughton-in-Furness	64
Banbury	263	Bruton	296
Banwell	280	Bude	25
Barnstaple	73, 74	Builth Wells	457, 458
Bath	1-4	Burford	257
Bedford	7	Burrington	281
Belford	241	Burton-on-Trent	315
Benenden	180-182	Bury St Edmunds	325
Betchworth	328	Caernarfon	441
Betws-y-Coed	438	Cambridge	16-19
Bicester	262	Canterbury	186
Biddenden	179	Cardigan	453
Bideford	76-78	Carlisle	47
Biggar	424	Carnforth	389
Birmingham	10	Castle Cary	297
Blagdon	282	Castle Douglas	410
Blairgowrie	428	Chale	170
Blakeney	132	Charlestown	44
Blandford Forum	119, 120	Cheltenham	146
Boat of Garten	418	Chichester	334-337

Chiddingfold	331	East Barkwith	197
Chippenham	360	East Hoathly	342
Chipping Norton	254, 258, 259	Eastbourne	344
Chipping Sodbury	131	Edinburgh	411-416
Cirencester	141, 142	Elgin	426
Clapton-on-the-Hill	144	Ely	21
Claverdon	351	Etchingham	346
Clevedon	279	Evesham	358
Clitheroe	191	Eye	317
Clynderwen	447	Fakenham	227
Cockermouth	48	Falmouth	40, 41
Colston Bassett	251	Faversham	189
Colyton	101	Fishguard	452
Corbridge	247	Fowey	45
Coventry	349	Frome	285-289
Cowes	168	Gainsborough	198, 199
Cranbrook	183	Girvan	409
Craven Arms	278	Glasgow	417
Crediton	95	Glastonbury	294, 295
Crewkerne	313	Gloucester	133, 134
Crickhowell	454	Godalming	330
Cullompton	104	Grange-over-Sands	63
Dartmouth	88, 89	Greenlaw	430
Daventry	239, 240	Grimsby	200
Deeside	439	Hailsham	343
Derby	192	Halstead	129
Dereham	229	Harlington	6
Ditchling	338	Harrogate	385, 386
Dorchester	108-115, 125	Haworth	383, 384
Dorking	329	Helston	37, 39
Driffield	379, 380	Hereford	160-162
Dulverton	302	Heriot	425
Dunblane	429	Herne Bay	187

Hertford	167	Lincoln	195
Hexham	244, 245, 248, 249	Linton	20
Hincaster	62	Llanwrda	437
Honiton	100	Lochgilphead	408
Hope Valley	65	London - Balham	215, 216
Horncastle	196	London - Battersea	211, 212
Hull	381	London - Brixton	213
Humshaugh	246	London - Chelsea	208
Hunstanton	225	London - Crystal Palace	217
Ilminster	312	London - Fulham	209, 210
Inverness	419	London - Greenwich	219
Ipswich	322, 323	London - Hammersmith	206
Isle of Harris	435	London - Holland Park	205
Isle of Mull	405	London - Kensington	204
Isleornsay	422	London - Knightsbridge	207
Kendal	55-57	London - Marylebone	203
Kennford	94	London - New Cross	218
Kilgetty	448, 449	London - Primrose Hill	201
King's Lynn	221-224	London - Queen's Park	202
Kingsbridge	85-87	London - Streatham Hill	214
Kington	163	Luckington	361
Kippen	434	Ludlow	273-277
Kirkby Stephen	58	Lyme Regis	106, 107
Lambourn	9	Lynton	72
Lanark	423	Maidstone	174, 175
Lancaster	388	Maldon	128
Lanchester	127	Malmesbury	359
Langport	299	Malpas, Wrexham	24
Lawrenny	450	Malvern	372, 373
Lelant	32	Marlborough	362, 363
Leominster	164-166	Matlock	67, 68
Lewes	339-341	Melrose	431
Leyburn	390, 391, 394	Melton Mowbray	193
Lifton	79	Midhurst	333

Milford on Sea	152, 153	Salisbury	366-369
Mold	440	Saltash	46
Monmouth	444	Sandwich	185
Moreton-in-Marsh	150, 151	Saxmundham	318-320
Morpeth	243	Sedbergh	61
Mousehole	34	Sevenoaks	173
Much Wenlock	271	Shaftesbury	117
Naunton	145	Sherborne	116
Neston	22, 23	Shipston-on-Stour	357
Newark	250	Shorwell	169
Newcastleton	432	Shrewsbury	266-270
Newmarket	324	Sidmouth	97
Newquay	30	Silverdale	190
Newton Abbot	81, 93	Sittingbourne	188
Northleach	143	Skipton	387
Norwich	228, 232-236	Sleaford	194
Oakham	264, 265	South Molton	75
Oban	406, 407	Southam	352
Oxford	253, 261	Southwold	316
Penrith	49-54	Sowerby Bridge	382
Penzance	33, 35	St Ives	31
Perranuthnoe	36	St Leonards-on-Sea	345
Peterborough	237	St Martin	402
Petersfield	158, 159	Stirling	433
Petworth	332	Stow-on-the-Wold	149
Pitlochry	427	Stratford-upon-Avon	353-356
Poole	123	Stroud	135, 137, 138
Radstock	283, 284	Sturminster Newton	118
Richmond	392, 393	Sutton Coldfield	348
Ridlington	230	Talaton	99
Ripon	395-397	Taunton	303-309
Rockbeare	98	Tavistock	80
Rushden	238	Tedburn St Mary	82
Saffron Walden	130	Tenby	451

Tetbury	139, 140	Woodbridge	321
Tewkesbury	147	Woodchester	136
The Lizard	38	Woodstock	255
Thetford	220	Worcester	371
Thirsk	398	Worthenbury	460
Tonbridge	171, 172	Yelverton	84
Totnes	90, 91	York	399, 400
Truro	42, 43		
Ullapool	420		
Usk	446		
Uttoxeter	314		
Wadebridge	29		
Wadhurst	347		
Walcott	231		
Wallingford	252		
Walsingham	226		
Warminster	5, 364, 365		
Warwick	350		
Waternish	421		
Wellington	310, 311		
Wells	290-292		
Welshpool	459		
West Lulworth	124		
Weymouth	126		
Whitby	374-378		
Wincanton	298		
Winchcombe	148		
Winchester	155, 156		
Windermere	59, 60		
Windsor	8		
Winterborne Kingston	121		
Witney	256, 260		
Woking	326, 327		

Photo opposite: Little Norlington Barn, entry 340
Photo overleaf: Swallow Barn, entry 286

What's in each entry?

① Surrey

② The Venison House
Drive through Surrey parkland grazed by rare breed cattle to reach this bijou hideaway. The circular cottage topped with a terracotta turret is quite unlike any other B&B you're likely to visit. It's set into a corner of Alison's lovely walled garden, with oval windows overlooking the park. Step through the sage green door into a country-chic bedroom with monogrammed pillows and crisp linen. Along a corridor leading to the sparkling shower room, there's a double-fronted cupboard concealing an immaculate kitchen. Alison provides homemade bread, marmalade, bacon, tomatoes and eggs, so guests can make a delicious, DIY breakfast.

③ Rooms	1 double with separate bathroom & kitchenette: £120-£150.
④ Meals	Pubs/restaurants 2 miles.
⑤ Closed	Rarely.

	Alison Bird
	The Venison House,
	Garden Cottage, Park Hatch, Loxhill,
	Godalming, GU8 4BL
Tel	+44 (0)1483 200410
Mobile	+44 (0)7768 745765
Email	agmbird@gmail.com

⑥
⑦

Entry 330   Map 4

Surrey

The Dovecote at Greenaway
An enchanting cottage in an idyllic corner of Chiddingfold. People return time and again – for the house (1545), the garden blooming with flowers, vegetables, hens and dovecote, the glowing interiors, and Sheila and John. The sitting room is inviting with rich colours, flowers, beams and a roaring log fire; the turning oak staircase leads to bedrooms that are cosy and sumptuous at the same time, and bathrooms with deep roll top tubs and a pretty armchair. Breakfast is a spread with homemade bread and home-grown tomatoes. Gorgeous countryside, walks on the Greensand Way… who would guess London and the airports were so close?

Rooms	1 double; 1 double, 1 twin, sharing bathroom: £115-£135. Singles £95, except weekends. Mid-week prices negotiable.
Meals	Pubs 300 yds.
Closed	Rarely.

Pets by arrangement.

	Sheila & John Marsh
	The Dovecote at Greenaway,
	Pickhurst Road,
	Chiddingfold, GU8 4TS
Tel	+44 (0)1428 682920
Email	info@bedandbreakfastchiddingfold.co.uk
Web	www.bedandbreakfastchiddingfold.co.uk

Entry 331   Map 4